Pacific Northwest Trail
Digest

2019 Edition

Tim Youngbluth

Tim Youngbluth

ISBN: 9781797809519:

DEDICATION

To all those who have tied their boots, shouldered their packs, hiked miles and miles, and then provided extensive notes about the wonders of the Pacific Northwest National Scenic Trail so that others may follow in their footsteps. Thank you.

CONTENTS

THE AUTHOR

Tim Youngbluth – Trail Name "Bravo." A retired Air Force Colonel, living near the PNT for about 10 years, he first became interested in backpacking 50 years ago with a 10-day hike in mountains of northeast New Mexico as a Boy Scout. He has sectioned hiked many parts of the PNT and plans to document the many trails within the Colville National Forest. He loves to explore and travel, as well as photographing historical sites.

MAJOR CONTRIBUTORS

Cathe Neuberger – Trail name "Pounce," she earned her Triple Crown in 2014. Her other backpacking trips include end-to-end hikes of the Long Trail, the Long Path, and the Pacific Northwest Trail. Pounce also enjoys bikepacking and packrafting. During the winter months she works as a ski patroller in Vermont and fills her free time with local backcountry ski adventures. You can find her on Instagram at @pounceonlife.

The things Pounce loves most about the PNT are exactly what makes it so challenging - isolation, navigating through trail-less sections, the huge sense of adventure, and needing to be 100% self-sufficient. There are no bail-outs on this trail! And, of course, there are incredible views.

Special thanks again to Pounce, who tirelessly proof read and corrected my mistakes, all in an effort to make the PNT your best hiking experience.

Ellie Stevenson – First-time thru-hiker, she tackled the PNT solo, experiencing the all the "ups and downs" of the trail. She found the rewards far outstripped the challenges and will be forever grateful for the unique experience. Raised in a family where vacation time meant a camping trip, she figured there's no way backpacking for two months could be a bad thing. A newly minted employee of a conservation non-profit in Durango, Colorado, she is working on plans to hike the Colorado Trail. Driven by her love of travel to discover new favorite places, she looks forward her next solo wilderness experience.

Katherine Cook –An avid backpacker, she completed her thru-hike of the PNT in 2013. A few years earlier she completed the PCT. She is also a seasoned mountain biker, with adventures including conquering the Great Divide Mountain Bike Route, solo and unsupported, riding from Banff, Alberta, Canada to Antelope Wells, New Mexico.

Greg Thompson – Trail Name "Goyo." Besides the PNT, he has completed the PCT and to plans complete the other two legs of the Triple Crown, the AT and CDT, in the future. However, he bets that in terms of attention to navigation, and rough/non-existent trails, none of the Triple Crown trails are quite the level of challenge as the PNT.

Brian Tanzman – Trail Name "Buck-30." A CPA by vocation and world-traveled hiker by choice. He has hiked over 20,000 trail miles including the PNT, the Triple Crown, and New Zealand's Te Araroa Trail. Just to change things up a little, he has also biked the Australian outback, kayaked the Mississippi River, and biked from Anchorage, Alaska across the Yukon to Banff National Park in Alberta, Canada.

Dick Vogel - Trail Name "Hike On." A retired U.S. Air Force Survival Instructor, he hikes 2000 miles for about nine months each year, completing eight of the 11 National Scenic Trails including the Triple Crown. He also backpacked in the Philippines (Luzon), Panama, Grenada, Canada, Alaska and Hawaiian Islands, trekking 34,000 total miles. When not on the trail, he pays back by volunteering to maintain trails.

Mark Davis - His 2015 westbound PNT hike ended abruptly at Port Townsend when he got news that an oak tree had fallen on the back of their house, necessitating a return home to deal with insurance adjustors and contractors. He thru hiked the PCT northbound in 2000 and the CDT southbound in 2005. The journal for his PNT hike is on www.postholer.com/markdavis.

Front Cover: View of Mount Olympus, from the Pacific Northwest Trail, on the High Divide Trail, Olympic National Park. Approximately mile 1121P, near the trail junction with the Hoh Lake Trail, below the summit of Bogachiel Peak. Photo courtesy Jeff Kish, Director Pacific Northwest Trail Association, PNT thru-hiker, 2014

ACKNOWLEDGMENTS

First and foremost I need to recognize the monumental work of Ron Strickland (aka "the father of the PNT") and his book *The Pacific Northwest Trail Guide* published in 2001. This book is not an attempt to replace his guide book, but only to build upon it.

I also wish to acknowledge Jeff Kish, Executive Director for the Pacific Northwest Trail Association, and Eric Wollborg, Communications Manager. They have worked tirelessly to grow the association and its members to protect and improve every mile of the trail. I would encourage every hiker to contact the Pacific Northwest Trail Association before venturing forth.

Thanks also go to the major contributors to this book. Their help has been invaluable. Also, I'd like to thank all the hikers who have shared their PNT experiences since 2007. I also need to thank the generous volunteers who offer support and local hikers who have added to this book and support the PNTA. I have tried to incorporate each and every comment from your journals and postings into the waypoint descriptions.

YOUR HELP IS NEEDED

This book now incorporates the notes, comments and trail updates from previous PNT hikers. Trail conditions change. This book is a cooperative effort by those who have taken the time to hike and document the routes described. The goal is to provide the best information to all those who want to hike along the Pacific Northwest Trail. Although the information is deemed to be reliable it is not guaranteed. Please plan your hike carefully, be prepared, and use good judgment on the trail.

Comments, corrections and suggestions are very welcome, and needed. I would like to be able to update this book each year. Please share your trail experience with me and the PNT community so we can build the best trail possible.

You may contact the author at **3dtrails@gmail.com**

Tim Youngbluth

FOREWORD

With the prime hiking season still months away, I've traded my trail runners for snowshoes to explore the North Cascades. On my last trip, some friends came along. As we climbed higher into the mountains, the snow grew deeper and we took turns breaking new trail. While hiking first, my lungs burned in the frosty air and my pace slowed. Before long, I fell back to let others lead and I realized that without their help, my trip would have ended short of the summit. Snowshoeing, like so many endeavors, is made better with a little help from our friends.

As Pacific Northwest Trail enthusiasts, we owe a lot to the friends in our trail community. It was just a few short years ago when I thru-hiked the PNT with my indispensable wife and hiking partner, Suzanne. To find our way, we carried a map and compass, GPS units — and pages from the Pacific Northwest Trail Digest, broken down into sections and mailed ahead in our resupply packages.

Today, the Digest remains an essential tool for every aspiring thru-hiker. It has been designed to work with the PNTA mapset and it pairs well with Guthook's hiking guide app through a common set of GPS waypoints, collected by author, Tim Youngbluth. Thousands of these invaluable waypoints have been incorporated into a shared data set which tells the story of the PNT by describing every junction and landmark along the trail. The most critical of these are compiled in text format in the pages of this handy guide.

This book also incorporates the notes, comments and trail updates from hikers, who have shared their first-hand experiences on the trail. In reading these descriptions, trail founder Ron Strickland's observation that every PNT hiker "walks with the ghosts of those who walked the trail before them," rings true to me.

Over the last forty odd years, many have made contributions to the PNT. Creating what Ron Strickland imagined would be "America's finest national scenic trail" has been a truly heroic effort that has touched and enriched many lives. All of the tools and tread we enjoy today were built on the bedrock foundation of those who came before us. While Strickland must be considered the father of the trail and acknowledged as the author of the first book-length guidebook, Ted Hitzroth, should be considered the creator supreme of all PNT maps. A professional cartographer, Hitzroth scouted and hand sketched what would become the first maps of the trail on his historic 1983 thru-hike with Strickland.

Yet, in 2019 every hiker should also give thanks to an unsung hero in the trail's history. Former PNTA staffer, Jon Knechtel delivered testimony before congress advocating for the PNT to join the national trails system. On March 30th, President Obama signed into law the Omnibus Public Lands Act of 2009, and the Pacific Northwest Trail became the Pacific Northwest National Scenic Trail after decades of advocacy work by the Association. This year, we celebrate Knechtel's achievement, and the 10th Anniversary of this momentous legislation.

With congressional designation, the PNT officially earned its place among the world-renowned, "triple crown trails," which have become household names today. The Appalachian Trail and Pacific Crest Trail celebrated their 50th Anniversaries just last year — and the Continental Divide Trail, its 40th.

Over the last fifty years, the triple crown trails have matured, with segments once made up of a hodgepodge of surfaces — not just trails, but also highways, cowpaths and overland routes — now much closer to becoming the continuous footpaths that we have come to expect of a national scenic trail today.

In the decade that has passed since the PNT earned congressional designation, the Association has also worked to refine the trail's corridor amidst a backdrop of sweeping change in the world of long-distance hiking.

What visitors will discover on the PNT this year is an experience that may feel both familiar yet new at the same time — the charm to be found on a "relatively young trail that's still a little rough around the edges."

With a renaissance in long-distance hiking unfolding around 2012, a new culture has emerged around these national treasures, one with the ability to assemble online, enhanced by smartphone technologies and affordable lightweight gear, and supported by trail-maintaining organizations and self-appointed volunteers.

On the PNT, good samaritans are lending more support to thru-hikers than ever before, but this too holds the charm of a trail still in its adolescence. With a smaller and more earnest network of "trail angels," long-distance hikers must be more self-reliant on the PNT than on longer-established trails. They also enjoy the pleasure of introducing locals — with long ties to the land — to the pathway which brings us together.

For those embarking on crown-to-coast adventures on this special anniversary year, I hope that you have an unforgettable summer. As a thru-hiker, you can help give back to the trail and enrich your experience in so many ways. First, by being a model ambassador for our trail community both on and off the trail. While you may never see another thru-hiker in person, tread lightly knowing that others will follow you. Prepare to marvel at scenic and untrammeled lands and to do your part to protect them for the wildlife for which they are home — and for the generations to come.

Happy hiking,

Eric Wollborg

Communications Manager, Pacific Northwest Trail Association
PNT (2016), CDT (2014), PCT (2012)

"The long distance hiker, a breed set apart,
From the likes of the usual pack.
He'll shoulder his gear, be hittin' the trail;
Long gone, long 'fore he'll be back."

M.J. Eberhart

CHAPTER ONE
INTRODUCTION TO THE TRAIL

Double Pacific Northwest Trail sign near Deception Pass, Washington

Pacific Northwest National Scenic Trail

For brevity throughout this book we will use "PNT" instead of the full trail name. The PNT traverses over 1,200 miles, highlighting a variety of mountain views, lush high meadows, river valleys, and the sea stacks along the Pacific Ocean beaches. Whereas other national scenic trails run north-south, essentially along the spine of mountain ranges, the PNT runs east-west. The trail hikes up and over the mountain ranges through high passes, on trails first made by Native Americans and miners, or on old wagon roads. An elevation gain/loss of 3,000 feet or more in a day, several times, for many days in a row, is very common.

The PNT is a long route filled with high adventure, unmatched beauty, solitude and personal achievement. The trail begins in the east at the continental divide in Glacier National Park. It ends near the western most point of the United States, at Cape Alava on the Pacific Ocean in Olympic National Park. Through our journey we hike through seven national forests, four wilderness areas, and three national parks.

The PNT has been hiked end-to-end by first-time thru hikers and by the most experienced long-distance hikers. With proper planning, equipment and physical training it can be the adventure of a lifetime. But let's ground your expectation in reality. The PNT has been called the "double black diamond" of all the national scenic trails.

The trail is very challenging for three reasons. First and foremost is that it is physically demanding. "You'll climb a total of more than 205,000 feet – that's [equivalent to climbing] Mount Everest more than eight times, measured from base to peak – as you hike from the starting point, about 200 yards inside the Canadian border on the east side of Glacier National Park. You'll also descend a total of more than 210,000 feet as you make your way up and down mountainsides to Cape Alava, Washington. It's an elevation change, to be precise, of 415,638 feet along the route. That's similar to the elevation change on the longer-established and better-known Pacific Crest Trail that runs from California to Washington, with one big difference. The Pacific Crest's elevation change of 489,418 feet happens over 2,650 miles. PNT's is crammed into less than half that distance."[65]

One 2013 thru-hiker, after covering only about one-third of the trail, penned in her trail blog, almost poetically writing:

> One of the more salient features of the Pacific Northwest Trail is its relentless pursuit of high views. If there is a mountain nearby with a view to be had, it seems the route goes up. So far the trail has climbed up and over the Rocky Mountains of Glacier and dropped down to the North Fork Valley, climbed up and over the Whitefish Mountains and dropped down to the Tobacco Valley, climbed up and over the Purcell Mountains and bobbed down once to the Yaak River Valley and then again to the Kootenai River Valley, climbed up and over the Selkirks and dropped down to the Pend O'reille River Valley ... and it would be out of character for the trail just to meander along flat for a while. What the hell, let's go climb another mountain.[KC]

A 2014 hiker, who has hiked 8 of the 11 national scenic trails, opined about the PNT by stating:

> Any trail that climbs over (instead of along) every mountain range on its way to the ocean, is bound to be more physically challenging. But that's only one part of the challenge. The PNT also traverses some very remote, "lonely" but beautiful back country. I hiked two days without seeing another human; four days without encountering another hiker. There are places on the PNT where you are starkly on your own, places where no one will be there to help if you get into trouble, no cell phone service, ... occasionally not even a trail! The PNT is not a trail for the faint hearted! But the PNT also offers rewards like no other trail.[DV]

Second, the trail is challenging because of the lack of logistics support and its isolation. Careful planning is required to ensure we carry all the resources we need. The trail is isolated because you will not likely see another hiker—or human being—for days while on some of the remote sections.

Third, the trail is challenging because there is a small seasonal window to complete the entire trail as a thru-hiker. Typically this is July 1 – September 15. Starting in Glacier National Park the trails are not open until middle of June or even July due to the snow levels. On the far side of the seasonal window it is common to find snow in the Olympic range in mid-September.

The good news is that the PNT can be accessed and easily hiked in sections. Although most hikers travel from east to west, some hike from west to east. The PNT is not a "super highway" national trail where you might meet many other hikers. There are no mileage markers and few trail signs. Resupply is available but it takes planning, with friendly towns and hamlets along the way.

Due to the weather and the higher mountain elevations, the PNT is a summer to early autumn hike. Snow is likely year round at some higher elevations, and we can expect the blistering heat in August hiking through the dry Okanogan Valley. The Olympic peninsula and the coast along the Pacific Ocean sit in a rain forest, with alternating days of bright blue sky changing quickly to fog and rain. The changing terrain, waterfalls, glaciers, river crossings, mountain summits and much, much more, make hiking the PNT an adventure of lifetime.

Why This Book?

This book is written for prospective thru-hikers, or end-to-enders, but also for those who would like to pick and choose portions of the Pacific Northwest Trail by section hiking. The book is written at two levels.

First, it allows you to quickly overview the ten sections of the trail and look for the major highlights, resupply points, permits, etc. Waypoints are used to help you quickly identify key trail junctions and landmarks along the trail.

Second, this book provides detailed information about the trail between the waypoints. In the description you will find precise GPS coordinates, the elevations, and other information to aid you in navigating the trail. Although many hikers just carry a map and compass, there are some sections of the trail that are more challenging where you must "bushwhack" between trails or roads. One criticism has been that too much detail has been provided in this *'Digest'* and it removes some of the "thrill of discovery" for the hiker. But for those of us who are not naturally born "mountain men," I've added the trail details for you to use, or not, as you like.

Detailed trail maps are not included; however, at the end of each chapter you will find graphic charts of the elevation profiles for the route described. The graphs include campsites and other key landmarks for your planning purposes.

Where Can I Find Trail Maps?

The best trail maps available are produced and distributed for free by the Pacific Northwest Trail Association. You can find their trail strip maps at pnt.org/maps. The ten trail sections of this book mirror the strip map sections of the PNTA. This book does have a map overview for each chapter, but it does not have the detailed trail maps. You should be able to correlate these maps to the waypoint narrative here easily.

Another excellent source for planning purposes is the USFS official website for the trail: https://www.fs.usda.gov/pnt/. The site includes several sources for overview maps and the current information about permits, the trail, and the communities that support it.

A new unofficial website for trail information and detailed maps for portions of the PNT in northeast Washington, is: http://newashingtontrails.com/pacific-northwest-trail/

The Pacific Northwest National Scenic Trail does not have an official established route yet. This book uses the terms "primary" and "alternate" to designate the trail routes. Trail and waypoint descriptions for both the primary and alternate routes are provided in each chapter.

How Much Climbing Is There?

The PNT starts on the eastern edge of Glacier National Park at 5,340 feet elevation and hikes west to the Pacific Ocean. Seems all downhill, doesn't it? From the start to the end, however, there are significant climbs to hike high to get the best views of the Pacific Northwest.

A good estimate of the total climbing following the primary route is about 135,000 feet over the 1200 miles of trail. This book offers descriptions of alternates routes and spur trails which offer more climbing to the summits of nearby peaks. Choosing these options could easily add another 5,000 elevation gain. Check the elevation profiles at the end of each chapter to get a better understanding of how steep your climbs may be.

Waypoint Descriptions

Each waypoint is formatted in the author's convention, as shown in the example below.

0006P 3.0mi 48° 55.997'N 113° 42.774'W 4680' Belly River Trail X Cosley Lake Cutoff Trail @ Gable Creek Camp

0006P = Waypoint number that generally refers to the total trail distance along the primary route. Waypoints start at 0000P at the trailhead near Big Chief customs in Montana and end with 1217P at Cape Alava, Washington. We can compare waypoint numbers to calculate an estimated distance between waypoints. For example, the distance between 0006P and 0025P is about 19 miles (technically it is measured at 19.2 miles, but 19 miles is close enough for our planning purposes). Waypoints on alternate routes have an 'A' as a suffix; for example, 0085A. Alternate route waypoints generally refer to the total trail mileage if we had only taken the primary route up until the point where we turned off onto the alternate route.

3.0mi = 3.0 miles from the last waypoint. Waypoints are repeated at the beginning of each chapter and for the beginning of alternate routes showing 0.0mi.

48° 55.997'N 113° 42.774'W = Geographic coordinates in the WGS84 datum plane, which is the same as used by the global positioning system (GPS). See section below on the waypoint and trail accuracy for more technical details.

4680' = Waypoint elevation above mean sea level. Comparing the elevation between two waypoints helps us determine if the route is level, climbing, or descending.

Belly River Trail X Cosley Lake Cutoff Trail @ Gable Creek Camp = Brief description of the point from map annotations to help you identify the waypoint location without plotting the geographic coordinates. The 'X' means "crossing" or "intersection." The @ means "at" or "very near" a landmark.

FR, RD, SR = For quick abbreviation and identification, this book annotates forest roads as FR, County or other non-forest roads as RD, and State Routes as SR. This will help you know if you are hiking in a national forest, or one that traverses private property.

Waypoint and Trail Accuracy – Disclaimer

This book is somewhat of an experiment. It combines new, three-dimensional satellite mapping technology, with on-the-ground hiker GPS tracking and observations. Together they are pretty good, but not perfect. The trail changes over time. Weather, fires, and nature constantly reshape the landscape and the trail. New trails are developed and hikers try different alternate routes every year. We have tried to cover the proven and common routing in this book.

As we noted, there is no complete "official" route for the Pacific Northwest National Scenic Trail at this time, so we have chosen to use the term "primary PNT route" as represented by the PNTA maps. Another term used is "original PNT route" which refers to the route first developed by Ron Strickland. Much of the original route remains as today's primary route, but we have tried to point out where they are now different.

The distance between waypoints is a computer estimate and is provided for your planning purposes. Although they are believed to be a pretty good estimate, the distances do not always account for unknown switchbacks, or some of the up and down distances. Please don't pace it off and then curse me for the mileage being too short!

For those who are interested in the technical details of the 3D mapping, here it is. The trail route and waypoints have been plotted from aerial photos using Google Earth, confirming the coordinates in both two and three dimensional views, using WGS84 datum. Many of the waypoints have been field tested to accuracy within 60 feet. For the best results set your GPS to use WGS84 datum. Waypoints where the accuracy cannot be measured as carefully are noted with (estimated) in the description. The estimated way points are very few, but still believed to be correct. GPS and maps are only tools. Always use your best judgment on the trail.

Special Note: This guide is written to add a narrative to the trail maps produced by the Pacific Northwest Trail Association (PNTA). Again, the official route for the PNT has not yet been established. Thus, the trail changes as route decisions are made by the PNTA, federal and state land managers, and private property owners. Updating the waypoints on the map and in this guide each year until the trail is finalized is a daunting task. Some waypoints numbers may differ from the nearest trail mile, particularly as the numbering moves west. The waypoint numbers here reflect those shown on the PNTA maps. The actual mileage between waypoints, as shown in this guide, is deemed to be as accurate as possible.

What Time of the Year is Best to Hike the PNT?

Of all the national scenic trails, the PNT perhaps has one of the shortest windows of opportunity for a complete through hike. Traditionally you start in Glacier National Park, with its high peaks in the Rocky Mountain Range, and conclude your hike in Olympic National Park, with its high peaks in the Olympic Range. Plus, just past the midpoint of the trail, the PNT crosses through the North Cascades National Park. Each of these parks has permanent glaciers. Although the trail does not cross the glaciers, there is snow all year on the peaks, and spotty snow on the trail most of the year.

The United States Geological Service reports the annual snow levels at one measuring site within Glacier National Park. It shows that the peak snow levels are actually around the May 1st each year, with a rapid melt into July 1st. Snow graphs for North Cascades and Olympic National Parks show similar results.

The best time to hike the PNT is July 1 through September 15, approximately 75 days of hiking. Some hikers have started a few weeks earlier, but it is not advisable before June 15. Ending your PNT hike after mid-September you risk seasonal heavy rain and snow in the Olympics that begin in early fall in the northwest. Here is the best place to learn about choosing a start date and snow levels on the PNT:

https://www.pnt.org/pnta/know-before-you-go/plan-your-trip/snow/

PERMITS and RESERVATIONS

Backcountry permits and campsite reservations are required for only three areas of the trail. The PNT Association provides a very concise web page with links to information on hiking the PNT through the three national parks at: http://pnt.org/trail/pnt-national-parks/. Another excellent place to start planning is the USFS official website: https://www.fs.usda.gov/main/pnt/passes-permits.

Glacier National Park

Backcountry permits are required throughout Glacier National Park. A good place to start is to review the Glacier National Park's Backcountry Camping Guide at: http://www.nps.gov/glac/planyourvisit/backcountry.htm.

There are two ways to obtain a permit. First, use the Backcountry Permit Advanced Reservation process. All advance reservations requests MUST be submitted online. Applications are accepted beginning March 15. Application for the permit can be downloaded at:

http://www.nps.gov/glac/planyourvisit/backcountry-reservations.htm

There is a $10 advance application fee and a $40 charge for each confirmed trip request, in addition to a $7 per person/per night camping fee.

Second, walk-up permits and campsite reservations are also available for the day before or the day of your camp. Nearly half of all the backcountry campgrounds are held for walk-ins, but those with reservations have a better chance of obtaining their desired campsites. Permits may be obtained at Apgar, St. Mary's Visitor Center, Many Glacier, Two Medicine, and Polebridge ranger stations. Fees also apply to walk-up services.

The Park Service strongly suggests you develop a second itinerary that may explore some less popular areas, in the event that your first choice is not available. Applicants will receive a confirmation letter by mail or by email, if you have provided an email address on the application form.

Ross Lake National Recreation Area and North Cascades National Park

One Wilderness Information Center supports the North Cascades National Park, and the Ross Lake and Lake Chelan National Recreation Areas. A permit is required for all backcountry travel in these areas. Note: Permits are not required for day use or for camping in car-accessed campgrounds along State Route 20.

There is no cost for a backcountry permit. The primary objective of the permit system is to better manage the backcountry and prevent overcrowding and resource damage.

Good news and bad news. There are no backcountry permit reservations, although the NPS has announced that they plan a pilot program for reservations for their most popular backcountry camps. Check with the NPS before heading out. Official backcountry permits are issued only in person only up to one day before your trip, on a first come first serve basis. Permits must be obtained from the WIC in Marblemount, Washington. It is located across the Skagit River from the North Cascades Highway (State Route 20) near milepost 120 and the town of Newhalem, adjacent to Newhalem Creek Campground. Their phone number is (360) 854-7245 and they are closed during the winter.

The Park Service says that if you are not traveling through Marblemount you may obtain a permit at the closest ranger station for your trailhead. For PNT hikers going west the closest station is the USFS Methow Valley Visitor Center in Winthrop at 24 West Chewuch Road, Winthrop, WA 98862, (509) 996-4003. For those going east best station is the Glacier Public Service Center at 10091 Mt Baker Hwy, Glacier, WA 98224, (360) 599-2714.

Note: While in Oroville call the WIC at (360) 854-7245 and explain that you are a PNT westbound hiker. They have been generally accommodating and issued permits over the phone.[CN]

Olympic National Park

Wilderness Camping Permits are required for all overnight stays in Olympic National Park wilderness (backcountry) and reservations are needed for some campsites as noted in this book and discussed below. If fact, most hikers end up with two separate permits for Olympic. One up to Forks, and one for the coast. Beginning February 15, 2018, reservations for Wilderness Permits are now accepted via email, postal mail, or in person to the WIC in Port Angeles. Applications can be downloaded, completed and then faxed to (360) 565-3108. Follow the link at the bottom of the web page at:
http://www.nps.gov/olym/planyourvisit/wilderness-reservations.htm
Call the Wilderness Information Center (WIC) at (360) 565-3100 to check on station hours and seasons or for more information about getting your permit. The WIC is located at the Olympic National Park Visitor Center, 3002 Mount Angeles Road, Port Angeles, WA 98362.
The fee for each wilderness camping permit is $8 per person per night or $45 for an annual pass. There is no nightly charge for youth 15 years of age and under but they still count towards the group size. Wilderness fees are non-refundable.
A separate permit is required for each hike originating at a new trailhead. Fees can be paid at staffed ranger stations where wilderness permits are available; wilderness use fees may be paid by credit card, cash or check. Some ranger stations and a few trailheads have self-registration permit boxes. Contact the WIC for locations. Upon completion of your outing, mail your payment in the envelope. The Park Services advises not to leave payment in trailhead permit boxes.
Planning Note: Download the trip planner map for ONP at:
https://www.nps.gov/olym/planyourvisit/upload/wildernessmap-10-25-16.pdf
While hiking the PNT around Anacortes (or around this point) it is a good idea to call the Olympic Wilderness Center to get the required permits, if you have not already done so. The PNT trek through Olympic National Park is a long stretch. Also, bear canisters are required at some camps and along the coast beach walk in Olympic National Park.

Hiking the Pacific Ocean Beach

The PNT offers a unique opportunity not afforded by the other national scenic trails—42 miles of beach hiking and camping. For those who have not done an "extended walk on the beach," it is important to learn about the conditions for hiking this landscape and to prepare properly.

Olympic National Park strongly recommends that you "Hike by the Tide!" This requires a copy of the most current tide charts for the dates you will be hiking in this area. In preparation for hiking this section I recommend you visit the Olympic NP website at: http://www.nps.gov/olym/planyourvisit/wilderness-coast.htm.

The website provides links to tide charts that are selectable by date for the upcoming year. Olympic NP recommends that for hiking north of La Push in the Ozette area, you add 30 minutes to the tide table for an accurate reading near Cape Alava. Here is an example of the tide chart for La Push, Washington for August 30-31, 2019. In this example, the chart shows that the best time to hike the beach at low tide is early morning and early evening. Note that very high tides are predicted around midnight and noon each day. Low tides, and the best beach walking should be at dawn and early evening.

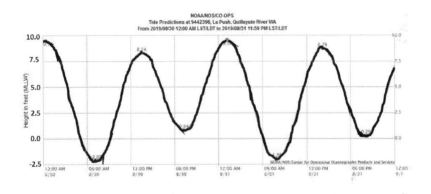

Trail Beginning

Getting To Glacier National Park, Montana

If you're lucky enough to have a friend or family member drive you to Glacier National Park, that's the way to do it. Barring that good fortune, let's take a look at other options.

Airlines: Glacier Park International Airport (airport code FCA) is near Kalispell, Montana, about 25 miles west of the west entrance to the park. The airport is serviced by Delta Connection SkyWest, Alaska Airlines through Horizon Air, and United Airlines through Denver and Chicago. Other airports include: Great Falls (200 miles), Missoula (156 miles), Spokane (300 miles), Calgary (266 miles).[32]

Train: Amtrak services both East Glacier and West Glacier. Download the Empire Builder planner at: https://www.amtrak.com/routes/empire-builder-train.html, showing service from Chicago, Portland, or Seattle to Glacier National Park. Shuttle service can be obtained at the lodges within easy walking distance from the train stations. The estimated lowest Amtrak fare from Seattle to East Glacier for 2019 ranges from about $83 to $139. (Cheaper fares can be found on other travel websites.) For those wishing to spend more time in Glacier National Park, after departing the train at East Glacier, consider hiking the Continental Divide Trail (CDT) north through the very scenic Triple Divide Pass. 2018 hikers report that this takes about 6 days on the CDT to reach the PNT, but it is very scenic and enjoyable.[80] The distance from East Glacier to intersect the Pacific Northwest Trail at waypoint 0021P is 78.5 miles.

Shuttles and Public Transportation: The park offers free transport to visitors to the park, allowing access to many destinations along the Going to the Sun Highway that bisects the park. Shuttles along the Going to the Sun Highway run every 15 or 30 minutes depending on time of day. The service is available between 7 am and 7 pm. There is two-way service between Apgar Center and Saint Mary Visitor Center. You can also take Glacier Park Inc.'s fee shuttles.[33]

One of the best resources for shuttle services is to contact Glacier Park, Inc. for the pickup and drop off locations, schedules, and cost. They have shuttles that take you right to the start of the PNT at Chief Mountain Customs. They have a hiker shuttle brochure. There is also a Hiker Shuttle between the Many Glacier hotel and the Saint Mary's Visitor Center, with stops all along Highway 89 and 17 on the east side of the park. The latest rate was $10 - $20 per hiker—cash only.[34]

Permits: Backcountry permits are required within Glacier National Park and may be obtained in advance for trips between June 15 and September 3—a very good idea. For details I suggest you read the Glacier NP Backcountry Guide and also watch their video (see Chapter 12).

Here's the gist of it. You can obtain permits for up to a $30 trip fee, plus a per person per night fee of $7. Permits *are not available* at the East or West Glacier train stations. Permits can be obtained from the Apgar Backcountry Permit Center, Saint Mary Visitor Center, Many Glacier and Two Medicine Ranger Stations, the Polebridge Ranger Station, and the Waterton Lakes National Park Visitor Reception Center (Canada). Note that none of them are near the start of the PNT. From March 15 to October 31, staff is available at 406-888-7857 if you need information or have a question.

Trail End

Leaving Olympic National Park, Ozette, Washington

This is a little difficult, but not impossible. There is no public transportation directly to/from Ozette. The nearest place for bus service is from Clallam Bay (22 miles), or Forks (36 miles). Many hikers head toward Clallam Bay and are able to pick up a ride along the way. There is an excellent Olympic National Park Travel Guide at: http://www.olympicpeninsula.org/page/transportation

Bus: New for 2019, there are trailhead shuttles on the Olympic Cast operated by Olympic Hiking Company (360) 457-2259, www.hikeolympic.com. Generally, they shuttle service for hiking groups to popular trailheads in ONP, but will offer service from Ozette that may connect with bus stops for Clallam Transit. Contact them directly for schedule and fare information.[79]

Clallam Transit services this remote county with limited bus service. Route 16 takes us from Clallam Bay to the transfer point at Sappho, then route 14 takes us to Port Angeles.[35] In 2018 there is a new bus service that transits between Port Angeles and the Bainbridge Island Ferry. From here the ferry service takes you to downtown Seattle with easy access to the train station, bus terminal and to SEATAC via Link Light Rail.

Also, the Olympic Bus Lines, an independent agent of Greyhound, operates between Port Angeles and Seattle's train and bus stations and Seattle's SEATAC airport twice a day.[36] Another option is to research Jefferson Transit which services Port Angeles with a brochure that describes the different transportation links into and throughout Seattle.[38]

Now that we've covered these planning and travel essentials, let's get on the trail in our next chapter.

This Book is too Heavy to Carry on The Trail

I couldn't agree more! This book is written first to be a planning tool and then to be torn apart and used on the trail with the sections you need. Each of the ten trail chapters, Chapters 2 – 11, is written to contain stand-alone information to help you while out on the trail. There are four sections to each chapter: key trail notes; detailed route narrative by waypoint; resupply options; trail support; and elevation profiles.

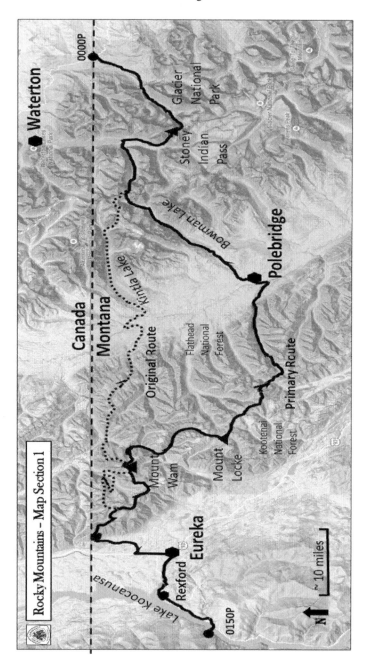

CHAPTER TWO
ROCKY MOUNTAINS – MAP SECTION 1
Glacier National Park to Lake Koocanusa

Pacific Northwest Trail, Glacier National Park

Key Trail Notes

<u>Highlights</u>: Stoney Indian Pass, Brown Pass, Boulder Pass, Mount Locke, Mount Wam, Tuchuck Mountain (highest point on the PNT).

<u>Primary Route Estimated Elevation Change</u>: 13,204' climb / 16,394' descent

<u>Route Alternates</u>: Boulder Pass – Kintla Lake, Ten Lakes Scenic Area

<u>Possible Resupply</u>: Polebridge, Eureka, Rexford

<u>Parks/Forests</u>: Glacier NP, Flathead NF, Kootenai NF

<u>Permits</u>: Glacier NP backcountry, reservations and $7 per night fee

<u>Other Notes</u>: Bear spray and bear canister

Before we start and hit the trail in Glacier National Park (GNP), double check our backcountry permit, camp reservations, bear spray, and all equipment. The PNT for the next 1,200 miles does not offer much chance to jump off the trail and run into REI to change out our gear.

0000P 0.0mi 48° 59.763'N 113° 39.551'W 5340' State Route 17 X Trailhead near Chief Mountain Customs

The trail begins at a parking lot about 300 feet south of the Big Chief border station on State Route 17. From the northwest corner of the parking lot, the trail leads downhill almost 800 feet and then follows the Belly River for a couple hours. This is a very pleasant walk with wildflowers and a short wall of green plants.

This trailhead is also a popular alternate starting point for the Continental Divide Trail (CDT). In just under 2.1 miles our descent ends and we intersect the Belly River Trail, which runs north-south.

0002P 2.1mi 48° 58.860'N 113° 40.646'W 4580' Belly River Trail (BRT) Split

Turn south on the BRT, and depending on the season, there may be many wildflowers on this section of the trail. We go about 1.1 miles as we come to the Threemile Campground and our next waypoint.

0003P 1.1mi 48° 58.021'N 113° 40.883'W 4620' Belly River Trail @ Threemile Camp

This camp is not one of the designated Glacier NP camps and there are no hiker reports on it. Keep hiking south on the BRT slightly uphill for another 3.2 miles to where the CDT branches south toward the Belly River Ranger Station on the Gable Pass trail at our next waypoint. The ranger station is part of the historic district first built in 1912 and there is no electricity here.

0006P 3.0mi 48° 55.997'N 113° 42.774'W 4680' Belly River Trail X Cosley Lake Cutoff Trail @ Gable Creek Camp

Gable Creek Camp is the first Glacier NP trail camp we find on the primary PNT route. The camp has four sites, two of which can be reserved after June 15 (hereafter shown in shortcut form as 4-2: 6/15). There should be a pit toilet and fire rings. Overnight backcountry fees for GNP are $7 per night.

The PNT turns west crossing the Belly River on a suspension bridge on the Cosley Lake Cutoff Trail as we hike 0.2 miles west to cross the Belly River on a park footbridge. Looking to the southwest we should see the prominent and distinctive Pyramid Peak at 8200'. Pyramid Peak will be our guide for the next several hours. Hiking southwest start a slight uphill climb and in 1.9 miles reach the north end of Cosley Lake.

About 0.5 miles before the next waypoint, you might take the time to visit the Gros Ventre Falls on the Mokowanis River. This is only a 400' long trail to see the waterfall. Continuing on the PNT we soon come to the junction with the Stony Indian Pass and Ptarmigan Trails.

0008P 2.1mi 48° 55.658'N 113° 44.794'W 4860' Cosley Lake Cutoff Trail X Stoney Indian Pass Trail (SIPT)

Note that camps along Cosley and Glenns Lake have been reported to be terribly windy as the predominant west wind funnels off the mountains and straight down the valley, with whitecaps often seen on the water. May the trail gods favor your stay here with a quiet night.

At this trail junction we bear right (southwest) following the shoreline of Cosley Lake for 1.4 miles. On the way we soon pass the Cosley Lake Camp on the north shore of the lake. The camp is about 200 yards south and not visible from the trail.[GT] This camp has 4-2: 6/15 sites, but no fires are permitted in this camp due to limited wood supply. You may also find stock at this camp.

After leaving the shoreline we enter a rocky wooded area between Cosley Lake and Glenns Lake. In about 0.6 miles we will see Glenns Lake and come upon the Foot Glenns Lake Camp at the north end of the lake. This camp is 4-2: 6/15, with a pit toilet, and again, no fires are permitted.

We keep to the SIPT southwest and slightly uphill for about 2.6 miles to the south end of the lake. Here is the Head Glenns Lake Camp, 3-2: 6/15 with a fire pit. Keep south on the trail for another 0.4 miles into our next waypoint at the Stoney Indian Pass Trail junction.

0013P 4.8mi 48° 53.288'N 113° 48.903'W 4880' SIPT X Mokowanis Lake Trail

Here the trail splits at a 'Y' junction. Note that the Mokowanis Lake Camp is 1.1 miles down this trail and reported to be far more scenic than the Junction camp.[GT] Although not directly on the PNT, you must get reservations for this camp after July 15. It has 2-1: 7/15 and fires are not permitted. There is a spectacular waterfall another 0.3 miles south of the camp and worth the short hike.[49]

The PNT keeps to the SIPT as it temporarily heads northwest into the Mokowanis Junction Camp which is 5-3: 6/15, and no fires are permitted. Stock is likely to be here, too. The primary PNT route along the SIPT heads southwest to start climbing just over 2000' to Stoney Indian Pass. In 1.7 miles past the camp, and just after climbing a short series of switchbacks, the trail opens to the small glacial Atsina Lake. Continue southwest climbing and look for the Atsina Falls due west. Hikers report that there may be a swift, thigh deep ford just past Atsina Lake.[GT]

A note of caution here; be prepared for ice, and blowing snow for this section of the PNT—even in early July. Check the weather and be sure you have the proper equipment to handle the climb.

The PNT will take you above the falls after more switchbacks with a 300' climb. The trail turns northwest to pass above the falls and into Stoney Indian Pass at 6909' at our next waypoint.

0017P 4.2mi 48° 52.900'N 113° 51.900'W 6908' SIPT @ Stoney Indian Pass

We know we're at the pass when we can look to the north and see Stoney Indian Lake below us and we begin to descend on a series of switchbacks that lead us down 550' to the east side of the lake. Here we find the gorgeous Stoney Indian Lake Camp on the north side, about 1.0 miles from the pass. The camp is 3-2:8/1 with a one night stay and no fires. The camp is 6370' elevation and likely has snow.

Continue northwest for another 2.3 miles past Stoney Indian Camp, dropping about 1800' elevation to reach the primary Continental Divide Trail junction at our next waypoint.

0021P 3.3mi 48° 53.862'N 113° 54.289'W 4600' SIPT X Continental Divide/Waterton Valley Trail

The PNT and the primary CDT join together for the next 3.8 miles as we hike north to Waterton Lake. The trail is also known in the park as the Waterton Valley Trail. In 0.85 miles we cross the Porcupine Lookout Trail that heads west. Continue north for another 1.4 miles to the side trail that takes you a quarter mile west to the Kootenai Lakes Camp. This camp is 4-2: 6/15 and fires are not permitted.

Continue north another 2.4 miles to the Goat Haunt Border Patrol/Ranger Station and the Waterton Lake Trail at our next waypoint.

Prior to the PNT starting at the eastside of Glacier NP and with the Belly River Trail, the original PNT "officially" started at Goat Haunt. Most of the hikers traveled to Goat Haunt from Canada, starting at the town of Waterton, traveling either via the Waterton Lake ferry, or by hiking the west side of the lake on the Canadian Waterton Lake Trail. This means carrying a passport to re-enter the U.S. and clearing customs with the Border Patrol.

If you take the boat ride from the town of Waterton, it will cost about $25 one-way. If you decide to go into Waterton from Goat Haunt for resupply, you will have to clear both Canadian Customs and then U.S. Customs upon your return.[GT] U.S. Customs meets every ferry docking at Goat Haunt. If you do not carry a passport issued by the U.S. or Canada, you are highly advised **_not_** to try to enter the U.S. at Goat Haunt do their limited ability to clear you into the country.

Even if you do not enter the U.S. from Canada, I still recommend you touch base with the rangers and the border patrol in any case. Some hikers have reported that they have later been stopped on the trail by the border patrol for questioning, even though they have never crossed the U.S. Canada border.[BT]

0025P 4.8mi 48° 57.468'N 113° 53.533'W 4230' CDT X Waterton Lake Trail

There are two camps in this area. The Goat Haunt Shelters are about a quarter mile northeast near the boat dock and are 7-4: 6/15. Shelters are three sided with a cement floor and will fit two small tents on the floor. The other is the Waterton River Camp, which is 5-3: 6/15 with fire rings. It is located down a spur trail a few minutes before our junction with the Boulder Pass Trail 6. Follow the Waterton Lake Trail a short jaunt of only 0.5 miles to join the Boulder Pass Trail 6 at our next waypoint.

0027P 0.6mi 48° 57.485'N 113° 54.223'W 4280' Waterton Lake Trail X Boulder Pass Trail

At the 'Y' junction we bear left (west) on the Boulder Pass trail as it heads into the valley created by Olson Mountain to the north and the prominent Citadel Peaks to the south. The valley extends and opens to the west as we gradually climb 2000' for the next several hours. In about 2.9 miles we come upon Lake Janet and the camp past the west end of the lake. This camp is small and is 2-1: 6/15 but will likely have stock. From the trail to the south we see Porcupine Ridge only 1.5 miles away as it rises almost 5000' above us.

Continue west for another 3.1 miles to Lake Frances and its camp on the northwest corner of the lake. This camp is beautiful and highly rated as one of the best in the park by thru-hikers[GT] with views of the lake and the mountains surrounding this small camp. It is 2-1: 6/15, no fires and only a one night stay. Few PNT hikers actually stay here simply because of their schedules and relatively short distance from Goat Haunt. Look to the southwest for the best view of the Dixon Glacier which feeds Lake Frances.

Around the corner from Lake Frances you will find the Hawksbill Camp and Thunderbird Creek, which is fed from the Thunderbird Glacier to the southwest. On a clear day you can easily see the Thunderbird Falls which is about half way up from Hawksbill Camp and the glacier. The camp is also small 2-1: 6/15 and no fires. Our next way point is 1.9 miles from Lake Frances Camp at the intersection with the Bowman Lake Trail.

0034P 7.8mi 48° 57.047'N 114° 02.135'W 6255' Boulder Pass Trail X Bowman Lake Trail

Decision Time. The primary PNT route now turns southwest to Bowman Lake and near the town of Polebridge, Montana. The more scenic and challenging route heads west to Hole-in-the-Wall, Boulder Glacier and Kintla Lake on the Boulder Pass Trail. In 2015, Backpacker Magazine proclaimed this original PNT route as some of the best 100 miles of trails in Glacier National Park. Unfortunately, this route is often closed and deemed too dangerous with ice and snow even into July. Plus, it bypasses a visit to Polebridge. The description of the alternate route along the Boulder Pass Trail follows at the end of the section. Instead of doing the entire alternate route, some hikers have done a very nice side trip up to Boulder Pass and returned to the primary PNT route.[80]

Back to the primary PNT route: Head west on the Bowman Lake Trail, thankfully at relatively level terrain for the first 0.5 miles. We should easily see the Brown Pass Camp to the north a few minutes after starting this trail. This camp is 3-2:7/15, and no fires.

Once at the top of the pass the trail plunges downhill losing about 1700' elevation loss in about two miles down to Bowman Creek. From this point the trail is relatively flat and easy to navigate for the next 3.3 miles to the north end of Bowman Lake and the Head Bowman Camp. This camp is 6-3: 6/15 with fire rings.

Bowman Lake is 6.3 miles long and the trail follows the western shoreline as it is one of the most popular and highest rated trails in the park. Unfortunately the views along the lake are often blocked by the trees. Also, pack horses and mountain bikers use this trail so it can be a muddy mess. About 6.0 miles down the lake we come to our next waypoint at the junction with the Numa Ridge Lookout Trail.

0047P 12.5mi 48° 50.239'N 114° 11.729'W 4040' Bowman Lake Trail X Numa Ridge Lookout Trail

The Numa Ridge Lookout Trail runs sharply uphill and to the northeast. This trail climbs 2900' in 5.1 miles to the lookout tower. The views are spectacular—but no PNT thru hiker has reported to have taken this climb, especially when the Polebridge and the Mercantile/Bakery is ahead!

In 0.8 more miles we come to the Bowman Lake Ranger Station and the Glacier NP car campground. The campground has no reservations. The camp has water and pit toilets. Primitive tent sites are $15 per night. At the south entrance to the campground we pick up the Bowman Lake Road. Here we'll be on our first of many dirt road walks on the PNT.

0048P 1.1mi 48° 49.684'N 114° 12.083'W 4040' Bowman Lake Trail X Bowman Lake Road

Hike southwest downhill on the dusty Bowman Lake Road for about 5.4 miles to Inside North Fork Road. Although this is a narrow dusty road, this is one of the more beautiful road walks on the PNT with Glacier NP to the east and the Whitefish Range to the west.[KC]

0053P 5.4mi 48° 47.216'N 114° 16.961'W 3580' Bowman Lake Road X Inside North Fork Road (aka Glacier Route 7)

We'll go to Polebridge by heading south for about 0.25 miles, looking to cross the bridge over the North Fork Flathead River. Along the way we pass the Bowman Creek Campground which is also primitive, but useable. We take the first right onto Glacier Drive.

Resupply: From here it is 20 minutes to the center of town and the Polebridge Mercantile with the Tavern/Café next door. Note: Due to the popularity of the PNT, beginning in 2018 the Mercantile will no longer accept resupply boxes sent to them. In return, however, they have improved their selection of supplies that a thru-hiker would need.[72] You can also follow the signs for the North Fork Hostel (406-888-5241) about a quarter mile away. A bunk bed at the Hostel is $22 or only $20 if you want to tent on the lawn. They will accept UPS shipped hiker boxes sent to 80 Beaver Drive, Polebridge, MT 59928. After our stop in Polebridge, we head west out of town on the dirt road.

0056P 2.1mi 48° 45.881'N 114° 17.525'W 3550' Polebridge Loop X North Fork Road

Decision Time. In 0.3 miles we come to the intersection with the North Fork Road. An alternative route is to head north back to the alternate original PNT route, a 13.7 mile road hike, to very near the border with Canada. But we're following the new primary PNT route and head south for 1.3 miles, and then turn back to the northwest. North Fork Road is a lightly used, tree-lined, dirt road. We want to look for the first road to the right (northwest), which is FR376 or Hay Creek Road. There is a house on the east side of the road and a driveway turning southwest 100' south beyond FR376. Our road and the junction we're looking for is just after the pavement starts on North Fork Road.

0057P 1.3mi 48° 44.851'N 114° 17.269'W 3560' North Fork Road X Hay Creek Road-FR376

Head northwest on Hay Creek Road for 3.4 miles staying on this dirt road, which is nicely graded and has little traffic.[GT] Soon after hiking on this road we enter the Flathead National Forest where camping is generally allowed anywhere, with caution. Next we look for a minor road bridge across Hay Creek, about 0.15 miles before our next road intersection with FR 1685. Water is generally available in the creek except after late July.

0060P 3.4mi 48° 46.160'N 114° 20.965'W 4070' Hay Creek Road FR376 X Forest Road 1685 (closed)

Continue west on FR376 Hay Creek Road, with Hay Creek to the south. You'll be climbing a gentle grade for the next 6.0 miles, gaining about 1100'. At the junction of FR376 and FR1680, we pick up the Hay Creek Trail 3. The trail may look very much like the road.

0066P 6.0mi 48° 45.425'N 114° 28.171'W 4710' Hay Creek Trail 3 X Hay Creek Road FR1680

If you're looking for water, FR1680 turns southwest and leads down to Hay Creek. Otherwise, continue southwest for another 0.5 miles to the trailhead at the end of the road.

0066.5P 0.5mi 48° 45.327'N 114° 28.748'W 4880' Hay Creek Road FR376 X Hay Creek Trail 3

TR3 follows the double truck tracks after crossing through the dirt mound barriers. Note that at the 3.0 miles, on an uphill grade, the trail/road turns to cross Hay Creek on a short bridge. Then it climbs southeast gaining 120' for 0.3 miles up to the ridge to an open U-turn at the top of the rise.

0070P 3.2mi 48° 44.222'N 114° 31.092'W 5310' U-turn on Hay Creek Trail 3

The PNT continues west on TR3 for another 1.2 miles to the swampy Hay Lake. In 0.15 miles after we pass the lake on the trail it turns north and climbs another 300' where the trail (old road) ends. Here we pick up the White Fish Divide/Ralph Thayer Memorial National Trail 26 at our next waypoint.

0072P 1.8mi 48° 44.309'N 114° 33.301'W 6040' Hay Creek Trail 3 X Whitefish Divide Trail 26

Check your map and directions; this is a confusing junction. In 2014 the sign for TR26 points the wrong way here. A hikers has marked the sign with "PNT W and E" arrow to help you.[DV] Turn right and take TR26 northwest where you should find that it drops downhill 500' to the intersection with Forest Road 115 in about 1.3 miles. TR26 is part trail and part road for the next 13.8 miles.

0073P 1.6mi 48° 44.955'N 114° 34.303'W 5560' Trail 26 X Red Meadow Road - Road 115 X Forest Road 318

Exiting TR26 we turn north on the gravel FR115 for 0.25 miles to where the road splits. To the right (north and then northeast) FR115 initially climbs slightly and takes us to the Red Meadow Lake and campground in 0.6 miles. This Flathead NFS campground has six sites, pit toilet, bear boxes, and no water except from the lake. A 2013 thru-hiker reported that there is a spring on the east side of the lake that you can hear draining into the lake.[43]

Our primary PNT route, however, bears left (north-northwest) on Forest Road 589 with a level grade. In only 0.15 miles FR589 turns west and begins to climb slightly uphill. We follow FR589 as it turns for another 0.4 miles and come to a sharp bend in the road. At the bend there are dual track that lead north, but we jog east for 60 yards and climb on the road. There is a culvert with water in another 200 yards ahead.[50] CAUTION: Depending on the season, this could be the last reliable water for the next 14 miles, which is at Blue Sky Creek.[66]

After the bend we hike uphill northwest for another 0.75 miles to come to our next waypoint at the trailhead for the Link Lake Trail 372 and the continuation of Trail 26. As we approach, we can see the trailhead parking lot on the east side of the road with the trailhead another 60 yards ahead on the west side.

0076P 1.5mi 48° 45.688'N 114° 35.524'W 6030' Road 589 X Link Lake Trail 372 X Whitefish Divide Trail 26

This is the trailhead for TR372 and TR26 with a large PNT sign.[61] TR372 climbs 600' to the northeast over a saddle in the ridge and down to Link Lake in about 1.0 miles.

The primary PNT route, now again TR26, starts on the opposite side of the trailhead parking area, and there may not be a sign. TR26 heads west uphill so be careful not to follow the more apparent trail northwest at what is a continuation of the road.

Climb west gaining 900' elevation on TR26 for about 1.3 miles to the top of the ridge that connects Whitefish Mountain and a 7045' Peak to its northwest. Next the trail climbs uphill into a clear cut area with an easy to follow tread-- when it is not snow covered—along the ridge west for 0.8 miles. The ridge is high and well defined, sprinkled with wildflowers, lustrous grasses, and thin, stubby trees.[KC]

0078P 2.5mi 48° 45.540'N 114° 38.110'W 7020' Trail 26 @ 7020' Peak

Navigation is relatively easy on this ridge, with the trail junctions signed.[GT] This waypoint is added just for reassurance as the trail crosses the top of a 7020' knob and then continues north. TR26 turns north with a few switchbacks downhill and then back up again at our next waypoint. For the next destination follow the ridge to the 7168' Butte that sits 1.5 miles to the northwest.

0080P 1.5mi 48° 46.598'N 114° 38.777'W 6920' Trail 26 Southeast of 7168' Butte

At this point TR26 departs the crest of the ridge and works downhill to the northwest along the western slope of the ridge for 0.6 miles. Then TR26 crosses over the ridge near the crest to work west on the northern side for about 0.25 miles.

Now TR26 returns to the north following the ridge downhill losing 420' elevation in 0.4 miles. This drops us into a 6367' saddle and our next waypoint. Look for an old pack trail that heads northeast and downhill into the valley. On a clear day looking east you should be able to see Huntsberger Peak at 7359' to the north across from Mount Young at 7284'.

0081P 1.2mi 48° 47.167'N 114° 39.952'W 6370' Trail 26 @ Saddle South of Huntsberger Peak

Just as we climb out of the saddle on a jeep road signed as "Whitefish Div Tr No. 26,"[50] look for the remnants of an old trail heading downhill to the east into the valley with Shorty Creek. We keep hiking past this northwest for the 0.7 miles as TR26 traverses below and to the eastside of the ridgeline, before climbing back over the ridge short of the 7051' butte to the east at the junction of Trail 374.[50]

0082P 0.7mi 48° 47.665'N 114° 40.407'W 6670' Trail 26 X Huntsberger Peak Trail 374

Staying on TR26 we continue northwest on mostly level tread, through dense forest, for the next 0.4 miles before descending. Along the way you might find on the map a small unnamed lake about 0.1 miles the west of the trail. Hikers in 2015 explored this for a trail camp, but it was horribly buggy and the water was fetid.[51] Continuing on the trail, at 3.2 miles you should come up to the intersection with the Whale Creek Trail 11 which drops you down nearly 700' in 0.6 miles to Whale Lake. Staying on TR26, in another half mile we intersect Trail 96 which comes up from the west. A small open area is here for a trail camp, but no water.

Caution: Beginning in this area, for approximately the next 3 miles, you may find evidence of the 2017 Gibralter Ridge Fire and hazardous trees.

Next, we press due north on TR26 along the ridge for another 2.2 miles to the top of Mount Locke. Although we have a clear view momentarily TR26 crisscrosses the ridge several times. In about 1.4 miles we should find the intersection with TR372, which has come again from the west to join TR26 to climb to the top of Mount Locke.

At the intersection with TR372 the PNT turns east temporarily into the switchbacks and begins the final 700' climb over the next 0.7 miles to come near the summit and to our next waypoint. The summit is reached by a spur trail about 100 yards off the main trail and worth the climb for the view.[49]

0086P 5.3mi 48° 49.695'N 114° 43.616'W 7205' Trail 26 @ Mount Locke

At the top of Mount Locke there is the collapsing Locke Cabin, originally built in 1929. From the top of Mount Locke the trails are well marked and we stick to TR26 downhill and northeast to where the PNT leaves TR26. Note that the trail junction with TR74 has moved east[DV] and your map may not be updated.

0087P 0.7mi 48° 49.933'N 114° 42.817'W 6640' Trail 26 X Blue Sky Trail 74

TR26 continues east while we turn to head north on TR74 as it drops down into the Blue Sky Valley. Look carefully for the turn north at TR74 which is signed and well-marked. The trail was reported to be cleared of blowdowns and in relatively good shape.[DV]

As we step off the ridge onto TR74 we leave the Flathead National Forest and enter the Kootenai National Forest. TR74 descends through deep forest about 900' for the first three quarters of a mile from leaving the ridge to crossing the Blue Sky Creek. After the creek the trail continues northeast for another 0.8

miles to reach the old forest road FR7020, which is still designated TR74. This area of Kootenai National Forest has a large population of deer and elk, with some grizzly bears mixed in to keep your interest in being trail aware.

0089P 1.6mi 48° 50.984'N 114° 42.492'W 5550' Trail 74 @ Big Sky Creek

Following TR74, now the old forest Road 7020, we head north and then west keeping the Big Sky Creek on our left. About 2.0 miles into this leg we break out of the forest due to fire damage and should be able to see a sheer rocky ridge that wraps around the creek in our direction. It rises 2100' above us. Continue for another 3.3 miles to the confluence of Big Sky and Graves Creeks. There is gate and a footbridge that leads to the trailhead parking lot on Forest Road 114. Note that there are a few excellent spots for a trail camping about 0.1 miles before reaching FR114 on TR74.

0094P 5.4mi 48° 53.806'N 114° 46.484'W 4120' Trail 74 X Forest Road 114 / Trail Camp

For the next 24 miles or so, we'll be hiking in the Ten Lakes Scenic Area. The Ten Lakes Scenic Area is beautiful and worth a more thorough visit. The landscape is mountainous but gentle, with long views across the basin ringed by mountains. The trails are in great shape with a couple cool lookouts to visit. [KC]
From the trailhead parking lot we head north on FR114, which is a well maintained hard-pack road.

0097P 2.6 mi 48° 55.760'N 114° 45.136'W 4530' Forest Road 114 X Therriault Lakes Road FR319

At this waypoint FR114 turns east, while the PNT continues north on Forest Road 319. In other words, keep going north in the same direction—do not turn. Follow FR319 north for another 1.6 mile to reach Forest Road 7032 and the trailhead for Trail 77 at our next waypoint.

0098P 1.6 mi 48° 56.904'N 114° 45.651'W 5110' Forest Road 319 X Foundation Camp Trail 77

The trailhead is a short 90 yards west on the unsigned spur road FR7032. The trail is at the west end of the parking lot where we follow it for about 0.7 miles west to the bridge that crosses Foundation Creek at our next waypoint.

0099P 0.7mi 48° 56.842'N 114° 46.554'W 5270' Trail 77 @ Foundation Creek

After crossing the bridge TR77 turns east and climbs the 250' ridge with a reasonable incline. This is a very brushy area so we keep following the old road[50] TR77 as it rounds a corner and continues a slight climb to the west. In another 1.1 miles TR77 turns south at our next waypoint.

0101P 1.6mi 48° 56.622'N 114° 47.172'W 5810' Trail 77 Waypoint – South Turn

TR77 has a fairly well defined tread and turns south and southwest. To your left (east) there have been some old overgrown logging tracks but we continue southwest. The next waypoint is only about 0.6 miles ahead and is added for reassurance. This point reflects where TR77 turns back to the northwest.

0102P 0.7mi 48° 56.361'N 114° 47.573'W 6190' Trail 77 Waypoint – Northwest Turn

The trail progresses with only slight ups and downs northward, past a small lake for the next 0.7 miles; fill your water as this is the last good water for 10 miles. Next TR77 intersects the Highline Trail 339 where the original PNT route rejoins (see alternate routing at the end of this section).

0103P 1.1mi 48° 56.925'N 114° 48.116'W 6340' Trail 77 X Highline Trail 339

As you turn on to TR339, don't be surprised if it has patches of snow even in July. From here the trail circles and climbs inside the bowl ridge counter-clockwise gaining over 600' in about 0.7 miles. We pass under Mount Wam as we climb toward the southwest and to the top of the ridge. Here we can find the spur trail that leads back up to the north and to the old cabin on top of the summit at our next waypoint. The trail only takes about 5 minutes to hike[BT] with enough space for a single person shelter near the locked rental cabin.[80]

0104P 0.7mi 48° 57.178'N 114° 48.687'W 7040' Trail 339 @ Mount Wam

The 0.15 mile spur trail climbs straight up 160' to the top. The USFS provides the following information about the cabin:

> *This 196-square foot cabin sits atop Mt. Wam on a rocky point in the middle of the Ten Lakes Proposed Wilderness Area. It has been used as an observation point for spotting forest fires since 1931. It was abandoned in 1951 and only used periodically until 1999 when it was restored. The cabin sleeps four and is equipped with a woodstove. The lookout is not wired for electricity and has an outdoor toilet. A small spring is located 0.8 mile from the cabin; we recommend bringing your own drinking water as all open water is considered contaminated. The cabin can be reserved 180 days in advance of your stay at $20 per night.*

From the intersection with the spur trail the PNT continues to follow TR339 along the ridgeline south, dropping about 130' in 0.3 miles. TR339 turns sharply west and down off the ridge to pick up the adjacent ridge protruding from Mount Wam to the southwest. Follow the southern side of this ridge for the next 1.3 miles at which point we intersect the Clarence-Rich Creek Trail 78.

As you continue west slightly downhill on TR339 in a thick forest, look carefully in 0.1 miles for the intersection with TR78.

0105P 1.9mi 48° 56.708'N 114° 49.739'W 6230' Trail 339 X Clarence-Rich Creek Trail 78

Decision Time. The new primary route, as established by the National Forest Service in early 2014, continues west on TR339. The original PNT alternate route has us turn north on TR78 to explore the Ten Lake Scenic Area. The Ten Lakes Scenic Area is dominated by a high ridge of the Whitefish Mountains, and although not officially a wilderness, the Kootenai National Forest manages it as such. The alternate route offers spectacular views of the Therriault Lakes and the Bluebird Basin areas.[41] The description of the Ten Lakes route is at the end of this section.

Back to the primary PNT route. There are no reports of a trail sign at this junction with TR78, but we continue west on TR339 and slightly downhill. Soon the trail turns southwest on an easily identifiable tread. After only about 0.3 miles the trail levels and winds along a soft ridge. For the next 6 miles you may be buried in the green along a wide heavily treed ridge line with mostly obscured views. Most of the time it feels like you could be walking in flatland forest anywhere. Finally, you pop out on the treeless scree slope, and can see something, but not views that make me want to throw my hat in the air.[47]

0107P 1.3mi 48° 56.509'N 114° 51.114'W 6590' Trail 339 @ Ridge Turnpoint

There are no significant landmarks here and this waypoint is added for reference. Turning southwest TR339 remains level around the 6600' contour before beginning a slight climb. In 0.4 miles the trail turns south to climb over the 6811' Butte and stays generally along the ridge crest. We should begin to see Stahl Peak, with its barren rock summit at 7,435', to our south. In 1.0 miles after turning south we intersect the Stahl Peak Summit Trail 81 coming up from the south.

0108P 1.5mi 48° 55.471'N 114° 51.474'W 6810' Trail 339 @ Stahl Peak Trail 81

The Stahl Peak Trail 81 is 0.8 miles long and climbs a little over 600' to the lookout, which has a wood burning stove.[49] This is a can't miss sidetrip.[80] There are "plenty of heart-pumping views at the summit. The north face drops over 1,000 feet to an unnamed lake. The lookout was built in 1926 and used for emergencies into the 1960's. Views from the summit include Mt. Wam, Green Mountain, Poorman Mountain and the Ten Lakes to the north. Mt. Gibralter, Mt. Scotty, Deep Mountain, Krinklehorn Peak and Krag Peak to the south. Mt. Barnaby, St. Clair Peak, Ksanka Peak, Independence Peak and Lake Koocanusa to the west."[42] The lookout and privy were reported to be in good shape in 2016 and well worth the hike up for a cozy night's stay.[CN]

Back on the PNT on TR339 we head southwest downhill for 0.6 miles into Therriault Pass. Within the next 0.5 miles into our next way point we pass a series of trail junctions. First is the Stahl Creek Trail 80 which comes uphill from the southeast and Baboon Lake. Next is the Gibralter Ridge Trail 335 from the south, and soon thereafter with the Big Therr/Highline Trail 190 coming uphill from the north and the Therriault Lakes and campgrounds. The next trail junction is at our next waypoint at the junction with the Therriault Pass Trail 87.

0109P 0.9mi 48° 54.982'N 114° 52.524'W 6360' Trail 339 X Therriault Pass Trail 87

TR87 turns west, then south, downhill into the valley. The PNT stays on the highline ridge leading us northwest as Mount Barnaby rises well above us to the west. The trail is generally level on the ridge just above the 6400' contour for the next 0.8 miles. Here TR339 turns north and descends 200' elevation over the next 0.2 miles to reach an unnamed glacier pond at the foot of Saint Claire Peak. About 200 yards east of the trail there is good trail campsite at the north end of the pond.

Climbing back up the 200' elevation we now hike north along the eastern shoulder of the mountain. Close, but not quite "billy-goat" style, the trail does lead us through a rock and scree field with incredible views east to the Therriault Lakes and valley.

About 0.3 miles before our next waypoint, TR339 turns west and we climb away from the 6400' contour we've been hiking and enjoying.

0112P 2.5mi 48° 56.209'N 114° 54.525'W 6590' Trail 339 x Sinclair Creek Trail 88

In August 2013 the NFS changed the primary route for the PNT at this trail junction. The original PNT hiked this section of TR339 south. Now the primary route reverses this as we hike north.

We meet TR88 as it comes in from the east. Do not descend on the old primary route here or you will miss the only decent views up here. Continue ascending and back in the trees again, where the environment begins to feel more truly alpine. There are lots of awesome flowers on display in the early summer.[47]

We continue southwest on the "trusty" TR339 with its good tread as it leads us still along the ridge with good views to the north. After working west for about 1.0 miles TR339 turns north at the junction with the Bluebird Trail 83.

TR83 would drop us lower on the ridge down to Paradise Lake and into the Bluebird Basin. It reconnects with our PNT TR339 in about 0.9 miles. We stay higher on TR339 to find Bluebird Lake in 0.7 miles.

0113P 1.7mi 48° 56.706'N 114° 55.881'W 6850' Trail 339 @ Bluebird Lake Camp

Bluebird Lake is not visible from the trail. There is an unsigned spur trail on the southeast outlet side of the lake. Don't be surprised if you find ice still on the surface even in July![GT] This an excellent place to trail camp, if this area doesn't have snow or is not flooded from the runoff.

For the next 1.5 miles we steadily climb on gradual uphill tread along the east side of the ridge shoulder, gaining about 400' into our next waypoint. Along the way there will be two trail junctions which would take us down the ridge to the east. Ignoring these junctions, we stay higher on the ridge looking for our next waypoint just after crossing a saddle in the ridge where TR339 turns northwest and downhill.

0115P 1.5mi 48° 57.800'N 114° 55.780'W 7270' Trail 339 X Blacktail Trail 92

The primary route now continues northwest on TR92, leaving TR339. This is the trail junction where the Ten Lakes Basin alternate route returns to the PNT primary route. TR92 has a poor tread and it hard to follow.[50] This new route brings us into Eureka from the north side of town. This reroute was necessary to keep hikers from trespassing on private property, and to avoid the short bushwhack east of Eureka.

Before we turn north on TR92, if you want one last excellent view of the Wolverine Creek Valley, just scramble another 60 yards up to the top of the ridge on TR339/TR92. Or, if you want to camp down near Wolverine Lakes, just follow TR92 east and downhill.

Coming off the ridge heading northwest on TR92 we rapidly drop down into a valley between Poorman Mountain and the north shoulder of Green Mountain. Unfortunately, in 2018, the trail was reported to have a number of blowdowns.[80] We'll descend 1250' over the next 1.3 miles into our next waypoint.

0116P 1.3mi 48° 58.388'N 114° 57.207'W 6040' Blacktail Trail 92 @ Old Mining Road

Just before TR92 begins to round to the south along the ridge, the trail picks up an old mining road as its tread. In about 0.5 miles TR92 crosses a small arm of Blacktail Creek on a wood bridge. The stream below usually has a good flow throughout the summer.[50]

After crossing the creek TR92 climbs as we transition to hike northwest again along the eastside of the ridge above Blacktail Creek. We still follow the old mining road and in 2.1 miles from our last waypoint we cross over the ridge in a small saddle at a 6152' marker on the map.

From here we progress down the ridge for another 1.7 miles with a western view, albeit somewhat obscured through the thick forest.

0121P 4.0mi 48° 59.972'N 115° 00.387'W 5290' Blacktail Trail 92 @ Northern Turnpoint

PNT Factoid: At this sharp U-turn in TR92, we are at the closest point the PNT comes to the U.S.-Canada border. A mere 100 feet to the north is the demarcation line.

We now follow TR92 south and downhill as the old grassy mining road is easy to follow. We have three major switchbacks over the next 3.0 miles before we descend another 1200' down the steep ridge. Some hikers have thought it would be much easier to hike straight west and downhill along the cleared border, however, that probably isn't such a good idea if you don't want to meet up with the U.S. Border Patrol. We'll stick to TR92 as we descend into the Tobacco Plains, as this broad valley is named.

0123P 3.0mi 48° 59.918'N 115° 01.098'W 4080' Blacktail Trail 92 X Burma Road 1001

The trailhead is just a small vehicle turnaround with no facilities. We turn south on this county road still descending for the next 0.6 miles to where we finally level in the valley floor.

NOTE: In 2015 a hiker was camped in this area and in the middle of the night was temporarily detained and searched by the U.S. Border Patrol. Being this close to the border with Canada the Border Patrol is especially vigilant north of Eureka.

There is a small pond formed by a dam just 1.1 miles south of the trailhead. There is a vehicle turnaround at the dam and on the east side of the pond there may be a good spot for a trail camp.

Trail Angel: About 0.75 miles south of the pond there is a new resort/camp off Gould Road. See details at the end of this chapter.

Most hikers at this point are ready to push on, however, to get into Eureka for rest and resupply. Moving on, we continue due south on Road 1001 and in 0.6 miles past the pond, we exit the Kootenai National Forest.

The road next jogs to the west and then south again to follow DeRozier Creek for about 1.3 miles. This is cattle and farming country along the road with the creek fenced off.[50] We follow the road as it turns west for 1.8 miles to take us to our next waypoint at the junction with highway US93 (aka Dewy Avenue).

There is a new Indian Springs Public Trail which you can take to avoid the initial road walk on Highway US93. As the Burma Road turns north and downhill, we begin to see some houses to the west (left). The is an entrance to the housing development is just prior to where Burma Road turns west. Only 20 yards past the entrance to the housing development, there are some two-wheel tracks heading west. Follow the tracks to the opening in the fence were the tracks turn south. Follow the trail for 2.3 miles around the edge of the golf course. The trail exits the trees onto a golf cart path by a small bridge. Follow the path, and then the road, west to US93. This route is 0.9 miles longer than the primary PNT route, but it offers much more shade for the second half of the trail—and no highway traffic.[76]

0130P 6.5mi 48° 56.272'N 115° 03.514'W 2690' Burma Road 1001 X Highway US93

Trail Angel: There is a trail angel north of Eureka that will give rides to PNT hikers. See details at the end of this chapter.

We enter US93 4.0 miles north of the center of Eureka, which is spread out along Dewey Avenue. The good news is that the two motels used by hikers are on the north side. The first is the Silverado Motel about 2.2 miles south. The room rates are around $45-$60 per night.

Hiking along US93 is not the best part of the PNT. The road walk is hot and dry but there is a wide but rocky shoulder on the east side of the road. Just hammer it out and get into town for ice cream and beer!

If for some reason you want to bypass Eureka, there is a short cut on a new bike path beginning at the junction of US93 and Highway 37. Follow the bike path as it parallels along the north side of the highway for about 2.1 miles to the end. Here we cross the road to walk on the wide south shoulder until we cross the bridge over the Tobacco River in about another 0.8 miles. Scramble down the slope to the PNT below, heading west along the river to Rexford on the Tobacco River Memorial Trail.[66]

Back to Eureka. The center of Eureka is around Dewey Avenue and 3rd Street, one-half block south of the Montana Market. Dewey runs north-south and most of everything we might need is on this major road in town.

The post office is about a mile north of town center. It might be a good idea to check in with the Rexford District National Forest Service office in Eureka to check on the trail conditions, forest fires, road closures, bear reports, etc. They are located at 949 US Highway 93 North (Dewey Ave.), phone 406-296-2536. You can also make reservations with the NFS to stay at the lookout at Webb Mountain—highly recommended.[GT] There are also several places where camping is possible.[80]

0134P 4.0mi 48° 52.848'N 115° 03.201'W 2595' Eureka Montana

Trail Angel (Eureka): See details at the end of this chapter. From the center of Eureka navigation is very easy for the next 10 miles. Head south on Dewey Ave (US 93) three blocks where Dewey Ave crosses the Tobacco River. Immediately after the bridge look to the right for the markings of a trail that heads north following the river. This is named the Kootenai Trail, but it is not so much a formal city trail but an abandoned rail corridor. Always keep the river to your right. There are occasional picnic tables and toilets.

In 3.2 miles the "trail" crosses under the paved SR37 just south of the highway bridge over the Tobacco River. You'll be walking this highway soon enough, but for now, cross under the road and stay on the trail for another 0.45 miles to Pigeon Bridge Road.

Soon we should be able to see the eastern edge of Lake Koocanusa. The lake is manmade, completed in 1972, and is 90 miles long. Its name is derived from three words put together: Kootenai, Canada, and USA.

Follow Pigeon Bridge Road west for another 0.5 miles into a housing development built on the southern slope of a small ridge. Follow the road southwest then west past the houses, but there is no need to exit out to SR37 yet. Pick up a path in the west corner of a loop in the housing area. The path will lead us 0.6 miles west into the Rexford Bench Campground.

0140P 6.4mi 48° 53.909'N 115° 09.417'W 2560' Kootenai Trail 255 @ Rexford Bench Camp

The NFS Rexford Bench Campground is suitable for RVs with 55 sites, with flush toilets and water. The fee is $12. From here we can easily hike the perimeter of the campground on the local path that generally goes just above the lake, or you can go into the small hamlet of Rexford. Rexford has a convenience store and two restaurants, but it is nothing like Eureka that we left a few hours ago. Want a shower/laundry and a shot of whiskey? Try the Frontier Saloon—they were reported to be very friendly to hikers in 2016.[67] For camping, there are opportunities for a "stealth" campsite along the lake.[43]

As we circle south around Rexford we come to the private Mariners Haven Campground, which has 65 RV and tent sites, laundry, showers, and a very limited store. The fee is unknown. Hike east past the campground on the dirt Mariner's Drive to our next waypoint, the junction with State Route 37 in 0.6 miles.

Water may be scarce for the next few days as we head up Webb Mountain. Good water was reported to be in Pinkham and Boulder creeks heading to Webb Mountain, with Pinkham Creek being the easiest to reach.[50] If you are cautious, I recommend filling up and carrying water before leaving Rexford.

0142P 2.1mi 48° 53.554'N 115° 10.894'W 2580' Mariner's Drive X State Route 37

Major road walking ahead. Follow the paved, high speed SR37 south for 6.7 miles; this is the only major access road along the eastside of Lake Koocanusa. Look for the massive steel structure of the 0.4 mile long bridge that crosses the lake. This is the highest and longest bridge in Montana and is the only bridge across the lake for 30 miles either up or down the lake.

0149P 6.7mi 48° 49.418'N 115° 15.716'W 2530' State Route 37 X Lake Koocanusa Bridge

There is a separated pedestrian walkway on the bridge for a safe crossing. Our next way point on the west side of the bridge is the 'T' junction with the paved Forest Road 228, 0.4 miles on the other side.

0150P 0.4mi 48° 49.679'N 115° 16.245'W 2600' Lake Koocanusa Bridge X Forest Road 228

This concludes the primary PNT route for our first section. For now, let's jump all the way back to Glacier National Park and our decision point at Browns Pass. The primary PNT heads southwest, but let's explore the alternate route that takes us northwest to Hole-in-the-Wall and Kintla Lake.

Alternate Route: The Original PNT Northern Route to Kintla Lakes and Beyond

This alternate route follows the original PNT route taking us north and west to Hole-in-the-Wall, past Boulder Glacier and Kintla Lake on the Boulder Pass Trail. Unfortunately, this route is too often closed and deemed too dangerous with ice and snow even into July. Plus, it bypasses a visit to Polebridge. If it is open, many PNT hikers have used this route and say the extra miles are worth it.

Start: 0034P Boulder Pass Trail (BPT) X Bowman Lake Trail

Rejoin: 0103P Trail 77 X Highline Trail 339

Mileage: 61.0 miles; shorter than the primary route by 6.4 miles

Highlights: Hole-in-the-Wall, Boulder Pass, and Tuchuck Mountain (Highest Point on PNT)

0034P 0.0mi 48° 57.047'N 114° 02.135'W 6270' Boulder Pass Trail (BPT) X Bowman Lake Trail

At this trail junction we turn northwest following the Boulder Creek Trail up hill to about the 6600' contour where the grade then levels. It is 1.6 miles to the spur trail that slopes downhill to the Hole-in-the-Wall Camp.

0036A 1.6mi 48° 57.725'N 114° 03.497'W 6590' BPT X Hole-in-the-Wall Camp Trail

The spur trail to the camp drops us down about 250' elevation in 0.3 miles. This camp is highly rated and desired by many GNP hikers[GT] but reservations may be difficult to score. It is 5-3: 8/1 with no fires and only a one day stay. Take some time to look both across the amazing expanse of the old glacial bowl and to the peaks and glaciers to the south. To the northeast is Chapman Peak rising almost 2800' straight up a cliff wall above us.

Back on the alternate original PNT route our next waypoint is at the Upper Kintla Lake Camp. Walking on the narrow rocky trail on the edge of the massive glacial bowl we continue working counter-clockwise to the west along the steep slope. In about 0.5 miles you will climb to the edge of the tree line and into the rocks and possibly snow for the next 3.5 miles. In about another 1.1 miles you may see the remnants of the older unmaintained trail that traverses higher on the ridge. Keep to the better lower trail.

We reach Boulder Pass 2.6 miles from the Hole-in-the-Wall Camp spur trail, and we continue northwest and west. Coming down from the pass at about one quarter mile west you will find Boulder Pass Camp on a rocky shelf. This camp, rated as one of the best in the park by backpackers, is 3-2: 8/1 with no fires. Soon thereafter you will begin a series of downhill switchbacks dropping you about 1000' over the next 2.1 miles of trail. From there the trail runs straight northwest and downhill another 1100' for 1.7 miles to reach the eastern edge of Upper Kintla Lake and the camp.

0045A 8.6mi 48° 58.820'N 114° 09.274'W 4380' Boulder Pass Trail @ Upper Kintla Lake

The Upper Kintla Lake Camp is 4-2: 6/15 with a pit toilet and fire ring. Hiking along the northern shore of Upper Kintla Lake gives us about 2.3 miles of "level" trail. Here we reach the portion of the Boulder Pass Trail that connects the Upper and Lower Kintla Lakes, which continues downhill 300' over the next 2.1 miles through the rocky forest following Kintla Creek to the south.

Hikers have reported that the trail along Kintla Lake is badly overgrown.[43] Soon we come out of the forest to where the trail opens to the larger Kintla Lake and the Kintla Head Camp, which is 6-3: 6/15. Past the camp the trail follows the northern shoreline and in another 2.6 miles we come to our next waypoint at the junction with the Kintla-Starvation Ridge Trail.

0052A 7.4mi 48° 58.291'N 114° 18.147'W 4190' Boulder Pass Trail X Kintla-Starvation Ridge Trail

The Kintla-Starvation Ridge Trail is another of the multitude of alternative trails, which would be a short-cut west to Abbot Flats in a little over 7.0 miles. It reportedly has a faint metal tag on a tree with a faint tread, but the trail improves as it climbs the ridge about 800'.

Our original PNT alternate route continues along the shoreline for another 3.3 miles to southwest end of the lake and to the short spur trail south to the Kintla Lake Campground. This is one of the most remote car camps in Glacier NP and it is rarely filled; no reservations are taken. The camp has a hand pump for water and a pit toilet. Past the spur trail we hike only 0.5 miles to the south trailhead on Glacier Route Seven (aka Kintla Lake Road).

0056A 4.0mi 48° 56.118'N 114° 21.164'W 4070' Boulder Pass Trail X Kintla Lake Road

Follow the GNP road south 1.5 miles to our next waypoint, the Kishenehn Trail. The trail is really an old forest road with no real trailhead. Our waypoint is a triangle road junction where we bear to the right (west). For those who want to go to Polebridge, bear to the left (southeast) to hike south on Glacier Route Seven for 12.1 miles to pick up the routing into town just north of the bridge over the North Fork Flathead River.

0058A 1.5mi 48° 55.220'N 114° 22.132'W 3990' Kintla Lake Road X Kishenehn Trail

Before we continue to describe the route for the Kishenehn Trail a word of caution is advised. This route takes us north where we will have to ford the river at Abbot Flats, which can be very dangerous with cold waist-deep, fast water. You might want to hike down the trail for about 0.2 miles to get a better view of the river 150' below. From this point you can judge the speed and flow of the river, albeit from afar. Unless it has been dry for a few weeks in Glacier NP you should be able to see the water far below. I recommend taking a safer route and turning toward Polebridge if you have any doubts.

Continuing, we hike north on the Kishenehn Trail following the river high above it on the bluff. At 1.6 miles from the trailhead we'll begin a "U-turn" back toward the river and begin our descent down a ravine. We descend from the bluff losing 180' elevation to reach the river's edge in 0.6 miles. At this point you are directly east of your goal on the far west side to reach the private road.

The Kishenehn Trail continues north for another 1.5 miles to reach our next waypoint, or another 2.2 miles to reach the Kintla-Starvation Trail described earlier. If at any point from here north you can find a safe, easy place to ford the river, I would take it and then pick up the south bound routing.

0062A 4.2mi 48° 57.042'N 114° 24.579'W 3880' Kishenehn Trail X Kintla Creek Trail

The Kishenehn Creek Trail (KCT) reportedly heads northwest and diverts for your current trail right around the Kishenehn Creek. The KCT has a very faint tread if it has not been washed away by the spring runoff. After crossing the creek follow the North Fork Flathead River around to the west. We are at the top of a backward 'S" turn in the river. In 0.5 miles you should come upon a flat wide area of the river. Hopefully it is shallow at this point with an easily managed current to reach the far side of the river at our next waypoint.

0063A 0.7mi 48° 57.078'N 114° 25.344'W 3880' Fording North Fork Flathead River

Ford the river heading due south, if possible. There should be sandy flat soil here and unfortunately no stepping stones. The far bank should only be about 40 yards across. "Rafties" have been known to launch from this area to enjoy riding the river south to Polebridge. Once on the west bank continue southwest away from the river about 120 yards to find the markings of a sandy parking area with tire tracks. This may offer a good place for a trail camp. Follow the tire tracks south 1.3 miles to find a gravel road running northeast-southwest. Turn southwest on this road slightly uphill for 1.0 miles to reach the North Fork Road 486.

0065A 2.4mi 48° 55.445'N 114° 25.388'W 3980' Private Road X North Fork Road 486

From this point we'll be doing some more PNT road walking for a while. Head northwest up the North Fork Road 486 for only 0.25 miles looking for Trail Creek Road - RD114. Trudge up this dusty dirt-gravel road past some small ranches for 2.0 miles to where the road turns due west and crosses a small creek. I suggest you check your water supply and the flow in the creek. There will be few opportunities for water after leaving the creek. Also, at this bend in the road and creek you should cross the Cleft Rock Trail 13, which heads southwest from the road.

Disregard the TR13 and after the road turns west road walk another 1.3 miles to find the trailhead for the Thoma Trail 15. Be careful as there may be a homemade "3 mile" sign with two tracks that look like the trail. There is a new trailhead another 0.35 miles west on the road.[BT]

0068A 3.6mi 48° 56.525'N 114° 29.663'W 4210' Trail Creek Road X Mount Hefty Trail 15 (New Trailhead)

TR15 is a 13.4 mile loop that goes to the top of the Thoma Lookout at 7104', or a 3000' climb from the trailhead. After the lookout the trail goes north before heading back southwest on TR18 and then on to TR19. Depending on the weather, their mood, and schedule, some hikers prefer to take pass the Thoma Trail and walking Trail Creek Road RD114 and RD114A to reach TR19. This route offers more opportunity for water and is only about 5.0 miles long. There is reportedly a piped spring 0.4 west on RD114.

Let's look closer at TR15 and climb to the Thoma Lookout. The trail starts north with a flat or gentle grade uphill. After about 0.4 miles it turns northwest where you will begin a continuous 2800' climb for another 3.5 miles to reach the lookout. Again, there is no water on this climb. The last 0.4 miles is a series of four major switchbacks gaining the last 240' elevation. Stay to the right of the small melt pond with the trail just off to the right of ridgeline, or just scramble up the ridgeline.[BT]

0072A 3.8mi 48° 57.722'N 114° 32.879'W 7104' Mount Hefty Trail 15 @ Thoma Lookout

There is a cabin at the lookout but it is locked, so don't plan to stay there, but there is a new cedar privy.[BT] Other hikers report that while at the Thoma Lookout take in "…the commanding views of the Whitefish Range to the west and south and the rugged peaks of the Northfork area of Glacier National Park to the east and the pristine southern Canadian Rockies to the northeast. Views to the north are blocked by the continuation of the ridge to Mount Hefty, which actually straddles the border between the USA and Canada."[12]

After crossing over the Thoma summit, TR15 leads north along the crest of the ridge for 1.8 miles with ups and downs. Our next waypoint is the junction with Thoma-Colts Creek Trail 18.

0074A 1.8mi 48° 58.917'N 114° 33.101'W 7010' Trail 15 X Thoma-Colts Creek Trail 18

At this trail junction TR15 keeps immediately west and then turns northwest to Mount Hefty. Our new trail for the original PNT alternate route takes TR18 temporarily east for 0.1 miles as we start down the south side of the ridge. Soon the trail turns south through a thinned forest. At 1.1 miles on the trail we should cross Colts Creek around 5800' elevation. TR18 follows the creek and the ravine southwest downhill for a total of 2.0 miles to reach the trailhead on FR114A, dropping 2600' elevation.

0076A 2.0mi 48° 57.937'N 114° 34.548'W 5400' Trail 18 X Forest Road 114A (decommissioned) and Creek Crossing

The trailhead exit for TR18 is a little farther north on FR114A than shown on the map. This is an old forest road that is not well maintained. Follow it south above the creek for 0.8 miles to come to a "U-turn" in the road. At the northwest corner we should see a set of truck tracks at our next waypoint.

0077A 0.8mi 48° 57.329'N 114° 34.726'W 5100' Forest Road 114A X Thoma-Tuchuck Trail 19

The trailhead for the TR19 is 0.1 miles down the truck tracks. We'll follow TR19 northwest initially climbing the slope and gaining about 1400' over the next 2.6 miles. Here the slope turns to the southwest and we climb another 300' to hike the crest of the ridge, enjoying the views to the north and south of the Flathead National Forest. Hike the crest of the ridge for 1.0 miles to our next waypoint just north of the crest of the 7285' Butte at the junction with the Tuchuck Ridge Trail 114.

0081A 4.1mi 48° 57.846'N 114° 38.874'W 7260' Trail 19 X Tuchuck Ridge Trail 114

While TR114 heads downhill to the southeast, we stay high on the ridge on TR19 and turn northwest. Coming off the 7285' butte, the trail drops steeply about 50' rapidly on a switchback before turning back to the ridgeline leading to the northwest and Tuchuck Mountain. (Tuchuck is pronounced "too-chuck.") We leave the crest of the ridge and follow the trail up the eastern slope of the mountain. Enjoy the good trail with many switchbacks and the 500' climb over the next 2.2 miles—well worth the climb—***Tuchuck Mountain is the highest point of the 1200 mile PNT!***

0083A 2.3mi 48° 58.564'N 114° 40.516'W 7745' Trail 19 @ Tuchuck Mountain – Highest Point on the PNT

Let the bushwhack begin! Descend to the west coming off Tuchuck Mountain following the prominent ridge. We should see the 7216' peak ahead to help guide us, however, we don't need to climb the peak. But, since you've come this far I will assume you want to enjoy one of the best parts of the PNT. We'll climb some peaks for the rest of the day. Climb the rocky ridge spine southwest to the summit of the 7216' peak and our next waypoint.

0084A 0.5mi 48° 58.385'N 114° 41.085'W 7216' Bushwhack @ 7216' Peak

Here our bushwhack turns northwest to follow the crest of the ridge dropping about 220' elevation into a ridge saddle in 0.2 miles. Back up we go to climb a 100' elevation in 0.1 miles over a hump and then immediately back down 100' into another saddle. Now we climb 220' up the rocky treeless scree in the last 0.2 miles to bag 7125' Peak at our next waypoint.

0085A 0.8mi 48° 58.798'N 114° 41.816'W 7125' Bushwhack @ 7125' Peak

We keep up our bushwhacking and turn due west descending steeply 1860' on the ridge from the 7125' Peak for the next 1.3 miles. In 0.4 miles we leave the almost barren ridge and enter the trees where the ridge crest becomes less well defined. We keep bushwhacking due west being careful to stay on the crest of the ridge as best we can and not drift off to the north or south. When we lose the crest it is better to head west or slightly southwest to avoid the worst bushwhacking.[GT]

The descent is steep with lots of loose rock. You might be able to follow the old telephone bare wire that is still there. The last mile or so just before Frozen Lake Road was a hellish mess of tangled trees and vegetation.[BT] The next way point should put you directly at the right spot on Frozen Lake Road – FR114Y.

0086A 1.4mi 48° 58.777'N 114° 43.558'W 5270' Bushwhack X Frozen Lake Road - FR114Y

We're now entering the Kootenai National Forest. Follow the road to the southeast and downhill. If you're on track, in about a quarter mile Forest Road 7010 extends to the east, while our road, now shown as RD414Y U-turns back to the west and continues sloping downhill. In another 1.0 miles you'll find the junction with Forest Road 7000. The Weasel Cabin is about 0.1 miles east on RD7000 and offers a good place for a trail camp. The Weasel Cabin a wonderful place on a lovely stream. It has a wood burning stove, foam mattress, picnic table and fire ring. This is a great place to rest after the Tuchuck section.[BT]

Back to FR414Y we cross Weasel Creek on a bridge and continue northwest on a slight downhill grade. At this point Forest Road 319, our next destination, begins to parallel our track and is 100 yards to the west but is 120' elevation above us. Some PNT hikers have scrambled up to FR319, but the planned track continues on FR414Y north for another 0.7 miles.

0088A 2.2mi 48° 59.015'N 114° 44.939'W 5120' Forest Road 114A X Forest Road 319

Once on FR319 we only need to hike west about 0.3 miles to find the Foundation-Camp Creek Trail 77.

0089A 0.3mi 48° 59.064'N 114° 45.339'W 5070' Forest Road 319 X Foundation Camp Trail 77

Initially the trail looks like an old forest road parking area but it turns into a Kootenai National Forest trail soon enough as we head west. The trail generally follows Camp Creek, staying on the north side with intermittent switchbacks. After 2.2 miles TR77 crosses Camp Creek to climb east uphill in a relatively easy slope. In another 0.4 miles TR77 turns back to the southwest leading us to rejoin the primary PNT route. At this point you should begin to see through the forest to the ridgeline to the south that parallels TR77.

In another 1.4 miles TR77 begins its 220' climb over the ridge and down the other side leaving the small Camp Creek valley. Next TR77 follows an 'S' shape path in a bowl and ridge with two small ponds below the trail. From the beginning of our descent into the bowl we hike 2.1 miles to complete the 'S' and find our junction with the Highline Trail 339.

0103P 6.3mi 48° 57.083'N 114° 48.069'W 6390' Trail 77 X Highline Trail 339

This completes our review of the original PNT, now alternate routing, and puts us back on the primary PNT about 0.7 trail miles southeast of Mount Wam.

Alternate Route: The Original PNT to the Ten Lakes Scenic Area

This alternate route follows the original PNT north into the very scenic Ten Lakes Area. Although there are a few miles of road walking, you will hike north to about 1.5 miles south of the border with Canada. The trail parallels the border with stunning views of the Therriault Lakes and the Bluebird Basin.

Start: 0105P Highline Trail 339 X Clarence-Rich Creek Trail 78

Rejoin: 0115P Highline Trail 339 X Blacktail Trail 92

Mileage: 14.3 miles; longer than the primary route by about 4.4 miles

Highlights: Poorman Mountain, Wolverine Lakes

0105P 0.0mi 48° 56.709'N 114° 49.746'W 6220' Trail 339 X Clarence-Rich Creek Trail 78

The primary PNT route continues west on TR339 while we turn north on TR78 following the west side of a ridge dropping down toward Rich Creek, descending about 800' in 0.6 miles. Here the trail parallels the creek going north. In just over 1.0 miles from our last way point we cross a small stream which may offer water. Next, we either find a safe relatively level place to bushwhack west 0.1 miles to FR 7103, or continue north on the east side of the creek on the good, old forest road. Following the road in about 1.9 miles we come to the next waypoint, a very safe way to cross the creek, and return to the PNT.

0108A 2.8mi 48° 58.936'N 114° 49.396'W 4950' Trail 78 X Old Mount Wam Road

The old forest road intersects with the closed Mount Wam Road, where we take a sharp turn south to find FR319 in 0.2 miles and the trailhead.[50] About 0.1 miles down FR319 there is a bridge over Rich Creek which may supply water and a good trail camp.

0109A 0.3mi 48° 58.776'N 114° 49.661'W 4900' Trail 78 X Old Mount Wam Road

From there turn south on FR319 for another 1.2 miles looking for Forest Road 7086 and our next waypoint.

0110A 1.2mi 48° 58.111'N 114° 50.524'W 4990' Therriault Lakes Road X Wolverine Creek Road FR7086

As we turn southwest on FR7086 we begin our trek into the Ten Lakes Scenic National Area in the far northern portion of the Kootenai National Forest. Soon we will hike north to be only 1.2 miles south of the U.S.-Canada border. But first we have some climbing to do--of course we climb, this is the PNT!

RD7086 starts as a gentle down slope to cross the Wigwam River in 0.5 miles. The river is a good place to top off your water supply, especially during August, as the next reliable water is 10 miles distant at Bluebird Lake. Some hikers have made a trail camp near the creek.

After crossing the bridge over the river we start a 2900' steady climb for the next several hours to reach the trail near the top of the ridge. Our next waypoint is 1.6 miles after the bridge where FR7086 meets FR7091. Look for where the road makes a U-turn from west to northeast at a road junction with an unnamed forest road.

0112A 2.1mi 48° 58.215'N 114° 52.555'W 5550' Wolverine Creek Road FR7086 X Ten Lakes Road FR7091

You may likely think you should continue west on the more level route, but don't be fooled and turn northeast and keep climbing. Hike straight climbing the grade for another 1.7 miles to a parking area on the right side of the trailhead for the Rainbow Trail 89. So far we've climbed about 1000' with much more to go.

0114A 1.8mi 48° 59.034'N 114° 50.659'W 5990' Forest Road 7091 X Rainbow Trail 89

TR89 starts west and climbs immediately to then switchback to parallel the ridgeline above us and to the north. After another switchback keep working west along the trail as the forest begins to thin and offers excellent views to the south. For the next 2.0 miles you'll climb another 1100' to be near the top of the ridgeline. At this point we should be in a shallow saddle with exceptional views to the north and Rainbow Lake, which sits only 0.15 miles to the north. Unfortunately Rainbow Lake is 650' below the trail.

Continue on TR86 with a relatively level grade as the trail flows west just below the ridge crest and below a 7626' Butte. In 1.3 miles the trail rounds southwest along the ridge to head toward our next waypoint just north of Poorman Mountain and the intersection with the Highline Trail 339.

0119A 4.5mi 48° 58.711'N 114° 55.501'W 7490' Trail 89 X Highline Trail 339

TR339 runs north-south under Poorman Mountain to our southwest. Barring poor weather, you should have exceptional views of the two Wolverine Lakes to your southeast. Although tempting, the lakes are 600' below you down a steep rocky cliff.

Hike south now on TR339 along the ridge line for 0.6 miles. Here TR339 slopes downhill to the west side of a 7686' peak, and in another 0.4 miles, you climb back toward the crest of the ridge. The trail crosses over the ridge to lose sight of the lakes. Soon after we intersect the Blacktail Trail 92 coming up from the west.

0115P 1.1mi 48° 57.800'N 114° 55.780'W 7270' Trail 339 X Blacktail Trail 92

RESUPPLY OPTIONS

0053P 48° 47.216'N 114° 16.961'W 3580' Bowman Lake Road X Inside North Fork Road (aka Glacier Route 7) **Polebridge:** Follow the primary route south for about 20 minutes to reach the town along the primary PNT route.

0134P 48° 52.848'N 115° 03.201'W 2595' Eureka Montana: This is the center of town along the primary PNT route.

Trail Support

0123P North Eureka: Mary Carvey, mmcarvey@yahoo.com, (406) 871-0887 (cariboutrailwagoncamp.com), fee resort. From Burma Road, head east on Gould Road for 0.5 miles to the second right turn. Go past the brown house to the open gate and you will find the campground. Set up your own tent and have access to the facilities or stay in some of the wagons that are available.

0130P Eureka: Stan and Betty Holder, bettyholder56@yahoo.com, stan.holder@hotmail.com. Home: (406) 889-5268, Stan (406) 788-4973, Betty (406) 788-5269. Can give rides, offer hot showers, and a place to camp. Will keep packages for people. Highway 93 about 3 miles south of the border.

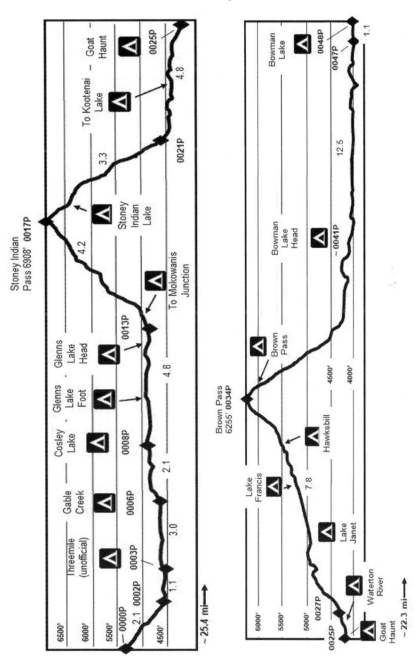

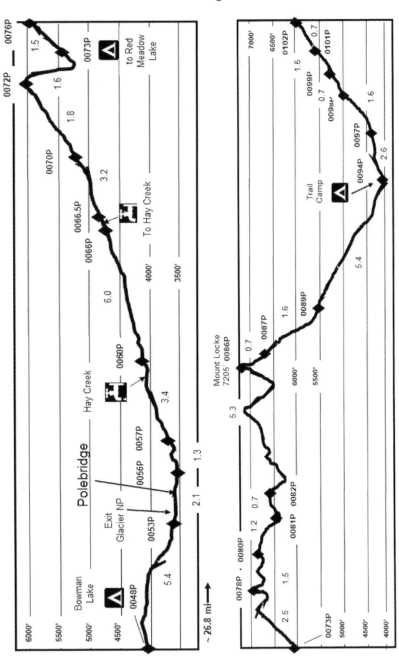

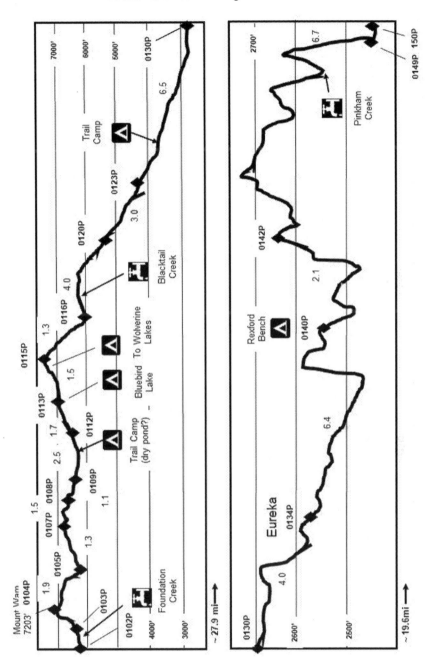

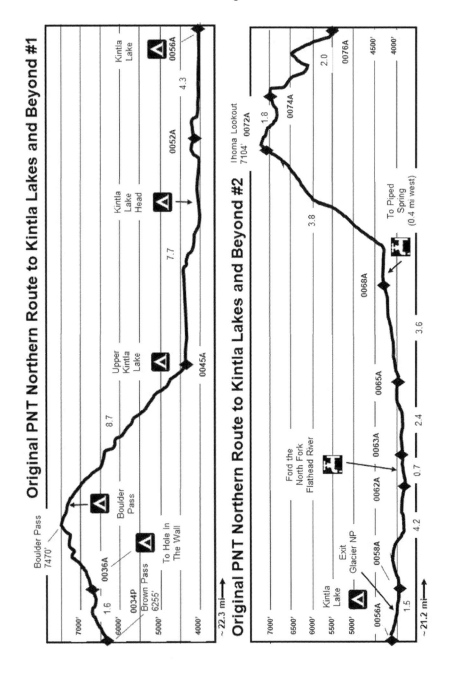

Original PNT Northern Route to Kintla Lakes and Beyond #3

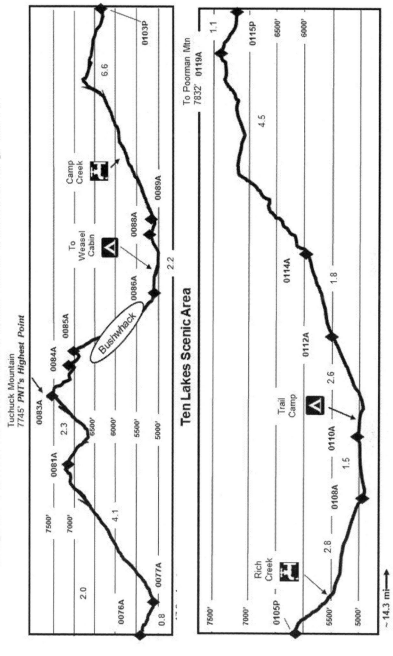

Tuchuck Mountain
7745' *PNT's Highest Point*

Camp
Creek

To
Weasel
Cabin

Bushwhack

Ten Lakes Scenic Area

To Poorman Mtn
7832' 0119A

Trail
Camp

Rich
Creek

~ 14.3 mi→

Tim Youngbluth

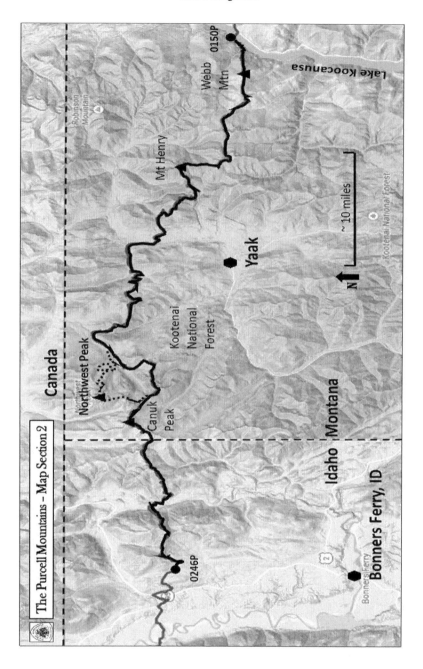

46

CHAPTER THREE
THE PURCELL MOUNTAINS – MAP SECTION 2
Lake Koocanusa to Kootenai River

Bushwhack on ridge, Tuchuck Mountain in background, Flathead NF

Key Trail Notes

Highlights: Webb Mountain climb, Northwest Peak

Primary Route Estimated Elevation Change: 15,334' climb / 14,994' descent

Route Alternates: Northwest Peak

Possible Resupply: Yaak, Bonners Ferry

Parks/Forests: Kootenai NF, Kaniksu NF

Permits: None

Other Notes: Bear spray recommended, scarce water sources

As we begin our journey through the Purcell Mountains plan your water use carefully. This is a hot dry section of the PNT, particularly in July and August. You'll be walking on a number of ridgelines well above seasonal creeks. Lakes are generally located far below the trail. Water is available, but look carefully for every opportunity to fill up.

0150P 0.0mi 48° 49.679'N 115° 16.245'W 2600' Lake Koocanusa Bridge X Forest Road 228

After crossing the Koocanusa Bridge, turn southwest on the paved RD228. The road is at least 100' above the lake. Walk the road for 1.3 miles looking for the trailhead to the Webb Mountain Trail 435. Just before the trailhead we cross Boulder Creek, which has been diverted under the road. You'll have to scramble down a slope about 50' to reach the creek.[BT]

0151P 1.3mi 48° 49.091'N 115° 17.433'W 2630' Forest Road 228 X Webb Mountain Trail 435

The trail head is marked by a small parking lot on the west side of the road, just big enough for one or two cars. There is a PNT logo at the trailhead.[50] Get ready for another big PNT climb. There is a good place for a trail camp about 10 minutes up the trail.[BT] For the next 4.3 miles we climb to the top of Webb Mountain, gaining almost 3400' in elevation. Depending on the time of year we might find our first ripe huckleberries along this trail. A hiker in 2015 said, "There was some good berry action, albeit on plants more like ground cover than bushes. Still tasted good."[47]

It is good to report that in 2015 it appears that there are PNT markers at just about every trail junction from here to Idaho.[47]

0155P 4.3mi 48° 49.130'N 115° 20.611'W 5950' Trail 435 X Thirsty Mountain Trail 436

TR435 ends near the top of Webb Mountain where it is a short finish to climb on the old road to the summit. Here you find the lookout cabin, with bunks for five people. There is no electricity or water. The fee is $35.00 per night and reservations can be made at the Eureka Ranger Station. Reservations for the Webb Mountain lookout tower are extremely hard to get and may have to be made months in advance through the Kootenay NF.

Head down the service road a few minutes to find a big sign that says "Trail." This obvious track turns out to be TR436.[KC] We follow the trail west and downhill for 0.8 miles, losing 300' elevation to cross Forest Road 1921.

0156P 0.9mi 48° 49.127'N 115° 21.612'W 5680' Trail 436 X Forest Road 1921

We cross the road and continue on TR436 hiking uphill through a clear cut area for about 0.3 miles. Just before entering the trees and climbing the slope, we should be able to see Thirsty Mountain, about 0.8 miles ahead. TR436 takes us around the south side of Thirsty Mountain—thankfully we don't have to climb another peak, just yet anyway.

A little over 0.5 miles from our last waypoint there are two small ponds about 100-150 yards north of the trail that offer water and a fairly good trail camp. You may have to hike west past them and double back to the northeast following a game trail to find the ponds.[CN]

Continue west on the signed and easy to follow TR436[50] as it turns south to traverse a saddle on the south side of Thirsty Mountain. From the saddle we descend about 400' over the next 1.2 miles into our next waypoint.

0157P 1.5mi 48° 49.825'N 115° 23.140'W 5960' Trail 436 X Boulder Lakes Trail 62

Look for a sharp right turn (northwest) onto the old forest road. TR436 continues to descend southeast on a clear tread back towards lake Koocanusa. FR7183L is relatively level for the first 0.3 miles when it turns southwest and descends 300' for about 0.4 miles. Here the road turns northwest again to roughly follow the 5600' contour. Look for a small spring on the trail that was flowing well in August 2017, about 0.5 miles up the trail after it turns to the northwest.[ES]

0159P 2.0mi 48° 49.720'N 115° 24.539'W 5450' Boulder Lake Trail 62 X Forest Road 7183

Cross the road staying on TR62, a decommissioned forest road. There may be a gate just after crossing FR7183. Look to cross Boulder Creek in 1.0 miles. If you need a camp, this is a good place to set up. It is east of the trailhead for the Boulder Lake Trail 62.

0161P 1.0mi 48° 50.257'N 115° 25.412'W 5500' Boulder Lake Trail 62 @ Boulder Creek & Trail Camp

We hike TR62 northwest on a slow climb for another 0.3 miles to where the trail rounds to the west. Look for a hiker registry 1/4 mile after the beginning of the Boulder Creek trail.[61] After 1.0 miles on TR62 we come upon a small spur trail that leads to the south and to the Boulder Lakes, which offer water and a good trail camp as reported in 2016.[CN] There are primitive campsites at the south end of the lake, too. Huckleberries ripen in August, but note that moose and grizzly bears are known to frequent these two lakes. In 2012, one hiker met two researchers who were gathering bear fur from barbed wire. The fur is then analyzed for info about the bear population around Boulder Lakes.[GT] No hikers have seen a bear here since.

We continue west and soon climb on switchbacks up 1000' to the crest of the ridge and a complex trail intersection. Once you reach the crest of the ridge, turn north (right) for about 30 yards, looking for Trail 91 which runs to the west downhill.

0162P 1.5mi 48° 50.161'N 115° 27.198'W 6640' Trail 62 X Trail 337 X Purcell Summit Trail 91

The trail junction may not be apparent, but the PNT route in this area is obvious.[50]   We turn west and downhill on TR91 for 1.8 miles to Gypsy Meadows, which has a good creek and a fine trail camp, although reportedly not readily visible from the trail.[GT]   In 2015 the camp was reported to be just a soggy swamp, so things may have changed.[47]   From the meadows we climb again about 760' in about 1.4 miles to reach the trail junction with TR251. The junction lies in a saddle between a 6733' and a 6800' Butte.

0165P 3.2mi 48° 49.939'N 115° 30.439'W 6680' Trail 91 X Marble Creek Trail 251

Continue north on TR91, which perhaps is the same now as TR251. The trail generally follows the natural crest of the ridge and passes just west of the 6903' Butte in 0.5 miles. From there the trail and the ridge bend to the northwest. You may be able to see Mount Henry 2.7 miles to the north, which we will climb later. For now we're going downhill, then uphill to cross near the 6575' hump and into our next waypoint crossing Purcell Trail 7.

About 0.2 miles from the top, there is reportedly an excellent cleaned-out flat spot, inside a small circle of trees. It is on the right side of the trail with lots of cushy pine needles, along with the classic exposed tree root in the middle.[47]

0167P 1.3mi 48° 50.716'N 115° 31.204'W 6560' Trail 91 X Purcell Trail 7 Saddle

Be prepared for a sharp 600' descent and a 500' climb back up over the next 1.5 miles.[66]   We now join TR7 watching for the cairns marking the right turn at junction. From the 6575' hump, the map shows the trail doing a U-shape loop to the west, however, some hikers have found an unmarked trail due north down the ridge. Follow the best marked trail knowing that your major direction is north. Look for the junction with the Basin Creek Trail 233 and the Turner Creek Trail 161.

0168P 1.3mi 48° 51.233'N 115° 31.005'W 5980' Trail 91 X Swastika Trail 233 / Turner Creek Trail 161 (signed)

TR233 heads northeast, while TR161 heads west to Turner Falls in about 3.5 miles. TR161 was reported unmaintained in 2017 and in extremely bad shape (there is a sign on the west end of the trail warning that it is not maintained).[ES]

The primary PNT continues north for the views and the opportunity to climb Mount Henry. Soon the trail descends slightly into a saddle as we then climb north on a gentle grade to intersect the Vinal Creek Trail 9. There is an obvious trail junction and a sign for the Vinal Creek Trail, which continues straight ahead and downhill. Turn right and uphill at this junction for the PNT.[CN]

0169P 2.0mi 48° 52.693'N 115° 30.863'W 6460' Trail 91 X Mount Henry Trail 17 X Boulder Lakes Trail 7

At this 'Y' junction, TR7 breaks away to the northeast along the eastside of Mount Henry. The lake is to the right (northeast); some hikers have left the primary PNT route for the night and hiked the trail downhill losing about 250' elevation to get water and camp at Lake Henry.

The primary PNT route bears left (northwest) on TR17, looking for a spring with water in 0.4 miles; water is seasonal and was running very slow in 2016.[CN] Just prior to the spring there appears to be an unmarked trail west that follows the 6640' contour to bypass the climb to Mt. Henry and takes you to TR9 in about 0.2 miles. The spring is just past this unmarked junction uphill, and it had water in the dry 2015 summer.[50]

As we climb on the PNT past the spring look for the trail junction with the spur trail that leads to the lookout. Be forewarned that this approach to the summit is 800' up in 0.4 miles. The lookout at Mount Henry was reported to be in bad shape in 2013[KC] and has remained so through 2016.[CN] If you were returning from the lookout on the side trail, there is a new trail sign here with "Spring 1/8 MI. and Mt. Henry Lake 2 MI." with a PNT blaze tacked on the tree under the sign. The sign has no arrows! Turn east to go back to the Boulder Lakes Trail 7, or turn west to continue to the Vinal Creek Trail 9.

0170P 0.8mi 48° 53.056'N 115° 31.242'W 7060' TR17 X Vinal Creek Trail 9

The PNT will follow TR9 west and down the slope heading to Turner Falls. But for now, let's turn north up to the summit of Mount Henry. From here our climb is 350' elevation gain to reach the lookout tower in just less than 0.5 miles. Mount Henry at 7243' is the highest point between Lake Koocanusa and Yaak, Montana. If you look ESE you will see Webb Mountain only 9 miles distant, but seemingly many miles on the trail.

Back downhill on TR9 we'll hike southwest downhill for about 0.5 miles to s spur trail that heads west for 90 yards to a trailhead parking area at the end of Solo Joe Road.

0171P 0.5mi 48° 52.846'N 115° 32.235'W 5860' Vinal Creek Trail 9 X Spur Trail to Solo Joe Road Trailhead

From the spur trail TR9 drops down the ridge where the PNT route in this area is now obvious and easy to follow.[50] We keep descending the ridge to the southwest and occasionally west for about 2.2 miles to temporarily join a Forest Road 6072.

We follow the trail across the closed road twice as we descend.[50] The trail now generally heads west for the last 0.8 miles into Turner Falls.

0174P 3.3mi 48° 51.992'N 115° 35.051'W 3550' Trail 9 @ Turner Falls X Bunker Creek Trail 51

At this way point on TR9 we find a short spur trail to Turner Falls—a nice resting spot for sure, but a hiker reports that rodents inhabit this camp area.[GT]

Also at this trail junction there is a brief "unofficial" alternate route to consider. The Vinal Creek Trail 9 continues to the west for just over 3.0 miles. A 2016 thru-hiker reports, "The Vinal Creek Trail 9 plus FS 746 to Bunker Hill was a great alternate, and a very welcome respite from the demands of the trail thus far."[CN] On this alternate route we would then hike from the end of the trail north on Forest Road 746 for 3.2 miles to Bunker Hill.

The primary PNT route, Bunker Creek Trail 51, takes us also to Bunker Hill in a perhaps more challenging 7.2 mile route. Off we go, heading north on TR51 with Fish Lakes to the east and then climbing up the ridge. There is good camping shortly upstream at the start of TR51 with an elaborate campsite with hand-hewn tables. Caution: Hikers report that the camp from 2013 through 2016 had rodent problems and securing your gear in your tent and also hanging food is advised.[CN]

TR51 climbs through a lengthy burned zone and fortunately all the blowdowns have been cleared and the trail is easy to follow.[50] In about 2.5 miles the trail may be a little difficult to follow through a clear cut area. Our next waypoint is the intersection with Forest Road 6047.

0178P 4.5mi 48° 53.980'N 115° 36.261'W 4570' Trail 51 X Forest Road 6047

After this point you should be traveling along the slopes downhill; if you are climbing for any extended period of time, check your position. There are multiple old forest roads in this area and some offer alternate easy navigation to the west, albeit not the most direct route.

The PNT follows RD6047 downhill northeast for about 0.7 before picking up TR51 again. FR6047 offers the easier path to follow, but it adds about an extra mile to our journey.

0180P 1.0mi 48° 54.196'N 115° 37.136'W 4040' Trail 51 X Forest Road 6047 Again

Staying on TR51 we descend west into a heavy forest and to our next waypoint. The trail is now well marked and easy to follow as we cross the closed road.[50]

0181P 1.0mi 48° 54.329'N 115° 38.084'W 3550' Trail 51 X Old Forest Road 14107

We continue downhill on TR51 on a southwest heading to cross the well-defined Forest Road 746, which runs north-south.

0182P 1.1mi 48° 53.860'N 115° 38.874'W 3180' Trail 51 X Forest Road 746

In 2016 the USFS Three Rivers Ranger Station posted a notice that the PNT maps are incorrect showing a trail crossing the road. There is no trail. Hikers should turn north on FR746 following a 1.9 mile road walk down to the West Side Yaak River Road. We start with a slight uphill climb into our next waypoint.

0182.3P 0.7mi 48° 54.468'N 115° 38.977'W 3230' FR746 X Forest Road 5812

Bear left at this 'Y' intersection to follow the unmarked FR5812 downhill. There are two major switchbacks that will take us down to the valley floor and Upper Ford Road.

0183P 0.9mi 48° 54.743'N 115° 39.413'W 3010' Forest Road 5812 X Upper Ford Rd

We turn south again to begin our road walk for the next 14 miles. In 0.4 miles a bridge crosses the Yaak River with easy access. In a short 0.4 miles after the bridge we come to our next waypoint.

0184.5P 0.8mi 48° 54.215'N 115° 39.820'W 3000' Upper Ford Road X Yaak River Road – FR92

Trail Angels (Yaak): There is a possible trail angel. See details at the end of this chapter.

Resupply: To get to Yaak, Montana do not turn north on RD508, but instead continue south on RD508 for 6.8 miles. Yaak only has a limited general store and restaurant. It may be a good place to send a resupply box to the Yaak River Mercantile, (406) 295-5159, but check first.

Back to the PNT, turn north at the first road, which may be designated RD92 or RD508, or both. We hike this road north for 2.3 miles to cross the West Fork Yaak River and then Yaak Valley Ranch Road. In 0.15 miles after the creek, head west on RD276.

0186P 2.9mi 48° 56.159'N 115° 40.415'W 3110' Yaak River Road FR92 X West Fork Yaak River Road FR276

More roads ahead as we continue uphill and west on RD276. The road parallels the West Fork Yaak River, which unfortunately, is too far below us to scramble down and back up if you need of water. We are on this unremarkable road for 2.3 miles to reach RD5857, or next way point.

0189P 2.3mi 48° 55.884'N 115° 43.273'W 3420' FR276 X French Carver Rd FR5857

Note: Due to the lightning-caused Davis Creek wildfire in July 2018, the PNT was closed between French-Carver Road – FR5827 and the Rock Candy Mountain Trail 461. At publication, there are no reports of the trail conditions.

We go straight ahead on the road then around a "horseshoe" in the road to cross West Fork Yaak River in just under 0.3 miles. There may be access to the river here. Soon RD5857 turns back to the southwest where we keep climbing on a steady grade. For the next 3.6 miles the road climbs on long switchbacks edging along several clear cut sections of timber. Our next waypoint is the intersection with RD5861.

0193P 3.8mi 48° 55.539'N 115° 45.046'W 4220' Forest Road 5857 X Forest Road 5861

At this 'Y' junction, the PNT takes RD5857 as we bear right (northwest). Soon thereafter in less than 0.4 miles we find RD5857A intersecting from the east. We continue northwest staying on the road steadily climbing. After 1.7 miles from our last waypoint we turn southeast and meet an old unnamed forest road signed "French Creek Trailhead." Keep to RD5857 headed southwest then looping back to the northwest, steadily climbing the entire time. About 0.5 miles from the next waypoint, RD5857 is gated and locked. There is a big sign "Trail 33 Obermayer Mtn."[50] We continue west to reach our destination for the trailhead and our next waypoint.

0197P 4.3mi 48° 56.007'N 115° 47.891'W 5440' Forest Road 5827 X Garver Mountain Trail 8

Finally we're off the roads and back on a trail! Well, at least for the next for 3.4 miles that is, as we head west and northwest on TR8.

For a side trip, you can take the trail due south from the trailhead for about 0.3 miles to the top of Garver Mountain. Here you'll find a lookout tower where you can stay overnight with reservations. The fee is $35.00 per night for a pit toilet, but no water.

Back to TR8, we're hiking on the northern slope of a rounded ridge through fairly thick uncut forest. The crest of the ridge is about 200' above us until we work our way to the top in 1.2 miles. Here TR8 turns north along the ridge for about 0.7 miles where we begin our 900' descent down to Pete's Creek Camp at Forest Road 338

0200P 3.4mi 48° 57.399'N 115° 50.505'W 4310' Trail 8 X Forest Road 338 @ Pete Creek Trail Camp

To get to the campsite on the map, walk the road about 100 yards north, then turn left on a spur road curving back towards the south. At the end of the spur road, in only about 50 yards, we find the trail camp near the creek.

The primary PNT route now turns north on the well-defined RD338, which is paved for the first mile or so.[50] Fortunately we're on fairly level tread only slightly climbing here as it rounds to the southwest. Our next waypoint is the 'Y' junction with Forest Road 5902.

0204P 3.3mi 48° 57.225'N 115° 52.484'W 4660' Forest Road 338 X Forest Road 5902

Decision Time. The primary PNT continues southwest on RD5902, where the original PNT bears right (west) on Forest Road 338. The original PNT route takes us higher in elevation with some excellent views at the summit of Northwest Peak and Davis Mountain, and then rejoins the primary PNT route in 13.3 miles. The description of the alternate original route is at the end of the section. The Northwest Peak Scenic Area is beautiful and should seriously be considered.[KC] "Not to be missed. The Norwest Peak Lookout is an excellent place to spend the night."[80]

Let's proceed with our description of the primary PNT route, which has more trail, is less difficult, and still has good views. Continue southwest on the slight uphill grade of RD5902 for 2.0 miles. The road parallels the West Fork Yaak River, which lies about 80' below us to the north. Our next waypoint is the trailhead for the Midge Creek Trail 177. If you find the bridge over the river, you have gone too far. The trailhead is about 100 yards east of the bridge.

0206P 2.0mi 48° 56.343'N 115° 54.687'W 4860' Forest Road 5902 X Midge Creek Trail 177

In 2016, TR177 was cleared, signed, and in great shape.[61] There is a reported good trail camp 0.1 miles west on FR5092, just south of the bridge on the Yaak River. Given the scarcity of water for the next 18 miles, it might be a good idea to visit the river whether camping or not.

Follow TR177 south and southeast through thick uncut forest, climbing 1100' to our next waypoint in 1.9 miles. Hikers report that the trail is actually west of the trail line on the map. Again, check your water here and look for a seasonal branch of Midge Creek where the trail crosses about 0.3 miles before our next waypoint. This is your best last chance for easy access to water.[47] At our next waypoint, TR177 is on the second of two forest roads that the trail directly crosses.

0208P 1.9mi 48° 55.219'N 115° 53.834'W 6060' Trail 177 X Forest Road 5926

After crossing the old forest road we continue on TR177 which will be a long steady pull uphill. We continue south and keep climbing to 6600' elevation just west of the 6650' butte. The trail approaches near the crest of the ridge and turns west into a saddle marked on the map as 6530' in a U-turn before the trail heads west. As the trail leads west the forest becomes sparse on the rocky terrain and the trail reportedly is clear below the scree field but fades in the flat.

Just head for the ridge where you climb south.[50] Keep hiking around the bowl and along the ridge near the 6850' contour.

As the trail rounds south in the bowl you should be able to see Rock Candy Mountain at 7204'. Toward the end of TR177 it becomes faint, but there are a few blazes on the trees and rock cairns to guide you.[50] Hiking into a saddle very close to 7000' we come to a large rocky, treeless bench, where we look for a trail, downhill to the west and our next waypoint.

0212P 3.8mi 48° 54.199'N 115° 57.039'W 6980' Trail 177 X Rock Candy Mountain Trail 461 (signed). Note: some maps show this as Trail 174.

This junction is well signed and west of the saddle.[ES] To climb Rock Candy Mountain summit turn south on TR461 for about 0.5 miles. Instead, however, we turn northwest and follow the new TR461 following the PNT markers. Head downhill losing about 400' elevation before contouring into our next waypoint.[61] In mid-August 2016, a small water source was found about 0.1 miles before our next waypoint.[66]

This is the junction of TR461 and TR174 where the original PNT route, coming from Northwest Peak, rejoins our primary PNT route.

0213P 1.1mi 48° 54.941'N 115° 57.989'W 6390' Trail 174 X Trail 461

Fortunately hikers report that things improve greatly on TR461 from this waypoint. Following TR174 we head northwest along the ridge close to the 6400' elevation through intermittently sparse forest for 2.0 miles. In 2016 and 2018 a small water source was found along the trail about 0.7 miles from our last waypoint.[66]

0215P 2.1mi 48° 55.951'N 116° 0.055'W 6400' Trail 461 X Bushwhack from Climber's Route Northwest Peaks Scenic Area

At this point TR461 follows the crest of the ridge west for 1.1 miles to Canuk Peak as we climb 500'. There is a fallen-down lookout cabin at the summit. Looking west you can see far into Idaho and the upcoming PNT route.

0217P 1.1mi 48° 56.008'N 116° 01.286'W 6934' Trail 174 X American Mountain Trail 440, Near Canuck Peak

The PNT turns sharply left (south) and descends rapidly on TR440.[60] In 2016 the trail was reported to be cleared in Montana, but not in Idaho, with some blowdowns there.[61] In any case, we descend rapidly to the south. In 0.2 miles TR440 begins its switchbacks down the western slope of the ridge dropping 850' by the time we reach the old forest road, Spread Creek Road - RD435 in 1.1 miles from the summit.

0218P 1.1mi 48° 55.521'N 116° 01.525'W 6080' Trail 440 X Spread Creek Road 435 X Trail 44 and Camp (dry)

Look for the new trail registry here[61] for TR44. There is a flat, large, dry trail camp just after the road crossing.[61] Crossing the road, we head southwest to our next waypoint in Idaho. Continue climbing southwest where in 0.5 miles the trail climbs another 200' steeply up the ridge to the top of a hump. Next, TR44 makes a brief U-turn to the north, then south before descending down the ridge to the southwest. After the trail levels off go another 0.5 miles to find a small creek and a flat area for a trail camp. This area maybe swampy some seasons, but it is extensively bridged making for easy navigation.[50] Dry, flat, spots are scarce, perhaps non-existent during early season snow melt. In reference to the claimed trail camp 0.5 mile after the trail levels off, yes, one could camp there, but not very comfortably."[GT]

Our next waypoint is just over the Idaho state line as the trail climbs again into a small saddle on the ridge at the junction with the Ruby Ridge Trail 35.

0220P 2.1mi 48° 54.704'N 116° 03.017'W 6000' Trail 44 X Ruby Ridge Trail 35

The PNT is now in Idaho and the Kaniksu National Forest. Technically TR44 has become TR35 as we enter the new forest nomenclature. We'll follow TR35 for the next 9.2 miles. In 2016, TR35 was reported clear all the way to the forest road and in fine shape.[61/66]

We continue northwest following the trail along the ridge and eventually descend about 160' to cross Deer Creek Road. There is a decent spot for a dry roadside camp here.[81] If our navigation is on target we cross the road at the top of the U-turn where the road hits the crest of the ridge at Canuck Pass. We hike northwest still on TR35 following the trail and the ridgeline to the west. In 1.2 miles after the Canuck Pass we reach Copper Ridge Road RD403.

0222P 1.9mi 48° 55.228'N 116° 04.802'W 5880' Trail 35 X Copper Ridge Road 403

You may find a relatively small, but adequate flat area, after crossing the road to set up a trail camp without water. TR35 traverses southwest along the crest of the ridge, or near the top. In 0.8 miles we are south of Spruce Lake, down in the bowl created by the humps and buttes, but unfortunately it is about 420' below us.

Keep following the trail along Ruby Ridge to the southwest hiking at times through sparse forest with excellent views to the south. The trail has a fairly level grade at 5800-5900' elevation for the next mile where it begins a slow downhill approach almost to our next waypoint. About 2.1 miles past our view of Spruce Lake the trail descends rapidly 500' on switchbacks to cross Forest Road 2517. With luck you'll be here during huckleberry season with some of the best picking on the PNT along Ruby Ridge.

The trail meets Forest Road 2517 at a point just prior to the road's turn south. There is a seasonal spring near the bend in the road. Hike on FR2517 northwest 0.1 miles to find TR35.

0226P   4.1mi   48° 53.936'N   116° 08.105'W   4740'   Trail 35 X Forest Road 2517

Back at the trail-road junction, we follow Ruby Ridge on TR35 to the west as we keep descending for the next 2.4 miles. Along the way as TR35 turns south it descends 760' elevation to our next waypoint. Here we meet TR205.

0228P   2.4mi   48° 53.357'N   116° 09.326'W   2980'   Trail 35 X Trail 205

The primary PNT keeps us heading north on TR35 at this trail junction for 1.7 miles. After three major switchbacks, we meet Moyie River Road 34. Just prior to reaching the road, there is a trailhead on a spur road. Hikers report that there is a camping option here at the trailhead, albeit very close to the railroad tracks.[ES] There are picnic tables at the trail head and a creek can be accessed nearby for water.[GT] Follow the jeep tracks out of the campground east about 200 yards to Kreist Creek.[50]

0230.5P   1.8mi   48° 53.963'N   116° 10.280'W   Trail 35 X Moyie River Road 34

Once on the paved road we head north for 0.75 miles looking to turn west and cross the bridge over the Moyie River on Earl Lane Road RD348.

Hungry? You may want to keep going north another 5 minutes to the Feist Creek Resort (restaurant), which might also serve as a possible resupply box shipping point.[BT] Their phone number is (208) 267-8649. Cliff is generous and welcoming, providing wonderful lawn space for camping. Good food![48] Be sure to sign their PNT hiker notebook with entries all the way back to 2014.

Back to the PNT. In only 0.1 miles after crossing the river turn north on Bussard Lake Road, which we follow for just under 0.4 miles to reach Forest Road 2202. FR2202 leads us west to the trailhead for the Bussard Mountain Trail 52. Be careful not to cut through the private property to the east of the trailhead.

0231P   1.5mi   48° 54.790'N   116° 11.139'W   2620'   Forest Road 2202 X Bussard Mountain Trail 32 / Trail Camp

Note: Maps indicate that this is TR52, but the trail sign shows "Bussard Mtn Tr. No. 32."[66] We pick up TR32, but before we start the strenuous climb, note that there is a good spot for a trail camp in the trees a few yards north of the trailhead and a creek nearby running in 2017.[ES] Unfortunately, dirt bikers have trashed this section of the trail.[50] TR52 begins and we continuously climb to gain 3130' over the next five miles with many, many switchbacks. About 1.6

miles into our climb the trail crosses the Sidehill Trail 415, which runs north-south along the 3900' contour. We keep climbing west on TR52.

In another 2.8 miles TR52 levels slightly at the top of the ridge and skirts east of and slightly above the old forest RD2485, the Tilly Mine jeep road.

0235P 4.5mi 48° 53.824'N 116° 13.465'W 5710' Trail 32 X Old Jeep Trail

Follow the old jeep road, still on TR52, or now perhaps TR32, climbing southwest along the ridge for about 0.5 miles. Here the old jeep trail turns south on a level grade, and eventually turns into the Rutledge Creek Trail 152. If you want to climb Bussard Mountain then take the old road for 0.1 miles south then find the easy clear approach to the summit. Great views are reported from the summit and well worth the little side trip.[KC] "Don't miss this unexpected summit views here after a short side trip."[80]

0236P 0.5mi 48° 53.524'N 116° 13.838'W 5930' Trail 32 X Danquist Trail 225

The PNT does not climb to the top of Bussard Summit, but turns west from the old jeep trail on the TR225. The 200-yard hike to the summit, however, does offer some good views. The top of Bussard Mountain also has plenty of flat room, albeit dry to camp. Although you might be able to beg some beer from the off-roaders who clearly frequent the spot.[81]

Back to the PNT on TR225. This trail generally follows the crest of the rocky open ridge for 0.5 miles before descending on the northern slope into the trees. In another 2.0 miles we have climbed back up to the top of the ridge at our next waypoint.

0238P 2.4mi 48° 54.184'N 116° 16.445'W 5300' Trail 225 X Trail 23

TR225 turns north toward Tungsten Mountain. The primary PNT route, however, turns west on TR23 over the ridge for about 120 yards before turning south and then dropping dramatically downhill on tight switchbacks. "This would be a double black diamond run for skiers."[GT] We descend 440' in just over 0.5 miles where the trail levels off around the 4800' contour. The map notes that there is a spring in this area but hikers report that it may not be flowing. At this point the map shows an old forest road that runs northwest to Bethlehem Mountain, but it is very faint.

TR23 follows this old road bed south another 1.9 miles downhill on a gentler grade than the one we just experienced. After about 1.1 miles the trail comes near Rock Creek just to the west which may offer the first opportunity for water in some time. The road bed diverges south from the creek for another 0.9 miles and into our next waypoint at the junction with Camp Nine Mile Road RD397.

0241P 2.3mi 48° 52.696'N 116° 17.025'W 3840' Trail 23 X Camp Nine Mile Road 397

We turn northwest on RD397 on a relatively level grade for the next 0.6 miles. Look for good water in Rock Creek in about 0.2 miles, but it was dry in August 2017.[ES] In 1.8 miles after starting on RD397 we leave the road and venture west on a short bushwhack.

Note: Some hikers have found a dry bushwhack west to Brush Lake by leaving the road about 0.3 short of the upcoming waypoint. Bushwhack uphill a little then circle counter-clockwise to the east side of Brush Lake. Turn south to the end of the lake.[KC]

0242P 1.8mi 48° 53.647'N 116° 18.504'W 3470' Road 397 @ Brush Lake Bushwhack

The exact start for our bushwhack is across the road from old truck tracks which lead east uphill to the Bethlehem Mine. You may choose another option and keep road walking 4.1 miles by skipping the Brush Lake Campground and staying on RD397. This will take you to intercept Forest Road 1004 at a point which is described in Section 3. In 2015 a hiker wrote in his journal, "What was I thinking? I failed to note the additional road walking time incurred after the bushwhack, when added to the ninety minutes that the bushwhack 'shortcut' took me, made this the longer choice. Walk the 4.4 miles on FR397, don't take this so-called 3.1 mile 'shortcut'."[47] Another 2015 hiker stated, "Having done the bushwhack to the ugly Brush Lake and then more road walk to the highway, I realized I would have been better off to just walk RD397 north all the way."[50.]

The map shows bushwhacking due west, but there are two other better options. First, there is a mountain bike path that is on the southeast side of the lake. To intercept the bike path leave Road 397 about 0.3 miles south, before our next waypoint. From the road we bushwhack due west to intercept the bike trail.

The second bushwhack option begins at our next waypoint and takes a more northwest track. Brush Lake's north side has been reported to be very swampy and impassable. Here's my recommendation if you don't choose to bushwhack to the bike path. From our waypoint bushwhack northwest staying on the higher ground on the slight ridge above the lake and the swamp. Aim for the best crossing down the ridge between the swamp and the pond to your north. You should be able to see a large rock outcropping on the far side of the dip that goes down into the creek. This is our target.

0243P 1.1mi 48° 53.982'N 116° 19.653'W 3030' Bushwhack @ Brush Lake Creek

After crossing the creek (or lowest swampy area) keep bushwhacking up the ridge to dry footing trying to pass to the west of the large rock outcropping. If you come up south you'll be fine and should be in a very rocky, treeless western sloping grade. Keep working southwest looking to come closer to Brush Lake. It may not seem like it, but when you get due north of the lake, there is an ATV trail on the side of the slope about 60' above the lake. There is also a dirt road between the ATV trail and the lake.

Our bushwhack adventure ends, as does this portion of the primary PNT route, at the treeless intersection of Forest Road 1004. FR1004 runs west to the campground road, which then would take you south to the Brush Lake Campground. This NFS campground is a no-fee fishing camp with only four sites, but with vault toilets.

0244P 0.8mi 48° 53.428'N 116° 20.121'W 3010' Bushwhack X Forest Road 1004 @ Brush Lake

Alternate Route: The Original PNT Northern Route to Northwest Peak

This section discusses the navigation for the alternate route, previously the original route, up to Northwest Peak and then returns south to the primary PNT route. It is a little longer, with more road walking but it is more scenic, and the trail-less ridge walk is amazing.[BT]

In 2016, a thru-hiker wrote about this alternate route:

> *"Whoooo! NW Peak Scenic Area original route is the real deal. PopStar and I hiked that route on July 3rd and I do suggest it, but know it is a work out!*
>
> *The trail is in great shape all the way to the summit. We found the ridge walk to Mt. Davis to be a breeze, but give yourself plenty of time for the bushwhack/scramble from the summit of Davis around the bowl to the saddle where you meet up with the new primary route. Plenty of stunning camping above the tree line if it takes longer than you'd hoped!"[59]*

Start: 0204P Forest Road 338 X Forest Road 5902

Rejoin: 0213P Trail 174 X Trail 164

Mileage: 12.5 miles; longer than the primary route by 4 miles

Highlights: Northwest Peak 7705' and the amazing "knife edge" ridgeline bushwhack

0204P 0.0mi 48° 57.225'N 115° 52.484'W 4660' Forest Road 338 @ Yaak River

At this junction RD5902 heads southwest in line with the direction we've been hiking, while our alternate original PNT route turns to the west staying on RD338.

In 0.5 miles RD338 crosses a bridge over the West Fork Yaak River. Keep hiking on RD338 for another 6.2 miles past the bridge, with easy navigation, to reach the trailhead for the Northwest Peak Trail 169, having gained 1630' elevation. The trailhead has parking for only two vehicles so look carefully for it. As you get close to the trailhead RD338 does a series of climbing 'S' turns with a creek centered in the turn. There was good flow in the creek in dry 2015.[51]

0210A 6.0mi 48° 57.799'N 115° 55.704'W 6120' Forest Road 338 X New Trailhead - Northwest Peak Trail 169 (new trailhead)

There is new trail head without a log book in 2017. TR169 immediately heads uphill and then finally turns back west as we begin our climb to the summit of Northwest Peak. In the next 2.0 miles you will gain about 1460' in elevation. After the first 1.0 miles the trail breaks out of the forest and onto a spotty and then treeless rocky slope.

The trail may be difficult to find at times due to snow and rock slides. Nevertheless keep climbing the ridge higher, gaining glimpses of the summit. Good cairns mark the way for us. About 0.3 miles from the summit the trail takes us through a treeless boulder field, but on a defined tread up to the lookout cabin at the summit.

0213A 1.8mi 48° 57.796'N 115° 58.096'W 7709' Trail 169 @ Northwest Peak

The tower is a spectacular spot to spend the night. Look for tools to lower the shutters.[49] There is a pit toilet nearby. Northwest Peak offers unobstructed spectacular views far north into Canada and of the glacier bowl carving Upper Hawkins Lake, about 1000' below us. Unfortunately, according to the USFS, the old lookout tower on Northwest Peak. USFS crews worked on the tower in 2017 and it looks like a great place to stay.[CN]

As we depart Northwest Peak you find that there is no trail to follow. Instead the PNT heads southwest along the almost "knife-edge" crest of the ridge leading to the hump at 7360' which lies about 0.45 miles ahead. The slope on either side of the ridge crest is dramatic, falling over 800' in just over 0.1 miles—let's stay on the crest.

0214A 0.4mi 48° 57.505'N 115° 58.448'W 7360' Bushwhack Point on Northwest Peak

The ridge line turns south as we follow it and climb for the next 1.5 miles to reach the summit of Davis Mountain. Hike along this bumpy backbone with numerous PUDs to where we eventually climb up to the summit of Davis Mountain.

0215A 1.7mi 48° 56.298'N 115° 58.105'W 7583' Bushwhack @ Davis Mountain

Davis Mountain has no facilities and the western edge is a sheer drop off. From the summit we bushwhack downhill to the southwest, rounding the bowl along the eastern slope of Ewing Mountain. We need to carefully descend on the ridge down to the edge of the tree line. Other hikers have continued to follow the ridge to the west, rather than descend, as a shortcut to find TR174.

As we follow the base of the rockslide at the edge of the tree line we'll be turning southeast trying to stay around the 6400' contour. After turning south for about 0.5 miles start looking for the small shallow saddle in the ridge at our elevation to our west. Our bushwhack takes us into the small open saddle about 150' in diameter where we should find TR174 and rejoin the primary PNT route.

0213P 1.2mi 48° 54.941'N   115° 57.989'W   6390' Trail 174 X Trail 164

RESUPPLY OPTIONS

0184P 48° 54.525'N 115° 38.508'W 2990' Trail 51 X West Side Yaak River Road **Yaak:** The town is 7.3 miles south of this waypoint following Road 508.

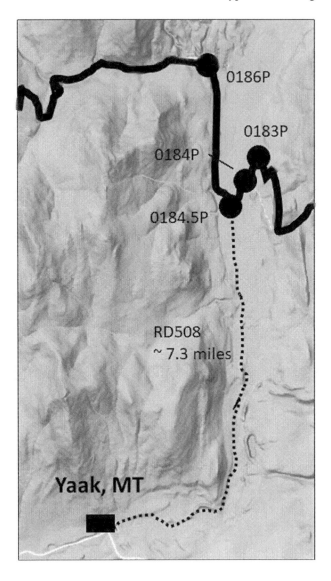

0244P 1.7mi 48° 54.546'N 116° 21.066'W 2500' Forest Road 1004 X Camp 9 Road – Old US Highway 95 **Bonners Ferry:** Turn south on US95 for about 15 miles.

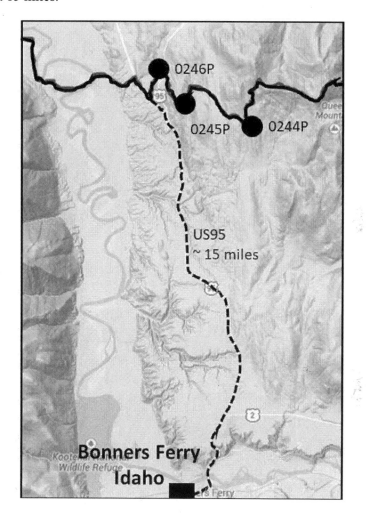

Trail Support

0184P   Yaak: Randy Beacham, beachamphoto@yahoo.com, (406) 295-9320. Knows the trails and weather. Can help with rides early in the morning and in the evenings and people can camp out at my place. Since we don't have cell phone service here, and I'm not home often, contact me a few days ahead of time, perhaps when in Eureka.

0244P Bonners Ferry: (previous support, unknown for 2019) Sharlene Delaney, sharlenedelaney@ymail.com, 208-660-7389 cell.

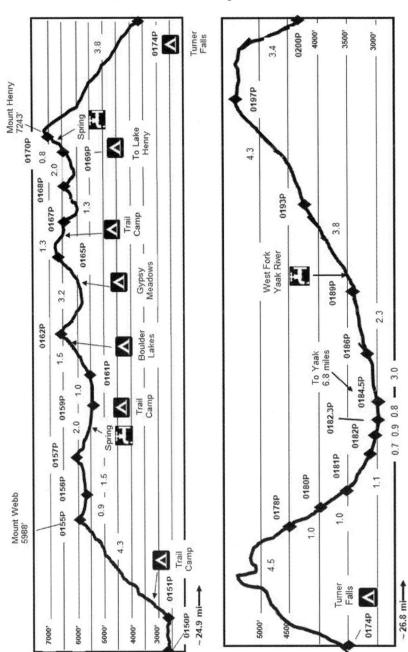

Tim Youngbluth

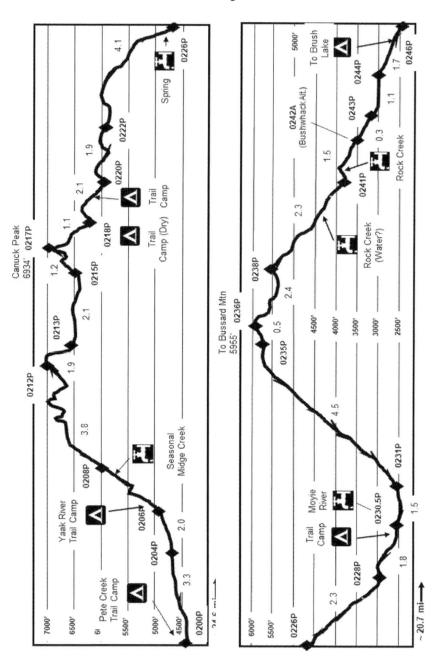

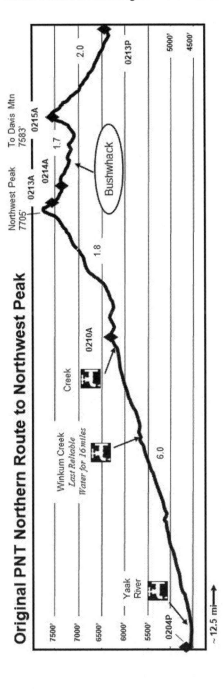

Original PNT Northern Route to Northwest Peak

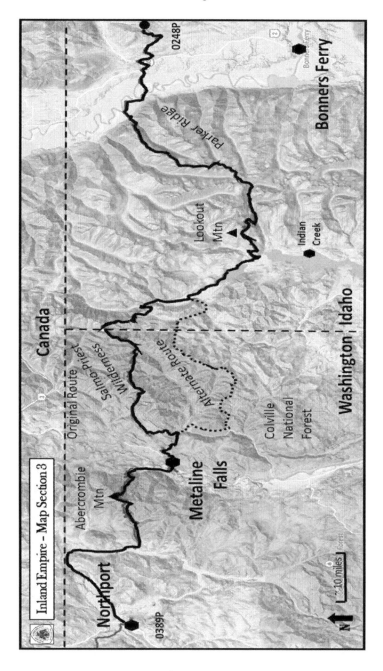

CHAPTER FOUR
INLAND EMPIRE – MAP SECTION 3
Kootenai River to Columbia River

Ascending Abercrombie Mountain, Colville National Forest

Key Trail Notes

Highlights: Parker Ridge, Lion Creek Bushwhack, Lookout Mountain, Abercrombie Mountain

Primary Route Estimated Elevation Change: 23,280' climb / 21,520' descent

Route Alternates: Hughes Meadow, Leola Creek

Possible Resupply: Bonners Ferry, Metaline Falls, Northport

Parks/Forests: Kootenai NF, Colville NF

Permits: None

Other Notes: Bear spray recommended. The Parker Ridge Trail 221 was reopened in 2016 by the USFS after monumental work to clear the trail from the devastation from the 2015 wildfire. Trail Angels in Metaline Falls.

0244P 0.0mi 48° 53.428'N 116° 20.121'W 3010' Bushwhack X Forest Road 1004 @ Brush Lake

The PNT now embarks on more road walking with an easy section across the Kootenai Valley. Follow Brush Lake Road RD1004 first southwest and then northwest for 1.6 miles. Next, we cross RD397 which has come from the northeast. If we had road walked RD397 instead of bushwhacking, this is the junction where we rejoin the primary PNT route.

Continue north and downhill on FR1004 for another 0.5 miles crossing the new US95.

Possible Trail Angel, (Bonners Ferry). See details at the end of this chapter.

Resupply: If you turn south on US95 instead of crossing, in about 15 miles you come to Bonners Ferry, Idaho. Although a little off the PNT, this is the largest town even near the trail for about the next 600 miles until you get close to Sedro-Woolley, Washington. For hikers planning to go into Bonners Ferry, 0.9 miles south of the PNT on US95 there is a scenic overlook with a wide turnout that offers the best place to hitchhike. It also has better cell phone service.[47]

Back to the PNT primary route, FR1004 intercepts US95 at an angle in an 'X', rather than straight '+'. Although FR1004 stops at US95 cross the road and hike north about 0.1 miles looking for break in the fence. "Bushwhack" west down the slope. You should see the definitive markings of the old FR1004 through the trees as we hike down the slope to Camp 9 Road – Old US95.

0246P 1.7mi 48° 54.546'N 116° 21.066'W 2500' Forest Road 1004 X Camp 9 Road – Old US Highway 95

Follow Old US 95 Road south and downhill for 1.3 miles to find State Route 1. Back to the north hike 1.0 miles on SR1 to Copeland Road. Head west on to reach our next waypoint in Copeland.

0249P 3.2mi 48° 54.159'N 116° 23.353'W 1790' Copeland Road X Farm to Market Road

Although the map shows "Copeland" there are no service here. At the 'Y' junction keep straight northwest, and then west to cross the bridge over the Kootenai River in 0.7 miles. There is a boat launch and picnic table under the bridge to provide easy access to the river if you want to cool your feet.

The U.S. Border Patrol frequently checks the outhouse and area under the bridge. Stop at the wheat farm just before the bridge. Vance, the owner of the property, likes hikers and may give permission for you to hike by the picnic table on his property.[48]

After crossing the bridge follow the road and the river 0.8 miles west to Kerr Lake Road - RD45C, which we take west while RD45 turns southwest. In another 1.3 miles RD45C intersects with a short spur road that climbs 40' up to West Side Road RD18. Head north on Westside road in the afternoon shade.

Strong recommendation: Instead of turning north on Kerr Lake Road, a dusty farmer's driveway, continue west on RD45 directly to Westside Road. This is 0.3 miles longer than the primary route, but it offers shade in only 0.9 miles.

0253P 2.9mi 48° 54.050'N 116° 26.578'W 1770' Kerr Lake Road- 45C X West Side Road 18

After this triangle intersection we keep west for a quick 0.15 miles to Westside Road. Nest we head northwest 2.7 miles to reach the trailhead for Trail 14. There are two points to help find the trailhead. About 100 yards before the trailhead you will pass over Parker Creek and about 40 yards before it you will come upon a small connector road or driveway to your right (east). The trailhead, of course, is to your left (west).

0255.2P 2.6mi 48° 55.135'N 116° 29.634'W 1900' West Side Road X Trail 14 / Parker Ridge Trail 221

A word of caution, Parker Creek may be the last point to fill up on water for the next 16 miles. 2016 hikers confirmed that there is no water until Parker Lake, which requires a very steep 500' descent over 0.5 trail miles off the primary PNT route.[64] At the TR14 trailhead here is a small camp area west of the road at Parker Creek. Now we're ready for one of the PNT's epic climbs as we enter the Kaniksu National Forest.

Follow TR14 for only about 0.3 miles to pick up TR221. TR14 stays lower following Parker Creek to the west. The PNT, of course, climbs higher on TR221. A 2015 thru-hiker reported that the trail was "clean as a whistle."[48]

After climbing 3300' in 4.4 miles on TR221, at about the 5200' contour, there is an unmarked side trail to the north to Parker Ridge Spring. The spring is easy to find, but barely running in 2017.[ES] The trail is in the 'U' of a sharp switchback; water is not guaranteed and there is no good campsite at the spring. We continue climbing on TR221 for another 2.1 miles to our next way point, which is a small clearing in the thick forest that offers a relatively good trail camp, albeit without water.

0262P 6.8mi 48° 54.128'N 116° 33.374'W 5940' Trail 221 @ Parker Ridge Trail Camp

After passing through the small clearing our climb becomes "friendlier," but we're still climbing for the next 4.0 miles following the ridge line as it turns to the south and close to Parker Peak. There once were lovely campsites on the trail, but these were burned in the 2015 wildfire and are now unsuitable.[CN] About 1.0 miles from Parker Peak the PNT turns south and follows the eastern slope of the peak at about the 6800' contour. As TR221 turns south, you might find a trail that would take you to the summit of Parker Peak, at 7670'.

After leaving the crest of the ridge we traverse the very rocky eastern slope for 1.6 miles, but the trail is fairly well defined. We might find water along the way from the snow melt on the peak, but this is unlikely from mid to late summer.[LB] Our next waypoint is crossing the unnamed trail that heads up the west side of Parker Peak to the summit. "Highly recommended side trip for lunch."[80]

0265P 3.3mi 48° 52.020'N 116° 35.529'W 7060' Trail 221 X Parker Peak Summit Trail

On the ridge near this waypoint there is a small, dry campsite. If you want to "bag" another PNT peak, turn back north and climb up about 610' in a little over 0.5 miles. The summit trail is easy to miss. At the campsite look north for faint trail and an old trail sign nailed to a tree.[64] On the summit of Parker Peak there are only the remnants of a 1932 log cabin at the top. Back on the primary PNT route we're heading southwest for a little over 0.5 miles descending on Parker Ridge. Here we cross the Parker Lake Trail 203 at our next waypoint.

0266P 0.5mi 48° 51.581'N 116° 35.745'W 6860' Trail 221 X Parker Lake Trail 203

TR203 is not on the PNT route, but if you're in dire need of water, it drops steeply down 540' from the top of the ridge to the pristine Parker Lake. The trail switchbacks down the slope to reach the lake in about 0.6 miles.
It is about this point we should emerge from the burn area. 2016 hikers describe leaving the burn area to find the Selkirk mountains here as "downright brazen, revealing long expanses of exposed granite, Sierra-like in their sparse attire of white pine, larch, firs, and spruce. We hadn't been so delighted by a mountain range since the Northern Rockies of Glacier National Park."[67]
Keeping to the primary PNT route on TR221, we continue west along the ridge line for the next 0.9 miles before turning predominantly south for the next 5.0 miles and to our bushwhack point. Before we get there, however, our next waypoint is crossing the Long Mountain Trail which would take you down the ridge to Long Mountain Lake.

0269P 3.5mi 48° 49.850'N 116° 36.851'W 7110' Trail 221 X Long Mountain Lake Trail 15

The TR15 spur trail drops east 500' in elevation on many switchbacks down the ridge to the lake, where there is an excellent place to trail camp. The lake is nestled in a rocky knob between Parker Ridge and the Parker Creek headwaters. Long Mountain Lake is a piercing blue bowl of water hanging high on the edge of Long Mountain in the Selkirk Mountains, and it makes a decent place for a campsite. It would be excellent except the site next to the lake is pretty trashed.[KC]
We stick to TR221 which stays high along the ridge descending south for another 1.0 miles to meet the junction of the Pyramid Pass Trail 13 and the Long

Canyon Trail 7 at the edge of a boulder field. TR7 runs down the western slope to the northwest.

0270P 0.9mi 48° 49.191'N 116° 36.992'W 6400' Trail 221 X Pyramid Pass Trail 13

TR13 is the main corridor trail that ties together the other trails in this area. We leave TR221 and turn south on TR13 along the west side of the ridge, climbing 320' elevation to the rocky ridge saddle in 0.4 miles. Next, we descend on the eastern slope for 0.5 miles to cross the Trout Lake – Big Fisher Trail 41. TR41 runs northeast toward Trout Lake. There is a creek near this junction.

TR13, our primary PNT route, takes a hard switchback to the west before working further south. In a short 0.4 miles on a fairly level grade, TR13 intersects with the Ball Lakes Trail 43 at our next waypoint. If you miss this waypoint, there is a trailhead/parking lot further on, and you can catch a trail to Ball Lakes, a popular spot for locals.[48]

0271P 1.1mi 48° 48.310'N 116° 36.395'W 5820' Trail 13 X Ball Lakes Trail 43 (signed)

The Primary PNT route is now on TR43 to the southwest while TR13 continues downhill to the east to Trout Creek and Forest Road 634. This is an obvious, but unsigned trail junction.[64] We follow TR43 for only 0.4 miles to the north end of Pyramid Lake, and an excellent spot for a trail camp. From here we keep to TR43 south for another 1.2 mile to our next waypoint.

Before we get there the trail climbs a steep 600' ridge to reach the Ball Lakes. The lower lake in particular has a large scenic waterside site. Arriving on a weekend might find the sites already full, however.[GT] Whether you camp or not, be sure, however, to fill up on water before leaving Ball Lakes. In 2016 hikers reported that Upper Ball Lake is the most the most beautiful lake in this area—three campsites with fire rings and crystal clear water.[64]

The Idaho National Panhandle Forests website provides the best trail description for the route between Ball Lakes and Pyramid Lake.

"The trail winds through spruce and alpine fir at a gentle grade. Bridges cross numerous creeks and seasonal drainages along the trail. At 3/4 mile the trail approaches Pyramid Lake at its outlet. The hour glass shaped lake is set in a sub-alpine cirque with head-wall and scree field on the southwest side. Trail 43 crosses the bridge at the outlet, then switchbacks into a steep, rugged ascent from the Pyramid Lake bowl. After reaching the top of the head-wall at the 1 1/4 mile the trail takes a short, less steep pitch through stunted trees and boulder strewn meadow to a trail junction. The right hand trail leads 100 yards to the upper Ball Lake (elevation 6708 ft). The left fork leads 1/2 mile down to the lower

Ball Lake. Both Ball Lakes sit at the base of another huge granite head-wall with large scree fields descending to their edges. "[26]

0273P 1.8mi 48° 47.398'N 116° 37.146'W 6630' Trail 43 @ Ball Lakes Bushwhack Start

Look for the cairn that marks the start of the bushwhack.[67] Several hikers recommend wearing long sleeves and pants for this bushwhack. Don't get frustrated and you don't need brute force. Choose your line carefully and plan to work slowly. If you find parts of the faded old trail then take it, but know that it is there only 50 percent of the time or less.

Another important point to consider is what time of the day you start your bushwhack. Several hikers have started in later afternoon and have been forced to overnight along Lion Creek. That part of the bushwhack is tough enough. There is no place to set up a tent or find a dry spot along Lion Creek 5.0 miles ahead. It may be better to camp at Ball Lakes and start the bushwhack fresh in the morning.

The bushwhack begins at the southern end of the lower Ball Lake near Spanish Creek by climbing the rocky scree field toward the west to find the crest of the ridge. Once on the crest we follow it south for about 0.5 miles looking for a good, safe spot to descend the ridge to the west. There is a small cairn at the drop off point.

While working west along the ridge, it is better to try to remain level around the 6800-6900' contour lines, then to try to scramble along the top of the ridge. Staying at this level in about 0.4 miles we reach the crest of the far ridge. Here, we follow this rocky ridge south for another 0.5 miles into our next waypoint.

0274P 0.9mi 48° 46.912'N 116° 37.733'W 6780' Turn Point West on Bushwhack

In 2018 a number of PNT hikers have chosen an alternate bushwhack route that descends into the valley for about 0.7 miles but then climbs to follow the Lions Head Ridge to The Lions Head, and then stays high along the ridge to Lookout Mountain to re-join the PNT there.

"Highly recommend the Lions Head route. Be sure to allow a full day for the ten-mile bushwhack. Spend night at Pyramid or Ball Lake, get water at creek in basin below Lion Head and carry to allow spending the night at Lookout Mountain. Said basin is a great place to putter around a bit. Rambled to the base of Lion's Head on a ledge. One of the best days of the PNT."[80]

Caution: This route stays high for the views but requires both Class 2 and 3 scrambles. Be advised that there is a 600' shear cliff drop off on the north side of the ridge at various points. There is not enough information to provide any further description of the route. Again, if you are solo, or not skilled enough to climb this route, descend to follow the primary bushwhack route.

Back to our primary route and bushwhack. We're looking for a safe place to descend the ridge. Our turn point is just about the last point on the ridge to do this. It sits in a saddle right before the ridge begins to climb to the south. To the east is a fairly dramatic rock cliff.

We turn west still on our bushwhack leg, as we descend losing about 1000' elevation in another 0.6 miles. Hiker warning: "In my opinion that plunge off the top would be the very worst place on the whole trail to hurt yourself. With the indistinct route location, the vertical terrain and the dense brush/forest you'd never be found if incapacitated there."[GT]

We go slowly and carefully—fully enjoying the experience of being a 19th century mountain man, or woman. This is a crazy bushwhack steeply down, and continuing difficulties with brush, muck and fallen trees along the creek. If in doubt on the descent, turn slightly southwest. Once at the bottom we should be around the 5800' contour and hopefully on the northern branch of Lion Creek.

Once we find the creek, prepare for some hard, tedious hiking.[48] We follow the creek southwest downhill, sometimes on the east side of the creek and sometimes on the west side, looking at another 1500' elevation loss over the next 2.0 miles to reach the 'Y' confluence with Lion Creek. We might be able to find occasional bits of trail to follow south along the creek, but they will keep disappearing.[GT] Some hikers report that it is better to stay a little higher and more in the trees where beating the brush was not as problematic. When we are at the creek junction we turn west and bushwhack a little bit more.

Never underestimate the time it will take to get through this section. The downed timber brings numerous challenges, the bushes are relentless, foot placement is critical with "drop-offs," with muck and slippery branches. The plants are tall and so dense you can't see even for short distances.[64] Make sure your pack is secure with any equipment on its side is tied down. You may find lost trekking poles, tents, and sleeping bags along the way snagged by the brush.

There are no definitive reports about where we can pick up the trail and end our bushwhacking. The best evidence appears to be about 1.5 miles west at our next waypoint. With good navigation and persistence, we find the Lion Creek Trail 42 which is closer to Lion Creek than shown on the map.[ES]

0278P 4.1mi 48° 45.792'N 116° 41.675'W 4370' Bushwhack X Lion Creek Trail 42

Once on TR42 follow it downhill and west. There is reported to be a good trail camp in about 0.4 miles where Kent Creek flows into Lion Creek. At this point TR42 is an abandoned forest road. If the trail is not here, keep bushwhacking west along Lion Creek to pick up the trail. The trail is about 80 yards north of the creek and 30-40' higher.

Look for the natural water slide and several good places to trail camp; easily seen from the trail this is a great rest spot. At the end of the trail we exit at a U in the road where it turns up hill about 100 yards to the road-end parking lot. Take the left branch for the PNT.

0280P 1.5mi 48° 45.492'N 116° 43.878'W 3720' Trail 42 X Lion Creek Road – RD42

Following the road downhill southwest for 1.2 miles we come to our next waypoint and to begin our climb up to Lookout Mountain at our next waypoint.

0282P 1.9mi 48° 45.276'N 116° 45.153'W 3210' Forest Road 42 X Forest Road 423

Before we begin to climb, you might take stock of your supplies and physical condition, and then consider a minor route shortcut. Instead of climbing Lookout Mountain you can stay on RD42 for 5.1 miles of road walking to re-join the primary PNT route at the Lion Creek Campground. The campground is located at the north end of Lower Priest Lake at the junction with Ross Creek Trail as described below.

Ah, but what the heck, we'll climb Lookout Mountain! We can get water from Lion Creek, but there are several stream crossings on our climb up Lookout Mountain.[50] Take the sharp turn northeast climbing over the Kelly humps on FR423 off Lion Creek Road.[GT] FR423 climbs on large switchbacks for 4.2 miles gaining 3270'. Navigation on the road is easy as ATVs have cut a defined path on the old road. Look for the mountain goats up on the hillside.[48]

0287P 4.7mi 48° 46.213'N 116° 46.152'W 6480' Forest Road 423 X Trail 37 below Lookout Mountain summit

We've hiked this far so we might as well take the side trip to the summit and continue on the road/trail another quarter mile gaining 300' to reach the lookout tower at the summit at 6787'. The tower is one of the Forest Service's newer ones built in 1977, replacing the original built in 1929. The tower may be manned; if so take a minute to chat with the ranger. Lookout Mountain is unique in that it has a very dramatic sheer rock face on the north side.

After visiting the summit, we find TR37 at the small turnout in the road, and descend on the trail for about 0.2 miles before angling to the west. Here the grade lessens for just a little bit before going downhill again.

At about the 5800' contour the trail levels and heads northwest and in 1.1 miles from the start, we cross Trail 36, which runs to the north and to Lookout Lake.

0288P 1.1mi 48° 46.453'N 116° 47.021'W 5510' Trail 37 X Lookout Lake Trail 36 X Lucky Creek Road

At this junction there is a small, dry trail camp with a fire ring. To return to TR37 we follow the road downhill, first southwest and then northwest a short distance into our next waypoint. Lucky Creek Road is not shown on the map.[ES] Just prior to the next waypoint, at a 'U' turn in the road, there is a small lake 90 yards north. In 2018 it was reported not to be the best, but serviceable.[80]

0288.2P 0.6mi 48° 46.449'N 116° 47.254'W 5350' Lucky Creek Road X Trail 37

TR37 is the southern point of a sharp 'U' bend in the road, where Lucky Creek Road turns north. TR37 heads southwest immediately downhill. Be looking to cross Lucky Creek Road RD43 in 2.6 miles as TR37 follows the ridge, generally along the northern slope. Once we're on the road, look carefully to turn south in about 0.1 miles at a wide spot in the road, or rock pit. Near there we should be able to pick up the trail downhill again to the southwest, even though it is not marked.[50] Follow TR37 for another 0.9 miles to intersect Lucky Creek Road 43 again.

0292P 3.4mi 48° 45.225'N 116° 49.797'W 3410' Trail 37 X Lucky Creek Road 43

Although there is an old, steep trail that leads down, it may be best just to follow RD43 downhill north, then south for just under 2.1 miles meet East Shore Road RD1.

0294P 2.1mi 48° 45.696'N 116° 50.603'W 2580' Road 43 X East Shore Road RD1

Hike south on RD1 downhill for only about 0.9 miles to find the Floss Creek Trail 42. There is a shortcut at 0.5 miles. Look for a single post trail sign, "FL TR 42," on the east side of the road, across from a single-car turnout across from the sign. It can be found at 48° 45.295'N 116° 50.714'W. Follow the shortcut west to save about a mile of walking to the south and then northwest back from the waypoint shown below.

Following the longer primary route, there is no sign at the trailhead, only a single-car turnout and a deep double berm. The sandy, wide trail is almost hidden when walking the road south, but it is very apparent looking back to the northwest.

0295P 0.9mi 48° 45.010'N 116° 50.588'W 2480' East Shore Road RD1 X Floss Creek Trail 42

Before we discuss TR42, note that if you continue south on RD1 for another 0.4 miles you will be at the Idaho State Lion Head Campground with 47 sites, toilets and water on the north shore of Priest Lake. There is a $21 camp fee.

Resupply: The nearest camp store is another 10.0 miles south on East Shore Road at the Idaho State Indian Creek Campground. This campground has hot showers and a small general store. Both campgrounds have fee sites only.

Back to TR42. The trail is the primary route for the PNT and is also the Idaho Centennial Trail. Unfortunately, this junction at RD1 is not well marked and there are few signs down the trail. Some flags are here to help. We head west on the dirt road/tracks for about 0.1 miles. From here there should be ATV tracks going north. We work our way north picking the best route for now. If we would have kept going west after 0.1 miles, the trail would have taken us down toward Caribou Creek. After fording the creek, or perhaps crossing on a log downstream, we turn north to intersect TR42. Our goal is to hike north on the best trail, keeping between the creek to the west and RD1 to the east.

In about 0.8 miles from RD1 we should cross the creek and then in another 0.15 miles cross an unnamed forest road heading E-W. At this point the only good trail is the one we want, TR42. In about 0.6 miles after crossing the unnamed forest road there is a spur trail to Geisinger Camp, which is 0.3 miles west on the southern shore of Upper Priest Lake.

0296P 1.6mi 48° 45.989'N 116° 51.395'W 2520' Trail 42 X Spur Trail to Geisinger Camp

Continue on the well-marked and easy TR42 – the Idaho Centennial Trail – for 1.0 miles to reach Trail 58. This area has some impressive old growth Cedar trees. The map shows TR42 branching to the northeast while the PNT primary route follows TR58 along the shore of Upper Priest Lake. The trail, according to the NFS, is named the Upper Priest Lake Trail 302 at this waypoint.

0297P 0.9mi 48° 46.612'N 116° 51.947'W 2760' Trail 42 X Upper Priest Lake Trail 302

Upper Priest Lake is accessible by boat and campsites are popular during the weekends in the summer.[ES] While hiking on the east shore of Upper Priest Lake, look for a great trail camp with a bench where the trail first hits the lakeshore.[49] TR302 follows the lake shore and in 2.3 miles we should find Trapper Camp, the last Upper Priest Lake Camp on the shoreline. In 2015, just before Trapper Camp, there is a major blowdown of trees for about 0.1 miles.[48] Just south of the camp the trail crosses Trapper Creek on a footbridge. From here on the trail has a good very tread and is easy to follow.

0299P 2.3mi 48° 47.814'N 116° 53.731'W 2450' Trail 302 @ Upper Priest Lake Trapper Camp

There is a privy and bear boxes at this camp.[CN] Continuing on the trail, within a mile north of the Trapper Camp on TR302 we come to the end of the lake and head into the forest to follow the Priest River north, but still on the east side. We trek along TR302 north for 4.1 miles on excellent tread to reach Forest Road 655.

0303P 4.1mi 48° 50.596'N 116° 56.728'W 2640' Trail 302 X Forest Road 655

Across FR655 there is a good open spot to trail camp with several rock fire pits. Look for a good spot just beyond the stock parking area. Hunters use this spot during deer season late in the fall.

The PNT begins more road walking and easy navigation for the next 5 miles or so. Head west on RD655 for 0.4 miles to Forest Road 1013 to our next waypoint.

0304P 0.4mi 48° 50.469'N 116° 57.175'W 2630' Forest Road 655 X Forest Road 1013

Decision Time. It is highly recommended that hikers use the alternate route following the Jackson Creek Trail to Sullivan lake, as described at the end of this chapter.

For now, we'll continue on with the primary PNT route. Here we hike FR1013 north on a fairly level remote, dusty forest road. In 4.3 miles we look for the trailhead for the Upper Priest River Trail 308, which should be marked as part of the Idaho Centennial Trail. FR1013 at the trailhead is fairly level with ample stock trailer parking on both sides of the road. In 2014 the trailhead was clearly marked and easy to spot on the west side of the road.

0308P 4.3mi 48° 53.895'N 116° 58.001'W 2770' Forest Road 1013 X Upper Priest River Trail 308

Continuing on the primary route, TR308 is a heavily used trail that runs to the north along the Upper Priest River, so it should be easy to follow. You may find a note from the NFS that says that Trail 317 and Trail 315 ahead are not maintained. There is a spot for a trail camp here.

TR308 starts by heading west downhill slightly toward the river for less than 0.2 miles before turning north for just under 0.5 miles. Here the trail turns west where we will have to ford the river.

0309P 0.7mi 48° 54.162'N 116° 58.187'W 2770' Trail 308 X Trail 317

Head west downhill to ford the Upper Priest River, which should be no more than 100' wide at this point. We find TR317 on the west side and climb approximately 100' in elevation up the west slope. Here TR317 turns south and climbs 730' for 1.1 miles to Cabinet Pass and intersects with old Forest Road 1343.

0310P 1.3mi 48° 53.362'N 116° 58.412'W 3540' Trail 317 X Forest Road 1343

FR1343 has not been used for several years but is still has a visible tread. From this point we turn west on the dirt portion of the road and within 100 yards come to a narrow 'Y'. The left (southwest) portion of the 'Y' is FR1114 slightly downhill and is a possible alternate route. The primary PNT bears right (west) on the 'Y' and climbs slightly. Although this is a road for about 0.2 miles it soon turns back into TR315.

TR315 traverses the western slope of a heavily forested ridge, but there are some open views to the west into Washington State. But, expect that the trail will be choked with Alders and progress will be painfully slow. A bit of hard maintenance work has been completed, but in 2015, it was still horrific and a tedious hike through grizzly country[48]. On the horizon to the northwest the highest peak is Shedroof Mountain, which is on the PNT in a few more hours. After 2.25 miles on TR315 the trail turns west on the ridgeline and then begins a series of major switchbacks on the southern face climbing in elevation.

After 2.8 miles of major switchbacks, TR315 returns to the north along the ridge just above the 5000' contour having gained about 900' elevation. Strongly consider using an alternate route instead of this bushwhack on TR315 until all the trail maintenance has been completed.[48]

0315P 5.0mi 48° 54.925'N 117° 00.463'W 5010' Trail 315 @ End of Switchbacks

Continue north on TR315 generally on the western slope just below the crest of the ridge. In about 1.5 miles the trail descends slightly into a shallow saddle in the ridge. Here we're looking for an unmarked trail junction to the west which climbs slightly over the ridge at a 'T' junction.

0317P 1.4mi 48° 56.000'N 117° 00.538'W 5390' Trail 315 'Y' Split

If you've missed this junction you would stay straight on the old road bed soon turning to the northeast on what looks like the better tread. TR315, however, turns left (west) to climb slightly around a small hump before climbing north again along a new ridge. As we head northwest TR315 takes us higher on the ridge and to the Shedroof Divide Trail 512 in 1.1 miles.

0318P 1.1mi 48° 56.844'N 117° 00.969'W 5940' Trail 315 X Shedroof Divide Trail 512

At this 'Y' intersection we bear left (northwest) following TR512 downhill for 0.8 miles dropping 400' in elevation. Here TR512 turns southwest and climbs for another 1.0 miles to reach the Idaho - Washington border and the Colville National Forest.

Congratulations, if you're a thru-hiker you've covered two states of the PNT, but are only about one-quarter of the way to the Pacific Ocean! Continue southwest, now in the Colville National Forest and the Salmo-Priest Wilderness, on the easy to follow TR512 for 0.9 miles to cross the Salmo-Divide Trail 535 at out next waypoint.

0320P 2.4mi 48° 56.385'N 117° 02.818'W 6300' Trail 512 X Salmo-Divide Trail 535

There reportedly is a trail camp spot on the north side of the trail junction, but without water. We still have more climbing ahead. TR512 leads south on many switchbacks on good tread climbing the north face of Shedroof Mountain. Almost due west of Shedroof Mountain, the trail will begin to descend. At that point you may find an old faint summit trail.

Although not part of the primary PNT route, you may have the energy and inclination to climb another peak. If so, take this unmaintained summit trail east and bushwhack as best you can to the top, gaining about 200' elevation in a little over 200 yards. From the summit of Shedroof Mountain you can see far into Canada to the north, your PNT route from Idaho in the east, and your PNT route through the Selkirk Mountains to the west.

After passing Shedroof Mountain TR512 continues south on a relatively level grade for 0.4 miles, then drops 900' on numerous switchbacks for the next 0.9 miles to reach the intersection with Shedroof Cutoff Trail 511.

0322P 2.2mi 48° 55.126'N 117° 03.202'W 5500' Trail 512 X Shedroof Cutoff Trail 511 (estimated)

TR512 runs south but we turn west on the primary PNT route on TR511. We descend for about 0.5 miles down to Sullivan Creek. TR511 exits onto an old forest road in what looks like a 'U' turn switchback to the southeast.

0323P 0.5mi 48° 55.099'N 117° 03.821'W 4980'' Trail 511 X Forest Road 850

The trail (aka old road) turns southeast to follow the creek about 70' below in a steep ravine. Follow the trail along the creek for just under 0.3 miles and then cross. Near this point there is a trail/road junction, but we keep working southwest following TR511 along the creek. Note that the creek is often fast even into to August due to the snow runoff from the higher elevations.

In about 1.0 miles after crossing the creek, TR511 comes to the trailhead, by our next waypoint. The trailhead sits about 40' elevation higher than the next PNT leg. Follow the forest road around a bend and downhill, and in a short 100 yards you will be on Forest Road 2220.

0324P 1.2mi 48° 54.425'N 117° 04.695'W 4340' Trail 511 X Forest Road 2220

If you turn east (left) and follow FR2220 downhill in 0.5 miles you will come to the old Gypsy Meadows Horse Camp with excellent grassy sites and a good stream.

Decision Time. The primary PNT heads west on RD2220 for 0.9 miles, which is easy to follow. From here you should find the old Leola Creek Road RD260, which has been described as **the worst section** of the PNT – "**Hell on earth!**" The unmaintained road has not been serviced in 15 years and is thick with alders, thistle and has a complete overgrowth. When I spoke to PNT hiker

"Feather" about this section in 2012, he described it as the worst four miles in ten years of hiking anywhere in the country. An alternate route, a long, long road walk, is described in the alternate routes at the end of this section.

The U.S. Forest Service needs to relocate the PNT to better trails in this area, but until they do I'll describe the route for you. Following RD2220 northwest for 0.3 miles to the 'Y' in the road. We bear left onto the lower abandoned Leola Creek Road 260. This road soon turns north to parallel Deemer Creek. We're headed north. We want to head south on this road on the west side of the creek. Find a safe place to cross the creek and scramble up the bank to the road on the west side. You can keep north to the end of the road to cross the creek, too.

Head south climbing away from the creek for 0.5 miles. From here the road holds a gentle grade to the west for 1.3 miles where it crosses Leola Creek, and then turns southeast climbing 200' above the creek in 0.6 miles.

By now you've probably had a great upper body workout by untangling yourself from each alder snag, first from yourself in front, and then from your pack behind you. Turning back to the west the road holds a relatively level grade around 5200' contour except for the last 0.4 miles where it loops from north to south climbing about 400' to finally reach the terminus for Forest Road 200 and the trailhead for the Crowell Ridge Trail 515.

0329P 5.2mi 48° 55.039'N 117° 08.352'W 5560' Road 260 X Crowell Ridge Trail 515

There is a trailhead parking area at the end for Forest Road 200, with the trail on the west side. TR515 is a welcome relief as it is easy to follow with a relatively good tread as it heads west and we enter the Salmo-Priest Wilderness area. This trail climbs steadily, then follows along the nearly treeless ridge. It has a rocky tread but is passable. TR515 follows Crowell Ridge to the southwest for 3.7 miles ending at the intersection with the North Fork Trail 507 at our next waypoint.

0333P 3.7mi 48° 53.996'N 117° 11.241'W 6630' Trail 515 X North Fork Sullivan Creek Trail 507

Note that the map shows the intersection of TR515 and TR507 a little south and lower on the ridge than the actual position. The USFS states that, "Due to a trail bridge failure, the Upper North Fork Trail 507 will be closed to public use until the structure is replaced."[44]

Nevertheless, TR507 continues the primary PNT route climbing along Crowell Ridge, although initially it grades downhill slightly. In 1.1 miles TR507 begins a series of switchbacks to descend down the south face of Crowell Ridge toward the North Fork Sullivan Creek. About 0.2 miles short and above the creek, TR507 levels out at 5500' contour and works west to cross the Slate Creek Trail 525 in another 1.1 miles.

0336P 2.7mi 48° 54.729'N 117° 13.224'W 4560' Trail 507 X Slate Creek Trail 525

TR525 heads north deeper into the Salmo-Priest Wilderness while we head west on the primary PNT downhill on TR507. In just under 0.5 miles from the trail junction TR507 comes very close to the North Fork Sullivan Creek. This offers an excellent point to fill your water and find a trail camp, if you desire.

Following TR507 west still generally downhill, we hike for another 0.7 miles into swampy ravine. Crossing the ravine, the trail climbs and then undulates along the east side of Crowell Mountain turning southwest into our next waypoint, crossing the Red Bluff Trail 553.

0338.3P 2.2mi 48° 54.148'N 117° 16.252'W 3620' Trail 507 X Halliday Trail 522 X Red Bluff Trail 553

The PNT primary route now takes the better trail south. TR507 may continue straight ahead but soon becomes an unmaintained trail. If you find yourself on a "bushwhack" you have missed the trail junction.

TR533 descends immediately east off the ridge and as it winds quickly to cross Sullivan Creek in 0.6 miles. From there TR533 turns and climbs slightly to the 3500' contour for the next 2.3 miles. We hike through thick virgin forest as the trail parallels the boundary of the Salmo-Priest Wilderness less than a quarter mile to the east.

Next, TR533 descends rapidly as it rounds to the east to cross an unnamed creek. We now make the final turn south following the TR533 through switchbacks into our next way point at the trailhead with Sullivan Lake Road.

0343P 5.2mi 48° 51.243'N 117° 17.267'W 2620' Red Bluff Trail 553 X Sullivan Lake Road 9345

Time to begin the road walk into Metaline Falls. As we turn west on Sullivan Lake Road, in 0.3 miles there is the entrance to the NFS Mill Pond Campground. The campground is small and has fresh water and toilets, but no electricity. The NFS fee is the standard for this "primitive" type. You may be able to find a ride here into Metaline Falls.

Continuing west on Sullivan Lake Road in another 0.5 miles there is the entrance to the Mill Pond day-use picnic area with an old interpretive trail near the pond. Keeping to Sullivan Lake Road the next waypoint is the first road intersection with Lime Lake Road in about 3.1 miles.

0346P 3.9mi 48° 51.865'N 117° 20.894'W 2530' Sullivan Lake Road 9346 X Lime Lake Road

From this intersection head northwest 0.8 miles to Highway 31. CAUTION: State Route 31 is one of the major truck routes from the Canada border about 10 miles north. As you hike south on SR31 there are several blind curves and no shoulder. This is rated as one of the most dangerous road walks on the PNT.

Descend the 1.9 mile hill dropping 410' elevation down to Metaline Falls. Take the first left uphill into town to find the local park and the stores on 5th Avenue. (Please don't think it is anything like 5th Avenue in New York City, but it is a welcome respite for a thru-hiker!)

0347P 4.8mi 48° 51.835'N 117° 22.345'W 2090' State Route 31 @ Metaline Falls, Washington

Trail Angels (Metaline Falls): There are two trail angels here. See details at the end of this chapter.

"Mary of Boundary Tours," a PNTA board member, is located at 124 East 5th Avenue, across the street from city hall. Boundary Tours runs guided kayak and canoe tours on the river, which can make for an interesting trip north on the river to the original PNT route. They can help you add 12 miles of the water trail to your trip and travel from Metaline to Boundary Dam and then resume the PNT from there.

Boundary Tours offers a Lodge (Teepee) set up in the yard. There is space for your own tent, plus a couple of amenities such as a crank powered washer, solar dryer, and the local sanitation business donates a port-a-potty. They also have a fire pit and BBQ available.

Note: The US Post Office does not deliver packages on Saturday. Metaline Falls has two restaurants within a block and one of them is a local social hot spot Coup

You might also look for the Washington Hotel (509-671-7906), with 15 rooms for rent and three camping spots in the yard. The Washington Hotel is a singularly special place: a 1906 old Craftsman building. The rooms are each uniquely furnished with period-appropriate pieces and the old wood floors are deliciously squeaky. I doubt I'll stay in another place so saturated with character on this trip, and I'm glad to have landed here.[KC]   Laundry service is also available for a fee. Breakfast is served next door starting at 6 am.[GT]

The town of Metaline Falls is exquisite, as far as hiker towns go. Everything is within one block, the park is beautifully kept, and the setting is rocky, mountainous, and generally lovely.[KC]

Departing Metaline Falls, walk across the high bridge that spans the Pend Oreille River on SR31. (For movie buffs, the area from the Pend Oreille Bridge at Metaline Falls north to the Boundary Dam is where Hollywood shot portions of the 1997 movie "The Postman" starring Kevin Costner.) Continue south on SR31, but note that some hikers have taken a shortcut to leave SR31 about 0.1 miles after the bridge, scampering west up a game trail just before the power line. You have to climb the steep slope up 400' to reach Boundary Road. This is a lot of effort but saves about 1.7 road miles.

The primary PNT route still road walks SR31 south for another 0.9 miles past the bridge to meet with the local Boundary Road – RD2975 at our next waypoint.

PNT Factoid: As we walk through Metaline Falls think back to the gold rush days and the miners that were in this area in 1859. At the time the town was actually on the river just below our next waypoint. Even before the miners, in 1809, David Thompson with the North West Company (fur trading) mapped this area.

0348P 1.1mi 48° 51.424'N 117° 23.293'W 2150' State Route 31 X Boundary Road

We turn slightly southwest and uphill to follow Boundary Road back to the north. Simply follow this road north for 3.6 miles on an uphill grade looking for the intersection with Flume Creek Road – RD350. The road intersection is at a turn in Boundary Road and right under the high wire power lines. Look for the stop sign and the prominent road sign "Flume Creek Road."[66]

0352P 3.6mi 48° 53.884'N 117° 22.849'W 2580' Boundary Road X Flume Creek Road – RD350

We hike RD350 northwest for the next 7.3 miles climbing the large ridge to the west to connect with our next trail, Flume Creek Trail 502, gaining 2550' in elevation. In 2015, a very dry year, good water was reported all along RD350,[49] but do not count on water above 4,000' elevation.[66]

About 0.9 miles into RD350 you will see a power line cut through the forest that runs straight uphill to the west. This may be a tempting shortcut, but I advise that you to stick to the longer and safer road walk on RD350. In another 0.8 miles the road comes close to Flume Creek with a chance for water.

Keep following rocky RD350 and its major switchbacks from south to north for the next 5.5 miles, crossing the power line cut several times, to finally reach the trailhead for the Flume Creek Trail 502. The trailhead is very small. FR350 comes to a 'Y' where you hook right for only 20 yards to find the trail.

0359P 7.2mi 48° 55.230'N 117° 25.039'W 5130' Forest Road 350 X Flume Creek Trail 502

TR502 leads you into a vast roadless section of the Colville National Forest which offers panoramic views of the Selkirk Mountains. Heading west on TR502 we keep climbing another 2000' over the next 2.6 miles to reach the southern base of Abercrombie Mountain. TR502 initially begins in a dense forest which thins the higher we climb.

At 1.8 miles into the trail, around the 6000' contour, the trail turns from west back to northeast to begin a series of major switchbacks up the south slope of the ridge. Right at the point where the switchbacks begin there is reportedly a spring, but it is not always flowing depending on the snowfall the previous winter. In 2015 it was dry but in 2016 it was running well.[CN]

Be advised that from this point you will likely find remnants of snow except for the period mid-July through mid-September. The switchbacks end in 1.3

miles as you come near the crest of an intermediate ridge and resume hiking to the west. There are opportunities for a trail camp on the intermediate ridge.[60] Abercrombie Peak should be clearly visible only 0.4 miles ahead. However, TR502 cuts south across the treeless eastern face of the mountain only 0.1 miles below the summit. Climbing to the summit at this point is difficult, especially with a full pack. Continue on the established TR502 for another 0.3 miles to meet the Abercrombie Mountain Trail 117, which will take you to the summit.

0363P 3.6mi 48° 55.548'N 117° 27.671'W 7130' Trail 502 X Abercrombie Mountain Trail 117

Turn north for 0.2 miles to climb the additional 180' elevation to reach the summit. This mountain is special in that it is one of only 57 peaks that have a prominence of greater than 5000' in the United States. Prominence is the elevation difference between the height of the summit and its base contour.

Again, a word of caution, if thunderstorms are present it is advisable not to climb to the barren summit. Abercrombie Mountain is the second highest in Eastern Washington (missing the tallest by only one foot to Gypsy Peak, which the PNT passed about 20 trail miles ago). At the peak you find talus rock and cairns, but not much else--except some of the best views on the PNT!

Returning to the primary PNT route we descend 1320' elevation to the southwest on TR117 for 2.0 miles. The trail down from Abercrombie is marked with cairns, and is well worn.[GT]

Time for another word of caution. ***Note: This is GRIZZLY BEAR and COUGAR (aka Mountain Lion) country!*** The proximity to Canada allows the bears to move back and forth along the Selkirk corridor quite easily. The dry 2015 summer reduced the amount of huckleberries. This effectively reduced the number of bear sightings in this area.[48] Normally black bears, caribou, elk, moose, coyotes and grey wolf are also found along TR117 and into our next waypoint at North Fork Silver Creek Trail 119.

0365P 2.0mi 48° 55.468'N 117° 28.848'W 5810' Trail 117 X North Fork Silver Creek Trail 119

TR117 meets TR119 on a level stretch of the trail in a shallow saddle, which makes for a good trail camp.[48] You may not recognize this topography due to the forest, but TR117 turns north while TR119, our PNT route, continues west exiting the forest onto the south slope of a rocky ridge. Follow TR119 west for 0.9 miles where the trail turns south and drops downhill 1600' in elevation on a series of switchbacks. At the bottom of the switchbacks we come to Silver Creek Road - RD070. The trailhead is actually on the western edge of the NFS Silver Creek Campground. To find RD070, drop down through the parking area and around the corner to the west.

0370P 5.7mi 48° 54.345'N 117° 31.124'W 3130' Trail 119 X Silver Creek Road – RD070

The campground is primitive with only a pit toilet and a few sites. Water is obtained from the creek. Silver Creek Road - RD070 parallels Silver Creek, both flowing downhill and west out of the Colville National Forest. Head west on RD070 for the next 3.6 miles, passing several other forest roads, but always following the main dirt forest road west. Just before reaching our next waypoint we pass by several homesteads and soon reach the paved Deep Lake Boundary Road – RD9445.

0374P 3.6mi 48° 54.613'N 117° 35.155'W 2130' Forest Road 70 X Deep Lake Boundary Road – RD9445

Hike RD9445 north through farm/ranch country on a level paved road. Traffic is likely to be sparse on this country road.

0377P 5.3mi 48° 58.809'N 117° 35.349'W 2120' Deep Lake Boundary Road X O'hare Creek Road (Driveway)

The original PNT routed hikers west through the gate of O'Hare Creek Road and into private timberland. Following this route is trespassing on private property. Instead, we continue our road walk north on Deep Lake Boundary Road.
In about 0.5 miles the map shows Cedar Lake near the road. Unfortunately, this is a private lake with no legal access. Sticking to the paved road we come to our next way point at the road intersection with Cedar Creek Road, which comes in from the east.

0381P 3.4mi 48° 58.809'N 117° 35.349'W 2120' Deep Lake Boundary Road X Cedar Creek Road

As we hike north on the road, we come to a large bend to the west. After the bend, you may see a dirt spur road to the north. Be advised that at this point the Canadian border is only 65 yards to the north. A little ways beyond the border is Pend O'Reille River we discussed at Metaline Falls. DO NOT attempt to go down the dirt road—the Border Patrol is very active in this area.
Keep hiking west on the road and then south to our next way point.

0383P 3.4mi 48° 59.488'N 117° 38.153'W 1470' Deep Lake Boundary Road X Northport/Waneta Road - Store

After a long road walk you can rest and get a "cold one" at the convenience store. In 2018 the owner was very helpful to PNT hikers as they hiked this new route. You may be able to find a ride into Northport from the store.
A few more miles of road walking to go. We keep hiking south on the same road, now designated the Northport/Waneta Road. The road parallels the Columbia River to the west.

0389P 4.9mi 48° 56.877'N 117° 42.420'W 1390' Upper Columbia RV Park/Campground – Store

This RV campground has high marks on by RV campers, but there are no reports from PNT hikers. It may be a nice rest stop on the Columbia River as you continue the trek into Northport. Of course, we keep south on the paved road we've been walking.

0392P 3.1mi 48° 55.506'N 117° 44.868'W 1370' Deep Lake Boundary Road @ Deep Creek

At this way point you may have access to Deep Creek. The best approach looks to be from the east side of the bridge. From here, the road walk continues for just another 2.2 miles. The road has a gentle descent and approach to the Columbia River as we hike south all the way into Northport. The shoulder of the road is narrow in spots, but with relatively light traffic in this rural area.

0389P 2.2mi 48° 54.967'N 117° 46.896'W 1360' State Route 25 @ Northport, Washington

This ends this section's discussion of the primary PNT route. For our discussion of Northport, see Chapter 5. See details about trail angels in Northport at the end of this chapter.

Alternate Route: Hughes Meadow to Sullivan Lake

This recommended alternate takes us west to Hughes Meadow then onto Sullivan Lake. Take this to avoid the horrendous Leola Creek bushwhack. This route takes us a little south and then back north through Hughes Meadow to then follow the Jackson Creek Trail west and on into Sullivan Lake. Although a little longer it provides more of the scenic high views along the Shedroof Divide in the Salmo-Priest Wilderness.

Start: 0304P Forest Road 655 X Forest Road 1013

Re-join: 0343P Red Bluff Trail 553 X Sullivan Lake Road 9345

Mileage: 35.6 miles; shorter than the primary below by 4.0 miles

Highlights: Good trails and tread, more time "up high."

This alternate route is highly recommended until maintenance work on Trail 315 has been completed. There is a total of 9.3 miles of road walking at beginning and at the end.

0304P 0.0mi 48° 50.469'N 16° 57.175'W 2630' Forest Road 655 X Forest Road 1013

We turn south to follow the bumpy dusty FR1013 downhill for 0.6 miles to cross the Upper Priest River on the road bridge. After the bridge FR1013 turns southwest and uphill, to turn again west to cross the signed bridge over Gold Creek. About 100 yards west of the bridge we turn north at our next waypoint.

0307A 2.6mi 48° 49.268'N 116° 58.928'W 2840' Forest Road 1013 X Hughes Meadow Road - FR662

Turn north on FR662, a rocky, curvy old forest road. We climb slightly for 1.5 miles staying about 70' above Gold Creek below us to the east. We're looking for a 'T' junction with Forest Road 1399 coming in from the west at our next waypoint.

0308A 1.4mi 48° 50.362'N 116° 59.510'W 2900' Forest Road 662 X Bench Creek Road FR1399

We stick to the alternate route and turn west, past the gate, and hike down RD1399. The road crosses the creek on a bridge in about 150 yards and then turns uphill to the northwest. In another 0.1 miles the road forks left into a parking lot, and right (north) as truck tracks. Follow the truck tracks to the end with the "No Motorized Vehicles" sign and across the berm.

0309A 0.2mi 48° 50.401'N 116° 59.839'W 2910' Forest Road 1399 X Jackson Creek Trail 311

No trail sign is posted here, but this is the beginning of Trail 311. We follow the old forest road bed that has a nice mossy tread, with some spots of major alder encroachment as we climb slightly uphill. Follow the trail north for 1.2 miles looking for a new wood "Trail" sign tacked to a tree, where we bear right. This trail is very faint as it enters a small rocky meadow. Look to turn east for about 25 yards and, after that, turn north to cross the creek.

0309A 1.3mi 48° 51.281'N 117° 00.406'W 2950' Trail 311 @ Jackson Creek and Trail Camp (Dual number with waypoint above).

The meadow before the creek offers a good spot for a trail camp as well as in the cedar trees across the creek. After fording the creek (just a skip and a jump) we enter a magnificent stand of old growth cedars, some eight feet in diameter and over 200 feet tall. Some of the trees in this area are reported to be over 2000 years old.

At the creek, the trail is not obvious. Head north about 20 yards and look carefully for the faint indications of a possible trail between the cedars and the ferns, probably slightly to your right (northeast). If you've wander too far to the east, you'll enter a swamp. Although somewhat dark and damp amongst the cedars, once you find the trail, it is easy to follow even with some monstrous blowdowns. If you wander too far to the east, you'll enter a swamp. Our next waypoint the trail junction is clearly marked with three distinct trail signs about 6' up at a 'T' trail junction.

0310A 0.3mi 48° 51.493'N 117° 00.555'W 2950' Trail 311 X Hughes Fork Trail 312

Our choice is to begin hiking on Trail 311 west and then follow another alternate to the south end of Sullivan Lake.

Caution: After TR311 diverges away from Jackson Creek, we climb to hike high ridgelines and steep mountain slopes for a potential 17 mile dry stretch.

TR311 is part of a series of trails through an area called the Shedroof Divide, which is a short range of peaks along the Washington-Idaho border. TR311 takes us near the southern end of the Shedroof Divide. We hike west and in 0.5 miles we begin to parallel Jackson Creek, which we'll follow closely for another mile gaining about 600' elevation. About half way, at a small stream crossing, we enter Washington and the Salmo-Priest Wilderness.

TR311 diverges from Jackson Creek as we continue to climb northwest with 1600' elevation gain over the next 1.9 miles into the next waypoint.

0315A 4.8mi 48° 51.322'N 117° 0.143'W 5530' Trail 311 X Shedroof Divide Trail 512

There are no reports if this trail junction has trail signs. TR512 leads us southwest, but first we must tackle some major switchbacks as we climb the northeast face of Helmer Mountain. In 0.5 miles the trail opens into a relatively treeless area from an old wildfire burn. After a short time hiking northwest, TR512 turns southwest, still on a treeless slope of the mountain. From this point looking east on a clear day, we find Lookout Mountain east of Priest Lake which we may have climbed a few days before.

Still hiking southwest on TR512, the trail temporarily crosses the crest of the southern arm of Helmer Mountain to give some views of the Colville National forest and the PNT to the west. Soon, however, we cross back over to now hike on the east slope of Mankato Mountain. Look for a 'U' where TR512 turns southwest.

TR512 provides us a good tread through the old burn area for another 2.3 miles. We hike on both the east and west slope near the crest of the Shedroof Divide giving us excellent views of the Salmo-Priest Wilderness. We exit the burn area waypoint.

0320A 4.9mi 48° 48.990'N 117° 07.394'W 6030' Trail 512 X Gold Creek Trail 320 (Abandoned)

On our final leg of TR512 we hike near the top of the ridge for another 0.7 miles. Next we begin our descent to exit the Salmo-Priest Wilderness at our next waypoint.

0321A 1.7mi 48° 47.866'N 117° 7.622'W 5440' Trail 512 X Forest Road 22

Just a quick road walk west around the corner to find Trail 503. There are no reports of a trail sign at the trailhead.

0322A 0.4mi 48° 47.897'N 117° 08.048'W 5390' Forest Road 22 X Grassy Top Mountain NRT Trail 503

The trail immediately drops off the road to the southeast and soon crosses Pass Creek. Water here may be seasonal but it has had a very good flow in late August in the past.

After crossing the creek we begin our climb to gain 650' elevation over the next 1.2 miles, topping out at the 6,000' contour. TR503 is level on the eastern slope of the ridge for the next 0.5 miles. Shortly the trail climbs about 200' to the crest of the ridge. The trail is level for the next 0.3 miles into our next waypoint at the junction with the Hall Mountain Trail 533.

0324A 2.5mi 48° 46.673'N 117° 09.341'W 6170' Trail 503 X Hall Mountain Trail 533

There are no reports of a trail sign at this junction. TR533 takes us west on a relatively level tread under a heavy forest canopy for about 0.4 miles into a small clearing. Keep following the good trail west for another 1.7 miles until it turns northwest and opens along a rocky ridge. The trail along the ridge goes about 1.2 miles to where it turns sharply west and downhill. We lose 300' elevation in the next 0.9 miles as we find the trail junction with the Noisy Creek Trail 588.

0328.8A 4.7mi 48° 48.024'N 117° 13.782'W 5560' Trail 533 X Noisy Creek Trail 588

This is a 'T' trail junction with TR533, TR540 and TR588. TR533 turns north to trailhead parking used by hikers and mountain bikers. TR540 continues west to the top of Hall Mountain in 1.6 miles. We keep to our alternate PNT route by turning south on TR588 to take trails all the way to Sullivan Lake.

TR588 descends for the next 5.0 miles on a suspect tread. Mountain bikers love this trail for the long descend and easy parking on top. Nevertheless, it is far better than road walking.

TR588 descends due south of 1.3 miles with a large eastern 'U' that takes us west and parallel to Noisy Creek. You can find numerous places to access the creek and small water falls for the next 1.8 miles. The trails turns south after the last creek crossing and continues downhill for the next 1.3 miles to the trailhead.

0334A 5.1mi 48° 47.291'N 117° 16.905'W 2620' Trail 588 X Noisy Creek Campground

This NFS campground has a $16 per night fees for 19 non-electric sites. There are no showers, but there is a privy at the trailhead and elsewhere. There is a swimming beach in the campground. We follow the loop to the privy by site #03 toward the lake to find the trailhead for the Lake Shore Trail 504.

0334.3A   0.5mi   48° 47.545'N   117° 16.885'W   2620'   Noisy Creek Campground X Lake Shore Trail 504

TR504 hugs the shoreline on the east side of Sullivan Lake with a gain/loss of only 250' over its 4.2-mile length. The trail connects two campgrounds and is very popular in the summer. The trailhead is on the main road of the NFS West Sullivan Lake campground. Hike north on the main campground road to Forest Road 22 then west into our next waypoint.

To get to Metaline Falls, walk 4.7 miles on Sullivan Lake Road to SR31. From there turn south for 2.2 miles into town. As you hike south on SR31 there are several blind curves and no shoulder. This is rated as one of the most dangerous road walks on the PNT.

0337A 4.4mi 48° 50.660'N 117° 17.236'W 2560' Forest Road 22 X Sullivan Lake Road

Here we simply turn north and follow Sullivan Lake Road to the trailhead for the Red Bluff Trail 533.

0343P 0.7mi 48° 51.243'N 117° 17.267'W 2620' Sullivan Lake Road 9345 X Red Bluff Trail 553

RESUPPLY OPTIONS

0295P 48° 45.010'N 116° 50.588'W 2480'   East Shore Road RD1 X Floss Creek Trail 42 **Indian Creek State Campground:** The nearest camp store is 10.0 miles south on East Shore Road. This campground has hot showers, a small general store, and a fee to enter. Follow the East Shore Road south—a very lightly travelled road. This resupply point is recommended for emergency situations only.

0347P 48° 51.835'N 117° 22.345'W 2090' State Route 31 @ Metaline Falls **Metaline Falls:** One of the best trail towns on the PNT!

Trail Support

0347P Metaline Falls: Kathryn Bowman, kathrynjobowman@gmail.com Can provide housing, transportation, meals, info, fun side trips, etc., and good FS trail advice.

0347P Metaline Falls: Mary of Boundary Tours, boundarytours@hotmail.com We are right on the Main Street at 124 5th Ave E. Camping in the yard with a few amenities. Can arrange to pick up resupply packages for people expecting to be in town during holidays and weekends. There is no package delivery at the post office on Saturdays.

0389P Northport: Jami and Josh Lord, jamilord1978@gmail.com, 1-509-732-6642, Jami Rose Lord on FB. Can provide camping in their backyard, laundry, shower, kitchen use and home cooking, wifi, zero day relaxing, fun conversation, garden treats, and possible rides. 721 Center Ave, Northport, four blocks south of the Post Office. Also accepting Hiker packages.

0389P Northport: Madonna Regis ("Fire Starter"), mregis2011@hotmail.com, (509) 481-8477. Can provide a back yard for over-night stays and live right in town, electrical plug in, and pets are great. If you need a night or a couple days to rest up, showers if needed. Will also provide rides for those who don't like the highway walking.

0389P Northport: Jael and Jada Regis , jjregis@outlook.com, (509) 732-6675. Can provide rides, showers, yard camping, laundry, meals, wifi, close to post office and large convenience store.

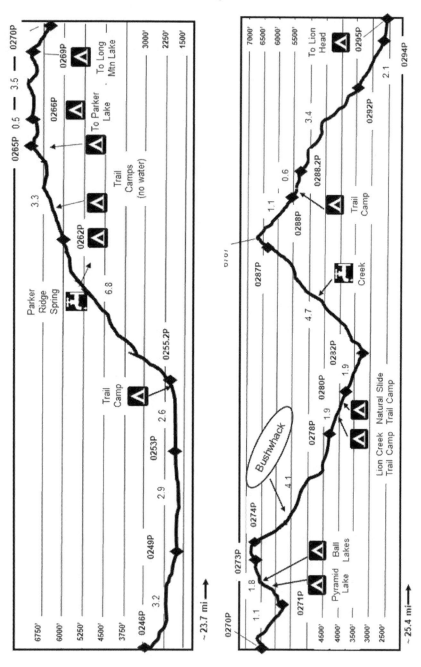

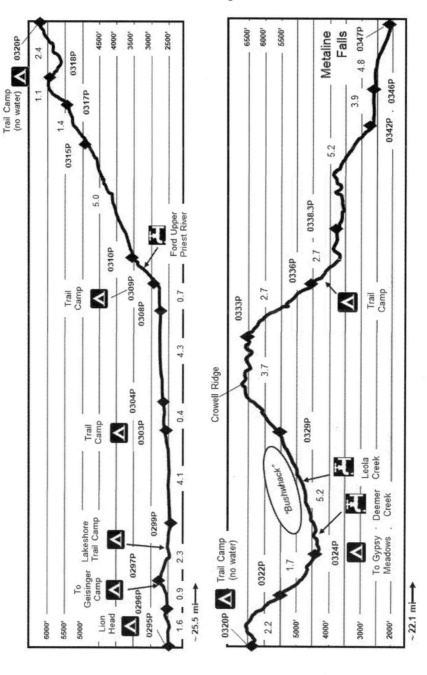

97

Tim Youngbluth

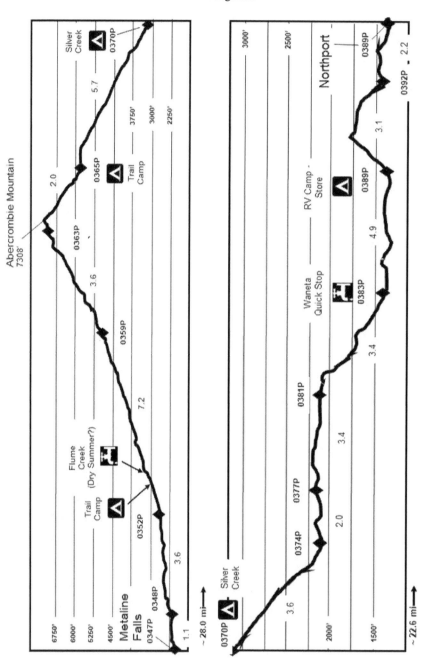

98

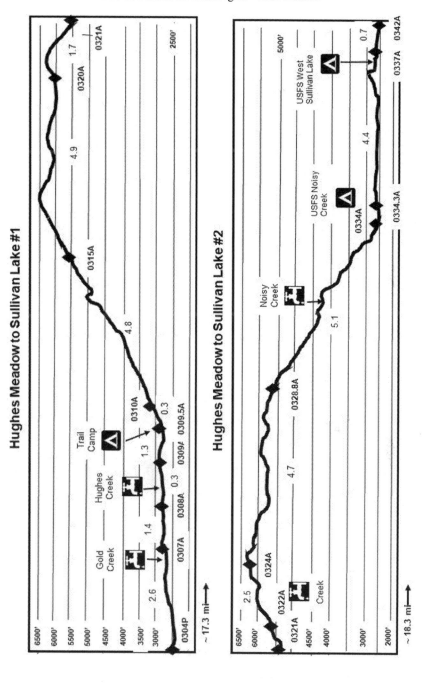

Hughes Meadow to Sullivan Lake #1

Hughes Meadow to Sullivan Lake #2

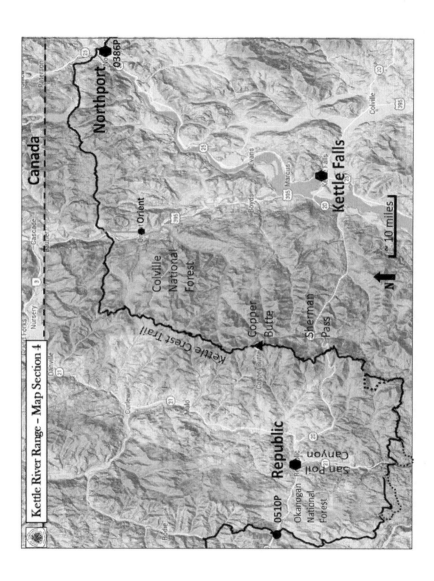

Kettle River Range – Map Section 4

CHAPTER FIVE

KETTLE RIVER RANGE – MAP SECTION 4

Columbia River to Sweat Creek

Kettle Crest National Recreation Trail 13, from Sherman Peak,

Colville National Forest, Washington

Key Trail Notes

Highlights: Kettle Crest National Recreation Trail and Copper Butte, San Poil River Canyon

Primary Route Estimated Elevation Change: 13,270' climb / 10,220' descent

Route Alternates: Thirteenmile Trail; Swan Lake Bypass

Possible Resupply: Northport; Orient; Republic

Parks/Forests: Colville National Forest

Permits: None

Other Notes: Known 2015 wildfire damage to the Kettle Crest Trail 13 and other trails north from Forest Road 450 to Copper Butte, and in the Swan Lake area.

0389P 0.0mi 48° 54.967'N 117° 46.896'W 1360' State Route 25 @ Northport, Washington

The town of Northport offers a good chance for resupply, even though you may have just stocked up in Metaline Falls. Tony's Market is right at our starting waypoint. The Matteson B&B, two blocks south at 607 Center Ave. is very "hiker friendly" with reasonable rates.[GT]
Sorry folks, but we're in for more road walks, uphill of course, but it is very much worth it to get to the Kettle Crest Trail. Leaving the center of Northport, hike 1.0 miles on SR25 crossing the bridge over the Columbia River, and then to the first intersection with Big Sheep Creek Road.

0394P 0.8mi 48° 55.700'N 117° 46.584'W 1450' State Route 25 X Big Sheep Creek Road 4220

The map shows the road as RD4220; nevertheless, it is easy to find the road. Stay north on Sheep Creek Road for the next 3.8 miles climbing over 500' to where the road turns to the west and enters a thicker forest with a little more shade. Here the road moves closer to Sheep Creek to the north, being sure to bear right at a 'Y'. In another 1.0 miles we come to the Sheep Creek Campground and picnic area.

0395P 4.4mi 48° 57.504'N 117° 49.958'W 1930' Sheep Creek Road @ Campground

The campground was closed in late July 2018 due to a wildfire. There is no report at the time of publication if it is open for 2019. The campground is free but requires a Washington State Discover Pass ($10 day use). The campground has a few sites, pit toilets, but the hand pump for water is broken in 2016.[60] There is a day-use picnic area across the bridge. We continue west on Sheep Creek Road which keeps us on the south side of the creek. In 1.3 miles, on a relatively level grade, we come to the junction with Forest Road 15.

0396P 1.3mi 48° 57.579'N 117° 51.497'W 2030' Sheep Creek Road X Forest Road 15

FR15 turns and climbs to the south, but we continue straight ahead to the west, where the road is now designated Forest Road 4220, but still Sheep Creek Road. Sheep Creek remains to our north. In about 4.0 miles the road opens to the flat area of Bennett Meadow to our north as we cross Forest Road 800. Keep headed west past a barren hill, reentering a strip of trees, where in another 1.2 miles, we come to our next waypoint at Forest Road 670.

0402P 5.9mi 48° 57.684'N 117° 57.809'W 2620' Forest Road 4220 X Forest Road 670 / 290

Continue through the intersection to the southwest, past a dry pond, on Sheep Creek Road which is now designated Forest Road 15. Keep hiking on a slight uphill grade to reach the crossing of Forest Road 600.

0403P 1.1mi 48° 57.091'N 117° 58.716'W 2880' Forest Road 15 X Forest Road 600

FR600 leads to the Elbow Lake Campground in only 0.3 miles, but the camp is not maintained by the NFS. It is free with five sites and a pit toilet. The lake in 2016 was marshy and smells a bit foul, but the campsites were nice.[CN]

Our PNT route, however, keeps us on FR15 heading west and on the slight uphill grade. In 1.6 miles FR15 intersects with Forest Road 460. Just about 150 yards before FR460 there may be a small spring on the southwest side of the road, and a small place for a trail camp. Turn left (west) on FR460 and hike only 130 yards to a three-road intersection. We're looking for Forest Road 170 at our next waypoint.

0405P 1.7mi 48° 57.098'N 118° 00.253'W 3310' Forest Road 15 X Forest Road 170

At this three-road intersection, FR15 continues west, Forest Road 445 shoots south, and the PNT takes FR170, which is the less defined road in the middle. We hike southwest and downhill into the ravine. In 1.3 miles FR170 intersects Churchill Mine Road – RD1520 at a switchback signed 1520 in both directions. Turn right here.[50]

0406P 1.3mi 48° 56.241'N 118° 00.949'W 3170' Forest Road 170 X Churchill Mine Road – RD1520

This is easy navigation, but more road walking. Keep southwest, then west on Churchill Mine Road on a level grade to pass the namesake mine in about 1.0 miles. Continue west passing through a clear cut area in another 0.4 miles, followed by an unremarkable downhill gravel road walk for the next 5.0 miles. Our next way point is crossing Pierre Lake Road – RD4013.

0412P 6.5mi 48° 55.420'N 118° 08.014'W 2150' Forest Road 1520 X Sand Creek Road – RD4013

We want to keep hiking west on RD4013, but if we turn south, in 1.4 miles there is the primitive NFS Pierre Lake Campground, which has 16 sites, tent pads, pit toilets, and drinking water from faucets.

Back to the primary PNT route as we continue west on RD4013 and our long road march downhill. You will pass a number of ranches along RD4013 for the next 3.7 miles as you walk downhill toward the Kettle River. Water may be scarce for the next 15 miles.

Just prior to reaching the road bridge over the Kettle River, we come to a road intersection where Sand Creek Road becomes Rock Cut Road at our next waypoint.

0417P 3.7mi 48° 54.951'N 118° 12.025'W 1470' Sand Creek Road – RD4013 X Rock Cut Road - RD4141

Resupply: There is the small hamlet of Orient 3.7 miles south with a small general store. In late 2016 the store changed ownership and should be open for the 2017 PNT hiking season. The stored used to have laundry and showers, but as of the time of publication, this has not been confirmed with the new owners. Follow the alternate route south on Rock Cut Road. This road is much safer than hiking on US395.

Let's get back to the primary PNT route. Heading west there is a steep river bank and the "no trespassing signs." This is not an optimal place to fill up on water, but some have done it. You decide. Cross the bridge and climb the road 0.25 miles up to cross highway US395.

0417.2P 4.1mi 48° 54.737'N 118° 12.351'W 1510' Forest Road 4013 X Highway US 395

After crossing US395 we hike west uphill on the Little Boulder Creek Road – RD595, following the Little Boulder Creek to our south. In 3.8 miles, after climbing almost 1300' we come to a 'Y' junction with Forest Road 9576 at our next waypoint.

0420P 3.8 mi 48° 55.060'N 118° 16.374'W 2800' Forest Road 595 X Forest Road 9576

This junction is a loop in the road with a creek flowing under it. There is reported to be a good place to trail camp here also. We bear to the left (southwest), still on Little Boulder Creek Road, but now designated Forest Road 9576. Continue climbing keeping the creek below us to the south. In just over 1.3 miles we cross Forest Road 240, which drops downhill to cross the creek in about a quarter mile. However, we need to continue climbing on FR9576 to gain 800' elevation in the next 2.0 miles and to reach our next waypoint, Forest Road 300. About 0.6 miles before the next waypoint the road loops to the southwest.

0424P 3.4mi 48° 55.100'N 118° 20.139'W 4170' Forest Road 9576 X Forest Road 300

FR9576 makes a sharp turn to the north, while we keep west now on FR300 (essentially stay on the same road only with a new designation). Over the next 2.1 miles you will pass a number of forest logging roads. At approximately 1.5 miles from our last way point there is a small 'U' in the road where we enter remnants of the 2015 wildfire until we cross Forest Road 930.

0426P 2.1mi 48° 55.402'N 118° 22.574'W 4920' Forest Road 300 X Forest Road 930 X Forest Road 450

Just south of this intersection there is a seasonal pond that may offer water and a good place to trail camp. After crossing FR930 stay west on FR450, but recognize that the dirt road begins to fade. In 2018, FR450 was reported to be in good shape, with signs of recent logging on both sides of the road.[CN] The "roads" in this area are mainly used by as a NFS winter recreation area for snowmobiles. You may find the blazes or trail signs to be about 8 feet up tacked to trees--with the heavy snows, that would make them eye-level for snowmobilers!

After 1.4 miles the road splits with FR400 branches to the left (east) while FR450 turns right and downhill. We follow FR400, the grassy less visible road uphill.[CN] Just prior to the top of the ridge look for another faint unmarked road junction.

0428P 2.1mi 48° 54.721'N 118° 23.613'W 5540' Forest Road 400 X Forest Road 425 / 430

We cross over the berm, around keep southwest through a small cut in the ridge before turning southeast and downhill on the faded old road. From here to our next way point we are hiking through the burn. This road winds its way south on Marble Mountain's western ridge through a thin forest. In 2.0 miles the old forest road comes to the junction with Forest Road 488. The road comes to five large boulders blocking the road followed by an old bare sign post with no sign.

0430P 2.0mi 48° 53.454'N 118° 22.628'W 4860' Forest Road 400 X Forest Road 488

We continue to hike in and out of the burn area for the next 3.6 miles. This grassy junction is a fairly nice place to trail camp. The nearest water, however, is Noonday Spring at 0.15 miles to the left (east) up the rarely used old FR488. The spring has just trickle in August. Look for the dry creek bed across the road where FR488 turns uphill. Follow the creek bed uphill to find a very small flow, not even enough though to make it downhill to the road.

Note that in 1.1 miles from the bare sign post at our waypoint junction you will find better water and trail camp as described below. Follow the prominent road to the right as it descends downhill winding its way on the slope from Marble Mountain until we cross Goat Creek Road – RD 215 at our next waypoint. Look for the old Forest Service Road sign with "Boulder-Deer Creek Rd", where we bear right. (I never could figure out the arrow for "Goat Creek Rd" which points deep into the uncut forest!)

0431P 1.1mi 48° 53.168'N 118° 22.491'W 4330' Forest Road 450 X Forest Road 215 (Goat Creek Road)

The road junction is in a level grassy clearing and an excellent trail camp. About 100 yards past the junction, and just before the road/trail heads uphill, look and listen for water from Goat Creek. There is heavy brush around the creek on either side of the trail, but the creek has a good flow in August as it passes under the road/trail through a culvert.

As we continue southwest, just after this junction there is another spot for a trail camp on flat ground. We climb about 500' over the next 1.1 miles to where the trail turns south again. Heading south we're still going downhill for 1.1 miles to the Deer Creek Summit Campground and the paved Boulder Creek Road.

The campground is to your northeast sitting above Boulder Creek Road, but it has been officially closed since the 2015 fire. It was another small primitive NFS camp that may offer a place to trail camp if needed. Water is across the paved road and down an old trail past the guard rail. You can hear the water but you can't see it from the trail.

0434P 2.5mi 48° 51.864'N 118° 23.799'W 4500' Boulder Creek Road X Kettle Crest Trail 13

You can expect to keep hiking in and out of the burn area (mostly in) for the next 12 miles. The trailhead is across Boulder Creek Road. The trail that looks more obvious to the right takes you to the toilet and the old forest road with significant logging activity after the 2015 fire. Look for the new trailhead sign.[CN] From the parking area turn east (left) and find the trail and a white blaze up in a tree. The Kettle Crest National Recreation Trail runs south for over 40 miles. It is used by hikers, horse riders, mountain bikers, and cross-country skiers.

TR13 in 2018 was reported to be in great shape through the burn area all the way to Old Stage Road.[CN] TR13 begins to climb immediately and for the first 4 miles or so only offers sporadic views to the west as you climb south along on the ridge, but after that it becomes a memorable hike. About 3.2 miles into the trail we come to an unmarked 'X' trail crossing, which is really the old forest Taylor Ridge Road – FR430. In the trees to the left, about 7 feet up, there's a map and a warning sign on our trail shown as "dangerous route." The dangerous conditions, however, only apply to TR13 winter cross-country skiers, so do not be too alarmed.

0437P 3.2mi 48° 49.792'N 118° 25.170'W 5430' Trail 13 X Taylor Ridge Road – FR430

From here the trail runs downhill for another 0.8 miles to cross the creek on a foot bridge. The creek usually has very good flow most summers and the best water on the Kettle Crest trail until you reach Neff Spring.[47] After crossing the creek the trail climbs again slightly as it weaves along the slopes of numerous unnamed "humps," crossing another good creek in about 0.9 miles. Our next waypoint is crossing the Big Lick Trail 30.

0442P 5.7mi 48° 46.510'N 118° 27.068'W 5180' Trail 13 X Big Lick Trail 30

TR30 is a NFS connector trail that crosses TR13 from northwest to southeast. The PNT on TR13 continues south, dropping down 50' into a dry creek and then begins another climb gaining 800' in 0.6 miles hiking towards Ryan Hill. Next, we descend (starting to get the picture of ups and downs?) for 0.8 miles to cross the Mount Leona Loop Trail 49a.

0443P 1.1mi 48° 45.977'N 118° 27.550'W 5510' Trail 13 X Mount Leona Loop Trail 49a

If you're interested in "bagging" another peak on your PNT trek, TR49a offers easy access to the Mount Leona summit. Stay higher on the ridge on TR49a for 0.7 miles then turn north on TR49 for another 0.5 miles to the top. There was a wildfire in this area in 2001 that allows excellent views from the summit. To return to the PNT, follow TR49 south from the summit for about 1.1 miles to meet TR13 again and continue south.

Back at our waypoint, we stay on TR13 as we continue southwest a little lower on the ridgeline, around the 5400' contour, working through the old burn area. In 1.1 miles TR13 turns to the west over a small ridge that gives us a clear view of Lambert Mountain. In another 0.3 miles TR13 crosses TR49 and then Stickpin Trail 71 at our next waypoint.

0444P 0.7mi 48° 45.487'N 118° 28.895'W 5510' Trail 13 X Stickpin Trail 71

TR13 continues south around the southern shoulder of Mount Leona and through an almost treeless area. In 0.7 miles we intersect the Mount Leona Trail 49, which heads west downhill. Next, we hike on the western ridge of Lambert Mountain, again with only patches of trees left standing from the 2001 forest fire. Most of the trail has open views on this ridge. In 1.1 miles past the Mount Leona Trail we cross the Lambert Trail 47, which also leads downhill west. Thankfully, this is the end of the 2015 burn area.

As we round the southern side the map shows Neff Spring and a possible trail camp in the trees on this portion of TR13. The spring has a pipe from it and is fenced to keep the range cattle out.

At 2.0 miles after crossing TR71, TR13 crests the western spine of the mountain and we have a clear view south to Copper Butte, which lies directly on the PNT. We keep climbing on TR13 along the western slope of Midnight Mountain, still in the cleared area from the forest fire. Look for the Midnight Spring just prior to the junction with the Midnight Trail 41 coming to meet TR13 uphill from the west. The spring was reported to be in good shape in late August 2018.[CN] Next, we keep south on TR13 for another 0.5 miles past TR41 to intersect with the Old Stage Road Trail 1 and Trail 75. These two trails are really one trail crossing from east to west.

0449P 4.3mi 48° 42.956'N 118° 27.834'W 6070' Trail 13 X Old Stage Road
Trails 1 / 75

The Old Stage Road is the remnants of the first state highway in
Washington, constructed in 1892. Supposedly the road can be used by horse
drawn wagons in the national forest, and although this sounds romantic, the old
stage road is wet, muddy and appeared to be cleared of blowdowns in 2015.[47]

For us, however, we pass TR1 to climb again heading south on TR13 for 1.3
miles to the summit of Copper Butte, gaining 1070' with only one major
switchback. On top of this 7140' peak there are some rock cairns and the
remnants of an old lookout tower. If it is a clear day, you might see the North
Cascades and the PNT route far to the west.

0450P 1.2mi 48° 42.161'N 118° 27.942'W 7140' Trail 13 @ Copper Butte
Summit

Descending from the summit, TR13 follows near the crest of the ridge for
1.1 miles before staying on the western slope of Scar Mountain. As we drop
down the side of Scar Mountain into a saddle before Wapaloosie Mountain,
TR13 crosses the Timber Ridge Trail 17. TR17 connects you with roads going
west as a possible shortcut to the resupply town of Republic. If you do divert
west at this point you will miss some of the best parts of the Kettle Crest Trail
and the San Poil Canyon area (Washington's Grand Canyon).

For now we continue south on TR13 and climb again for 1.1 miles,
thankfully for only 340' in elevation gain, to pass just under the summit on the
west side of Wapaloosie Mountain. We skirt the mountain and remain on a high
ledge before descending while crossing the Wapaloosie Mountain Trail 15 at our
next waypoint.

0453P 3.0mi 48° 39.793'N 118° 28.052'W 6870' Trail 13 X Wapaloosie
Mountain Trail 15

The PNT on TR13 stays on a high ridge around the 6800' contour for the
next 1.1 miles, and then drops slightly to cross the Jungle Hill Trail 16 coming
up from the east. About 0.15 miles beyond the trail junction there is reportedly
a small flat area to trail camp, albeit a little swampy and full of "skeeters."[47].
This camp is somewhat protected from the prevailing west winds as TR13 is
almost 200 yards below the crest of the ridge above. There is a piped spring a
couple of minutes down the trail past the camp site.[66]

TR13 descends on from the spring for 1.2 miles on a series of switchbacks,
dropping 720' in elevation into a saddle, where at the bottom TR13 crosses the
Sherman Trail 12. Like TR17 mentioned above, TR12 may provide a connector
route west to roads leading into the town of Republic. But for now, we have
more climbing ahead on TR13, gaining about 450' up the north face of Jungle
Hill in 0.75 miles. TR13 circles Jungle Hill counter clockwise around the 6300'

contour, finally heading south on a reasonable downhill grade through sparse forest.

In 1.3 miles after turning south TR13 rounds the ridge to cross over a crest and turn back to the southeast on the western slope of a bowl formed by Columbia Mountain. Half way through the bowl, we cross the Columbia Mountain Loop Trail 24 at our next waypoint. Above the trail intersection the map shows a spring, but it is unlikely that during the summer there would be much flow at this elevation on the ridge.

0458P 5.2mi 48° 37.397'N 118° 29.665'W 6130' Trail 13 X Columbia Mountain Trail 24

To climb another peak, turn east on TR24 climbing 660' along the ridge to the summit in just over 0.5 miles. Before you start up on this side trip, look for a spring about 100 yards up the trail, which was reported to have good water in 2018.[80] Columbia Mountain has a recently restored lookout cabin that may be suitable for use as a temporary shelter. The cabin is used by snowmobilers and skiers in the winter.

Back to the primary PNT route, TR13 heads southeast along the ridge passing two more springs on the map, but there are no hiker reports of water at either. Soon TR13 begins to descend the south face of the mountain on several switchbacks, dropping 500' over the next 1.1 miles.

TR13 crosses under a double wood pole power line and into a thicker forest. As you exit onto a dirt road there will be an old trailhead sign-in box. In 2014 the NFS completed a new horse campground about 0.1 north of where TR13 exits onto the spur road. There are a few sites, vault toilet but no water.

To your right (south) walk about 100 yards to be at Sherman Pass on the paved State Route 20. Here there is a story board that tells the history of Sherman Pass. Be sure to look up on the ledge above you and see if you can spot the wolves!

If you do not want to go to the highway, follow the trail east for another 0.3 miles into our next waypoint where TR13 continues on the south side of State Route 20.

0460P 2.2mi 48° 36.368'N 118° 28.476'W 5440' Trail 13 X State Route 20 @ Sherman Pass

Trail Angel (Republic): There are trail angels in Republic. See details at the end of this chapter.

We will cross SR20 several times over the next few weeks. Traffic at Sherman Pass is fairly light and it may be difficult to hitch. Most traffic is either farm trucks or 18 wheelers, and after making the long haul up to the top of the pass they are not likely to slow down and stop. There is room at the parking area for about four cars and I suggest that if you are hitching west on SR20 into Republic that you stand at the east entrance to the lot. SR20 after Sherman Pass has tight guard rails down the mountain and there is no safe spot to stop to pick up a hitchhiker.

The map shows the NFS Sherman Pass Overlook Campground 0.6 east of the pass. In 2014 this campground was closed by the NFS.

The trailhead for TR13 on the south side of SR20 is about 100 yards down the hill to the east. Carefully walk near the guard rail on SR20 to the yellow trail crossing warning sign to pick up TR13 south. You may also find a "shortcut" cross-country ski trail, about 50 yards down on the south side of SR20, which will connect you to TR13.[49]

The primary route, however, has us return the trail where we exited onto the dirt road near the horse trailer parking. If you take the trail you will have to follow SR20 for a short distance back uphill to TR13.

Once we're back on TR13 we climb—nothing new here! In about 0.75 miles the trail breaks out of the forest onto the east shoulder of Sherman Peak. At about 1.0 miles from SR20 you will cross the Sherman Loop Trail 72 that takes you around the west side of Sherman Peak. TR72, although perhaps shorter around Sherman Peak, is horse trail and very steep in sections.

The PNT on TR13 continues working along the eastern bowl of the mountain with good water just after the trail junction. We find pretty good views all the way back toward Northport on the east side of Sherman Peak. After climbing out of the bowl the trail takes a major switchback to the east before turning uphill to the west. Soon we're climbing on the southern slope of Sherman Peak.

If you want to "bag" another peak on the PNT, just look for the best spot to leave the trail to take the fairly easy bushwhack to the summit. This bushwhack will be through the burnt forest, grass and around rock outcroppings. The most likely spot to climb the additional 550' in elevation is just before the trail enters onto the southern slope, where it is 0.3 miles up to the top.

Back on the trail, TR13 works its way south of Sherman Peak and around to the west side of Snow Peak, staying relatively level around the 6200' contour. In about 0.7 miles after we cross over the western shoulder of Snow Peak, we come to our next waypoint, the Snow Peak Trail 10.

0464P 3.5mi 48° 34.825'N 118° 29.423'W 6330' Trail 13 X Snow Peak Trail 10

At this 'T' junction TR10 comes in from the west as we continue south on the primary PNT route on TR13, reaching the first of two springs in the area. In 0.5 miles from TR10, we should find the NFS Snow Peak cabin at 6240' elevation. Although the cabin is a bit off the trail, it is visible for a mile or two,[GT] and is available for $30 per night according to the NFS. It has a propane cook stove and solar lighting, but no water. There is a pit toilet and corral. The cabin is used mostly by horseman and cross-country skiers.

Still headed south past the cabin on TR13 we descend slightly, passing the second spring on the map. The second spring usually has good water and is only about 25 yards off the trail.[GT] We descend for the first 1.0 miles past the cabin before levelling. At 1.7 miles we meet the Edds Mountain Trail 3. A 2013 thru-hiker reported that, "the trail is ridiculously hard to spot where it turns off the Kettle Crest trail. I think you are just starting to head downhill when TR3 turns abruptly uphill to the right. The sign was knocked over too, which didn't help."[43]

0466P 2.2mi 48° 33.365'N 118° 29.787'W 5980' Trail 13 X Edds Mountain Trail 3

We turn west on TR3, leaving TR13 which continues south downhill. Hikers report that TR3 is easy to follow with well-placed cairns. It stays high with good views[27] as TR3 remains in grassy, rocky, open terrain on the south slope of Bald Mountain. We climb steeply over the next 0.5 miles, gaining about 600' in elevation. At this point TR3 is on the shoulder of Bald Mountain and the best place to bushwhack to the summit. The PNT, of course, offers plenty of other summits and continues to the west on TR3 on a very faint tread in spots. Our next waypoint is our bushwhack jump off point.

0468P 1.8mi 48° 33.341'N 118° 31.694'W 6120' Trail 3 @ Bushwhack Point

Decision Time. There is no exact point to leave TR3 and bushwhack south. The objective is to safely descend and find a rounded spine from Edds Mountain to your north. A longer but easier alternate route has been developed by hikers and it is described at the end of the chapter with the other alternates routes for this section

The following description applies to the original PNT route and as shown on the maps provided by the PNTA. On TR3 we come to an open grassy rocky spot about 0.3 miles long on the south slope of the mountain. There is a steep cliff to the south in the middle. Either go further west to the next ravine or take the preferred bushwhack into the slight ravine on the east side of this grassy spot. Hikers report that there is a black snag marking a potential starting point.

The first goal is to reach the low point in the ridge along the south shoulder of Edds Mountain. Once at the low point we follow the south shoulder ridge south for another 1.3 miles to reach the Hall Creek Ponds.

0470P 2.5mi 48° 31.616'N 118° 32.558'W 4650' Bushwhack @ Hall Creek Ponds

The ponds may offer a chance to get water even though access may be a little swampy. A trail camp here is possible. There may be a faint old trail near the ponds. If so, follow it south. Otherwise keep bushwhacking along the 'S' shaped rounded ridge to the south past the ponds. In about 0.2 miles the ridge seems to flatten and you should be able to see Hall Creek Road - Forest Road 600 is downhill to the west about 200 yards away. Keep bushwhacking down the shallow rocky slope to the west or southwest to meet Forest Road 600.

0471P 0.4mi 48° 31.422'N 118° 32.808'W 4590' Bushwhack X Hall Creek Road - Forest Road 600

Follow FR600 downhill south for 1.6 miles to find the trailhead for the Thirteen Mile Trail 23. FR600 is not well maintained, but it is used in the winter by snowmobilers. The road follows Hall Creek, which may not have water in the summer. Keep a careful eye out for the trailhead, although there are reports that a trailhead sign was erected here.

0472P 1.6mi 48° 30.278'N 118° 32.325'W 4330' Forest Road 600 X Thirteenmile Trail 23

TR23 tends to parallel FR600 south off and on for about 0.3 miles before turning to the west where it climbs. The trail is usually fairly well maintained and enjoyable.[AP] TR23 is advertised by the NFS to "wind through the rocky cliffs of the San Poil River Canyon." Unfortunately, there was a tremendous storm in 2012 with multiple micro-bursts that flattened much of the old growth on TR23, but with some work it is passable.

Continue west on TR23 climbing for another 1.5 miles until we are due south of Fire Mountain. From here we go downhill to our next waypoint in another 1.9 miles and looking for the intersection with the Bear Pot Trail 19. We cross a small creek (a fork of Thirteenmile Creek) and then find the trail on the other side.

0476P 4.1mi 48° 30.407'N 118° 36.166'W 4430' Trail 23 X Bear Pot Trail 19

Note: the PNTA map shows this trail junction north of its actual position. TR19 is a short quarter-mile trail that leads north from TR23 to an old hunter's cabin known as the Shelberg Cabin, which was once often visited by PNT thru-hikers. Unfortunately, a storm in 2012 crushed the cabin with Lodge Pole Pines. TR19 has been cleared but the cabin will likely not be restored. There is a footbridge crossing a very small creek just before the cabin remnants, but water is not reliable from late July - September. The nearest reliable water from the old cabin is in a pond at the TR19 trailhead, downhill another 0.5 miles north.

Back to the PNT, after crossing TR19, our next waypoint is 2.5 miles west on a pleasant undulating grassy, sandy trail to where we cross Forest Road 300.

0479P 2.5mi 48° 30.525'N 118° 38.221'W 4520' Trail 23 X Forest Road 300

FR300 is an old overgrown forest road that comes in from the northeast. You may not even recognize it. As we continue west on TR23 we are hiking along the bare southern face of Thirteenmile Mountain and find excellent views to the south. In 0.4 miles TR23 drops over the mountain's shoulder and continues west along a relatively level grade along the slope of the ridge. About 0.6 miles after passing the mountain's shoulder the trail meets the crest of this western ridge. From here we begin to go downhill toward Thirteenmile Road – FR2054 in another 1.8 miles.

0481P 2.7mi 48° 30.097'N 118° 40.887'W 3560' Trail 23 X Thirteenmile Road – FR2054

TR23 continues west across the road and up a rise to gain 140' in just 0.15 miles. At the top of the rise the primary PNT begins a bushwhack to the north, while the better TR23 continues southwest.

0481.4P 0.3mi 48° 30.081'N 118° 41.137'W 3750' Trail 23 X Bushwhack Point.

Decision Time. My recommendation is to follow TR23. This route is described in the alternate section at the end of the chapter. For now, we'll bushwhack north along the ridge on the primary PNT route.

We turn north as we climb on the ridge picking our best line heading to Cougar Mountain in 0.9 miles. Keep north, bushwhacking the slightly descending ridgeline for another 0.3 miles. Here the ridge drops more steeply to the north. We are at our next waypoint where the ridge begins to descend.

0482P 0.9mi 48° 31.065'N 118° 40.780'W 4040' Bushwhack @ Cougar Mountain

We bushwhack west into a shallow saddle and then right back up to the ridge. Keep bushwhacking west and northwest picking a line that drops down into saddles and then backup to the ridge. The forest is sparse along the ridge with relatively thicker growth down in the saddles. Our next waypoint puts us near one of the only landmarks out here, Dry Run Pond, about 1.7 miles from our last waypoint, depending on the bushwhack line you take.

0484P 1.7mi 48° 31.183'N 118° 42.716'W 3480' Bushwhack @ Dry Run Pond

The pond most likely will not have any seasonal water during the summer, but we should be able to identify it. Continue bushwhacking west another 0.4 miles downhill to the 3000' contour. At this point you should be near the face of a bare "hump" that leans to the north. There is a slight ravine only 0.1 miles west of it. Our task is to bushwhack down that ravine to the southwest into the thick growth. "My friend said 'I've see worse bushwhacks, but that was in the jungle. This was much worse than the Lion Creek bushwhack.'"[CN]

Try to pick a line on the south side of the canyon wall if possible, picking up a game trail or two. In this section you will descend about 1000' elevation over the next 1.2 miles.

Caution: The last 0.1 miles is treacherous as you lose almost 300' elevation. Loose rocks present a fall hazard here. You'll know you're at the bottom as you hit the swampy, chest-high grass and stinging nettles in the San Poil River basin. With a little luck you can ford the San Poil River in only about 60 yards wide at a narrow point, then climb the western bank to find paved State Route 21.

0485P 1.7mi 48° 30.488'N 118° 44.265'W 2110' Bushwhack X State Route 21

Time for a little road walk on the paved SR21 north through the San Poil Canyon. Sheer cliffs rise from 800' to 1200' above us on SR21 on both the east and west sides. We road walk just another 0.7 miles to the Ten Mile Campground and the Ten Mile Trail 25.

0486P 0.7mi 48° 31.106'N 118° 44.339'W 2170' State Route 21 X Ten Mile Trail 25

Resupply: If you continue north on SR21 past the Ten Mile Campground, for about "10 miles," you will find the great trail town of Republic, Washington. There is not a lot of traffic on SR21, but you can try to hitch a ride. About half way between the campground and Republic is a relatively large dude ranch and conference center. If they are headed that way, ranch hands have been known to give thru-hikers a lift into town.[BT]

The NFS Ten Mile Campground is on both sides of SR21 is closed. It is a good idea to fill up with water from the river before we head out on TR25. The trailhead is tucked back in the campground on the west side. There was a sign in 2017 warning of fire damage dangers, but the trail was clear.[ES] TR25 climbs north up the ridge before doubling back on switchbacks. Towards the top, directly above the campground, TR25 finally turns west to parallel Tenmile Creek, but it remains about 250' above it. The trail is only about 2.2 miles long where it ends at Forest Road 100.

0489P 2.2mi 48° 31.636'N 118° 45.972'W 3360' Trail 25 X Forest Road 100.

Decision Time. Let's get serious for a second. If you are a "purist" and want to walk every foot of the primary PNT route, then we'll describe it for you in the next few waypoints. If, however, you are out to experience the best of the PNT and want to hike the easiest route through some of the transition areas, then I recommend taking the alternate route on FR100. Yes, FR100 is more road walking, and the PNT certainly has too much of that, but I will try to accurately describe the primary route, and the alternate route, and let you decide. The recommended alternate route, on FR100, runs downhill to the southwest and is described at the end of this chapter.

On the primary route we begin our bushwhack by crossing the road staying on our westerly course and climbing up a hump gaining 120' elevation in a little over 0.1 miles. Pick a line that works west but stays on this soft ridge. Fortunately the crest of this "ridge" has less foliage than the ravines on either side. For the first 1.5 miles of the bushwhack it is very doable, at which point you will start to head downhill through very thick tangled forest with many fallen trees.

In another 0.1 miles you should cross an old dirt forest road that runs to the south. This gives you the first opportunity to bail out of the bushwhack taking it south for 0.6 miles to meet Rattles Snake Road and then west to Scatter Creek Road. But onward, bushwhacking west downhill now, more steeply dropping 170' in 0.15 miles through dark, wet moose-loving forest, to finally reach the paved Scatter Creek Road – FR53, just after crossing the creek.

0490P 1.8mi 48° 31.433'N 118° 48.197'W 3110' Bushwhack X Scatter Creek Road – FR53

If we're on target, we find an old forest road with a gate at this point on FR53. It looks tempting to follow the road, but it soon turns north, while our bushwhack takes us back up the steep hill straight west. Be prepared for slow progress for the next couple of miles as the bushwhack leads through very thick alders, nettles, poison ivy and over, under and along many fallen trees. Thankfully we've now climbed about 300' in elevation in 0.3 miles to reach the dirt "jeep trail" Ferry Lake Campground Road – FR100.

0491P 0.3mi 48° 31.506'N 118° 48.617'W 3430' Bushwhack X Ferry Lake Campground Road – FR100

Special Note: During the very dry summer of 2015 many major wildfires broke out along the trail in late August-September. National incident maps show that fires around Ferry and Swan Lakes and to the west engulfed all the PNT trails between Ferry Lake through Forest Road 3120. The following description is written about the trail before the fire.

No matter where you come out on the road, find the campground and get your bearings. The NFS Ferry Lake Campground has 9 campsites, toilets, but no drinking water. There is good access to the lake for water. This is another chance to bail out of the bushwhack by following the road south 11 miles to Scatter Creek Road. Beginning to get the picture here?

Let's keep up the bushwhack route by going to the north end of the campground and finding the north end of the lake. Climb over the barbwire fence and slide down the very steep hill into the swamp at the north end of the lake. Yes, I have the scrapes and bruises to prove it can be done! If the swamp looks too menacing, be advised that it extends about a mile north.

After crossing north of Ferry Lake, we bushwhack west-southwest to cross an unnamed forest road in about 0.5 miles at 3600' elevation. Keep working to the southwest, only gaining about 100' in elevation in 0.75 miles to reach Swan Lake and the NFS campground.

0492P 1.4mi 48° 30.946'N 118° 50.134'W 3710' Bushwhack X Swan Lake Campground – Forest Road 500

Swan Lake and the NFS campground is a good place to rest if you need it. The campground has 21 sites, vault toilets and drinking water, with all paved roads in the campground. There is also a small beach and a community pavilion on the north side of the campground. There are some tent-only sites right along the lakeshore.

The PNT map shows that you should take the Swan Lake Trail, just past the pavilion, and follow it around the lake counter-clockwise for about 0.3 miles before cutting to the west on an easily identifiable spur trail. Turning west if you go about 100 yards you will see an old forest road that heads north. This is not FR640. FR640 is still another 0.1 miles to the west up the ridge. Having scouted this area extensively, let me offer an easier alternative to get to FR640.

At the north end of the campground by the day use area, the paved road begins to go downhill to the pavilion. Instead, at the end of the parking area go through the man-gate looking for the gated dirt road to the east (your right). Follow the dirt road and pick up the trail. Go another 100 yards or so and bear left on the well-established old forest road trail. This will take you north of the lake and slightly downhill. About the point where the trail turns south in a curve, turn directly west and bushwhack uphill about 100 yards. Keep climbing until you clearly see the old remnants of FR640.

FR640 is overgrown and has not been cleared or maintained in at least ten years, but the road bed is visible. We may find it even easier to bushwhack and parallel the old road bed a little above it than to try to walk through the thousands of two to four inch saplings and alders that now choke it. Hike FR640 for about 0.7 miles as it rounds to the west. Bushwhack another 0.4 miles, shooting to get to our next waypoint in 0.4 miles. You may have to leave the FR640 old road bed in about 0.2 miles to take a west heading.

0493P 1.4mi 48° 31.695'N 118° 50.843'W 3880' Bushwhack X Unnamed Forest Road

This waypoint is the middle of a U-turn on an old unnamed forest road that is shown just south of the bushwhack section on the map. Follow the road northwest all the way to Forest Road 5314. The road is used by horse riders and is easy to navigate and quite a pleasant walk. At the end we have to cross two large berms just before the Forest Road 5314. Once on FR5314 turn south for 0.1 miles to find Forest Road 500.

0494P 0.5mi 48° 31.900'N 118° 51.310'W 3770' Forest Road 5314 X Forest Road 500

FR500 initially climbs and then levels for a pleasant hike, at least for a dirt forest road. It soon opens up just above the 3800' contour offering some excellent views to the south. In a short 0.9 miles we come to a cattle fence and sign stating that you are now entering the Okanogan National Forest. Just beyond the sign and around the corner you will see an excellent grass spot on the left for a trail camp. This is a favorite "deer camp" location for hunters in mid-October.

After crossing the forest boundary the road is now designated FR020. Look for the spring on the north side of the road about 0.5 miles after entering the Okanogan NF with a nice grassy spot for a trail camp.[ES] Although there are other upcoming water sources, this is the best one until you reach Granite Creek in 14 miles.[50] FR020 continues northwest on a generally level grade, passing Forest Road 060, and then crossing Forest Road 030 in the middle of a U-turn, at our next waypoint in 1.4 miles past the spring.

0497P 2.8mi 48° 32.495'N 118° 53.573'W 3750' Swan Lake Road FR020 X Forest Road 030

FR020 works southwest passing a creek just after the turn and stays level traversing around a "hump' and then turning back to the north. The forest here is thin and you may get a glimpse of the dark canyon walls to the southwest on the far side of the Aeneas Valley about 1.5 miles away. In 1.4 miles after crossing FR030 you will intersect with Forest Road 3120.

0498P 1.4mi 48° 32.763'N 118° 54.570'W 3660' Forest Road 020 X Coco Mountain Road FR3120

We turn north on FR3120, which we will follow for the next 5.3 miles. The road stays about 50' above Ogle Creek, but we cross the creek on FR3120 in 0.5 miles, where you might find water. Keep heading north slowly climbing and crossing other smaller forest roads. Sorry, but this section is another unremarkable PNT road walk. In 2.4 miles after crossing Ogle Creek we cross Forest Road 200. Just before FR200 there is a creek that may also offer water.

We keep north on FR3120 after the "U-turn" where we cross FR200, and we keep on our slow uphill grade. The road crosses another creek in 0.6 miles past FR200, but there are no reports whether this creek will provide water in mid to late summer. In another 1.8 miles we reach out next way point, Forest Road 3125.

0504P 5.3mi 48° 36.792'N 118° 54.797'W 4150' Forest Road 200 X Gardner Road FR3125

Hike west and then north on FR3125, slightly uphill, for only 1.2 miles to meet Forest Road 31.

0505P 1.2mi 48° 37.078'N 118° 55.846'W 4190' Forest Road 3125 X Fir Creek Road FR31

Next we turn north on FR31 as we keep going slowly uphill. In 2.0 miles FR31 crosses Forest Road 30, which has a creek 160 yards down the road, and a potential spring feeding the creek from the south. Our next water opportunity is about 1.7 miles north where FR31 crosses Forest Road 15. Fir Creek is a little over 0.1 miles east on FR15.

After passing FR15 we continue north, then northwest downhill for about 1,2 miles to cross Granite Creek, which usually has good water flow throughout the year. Near the creek you might see a "PNT" sign pointing to Fir Mountain, and the north end of the alternate route Corner Butte-Sweat Creek Trail 301 South, as described below. In 0.5 miles after crossing Granite Creek our road walk ends as we cross State Route 20, at the Sweat Creek Picnic area.

0510P 5.4mi 48° 40.794'N 118° 54.359'W 3520' Forest Road 31 X State Route 20 and Stealth Trail Camp/Trail 302

Resupply: Republic is 8.5 miles east on SR20.

The map shows that there is a NFS Sweat Creek Campground where FR31 crosses SR20, but the NFS has closed the campground and made it day use only. Nevertheless, you can find a fairly good trail campsite back in away from the road.

This concludes our review of the primary PNT route in Section 4. Below are five alternate routes for you to consider.

Alternate Route: Edds Mountain Trail 3 Bushwhack to Thirteenmile Trail 23

This route extends your hike on the Edds Mountain Trail 3 west about 2.0 miles before turning south to bushwhack down to FR600, which then leads us to the Thirteenmile Trail 23. This route has been followed by several thru hikers, and even though is a little longer than the primary route, it has a better bushwhack.

Start: 0468P Trail 3 @ Bushwhack Point

Re-join: 0471P Primary Bushwhack End at Forest Road 600

Mileage: 5.0 miles; longer than the primary route by about 2 miles

Highlights: Easier descent and route finding than the primary route bushwhack.

0468P 0.0mi 48° 33.348'N 118° 31.483'W 6110' Trail 3 @ Bushwhack Point

We continue west on the ridge on TR3, following the cairns that lead us through areas where the trail fades. In about 0.5 miles we are due south of Edds Mountain on its southern grassy slope. The trail keeps high on the ridge for another 1.2 miles. We look for the point where the ridge seems to end and the trail turns north. There may be indications of a slight ravine to our south down the slope.

0469A 1.7 mi 48° 33.230'N 118° 33.857'W 4890' Trail 3 Alternate Bushwhack Point

We begin our bushwhack looking for the easiest and safest route down the southern facing slope. Going down we try to stick close to the edge of the regrowth pines on the east.[BT] Our next waypoint is crossing an old mining road designated Forest Road 630. If we are too far to the west, we may find Forest Road 620. Look for the evidence of an old road running east-west at 4200' elevation or below.

0470A 0.6 mi 48° 32.781'N 118° 33.626'W 4300' Bushwhack X Old Forest Road 610

Once on FR630 we turn west looking for the junction with Forest Road 600 in about 0.7 miles depending on where we ended our bushwhack.

0471A 0.7 mi 48° 32.464'N 118° 34.120'W 3920' Forest Road 620 X Forest Road 600

Turn southeast on FR600 as this is the same road that we would have been seeking on the original PNT route, but we are about 2.0 miles north of that waypoint. FR600 starts level but after 0.5 miles we begin to climb on a good grade gaining over 600' elevation into our next waypoint.

0471P 2.0mi 48° 31.422'N 118° 32.808'W 4590' PNT Rejoin on Forest Hall Creek Road – Forest Road 600

Alternate Route: Original PNT Stock Route – Thirteenmile Trail 23

This alternate route follows the original PNT stock route to bypass the San Poil River ford and a rough bushwhack to Ferry Lake and Swan Lake. This alternate route follows Trail 23 southwest to its trailhead on State Route 21, and then road walking north to rejoin the primary PNT route just south of the Tenmile Campground and Trail 25.

Location:　　Chapter 5, Map Section 4, Shown but not highlighted on the PNTA maps.

Start:　　0481.4P Trail 23 X Bushwhack Point.

Re-join:　　0485P Bushwhack X State Route 21

Mileage:　　5.7 miles; longer than the primary route by 1.4 miles

Highlights: Trail 23 is a good trail with water and additional camp, and hikes State Route 21 north through the San Poil canyon.

0481.4P 0.0mi 48° 30.070'N 118° 41.069'W 3690' Trail 23 X Bushwhack Point.

Where the primary PNT route begins a bushwhack to the north, we will not turn north. Instead we will continue west on the well-marked tread of TR23 for another 4.4 miles. This portion of the Colville National Forest is still open, with park-like Ponderosa Pines, grass and rocky outcroppings.

About 0.9 miles past the bushwhack point you will come on the remnants of an old forest road running north-south in a slight depression. In another 0.8 miles TR23 turns south and begins to descend more rapidly. Soon the trail drops us into a canyon with a 500' sheer cliff next to the trail on the east. In the last mile the trail borders the creek which should have good flowing water. Hikers report that there are even pools deep enough to take a dip.[GT]

Coming out of the canyon you find the well-marked trailhead for TR23 on State Route 21 with room for horse trailers and a good place for a trail camp. There are two campsites, a toilet, but no drinking water. There is no fee, but the camp was reported to be somewhat trashed in 2013.[43]

0485A 3.4mi 48° 28.888'N 118° 43.743'W 2010' Trail 23 X State Route 21

To return to the primary PNT route, we just turn north on the paved SR21. It is about 2.3 miles to the waypoint where the primary PNT crossed SR21, and about "13 miles" north to the town of Republic. Enjoy this road walk through the San Poil Canyon on SR21 which has very light traffic.

0485P 2.3mi 48° 30.488'N 118° 44.265'W 2110' Bushwhack X State Route 21

Alternate Route: Forest Road 100 to Swan Lake and to Forest Road 500

This alternate route road walks in lieu of the two difficult bushwhacks to get west of Swan Lake to Forest Road 500. Although this route involves more road walking and is 3.5 miles farther than the primary PNT route, it is much faster and much less frustrating.

Start: 0489P Trail 25 X Forest Road 100.

Rejoin: 0494P Forest Road 5314 X Forest Road 500

Mileage: 8.6 miles; longer than the primary route by 3.2 miles

Highlights: Faster, albeit with a less frustrating road walk with little traffic, and still visits Swan Lake

0489P 0.0mi 48° 31.636'N 118° 45.972'W 3360' Trail 25 X Sunset Road FR100.

After exiting TR25 we turn southwest on FR100 downhill for 1.1 miles to meet the forest road, Rattlesnake Road – FR5320. Keep west on FR5320, which is the same direction as FR100 at that point, on a fairly level grade only gaining and losing 100' elevation over the next 1.3 miles where the road meets Scatter Creek Road – FR53.

0491A 2.7mi 48° 30.935'N 118° 48.038'W 317' Rattlesnake Road FR5320 X Scatter Creek Road – RD53 and Creek

The paved FR53 will take us southwest, then west into the NFS Swan Lake Campground. In 0.7 miles you will come to a triangle intersection with a sign that points to Ferry Lake. Continue west on FR53 for another 0.2 miles to see the gated old forest road FR500 heading to the north.

0492A 0.9mi 48° 30.580'N 118° 48.826'W 3330' Forest Road 53 X Forest Road 500

The dirt road FR500 will get you off the paved FR53, but there is only light traffic on FR53 anyway and the distance is the same. FR500 re-joins FR53 in another 1.3 miles. In either case we go uphill to end up just south of the NFS Swan Lake Campground. See the notes about this campground in the section above covering the primary PNT route bushwhacking into Swan Lake.

0493A 1.1mi 48° 30.423'N 118° 49.920"W 3640' Forest Road 53 X Swan Butte Road FR5314

To avoid the bushwhack section west of Swan Lake, we need to backtrack about 0.2 miles south of the campground on FR53 to Swan Butte Road – FR5314. FR5314 is the first road to the west, and leads us to Forest Road 500.

Follow FR5314 southwest and uphill about 0.9 miles where it turns to the northwest. You will cross several other forest roads but keep bearing to your right. After 1.6 miles on the road you will come to a small pond on the south side of the road. After passing the pond the road circles to the north for another 2.3 miles to intersect with FR500 and re-join the primary PNT route.

0494P 3.9mi 48° 31.900'N 118° 51.310'W 3770' Forest Road 5314 X Forest Road 500

RESUPPLY OPTIONS

0417P 48° 54.951'N 118° 12.025'W 1470' Sand Creek Road – RD4013 X Rock Cut Road - RD4141 **Orient**: This is as small hamlet 3.7 miles south on US395. Orient has a fairly good general store, with laundry and pay showers. US395 has a very narrow shoulder with blind corners, therefore, the better route is to hike south on Rock Cut Road.

Republic: There are three waypoints that offer paved road access to this great trail town.

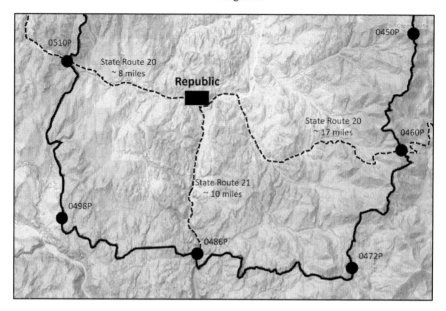

0460P 48° 36.368'N 118° 28.476'W 5440' Trail 13 X State Route 20 @ Sherman Pass. Republic is about 17 miles west of this waypoint at Sherman Pass on State Route 20. Traffic at Sherman Pass is fairly light and it may be difficult to hitch. Most traffic is either farm trucks or 18 wheelers, and after making the long haul up to the top of the pass, they are not likely to slow down and stop. There is room at the parking area for about four cars and I suggest that if you are hitching west on SR20 into Republic, that you stand at the east entrance to the lot.

0486P 48° 31.106'N 118° 44.339'W 2170' State Route 21 X Ten Mile Trail 25 To get to Republic follow paved State Route 21 north past the Ten Mile Campground, for about "10 miles" to find the great trail town of Republic. Traffic is very light on SR21 but you can try to hitch a ride.

0510P 5.4mi 48° 40.794'N 118° 54.359'W 3520' Forest Road 31 X SR20 Republic is about 8 miles east, following State Route 20. Traffic is light on the highway, but you may be able to hitch a ride.

Trail Support

0460P Republic: Artie and Mike McRae, themcraefamily@msn.com, (509) 680-1581 Cell (texting is best as both work full time). Can help with rides, shower, package mailing and pick up. Artie works at the post office and can retrieve packages on weekends. Big yard for tents and occasionally meal. One mile west of Republic on State Route 20.

0460P Republic: Karrie Stevens, karrieinrepublic@gmail.com or texts to 503-262-6864. Can offer rides and occasionally a bed and shower. Primary organizer for the PNT information board at the Ferry County Food Coop in Republic with info on where to obtain laundry, showers, stove fuel, clothing, hiking food, etc. The FC Coop will also allow hikers to charge phones, access internet, and leave their back packs while doing laundry, showers, etc

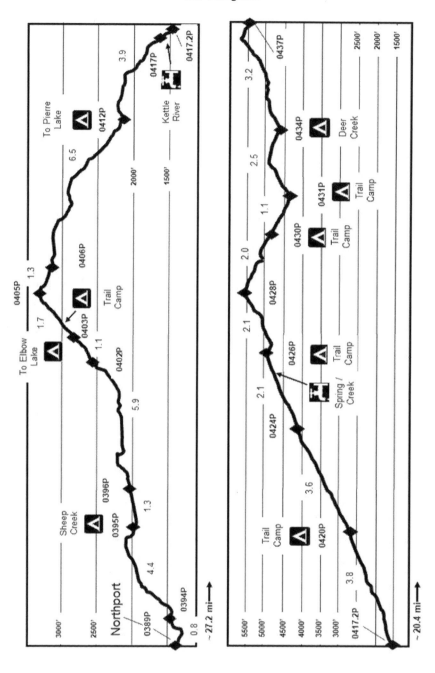

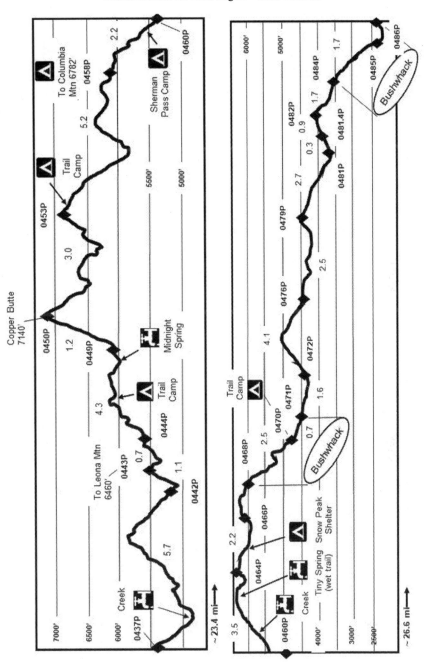

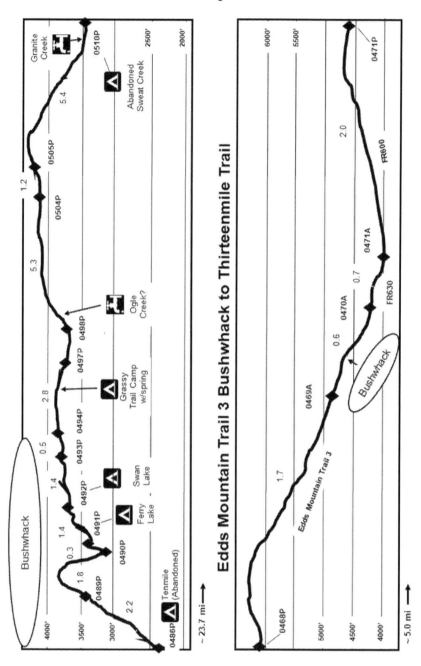

Edds Mountain Trail 3 Bushwhack to Thirteenmile Trail

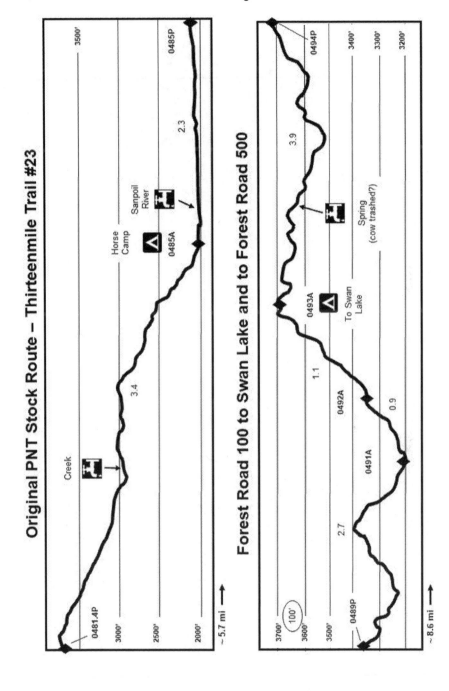

Original PNT Stock Route – Thirteenmile Trail #23

Creek

Horse
Camp

Sanpoil
River

0481.4P

0485A

0485P

3500'

3000'

2500'

2000'

3.4

2.3

~ 5.7 mi

Forest Road 100 to Swan Lake and to Forest Road 500

Spring
(cow trashed?)

To Swan
Lake

0489P

0491A

0492A

0493A

0494P

'100'

3700'

3600'

3500'

3400'

3300'

3200'

2.7

0.9

1.1

3.9

~ 8.6 mi

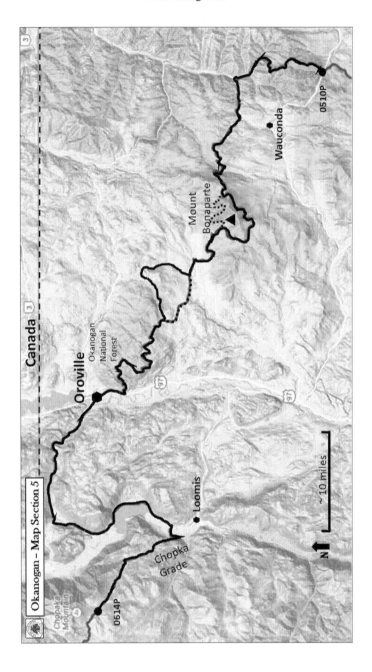

CHAPTER SIX

OKANOGAN – MAP SECTION 5

Sweat Creek to Cold Springs

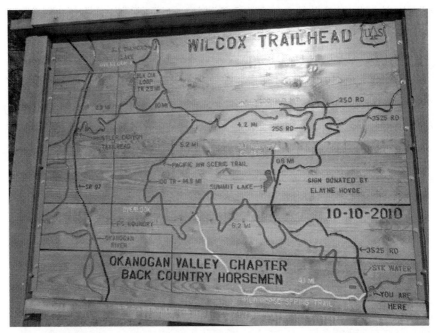

Trailhead sign for Trail 100 and Whistler Canyon, Okanogan County

Key Trail Notes

Highlights: Mount Bonaparte; Whistler Canyon; Chopaka Mountain Grade

Primary Route Estimated Elevation Change: 11,200' climb / 8,460' descent

Route Alternates: Bonaparte Mountain

Possible Resupply: Oroville

Parks/Forests: Okanogan NF, Loomis Natural Resource Conservation Area

Permits: None

Other Notes: None

0510P 0.0mi 48° 40.794'N 118° 54.359'W 3520' Forest Road 31 X State Route 20

The map shows that there is a NFS Sweat Creek Campground where FR31 crosses SR20, but the NFS has closed the campground and made it a day-use area only. Nevertheless, you can find a fairly good stealthy trail camp west of the parking area in the old campground, if you can sleep through the highway noise on SR20. There is a great stealth camp site just past the privy near a big boulder.[CN]

Finally, we're back on a trail, although don't get too excited because it is a horse trail. In the picnic area parking lot past the pit toilets there is a "PNT" sign to mark the route.[ES] Here are two choices: The original PNT route follows the Sweat Creek Trail 301, and would take us west and up to Clackamas Mountain. The primary PNT route puts us on the Maple Ridge Trail 302 and climbs the ridge to the east. The valley with Sweat Creek is in between the two.

Here's the description for TR302, the primary PNT route. This trail was reported to be in excellent shape from recent trail work in 2018.[80] From the parking area we head north into the woods to pass through a hiker zigzag cattle guard. Immediately after crossing through the fence, look for the generic "Trail" sign pointing to the right (east) and uphill for just a little bit. If you want to take TR301 to climb Clackamas Mountain, immediately turn left and cross the shallow creek

Sticking to TR302 it is described as scenic and quite nice.[BT] This area is used mostly for hunting, horseback, motorcycle, and ATV riding. There is also livestock grazing from June through September, so watch for cow paths. After a short uphill jump, the trail levels and follows the high wire lines east then it begins to climb up a steep, rocky bluff for the first 0.2 miles. Afterward it still climbs north steadily along the ridge with a total gain of 1200' in 1.2 miles.

From here TR302 follows the ridge to cross over the 4910' hump at our next waypoint.

0513P 2.8mi 48° 41.838'N 118° 53.360'W 4880' Maple Ridge Trail 302 X Trail 310A

As we approach the top there is a trail junction with a sign. We bear right (north) along the crest of the ridge for the next 1.5 miles before turning west and in 0.1 miles we should be near a rocky bluff, where we can look down the valley with Sweat Creek and up at Clackamas Mountain. Continue working downhill into a saddle dropping about 350', then climbing the far slope to join the Clackamas Mountain Trail 312. There are many cow paths in this area and a spring with decent flow into a trough is reported to be about 0.2 miles before the junction with TR302, but likely cow trtashed.[ES]

0516P 2.6mi 48° 43.430'N 118° 53.628'W 5170' Trail 302 X Clackamas Mountain Trail 301 and Pass Spring

Near this waypoint there is "Pass Spring," which is piped water flow into a cow trough, with little water in August 2017.[ES] This trail was reported to be in excellent shape from recent trail work in 2018.[80] Follow TR302 around the ridge to the north at about the 5100' contour, then drop down into another saddle and emerge on the eastern slope of the ridge. In the saddle you may find another trail that would take you to the top of the ridge and the 4876' butte, but afterward it would rejoin TR302. Rounding back to the east, the trail will break into a thinner forest and a "U-turn" where we might find "Easy Spring," another piped trough. This spring was reported dry in 2015.[50] Good water is 1.9 miles ahead in Cougar Creek.

Keep working north and downhill to reach our next waypoint intersecting Cougar Creek Road – FR3510-100. This section of the trail has been improved recently but it appears to cross private property right next to a cabin.[66] If you come to a cabin visible ahead veer left of it.[GT] As you exit the property there is a "no trespassing" sign.

About 0.1 miles from the road the trail crosses Cougar Creek, which offers the best flowing water around, but remembering the cows upstream, treating it is highly recommended. There is a place here to make a trail camp before reaching the forest road, but this could be private property.

0519P 3.1mi 48° 45.077'N 118° 52.816'W 3510' Trail 302 X Cougar Creek Road – RD3510-100

The primary PNT turns west on FR100, but note that there is a ranch about a quarter mile to the northeast uphill on the road. FR100 takes a slightly downhill grade through the forested valley with Cougar Creek always to our south. In about 0.5 miles there is a good place to trail camp near the creek. In another 2.1 miles we reach our next waypoint at the intersection with County Road 5495. About 0.8 miles before our next waypoint good water is reported in the creek. Fair warning: "The next few miles are the creepiest 'Deliverance/Hills Have Eyes' area on the entire PNT, by far. Yard signage does not make one feel very welcome. Move on through."[80]

0521P 2.7mi 48° 46.752'N 118° 54.760'W 2960' Cougar Creek Rd X Toroda Creek Road 9495

We turn west and uphill on the paved RD5495 following along Toroda Creek for 3.4 miles. There is not much endearing to this road walk, except after about 2.4 miles the road opens up into the central Washington grasslands with hardly a tree nearby. The road crosses a creek here but caution is advised because range cattle are in this area with several ranches along the road and with lots of "no trespassing" signs.[48] Our next waypoint is a mile ahead as we continue uphill and past the mine entrance.[50]

0525P 3.4mi 48° 46.310'N 118° 58.660'W 3570' Road 9495 X Bunch Road 4975

We turn northwest on the treeless RD4975, passing more ranches on our 2.5 mile road walk. Curiously, you might find RD4975 chalky white at the beginning from limestone or carbonate that is mined at the Wauconda quarry.[GT] Thankfully on this hot road, in 1.3 miles we enter some trees along the road and a little shade as we work the uphill grade. As we cross into the tree line the road changes designation to Forest Road 20. Navigation here is a series of dirt forest roads intersection close together. Stick to the main dirt forest road we're hiking on and look for the next road/trail, old Forest Road 030, at the waypoint.

0527P 2.5mi 48° 47.996'N 119° 01.136'W 4110' Road 020 X Forest Road (Trail) RD 030

The fastest and easiest way to the Bonaparte Lake Resort is to go straight on FR020. The more pleasant hike is to take the primary PNT route, which turns west along the old FR030. Going straight leads you to FR32 on the eastside of Bonaparte Lake on NFS property. Some hikers have stealth camped by the lake north of the resort. The resort has a restaurant and a very small store. Although "resort" is a bit of a stretch and the store is not really suitable for resupply. You can get a couple of meals from the restaurant, especially a giant hot breakfast.[ES]

Staying on the primary route, we head west following the old FR030 on a grassy tread slightly uphill for 0.5 miles where it then turns southwest. There has been logging in this area so look carefully for the main road. When I hiked this section in 2013 the grass was chest deep, with range cattle throughout. After 1.6 miles on FR030 you should intersect with the Washington DNR road that turns west. Toward the end the road fades and becomes confusing. Turn uphill looking for small NFS orange blazes, then west to find the very rutted DNR road. It begins a sharp descent for about 0.6 miles to reach Forest Road 010. Take FR010 south for 0.75 miles to intersect with Bonaparte Lake Road – RD 32.

0530P 3.2mi 48° 47.390'N 119° 03.368'W 3570' Forest Road 010 X Bonaparte Lake Road – RD 32

The NFS Bonaparte Lake Campground is 0.2 to the north. Hiking north 0.2 miles we enter the NFS Bonaparte Lake Campground which has 25 sites, water, and vault toilets, with a $12 fee. To continue the PNT we pass through the campground to find the utility road on the west side. We follow it to where the forest road turns north to parallel the west side of the lake and look for a big boulder. This is the trailhead for the Pipsissewa Trail 383 with a new sign.

0531P 0.5mi 48° 47.561'N 119° 03.766'W 3570' Bonaparte Lake Camp @ Pipsissewa Trail 383

TR383 starts southwest then turns north climbing on major switchbacks up the ridge. This is the beginning of our climb up Bonaparte Mountain. After 1.7 miles of steady climb, gaining 840' in elevation, we reach Lost Lake Road – FR

100. There is a small piped spring on the way up the ridge, and a place for a good trail camp just east of the road with a great view of the lake.[50] We head southwest on the forest road on relatively level grade for only 0.4 miles to the trailhead for the South Side Trail 308 at our next waypoint.

0534P 2.6mi 48° 47.911'N 119° 04.179'W 4560' Forest Road 100 X Southside Trail 308

TR308 starts southwest climbing 1300' in just 2.1 miles. We gain a little over 450' in the first 0.5 miles, which will put us just short of Duff Spring. You'll find the trail damp or even muddy just before the spring. In 2016 the trail was reported to be in good shape with evidence of recent trail work.[CN]

Continue southwest another 1.6 miles on TR308 toward our next waypoint at the junction with the Fourth of July Ridge Trail 307. About 0.2 miles before our next way point the trail crosses on a good wood bridge with a strong creek underneath.

In 2013 there was large windstorm that struck the east and south side of Mount Bonaparte, but 2015 hikers report that the trail is now clear.[50]

0536P 2.3mi 48° 47.618'N 119° 06.396'W 5830' Trail 308 X Fourth of July Trail 307

Decision Time. The primary route follows TR307 while the original PNT route keeps us on TR308 headed uphill and northwest. TR308 circles to the north and leads to the trail that climbs Mount Bonaparte. It is described at the end of this chapter. TR308 is the recommended route. The Bonaparte lookout is not to be missed for a historical lookout building with great views. It is the only manned forest service lookout in the Okanogan drainage.[80]

Nevertheless, sticking to the primary route along TR307, we head south on good tread climbing for about 0.6 miles to settle just above the 6200' contour. From here TR307 levels somewhat and in 1.3 miles puts us at Lightning Spring. There have been no recent reports on this water source. Continue clockwise as the trail takes us around Mount Bonaparte along the southern slope of the Fourth of July Ridge, descending slightly. In another 2.3 miles past the spring we come to our next waypoint at the southernmost point of TR307.

0540P 4.5mi 48° 45.419'N 119° 08.982'W 5710' Trail 307 @ Southern Most Point

The trail settles again, headed west around the 5600' contour where we pass the Roggow Cabin and the North Fork Siwash Creek in 1.5 miles. Soon TR307 turns back to the north and in 0.6 miles we reach the spur trail that leads west to the TR307 trailhead on Forest Road 3230. Around this point there may be a shelter along the trail.

0543P 2.2mi 48° 46.348'N 119° 10.661'W 5120' Trail 307 X TH Spur Trail X Cabin Trail 303

The primary PNT route stays north on TR307 for another 2.3 miles to reach the Antoine Trail 304 at our next waypoint. Just prior to reaching TR304 we cross a branch of Antoine Creek that reports to have good cold water.

0545P 3.3mi 48° 47.602'N 119° 09.293'W 4880' Trail 303 X Antoine Trail 304

Following TR304 we turn west and in 0.3 miles come to the old Napol's cabin. A tree fell on the old cabin and it is not useable.[49] There is no good place to trail camp in this area.[50] We continue northwest, dropping downhill about 250' elevation over the next 0.7 miles to reach Forest Road 150 and our next waypoint.

0546P 0.9mi 48° 48.087'N 119° 10.102'W 4410' Trail 304 X Forest Road 150

Approaching FR150 you might find that TR304 appears to continue across the road to the west. This is an untested alternate following cow paths and blue triangle markers that would take you to the next way point in about 1.7 miles. However, we'll follow FR150 north, then west, downhill through a less dense forest for 2.4 miles to reach Mill Creek Road - FR 3230.

0548P 2.6mi 48° 48.149'N 119° 11.932'W 3920' Forest Road 100 X Mill Creek Road – FR 3230

FR3230 leads north into farm and ranch land for 1.3 miles to the paved Antoine Valley Road – RD 9467. We turn east, and round the bend to the north on the paved road, crossing Mill Creek, going only 0.3 miles to Swanson Mill Road – RD 4662. This puts you about a quarter mile south of the unincorporated town of Havillah, which has no stores, but there is a church with a water spigot.[GT]

0550P 2.1mi 48° 49.522'N 119° 12.416'W 3460' Road 9467 X Swanson Creek Road – RD 4662

Get ready for another treeless road walk as we head west on RD4662 next to Antoine Creek. I suggest that if you can, fill up with water from the creek before turning north in 1.3 miles—if the cows haven't polluted it.[47] Turn north on Eden Valley Road – RD 4759 (aka Dry Gulch Road). Note: there is a road walk shortcut at this point. To take the shortcut, continue west on Swanson Creek Road for another 1.9 miles to Road 3525. Veer northwest on RD3525 for 1.7 miles to intersect Broser Way. Keep on RD3525 as it turns north for another

1.5 miles to find the Mount Wilcox Trailhead as described several waypoints below. The shortcut, although all road walking, saves you about 4.7 miles.

Back to the primary route as shown on the map, follow Dry Gulch Road north for 4.5 miles, passing only a few homesteads near the end.

Just before meeting our next waypoint we pass the triangle junction with Landen Lane running to the east. Around the corner as we hike west there are two ranch driveways, one to the south and one to the north. There is a creek on the map at the intersection with Mount Wilcox Road – FR 3524-100, but it was dry in 2015.[50]

If you are looking for a cabin for the night, albeit deluxe in nature, hike another 1.5 miles up Eden Valley Road to the Eden Valley Guest Ranch. The ranch has 10 cabins for rent, some on a nightly basis. Their phone number is (509) 485-4002.[39]

0556P 4.5mi 48° 53.165'N 119° 13.560'W 3410' Road 4759 X Haley Mtn FR 524-100

There is no road sign for the Mount Wilcox Road, but it is designated "FR3524-100".[50] This road thankfully leads into the trees and shade and into the Okanogan National Forest. We follow it initially west and then as it turns to the southwest on a reasonable uphill grade. In about 2.5 miles the road passes to the north in the shadow of Mount Wilcox, a 450' hump above the road. Keep west through thinning forest and in about 2.0 miles the road begins to fade.

Keep heading west, follow the clear ATV tracks as it approaches the top of the ridge.[50] It is easy to follow over and down to the new parking lot and outhouse on a spur road just off Summit Lake Road.[GT] Just prior to the road you should see a horse trailer parking area, known as the Wilcox Trailhead. Backcountry horsemen ride in this area of the Okanogan National Forest. As we exit at this trailhead, you'll find one of the best trail signs on the PNT, which displays your route for the next 12.4 miles.

0561P 5.2mi 48° 51.586'N 119° 18.357'W 3770' "Mount Wilcox Road" X Summit Lake Road – FR 3525

The Whistler Canyon Trail has been extended, which most maps do not show. You can still turn north on FR3525 and in 1.0 miles try to find Saddle Spring as the road turns to the west. There is a large bare spot west of the road opposite the spring. From here follow the road west on an uphill grade for another 1.4 miles, gaining 330' elevation to reach our next waypoint at Whistler Canyon Road – FR 100, aka the Whistler Canyon Trail. Do not turn at the first Trail 100 sign, but instead continue on the road another 200 yards to where the Whistler Canyon Road/trail 100 heads left.[GT]

At this junction we can follow the shorter FR3525 north, or use the White Horse Spring Trail. Using the horse trail we cross FR3525 and go west on the trail about 75 yards to where it turns north. There is a good water source a little beyond 0.2 miles up the trail. It is just off trail in the trees, maybe a hundred yards, on the left (west) side, where there is a remnant of signpost but no actual sign. Piped water flows into a trough. The pipe outlet doesn't quite clear the edge of the trough but you can easily catch water as it flows off the edge.[47] On the other hand, with all the cattle in this area, you may want to bypass this water unless you are desperate.[50] We follow this well marked horse trail north and northwest for 2.4 miles to our next waypoint.[30]

0564P 2.4mi 48° 52.523'N 119° 20.116'W 4230' Road 3525 X Forest Road 100 - Whistler Canyon Trail

The primary PNT route takes FR100 south. Maps show the NFS Summit Lake campground to the north about 1.0 miles. This campground is no longer in service. The lake is buggy and swampy.

We turn south on FR100, or now known as Trail 100. Thanks go to the Backcountry Horsemen for maintaining this trail. A water source at Twin Springs in 0.2 miles up the trail is signed "Stock Water."[50] The trail stays level for the first mile or so before beginning to descend, passing a seasonal pond soon after. The trail switches back north - south through almost open area for another 2.0 miles before reaching a shallow ravine.

The trail follows the ravine about 1.1 miles to the southwest through slightly more vegetation before looping back to the north to come near the edge of the rock bluff above the Okanogan River Valley. Expect a trail with thick dust here in August before you reach the bluff.[48] Next the road follows the edge of the bluff where the map shows a pond with perhaps an opportunity for a trail camp. It is unlikely to have water in this "pot hole," as they are known around this part of the northwest.

Special Note. In 2013 a thru-hiker had a close encounter with a cougar (aka Mountain Lion) in this area. Her trail journal is worth reading at this point:

The Whistler Canyon Trail through here is closed old road bed, wide and well-graded for walking. Maybe forty easy minutes later, I noticed a bit of movement on the road ahead and looked up, and a mountain lion with a long tail like a thick velvet theater rope was standing on the left edge of the road. Whoa! It's so rare to ever see mountain lions, and usually they run as soon as they see humans. This cat didn't run though. It ambled across the road, lanky and long-limbed, watching me. For a moment it paused on the right side of the road, and I thought for a moment it would head down the hill there. It turned and crossed the road again. I was sleepy, mouth agape, and fumbling with my camera to try get a picture, all the while distracted with the task of communicating to the mountain lion the terms of our encounter: I am not food, little kitty. Don't tangle with me. The mountain lion went left up the embankment about ten feet, and as it headed to where I had been standing I headed to where it been standing, a kind of two-species do-si-do. I turned and watched as it walked away up the road in the direction I had come, amazed by the extraordinary improbability of this strange encounter. I turned and walked down the road, happy to have seen a mountain lion so close, been stared down by its yellow eyes. I looked back, just to be sure, and the cat had turned around and was following me! I started making a lot of noise, waving my poles, and standing sideways so I would look big with my pack. It kept approaching. I made more noise. Bad kitty, I said. I will mess you up. It stopped, and then sat down in the middle of the road like a house cat. I glared at it a bit more, then walked away slowly, checking that it wasn't following. I continued to check for the next forty minutes or so, but I didn't see the cat again.[KC]

0569P 5.2mi 48° 52.831'N 119° 23.113'W 3180' Whistler Canyon Trail @ "Bluff Trail Camp"

From this potential bluff camp with no water, the trail rounds west and then in 0.5 miles turns north near the bluff's edge. In another 0.6 miles the trail enters a shallow ravine with more vegetation, which we follow into our next waypoint.

0571P 2.6mi 48° 54.272'N 119° 22.241'W 2920' Whistler Canyon Trail @ Spring (estimated)

Periodically there is a small creek at this junction[47] with a slight flow in August. A better water source is in the canyon 2.1 miles ahead.[50] The trail continues working west and downhill through a ravine for 2.1 miles before turning southwest into Whistler Canyon. In another 2.1 miles the trail drops us down 1250' elevation though a narrow canyon with openings to the west to give you a clear view of the valley and our PNT route ahead.

In 2012 the Pacific Northwest Trail Association, Backcountry Horsemen, Okanogan County and the Tonasket Ranger District teamed together to complete a two-year project to fund and build a new trailhead for the Whistler Canyon Trail at our next waypoint. Camping is permitted, but most thru-hikers want to get into Oroville for resupply. A Washington State Discover Pass is not required. In 2013 the PNTA raised money to purchase the land at the trailhead to preserve this access for PNT hikers. In 2015 there was a porta-potty at the trailhead.[47]

0576P 4.5mi 48° 54.131'N 119° 25.586'W 950' Whistler Canyon Trail X US Highway 97

Special Note: We road walk north on the very busy US97 for 2.6 miles to reach downtown Oroville. The Chamber of Commerce has worked hard to make PNT thru-hikers feel welcome. The town has a population of about 1,700 and lies only about 4 miles south of the US-Canada border.

In Oroville, US97 is Main Street as we enter the town from the south. For the sake of discussion, the shortest way to the trail is to turn west (left) at 12th street for one block, turn north (right) on Ironwood St. for one block and then west (left) on Kernan Road for about three blocks to the end of the road. This is behind the library and between The Old Depot Museum and the post office. The Old Depot Museum in Oroville is also the Visitor Information Center – great folks work there. The trail should be just ahead to the north about a half block. But, I'm pretty sure you will want to spend time in Oroville, so just ask anyone around Main and Central Streets and they will direct you the few blocks to the trailhead.

The Camaray Motel, 1320 Main Street, is excellent and hiker friendly and they will let you borrow a bike to get around town.BT   Rooms are about $50-$60. Reservations are suggested as they tend to fill up often, (509) 476-3684. You can do your laundry on-site for $4. The motel is centrally located and a short walk to supermarket and restaurants.GT

There is a city RV campground on the shore at the Osoyoos Lake Veteran's Memorial Park, with showers and all facilities. It is about 0.6 miles north of the center of town right off US97 – Main Street, with a $20 fee. Look for the road opposite Prince's Center (department store) and just before the gas station across the street. This road east will take you down to the lake and to the campground.

Gary Devon, Editor of the Gazette Tribune, is always interested in talking with thru-hikers and has actively promoted the trail. The Gazette Tribune is located at 1422 Main Street, (509) 476-3602.

Oroville has also worked hard on the Similkameen Trail to improve the hiking experience, but unfortunately there is only one PNT exit back to the road. The trail is rail-trail that follows the river gorge to offer incredible views of the canyon and crosses a 375 foot bridge about 90 feet above the river. There are interpretive signs along the 3.5 miles trail.

There are future plans to extend the trail into Nighthawk, but for now please do not attempt to cross the river and hike through the old tunnel. Although this is passable you end up having to trespass private property climbing a high security fence. In previous years, hikers have taken this alternate route by contacting one of the landowners to ask permission to cross his property. Unfortunately, this route also crosses the private property of several other land owners who have not been contacted. The local Public Utility District has notified the Pacific Northwest Trail Association in writing that they deem hiking this alternate route as trespassing.

0579P   3.0mi   48° 56.303'N   119° 26.662'W   940'   Similkameen Trail @ Oroville

Special Note: When hiking westbound, before leaving Oroville, be sure to call for Ross Lake Recreation Area Permits and North Cascades National Park camping permits (360) 854-7245. This is your last chance for good cell reception.

Be sure to have plenty of water as you leave Oroville for this is hot, exhausting 13 mile road walk, and beyond. We follow the old rail-bed trail for 1.5 miles west to exit at the trail at the Taber's trailhead on the Loomis-Oroville Road.[30] Please close the gate behind you.

0580P 1.5mi 48° 57.062'N 119° 27.823'W 1040' Similkameen Trail X Loomis-Oroville Road

We turn west on the paved road hiking far above the river. Our objective here should be to pound out the miles to get to Nighthawk, then past Palmer Lake, and make the climb to Cold Springs.

0592P 6.7mi 48° 57.995'N 119° 38.470'W 1170' Loomis-Oroville Road @ Nighthawk

The town of Nighthawk used to be a booming mining town at the turn of the century with hotels and a burlesque house, but the population now is about five people, with no stores or public water. You may be tempted to take a shortcut and stay to the west of side of the river rather than go across the bridge, but be forewarned that this dirt road south ends at an impassable cliff. It is better to keep to the highway, cross the bridge into Nighthawk, and trudge on down the road.

Good news, there is a good water access 1.3 miles after Nighthawk. There is a double track road down to a parking area with an interpretive sign that you can see from the road. It is the Greater Columbia Water Trail Access Site #3. Camping is allowed.[61]

About 3.2 miles after Nighthawk we cross Chopaka Road and have a clear view of the daunting task ahead where we will climb the steep dry barren ridge to the west.

0595P 3.2mi 48° 55.433'N 119° 39.068'W 1170' Loomis-Oroville Road X Chopka Road

At this point it is worth taking a timeout to consider a clearly "unofficial" shortcut. Two previous thru-hikers have turned west on Chopaka Road and climbed the ridge over to Chopaka Lake on the "Whiskey Trail." This alternate route traverses private property. One thru-hiker described her attempt to take the Whiskey Trail shortcut as follow:

> *"...I had planned to take an alternate, a steep scree gully up the side of a mountain, a route dubbed "The Whiskey Trail" that climbs something like 2300' in less than a mile. It sounded rough, but would cut out almost 9 miles of paved road walking and 6 miles of dirt road walking. The tradeoff sounded worth it, since the paved roads are crushing my ankle right now, though ultimately both options seemed kind of crappy. At any rate, just as I left the road and entered the*

private property at the base of the "trail", a truck barreled down the road, screeched to a halt, and the man inside said in no uncertain terms this alternate was not going to be happening. "The whole mountain's a rate snake den," he said. "Plus there are two grizzlies up there." "Plus it's private property." So much for that."[KC]

Back to the primary route on our road walk, in a short 1.1 miles past Chopaka Road we come to Palmer Lake and the primitive campground, which looks to me more like a treeless parking lot on a 140' wide strip of land between the highway and the lake. It might do in a pinch.

Continuing along the eastside of the lake we pass some small orchards and private summer cabins along the lakeshore. After 4.0 miles you are at the south end of the lake at the Split Rock boat ramp/picnic area, where there is water and a vault toilet. It is still another 2.2 miles along the highway to the southwest to reach our next waypoint, the Toats-Coulee Road. Look for a small road sign on the eastside of the Loomis-Oroville Road indicating the turn to the west (right).

0602P 10.4mi 48° 50.987'N 119° 38.780'W 1210' Loomis-Oroville Road X Toats-Coulee Road

Resupply: Having just left Oroville you will probably not need to resupply. But if you do, the very small village of Loomis is 2.3 miles south. The U.S. Post Office is open from 11:30 am to 3:30 pm. For 2018, there are no stores in Loomis.

After turning onto the dirt road in 0.2 miles you cross the Sinlahekin Creek, which is likely our very last chance to get water for the next 5 miles after a massive climb up the ridge. Be careful, however, because this is farm land with the potential for fertilizer runoff. *"It was a long walk from Oroville, past Palmer Lake with many 'No Trespassing' signs.*[48] Past the creek we follow the road as it rounds to the south for 1.1 miles to reach Chopaka Grade.

0603P 1.4mi 48° 50.472'N 119° 39.805'W 1310' Toats-Coulee Road X Chopaka Mtn Road – DNR Road 2200

Here's a big one—climbing 5000' in 8.9 miles. There is not much of a navigation challenge, or much to describe as this is a long hot pull up the grade for the first 3.3 miles when we reach a 'Y' road junction.

0607P 3.3mi 48° 52.812'N 119° 41.445'W 3050' DNR 2200 X Lower Chopaka Lake Road

The PNT primary route has been altered slightly here from the original route to avoid crossing private property. At this 'Y' junction we keep straight ahead on the road we've been walking. There is not a lot of shade on this section of the road, but it is a relatively easy uphill grade into our next waypoint.

0608P 1.6mi 48° 53.686'N 119° 42.562'W 3570' Chopaka Mountain Road X 'Y' Road Split

At this 'Y' we bear right (straight north) on the lesser traveled, but well defined road. The road is slightly downhill into our next waypoint, giving a slight reprieve from our uphill climb. Coming into our next waypoint, the road crosses Chopaka Creek in a "horseshoe" turn back to the east. Do not expect any water in the creek. Our next way point is the first road to the left, only 0.1 miles after the turn.

0609P 1.0mi 48° 54.247'N 119° 42.423'W 3360' DNR Road 2420 X Old Jeep Road 392504H

The PNT turns northwest, but if we continue east for 0.5 miles, and then north 0.6 miles, downhill into the valley we'd come upon the DNR Chopaka Lake Campground. The campground has 8 sites and vault toilets, and a hand water pump. The lake is reported to be beautiful.[43]

Back at our waypoint we turn back northwest on a dirt road which immediately turns into truck tracks. From here toward Cold Springs the route becomes a maze of fading old road and cow paths.

Keep heading northwest and climb for another 0.8 miles on the road/trail to pass a spur trail to the Tenderfoot Mine.

There are the remnants of an old mine building near the trail behind some trees. The actual location may be northwest of the point indicated on the map.

Here's mountain lion story for you from 2016 in this area:

"I had an encounter with a mountain lion! I was walking up the jeep road, and all of the sudden she appeared in the road not more than 50' in front of me, crossing from the meadow on the right to the left. We both stopped when we caught sight of each other, both of us a bit surprised to see the other. We stood looking at each other, trying to decide on the proper course of action. I decided that I wasn't in danger, and reached for my camera, and she chose to continue with her original plans, so I never actually got a picture. She bounded across the meadow, jumped into a tree, jumped back out of the tree, and ran downhill. Judging from the squirrel sounds coming from the tree, she missed her mark! It was pretty exciting and a special experience. I checked behind me as I continued to ascend the road, but I never saw her again." CN

0610P 1.1mi 48° 54.551'N 119° 43.707'W 4070' Old Jeep Road 392504H X Old Jeep Road 392505J @ Bear Pasture Cabin

Follow the jeep trail north and uphill for only about 300 yards, gaining another 130' elevation, and look for the faint jeep trail that diverts to the northwest while the jeep trail keeps north uphill. You're on the right track if you are on the edge of the tree line and cross evidence of a seasonal creek. There is a spring uphill about 100 yards in this area, but there are no reports of flowing water. Just past the creek is a collapsed cabin.[50] If your navigation fails, just head west through the trees to find the trail (old forest road) leading northwest.

The trail works west, climbing steeply on the ridge keeping on the north side of the tree line. The grass slope to the north uphill is treeless. In another 200 yards further, there is a standing cabin with a sign that reads "Beef Pasture Cabin."[50]

At this point turn uphill and head towards the spring, which is still intact, piped and running into a trough—good water![CN] Although it is piped, cattle have broken down the fence. Cold Springs is still about 3.6 miles ahead. Keep working northwest always near the trees on both sides, but hardly ever in them. It is 2.2 miles on RD392505J to our next waypoint.

0612P 1.7mi 48° 55.388'N 119° 45.910'W 5490' Old Jeep Road 392505J X Ninemile Creek Road

The "trail" now intersects with a bona fide dirt road, Ninemile Creek Road, which we can easily follow to the northwest. Soon we enter the trees and in 0.6 miles we cross another forest road that comes in from the north (right), but we keep on the northwest route and soon enter the Washington State Loomis Natural Resource Conservation Area. In another 1.3 miles, and another 600 elevation gain we finally reach the Cold Springs Campground, and our jump off point into the Pasayten Wilderness.

0614P 1.9mi 48° 56.409'N 119° 47.631'W 6260' Ninemile Creek Road X Chopaka Mountain Trail

This concludes our discussion of the primary PNT route for this section. The description of the Cold Springs Campground is at the beginning of Chapter 7.

Alternate Route: Original PNT Route to Climb Bonaparte Mountain

This original PNT alternate route takes us to the north side of Bonaparte Mountain to give us the opportunity to take a spur trail to the summit. After the devastating storm that blew down thousands of trees along TR307 the primary route, this alternate route is recommended, although not easy in itself. If you chose to climb Mount Bonaparte you will be rewarded with some great views. "It was worth it to camp at the lookout. There was a very nice ranger there."[48]

Start: 0536P Trail 308 X Fourth of July Trail 307

Rejoin: 0545P Trail 307 X Antoine Trail 304

Mileage: 5.5 miles; shorter than the primary route by 2 miles

Highlights: Opportunity to climb solitary 7257' Bonaparte Mountain

0536P 0.0mi 48° 47.618'N 119° 06.396W 5830' Trail 308 X Fourth of July Trail 307

Diverting from the primary PNT route we continue northwest. TR308 hovers around the 5800' contour for just under 1.1 miles into our next waypoint crossing the trail to the summit.

0537A 0.9mi 48° 48.064'N 119° 07.113'W 5760' Trail 308 X Bonaparte Trail 306

TR306 comes uphill from the north as we turn south on the trail and climb toward Mount Bonaparte. In this area Lookout Spring is accessible via a short spur trail, but in the very dry 2015 season, the water flow was reported to be minimal.[48] We keep climbing south for another 1.3 miles along the trail, which has seen more than its share of ATV use. After gaining almost 1200' elevation, you reach the Antoine Trail 304 and break out of the trees into subalpine terrain with excellent views at our next waypoint.

0538A 1.2mi 48° 47.353'N 119° 07.368'W 6910' Trail 306 X Antoine Trail 304

You've made it this far so let's keep going to the summit. Instead of turning west on TR304, keep south and climb to the summit in less than 0.5 miles. The trail becomes a little easier as you climb to the rounded top. Congratulations! You just made it to the third highest peak in Eastern Washington, on a high solitary mountain at 7257'. There is a spot for a trail camp on the summit, but without water.

There is a newer lookout tower, as well as the old forest service log cabin with hand-cut squared logs. You will have to climb the tower for the best views, but only if it is manned. When not manned, there is a drawbridge stairway that is pulled up to prevent you from climbing to the top level of the tower.[GT] If you look west, you will see the Okanogan River Valley and your destination along the PNT. About 30 miles to the east is the Kettle Range where we recently hiked.

After our summit climb and back on the original PNT alternate route, we take TR304 northwest downhill for 3.3 miles, dropping nearly 2000' elevation. We then rejoin the primary PNT route crossing Trail 307.

0545P 3.4mi 48° 47.602'N 119° 09.293'W 4880' Trail 307 X Antoine Trail 304

Tim Youngbluth

RESUPPLY OPTIONS

0579P 48° 56.303'N 119° 26.662'W 940' Similkaneen Trail @ Oroville
Oroville: This is the half way point on the PNT, with exceptional opportunities to resupply before heading into the Pasayten wilderness for a week or longer.

0602P 10.4mi 48° 50.987'N 119° 38.780'W 1210' Loomis-Oroville Road X Toats-Coulee Road **Loomis:** Loomis is a small village with a post office with very limited hours. The Loomis Kwik Stop should be open in 2019 (509) 223-3126 (closed Sundays). From the intersection with the Toats-Coulee Road keep south on the Loomis Oroville Road for about 2 miles.

Trail Support

None.

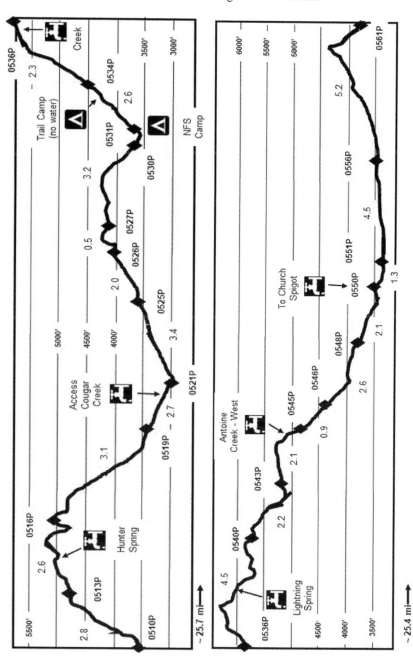

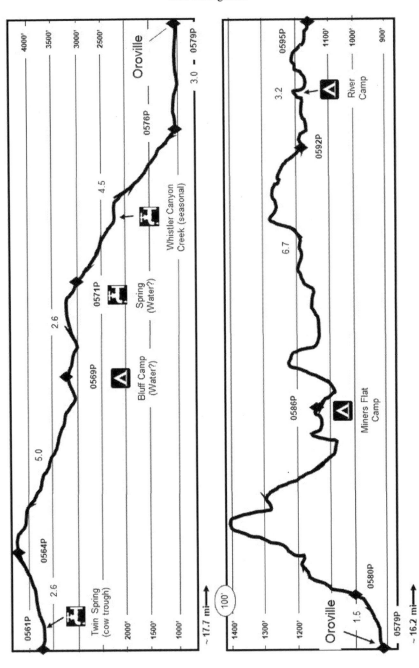

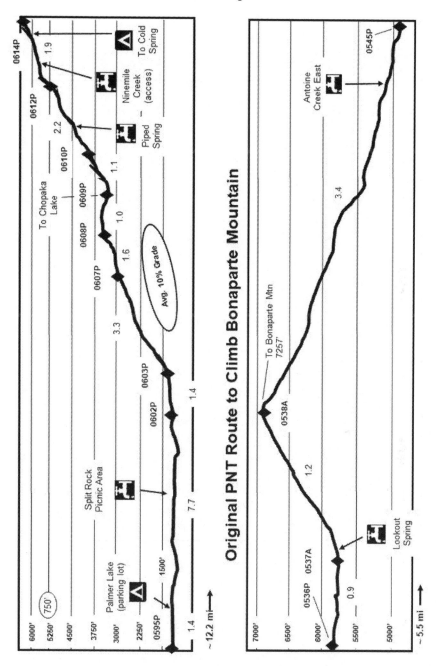

Original PNT Route to Climb Bonaparte Mountain

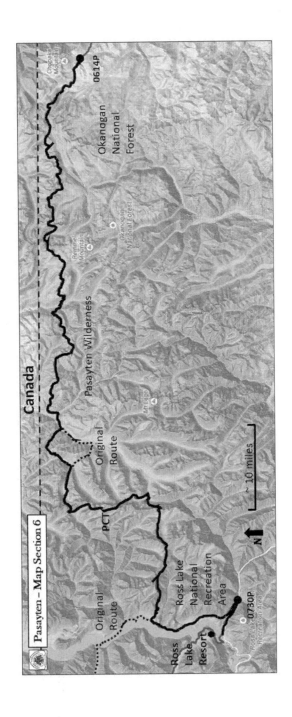

CHAPTER SEVEN
PASAYTEN – MAP SECTION 6
Cold Springs to Ross Lake

Amphitheater Mountain from Cathedral Pass, Pasayten Wilderness

Key Trail Notes

Highlights: Horseshoe Basin; Pacific Crest Trail Devil's Staircase; Devil's Dome; Ross Lake

Primary Route Estimated Elevation Change: 10,590' climb / 16,400' descent

Route Alternates: Harrison Camp Trail, Ross Lake Crossing – Little Beaver Trail

Possible Resupply: None

Parks/Forests: Washington State DNR - Loomis State Forest, Okanogan NF, Pasayten Wilderness, Ross Lake National Recreation Area

Permits: Pasayten Wilderness and Ross Lake Recreation Area Permits - (360) 854-7245

Other Notes: Bear canister recommended

0614P 0.0mi 48° 56.409'N 119° 47.631'W 6260' Ninemile Creek Road @ Cold Springs Campground

The Cold Springs Campground and picnic area are managed by Washington State's Department of Natural Resources in its Loomis State Forest, but it is not officially open. Camping is permitted with a Washington State Discovery Pass; $30 annual or $5 daily fee. The Backcountry Horsemen have done much work in the area including installing an exceptional new map board. Unfortunately the fence is down near the road and cattle have invaded the campground. There is a spring at the lower campground so treat your water. The upper campground has a prime camp spot on the hill top (this is a few minutes beyond the PNT trailhead, at road end).[GT]

Walk up the road past the campground to the trailhead.[50] There is a Loomis Natural Resource Conservation Area sign with a PNT symbol on it—probably the only one you will see for a while.

The original PNT route takes us on a higher, more scenic route, but it has been called one giant PUD (Pointless Ups and Downs). The new primary PNT route takes the Chopaka Mountain Trail, with lower elevations. The nice wooden trail maps unfortunately do not show the Chopaka Mountain Trail, but the entire trail is well marked with diamond-shaped blazes and is in good shape.[CN]

The trail begins just past the sign on a 5' wide trail leading to the northwest and downhill. In 0.6 miles there is a 'Y' junction and we turn left (west) continuing downhill, and shortly thereafter cross Disappointment Creek. After that the trail levels and hovers around the 5800' contour. In 1.2 miles past the creek the trail turns northwest for 0.5 miles to cross Swamp Creek, then west, downhill, to intersect with Forest Road E392404A.

0617P 2.9mi 48° 56.982'N 119° 50.386'W 5730' Chopaka Mountain Trail X Long Draw Trail 340

Follow FR392404A north for 0.2 miles where we come to a large open clear cut area on the west side of the road. There may be a trail sign for the Long Draw Trail at the north end of the clearcut. Keeping to the road we hike north for another 0.2 miles to come to a 'Y' on the forest road.

The 2015 wildfires that forced the evacuation of the PNT in this area makes navigation a bit of a challenge for the next few miles. There is a new parking area at the end of the road just after the "Y". The PNTA maps take us north here. There is a slight "shortcut" if you bear left (northwest) onto a new trail instead of following the truck tracks north. Nevertheless, we'll go straight here, linking up with a newer trail marked with orange diamond-shaped markers that takes us to our next waypoint.

0618P 0.7mi 48° 57.517'N 119° 50.354'W 5760' Long Draw Trail 340 X Spur Trail to Goodenough Trail (Creek)

Look for a new trail sign for Snowshoe Cabin pointing to the left. Water is available from the creek 70 yards west of our waypoint crossing the creek on a bridge. After a short distance there is another new sign for Snowshoe Cabin pointing to the right. Note: Snowshoe cabin is standing and fairly large, but it is not in good shape. It has been heavily occupied by cows. The "cabin" would provide shelter from the elements but it is not a good place to camp.[ES]

Instead of following the sign right, we follow the PNT going left onto an unsigned trail. Follow a line through freshly burned trees up the shoulder of Goodenough Mountain. There are cow paths contouring around the mountain and slightly uphill. Follow a good path as long it is headed northwest and uphill.

0619P 1.3mi 48° 58.113'N 119° 51.385'W 6870' Goodenough Trail @ Goodenough Park

If you overshoot and climb to the top of the ridge, just follow the crest west. Just for reference about a half mile along this trail you leave the Loomis State Forest and reenter the Okanogan National Forest.

The "trail" and cow paths can be indistinguishable through here. The cow paths contour up and around Goodenough Peak and slightly uphill, which we follow. Along the way to our next waypoint, you might pass an old cow trough without water and just uphill from that an old broken brown fiberglass marker. We can follow these markers on an old trail nearly to the saddle just east of Goodenough Peak.[CN]

Look for a moderately sized cairn with a brown marker with a PNT sticker on it! Just uphill from this cairn is a tree with the Pasayten boundary marker on it.

0620P 0.5mi 48° 58.344'N 119° 51.976'W 6920' Goodenough Trail @ Pasayten Boundary

In 2017 the trail from here is evident and the other side of the Goodenough Mountain was reported to be in good shape. USFS trail crews had cleared the trail from the boundary line west to Horseshoe Basin in early 2015. But, shortly thereafter a wildfire raged through this section of the wilderness.

On the west side of Goodenough Mountain we enter an area absolutely decimated by the 2015 fire. Navigation from here until just after the old Lone Wolf Camp can be challenging at times.[61] After traversing the north side of the peak, the trail turns due north and descends 300' in the next 0.4 miles to intersect the west end of Snowshoe Creek Trail 340.

0621P 1.2mi 48° 58.968'N 119° 52.855'W 7120' Snowshoe Creek Trail 340 @ Zig-Zag Gate Long View Trail 340

The trail is relatively open with intermittent trees for the next couple of miles as you hike along the middle of the ridge. You should have excellent views of the valley to the south. Just where the trail begins to turn south to go around Arnold Peak, there is the old site of Lone Wolf Camp. We can find good water here but no suitable place to camp.[61]

In another 0.4 miles we are between Arnold Peak and Horseshoe Mountain, with Smith Lake due south about 0.4 miles in the distance. Keep west for another 0.8 miles to find the junction with Trail 361 that takes you back 0.9 miles east to Smith Lake. This is also the trail junction with the Boundary Trail 533 at Horseshoe Pass.

0624P 3.1mi 48° 58.781'N 119° 56.118'W 7010' Trail 340 X Trail 533 @ Horseshoe Pass

Note that there is a place to camp by the trail junction with a stream for water, but there is a better site at Louden Lake 0.7 miles ahead.[61] The PNT keeps west now on TR533 for 0.5 miles to round the corner and view the Louden Meadow slightly below to the west. Next we climb slightly to reach Louden Lake (or pond) which offers the best campsite for the next 5 miles.

In 0.6 miles past Louden Lake, and after skirting along the edge of Rock Mountain, TR533 leads us to the Coyote Camp. After the camp, we follow TR533 south then back northwest along the ridge as we get a glimpse of the views into Canada to the north. Just before TR533 turns south to climb along the east side of Haig Mountain, we come to the Fireplace Camp. In another 0.8 miles TR533 rounds over the shoulder of the mountain having climbed 240' elevation gain.

From the shoulder we descend slightly but remain on the southern face of Haig Mountain on a clear tread, and in 1.2 miles, come to Dome Camp. Passing the camp TR533 remains along the ridge with great views to the south of the valley with Horseshoe Creek about 1150' below us. In 1.0 miles past Dome Camp TR533 turns north. At our turn there is another trail camp location on a relatively flat shelf. At this point on the trail you should have an excellent view of Teapot Dome to the west. Following the TR533 north for 0.4 miles takes us to our next waypoint at the Teapot Dome Camp.

0631P 6.9mi 48° 58.277'N 120° 02.037'W 6900' Boundary Trail 533 – Teapot Dome Camp

TR533 now heads underneath Teapot Dome on a generally level tread for about 0.7 miles to where we begin to climb into a bowl. This is along a ridge formed by Teapot Dome and Bauerman Ridge, right on the edge of the tree line. Next, TR533 turns west for 0.5 miles to come over the southern shoulder of Bauerman Ridge before turning northwest along the ridge just above the 7000' contour. In 1.4 miles after turning northwest, we should be near a small alpine pond with a potential trail camp. The trail circles north of the pond to the west for 0.2 miles to a "Pass" trail sign.[61] From here we descend north downhill for about 0.5 miles, dropping 180' into the "Scheelite Pass" saddle shown on the map and to our next waypoint.

0635P 4.1mi 48° 59.114'N 120° 05.311'W 6710' Trail 533 @ Scheelite Pass

Just northeast of the pass there are three seasonal ponds but the forest is fairly thick in this draw and perhaps not a good choice for a trail camp. TR533 continues working west on the southern side of the ridge, offering generous views of the Tungsten Valley to the south. This valley now runs east-west which is often affected by high winds funneling in from the Pacific Ocean. In 2.6 miles past Scheelite Pass we come to the old Tungsten Mine and the Tungsten Creek Trail 534 coming in uphill from the south. You know you're close when about 0.2 miles before the mine you pass the remnants of an old trail gate.

0637P 2.6mi 48° 58.583'N 120° 07.955'W 6720' Trail 533 @ Old Tungsten Mine

The remnants of the old mine are near the trail, but up about 60 yards there are two refurbished miner cabins where you can spend the night. Beware, make friends with the field mice that are known to live in the cabins; it is still worth the coziness.[ES] There is room to hang everything in the cabin.[48] The mine operated through the early 1940s. Many of the trails in this area of the Pasayten Wilderness were explored and developed thanks to the mining.

TR533 continues generally west as it diverts north, then south to stay on the ridgeline. About 0.9 miles past the old mine, we cross the headwaters of Tungsten Creek, which may offer water. There are many small, clear streams throughout this area so getting water is not a problem.[50] Far below us is the valley with Tungsten Creek, and then around the corner, the valley with Cathedral Creek. In 2.0 miles past the Tungsten Mine, after crossing the Apex Pass, there is a switchback on TR533 that drops you down about 130' in elevation where the trail turns to the northwest. At this point you should see Amphitheater Mountain a mile and a half to the west, and Cathedral Peak north of it. The best views of this approach to Cathedral Pass are in the morning, if your timing works.

In 2.6 miles after turning north, TR533 rounds the ridge to cross over our next waypoint, at Cathedral Pass. The last 0.5 miles to the pass is a climb of about 340' elevation as TR533 skirts near the face of Cathedral Mountain.

0642P 4.8mi 48° 59.120'N 120° 11.546'W 7580' Trail 533 @ Cathedral Pass - PNT High Point

At the high point of the pass you may be able, on a clear day, to see the tops of Mount Baker and Mount Shuksan far to the west, and our PNT destination down the trail in a week or two. TR533 rounds again along the ridge for about 0.3 miles before dropping down off the ridge directly toward Upper Cathedral Lake. There is an exceptional trail camp area off the trail on the north side of the lake.

In 0.8 miles past the pass you will cross the Cathedral Lakes Trail 545 that would take you north to the Lower Cathedral Lake. There is a good trail sign here. This trail to the Lower Cathedral Lake loops north to rejoin the PNT TR533 in 3.8 miles. But for our discussion we continue southwest on TR533, where in 0.5 miles, we may pass a second trail junction to take us to the Lower Cathedral Lake. Climbing slightly for about another 0.5 miles, we cross the unmaintained, probably unsigned, Remmel Lake Trail 565 coming across the bog from the southeast.

Next we bear right (southwest) and descend 400' on TR533 through a boggy area and in 1.1 miles crossing the creek on a good bridge. About 0.3 miles past the bridge TR533 intersects with the Remmel Lake Cutoff Trail 494, with a trail sign. This trail would take you southeast to Remmel Lake and beyond. Still on TR533 we go 0.5 miles to reach our next waypoint at Spanish Camp and crossing the Andrews Creek Trail 504. As you approach the camp there is a 'T' junction where you briefly follow TR504 north.

0646P 3.8mi 48° 57.680'N 120° 14.302'W 6740' Trail 533 X Andrews Creek Trail 504 @ Spanish Camp

In past years there was a wilderness ranger here checking for backcountry permits. Some backpackers do not realize you need permits, which are free and can be found at most trailheads.[51] Spanish Camp is a favorite spot for backcountry horsemen to camp with their stock. The cabin is unfortunately usually locked. A north tributary of Spanish Creek may be flowing near the camp. Leaving the camp to the west we cross the creek on a bridge, then in about 50 yards there is a 'Y' trail junction, where we bear right (north) on the newer trail, climbing uphill, not descending.

Hikers reported in 2018 that for the next 8 miles the trail was in very poor conditions from the 2017 wildfire that swept through this area. The tread is not hard to follow but the tread is destroyed and there are still many blowdowns.[80]

About 2.8 miles past the camp we climb a bluff on TR533 onto the treeless rocky area of the northwestern slope of Bald Mountain. The trail crosses the bluff and then descends for about 2.0 miles into the trees. About halfway down on the switchbacks we might glimpse the Ashnola River valley below, but soon the trail traverses through some quaking aspens. Continue down the ridge, following the many switchbacks, and dropping about 1900' elevation, we find the junction with the Ashnola River Trail 500 as it comes from the south.

0653P 7.2mi 48° 57.980'N 120° 19.300'W 5090' Trail 533 X Lake Creek Trail

There is an old Appalachian Trail type shelter, labeled as the Ashnola Shelter 0.2 miles north. In 2015/16 hikers found a big hole in the shelter roof and reported it to be "creepy." A better place to camp is in the live trees near the river. Nevertheless it has good water and some shelter from the wind. There is no longer a bridge over the Ashnola River.[61] In August the water level is likely to be flowing but shallow enough to cross easily.[ES]

After fording we climb out of the valley. Our climb is only interrupted where in 0.9 miles, we drop slightly into a ravine and cross the creek. The old bridge was destroyed and unusable. There was a stock crossing just downstream.[CN] Look for the clear reroute and use your best judgment on this crossing.

After crossing we immediately climb again for another 0.6 miles. Here we cross the Park Pass Trail 506 (abandoned), which joins from the west, just after you pass through an old broken gate. There is a spot for a good camp near the trail junction.

Next we keep climbing now to the south on TR533 for 0.3 miles to begin a series of major switchbacks to the southwest up the ridge. In 0.9 miles after the switchbacks end, we reach the 6600' contour to find a series of trails that seem to branch off TR533. Try to follow the trail that leads us directly west through the grassy brush in a depression. Otherwise take the better trail that is marked with a series of stakes as it climbs to the north, higher on the ridge in the open meadow area. Either way, all the trails take us eventually west and past the remnants of old Barker Brown's cabin. You can see the remnants well from the upper trail.

0658P   4.3mi   48° 57.795'N   120° 22.366'W   6910'   Trail 533 @ Barker Brown's Cabin

Only a few logs of the old foundation remain and it is not suitable for shelter. There are several good tent spots nearby on this grassy plane. The small stream 100 yards west might offer water.

The trail conditions improve for the next 8 miles. The 2015 fire damage this area but it has been logged out and pretty easy going.[80]

Follow TR533 west along the open alpine meadow of Sandy Ridge for about 0.7 miles to Peeve Pass where the trail begins to descend into the trees. Shortly after starting down it is advisable to get water at the creek crossing because the next available water is about seven miles down the trail. This creek is in a picturesque "calendar quality" meadow with a good campsite north of the trail.

In 1.3 miles past Peeve Pass we come to our next waypoint, a spur trail to Quartz Lake. There is an unsigned 'Y' trail junction about 0.2 miles before the spur trail.

0660P 2.1mi 48° 57.350'N 120° 24.267'W 6860'   Trail 533 X Quartz Lake Spur Trail

Although not on the primary PNT route, the more defined and used spur trail to Quartz Lake drops you down to the lake about 130' below in 0.5 miles. There are several decent campsites there. If you don't take the trail to the lake, bear to the left (west) at the 'Y' to stay on TR533. In 0.4 miles on TR533, you can bushwhack north up to the crest of the ridge just above you to check the views of the lake and Canada to the north. The views to the south of the Pasayten Valley from the ridge crest are even better.

From the spur trail junction we take the less traveled PNT trail. Look for a cairn up the ridge.[73] This leads us to climb again to the southwest up a rocky ridge and out of the trees on the south face of Quartz Mountain. The trail rounds the treeless mountain just above the 7000' contour for 2.2 miles, where it then descends again on switchbacks.

While on the ridge, the trail may be obscured but it has been marked with stakes and cairns. Take time to look around as this is one of the best views along the entire PNT.

Once we descend, the trail takes us into a small saddle at 6350' and then right back up again. There is a good place for a trail camp at the headwaters of Dean Creek. Climb west for 0.5 miles, gaining 230' to reach the crest of the ridge. TR533 then follows the crest of the ridge west for a short distance as the trail stays level but the ridge rises above us to the north. In 2006 there was a forest fire in this area and following the trail down is a little tough.[BT] Expect a few blowdowns on your descent to Dean Creek.[ES]

Keep working west as the trail gets within 1.5 miles south of the border with Canada and comes to Bunker Hill in 2.6 miles. This is a long slow climb on sometimes sandy soil. There were clusters of blowdowns in this area reported in 2017.[ES]

PNT Factoid: At Bunker Hill, a hiker without a GPS can still find their position by examining the arrangement of white rocks on the hillside that spell out latitude/longitude.[GT] You might note that the map places the old fire tower a little to the east of its actual position, but it is now just in ruins. Be careful not to turn south on the unmaintained Dean Creek Trail 456 which is another 0.2 miles past Bunker Hill. Plan to camp in this area to find some of the best views.[51]

0665P 5.7mi 48° 58.327'N 120° 29.259'W 7130' Trail 533 X Dean Creek Trail 456

About 0.5 miles up the trail there is an old trail campsite just east of the trail near a small pond, just before you enter the burn area. Navigation here is a little tricky with TR533 reported to be faded in 2017.[ES] The Bunker Hill fire must have been very hot. All the trees were killed and the ground eroded wildly in the intervening years. The trail is pretty much a mess, though you can follow it with a keen eye. It's clear a crew came through at some point after the burn and cleared some blowdowns, but not lately.[KC]

TR533 keeps heading west and in 1.4 miles from the trail junction it starts downhill steeply through the burnt forest area. We descend on the trail which was reported in 2017 to be in fair shape up to Bunker Hill Creek.[ES] From there the trail is faint. After crossing the creek, angle west to pick up the trail again in about 20 yards.

TR533, after crossing Bunker Hill Creek, rounds to the west for 0.6 miles before turning south to parallel the east side of the Pasayten River. From here to the Pasayten River you can expect clusters of blowdowns as reported in 2017.[ES] The good news is that there was evidence of a trail crew working in this area late in the 2017 season. Follow the trail south for 0.8 miles where it turns back to the west where we cross the Hidden Lakes Trail 477.

0670P 4.8mi 48° 58.903'N 120° 33.621'W 4010' Trail 533 X Hidden Lakes Trail 477

This area can be confusing and a non-alert hiker could accidentally follow the trail up East Fork Creek, away from the PNT and the Pasayten River.[GT] In 2017 there is a report that there are little ribbons at the junction. After turning to the East Fork trail and looking at the far side you can see the wire mesh that supported the old bridge. That is where you need to look for the trail. Look to crossed on a log upstream and then walk back to the wire mesh to find the trail there.[73]

0671P 0.5mi 48° 58.346'N 120° 33.632'W 3990' Trail 477 X Paysayten Trail 533.1

After crossing the creek, and hopefully finding the junction with TR477, we go west another 0.5 miles downhill to the Pasayten River at our next waypoint. As a last resort if you can't find the trail, bushwhack following East Fork Creek west to the Pasayten River and then follow the shoreline south about 1.5 miles to the old bridge abutment.[61]

0672P 0.8mi 48° 58.394'N 120° 34.233'W 3910' Trail 533 @ Pasayten River Crossing

In 2006 the bridge over the river was lost in the fire, but the pilings remain. Look to ford the river near the big concrete pilings. It is best to cross as soon as you can in knee deep water in August. In 2017 an easy crossing was reported to be just upstream from the old bridge.[73] Once across look to find the trail again about 30 yards beyond the river bank. Originally the trail went slightly northwest up to Trail Creek in only 0.1 miles and here it turned back southwest to parallel the river. Unfortunately, in 2016 Trail Creek washed out the trail at the turn point southwest.

If you can't find the trail after crossing the river, expect to just hike 0.1 miles, through fireweed, up the small rise to intersect a good trail on the west side of the Pasayten River. A 2013 thru-hiker reported that the distance to the trail is a little bit longer, "After crossing the Pasayten River just keep moving away from the river .2-.3 miles up onto a small bench. The trail is right there."[43] Once on the trail we turn southwest. The map may show the old Pasayten Cabin to the north, but it is gone and TR461 is obliterated with blowdowns in 2017.[ES]

Back on the PNT on TR533 you can expect blowdowns through this burnt area for about 0.7 miles from the river crossing. A USFS trail crew was cutting through the blowdowns in late 2016, and it was reported to be in good shape in

2017.[ES] We follow TR533 and the river southwest for 1.0 miles to the junction with the Robinson Creek Trail 478.

0673P 1.1mi 48° 58.168'N 120° 35.400'W 4000' Trail 533 X Monument 83 Trail 454

Decision Time. At the trail sign the original PNT route continues southwest on TR533. This alternate route is highly recommended and described in this chapter below.

The new primary route turns west and climbs to follow Harrison Creek. The USFS does not have an official designation for this trail. Although it is designated as the primary route, it is not "hikeable."[48] A 2015 hiker exclaimed, "Taking this route was one of my biggest mistakes of this hike."[50]

Nevertheless, here is the description of this route. We take the higher track southwest for only about 0.1 miles before it turns northwest and climbs along the ridge above Harrison Creek. Prepare for a very difficult bushwhack all the way to Rainy Camp.[50] The whole hillside appears littered with fallen logs that have toppled since the fire and the trail did not appear to have had any maintenance.[GT]

We climb almost 500' elevation in the first 0.5 miles, and head through one major switchback to the north. From there we keep climbing as the trail returns toward the creek and northwest. After the switchback, the trail levels temporarily but then resumes uphill, but at a more gradual grade.

In 1.6 miles after the switchback we come to Rainy Camp at 4850' elevation. The camp no longer exists as it has been abandoned for a long time.[50] The trail from here is easy to follow but there are a lot of blowdowns that have not been cleared. We go downhill to cross Harrison Creek and then head back uphill to the west on a steep steady climb. In 1.0 miles we gain 1160' elevation and come to our next waypoint crossing the Monument 83 Trail. The sign for the trail is partially burned, somewhat illegible, and easy to miss.[50]

0677P 3.6mi 48° 59.475'N 120° 38.149'W 5990' Monument 83 Trail 454 X Chuchuwanteen Trail 482

At this trail junction, turning north leads uphill to Monument 83 at the Canadian border in 1.0 miles. There are Border Patrol cabins on both the U.S. and Canada sides of the border.

Our primary PNT route, however, turns downhill southwest on TR482 along the western side of the ridge toward the Chuchuwanteen Valley. The trail here is recognizable but with lots of blowdowns to scramble over or around almost until you reach Chuchuwanteen Creek.[50] We descend 1550' in about 2.2 miles to reach the Chuchuwanteen Creek to cross on fallen logs at our next waypoint.

0679P 2.2mi 48° 58.083'N 120° 39.621'W 4440' Trail 482 @ Chuchuwanteen Creek

After crossing the foot bridge, we follow TR533 along the west side of the creek for about 130 yards before turning west momentarily and beginning our climb out of the valley. A 2015 hiker reported that the trail here was hard to find, and it was located on ridge above.[50] The trail climbs about 100' up and then turns southwest again to parallel the creek but higher on the western ridge. The forest is thick in this area and we're likely hiking through the proverbial "green tunnel" without much of a view with plenty of blowdowns to navigate around. This is a relief from the burn area we've been hiking in as the forest has green, lush, broad leaf plants that foretell of what we'll see in western Washington.[KC]

We keep working southwest for another 0.6 miles to where the trail opens into a rocky cleared area, but quickly returns back into the deep forest. The trail stays relatively level for 0.2 miles and then begins a gradual descent back down to the creek. In only 0.1 miles after crossing the creek again, TR533 comes to junction with the Middle Mountain Trail 462 near the Chuchuwanteen Cabin.

0681P   1.6mi   48° 57.194'N   120° 40.620'W   4600'   Trail 482 @ Old Chuchuwanteen Cabin X Boundary Trail 533

The cabin is marked on the map, but it is really the site of the ruins, if even that. The only suitable camps in the vicinity are down TR453 about 100 yards near the creek crossing where there is a good site on the near bank and marginal sites on the far bank.[GT]

The trail is easy to follow here, but unfortunately for the next several miles, you can still expect blowdowns on the trail, even though there is a good tread and some maintenance. TR533 heads west up the valley formed by Frosty Creek, climbing first on the south side but in 0.7 miles crosses over to the north side of the creek. We keep climbing through the thick forest for the next 2.6 miles to reach Frosty Lake.

Just before we reach the lake the trail breaks into the open to give us a view of the massive east sheer shoulder of Mount Winthrop and an idea of the rock climb that is coming up. About 0.2 miles prior to our next waypoint you might find the junction with The Parks Trail 495 coming downhill from the north.

0683P 3.2mi 48° 57.823'N 120° 44.458'W 5330' Trail 533 X The Parks Trail 495

Continuing west, the trail leads us past Frosty Lake to the south, but it is hidden by a rise in the terrain. To get to the lake, leave the trail when north of the lake. Cross a damp meadow to a line of trees which hides the descent to the lake. There is a very decent camp spot on the southwest corner of the meadow just in the line of trees. Scramble down to get to the water, but there is better water on the trail two-thirds of the way up to the pass.[78]

We now are on our last leg of the Boundary Trail 533 as we begin a tough climb up the switchback on the face of Mount Winthrop. The switchbacks take us up about 630' elevation gain in 0.7 miles, but only about 0.3 miles forward progress. TR533 "levels" about the 6100' contour and turns to the west toward Frosty Pass in 1.5 miles.

0686P 2.1mi 48° 57.399'N 120° 46.064'W 6490' Trail 533 @ Frosty Pass

Hopefully the weather is clear because ahead lies some of the best views on the PNT. After crossing over Frosty Pass TR533 turns downhill on another series of switchbacks, dropping 1000' elevation in 1.5 miles to intersect with the Pacific Crest Trail 2000 at Castle Pass.

0687P 1.5mi 48° 57.431'N 120° 46.758'W 5520' Trail 533 X Pacific Crest National Scenic Trail 2000 (PCT 2646)

The primary PNT route now joins the PCT2000, at a point 3.5 miles south of its northern terminus at Monument 78. We follow PCT2000 for 13.3 miles over some of the best views on any of the national scenic trails, and with some luck, you might pass some PCT thru-hikers finishing their 2650 mile trek from Campo, California. There is a good campsite 0.1 miles north on the PCT from this junction.

The junction with PCT2000 is just south of Castle Pass and about 150 yards south of the Castle Pass Trail 749, which leads west, paralleling the border with Canada. Turn south on PCT2000, hiking on a slight uphill grade along the western ridge below Blizzard Peak. Looking southwest toward the end of the valley you may get a glimpse of our next big climb above Hopkins Lake along the Devils Stairway. Keep working south and in 1.2 miles expect to pass over a small creek running down the ridge. Then, still hiking uphill, in 1.0 miles you are at our next waypoint on PCT2000 at Hopkins Pass.

0689P 2.3mi 48° 55.714'N 120° 45.714'W 6140' PCT2000 @ Hopkins Pass

Hopkins Pass sits in a really sharp saddle along the ridge, which also has the Middle Mountain Trail 462 coming uphill from the southeast. PCT2000 turns to the southwest toward Hopkins Lake, which we can see well below us, as we climb up the ridge above the lake. At the first major switchback there is a trail down to the lake and an area for a trail camp. (There are a lot of places to camp around the lake—a beautiful spot! There may be, however, a few PCT hikers and not your typical all-to-yourself PNT camp!)[ES]

We follow the switchbacks along the "knife-edge" crest of the ridge above the lake around the ancient glacier bowl. In about 1.5 miles from the pass we tackle the Devils Staircase.

The Devils Staircase is a series of tight switchbacks that takes us the final 150' elevation gain to the top of the ridge. Once on top of the ridge you feel like you're almost at the top of the world, with spectacular views in all directions. The trail turns southwest along the Lakeview Ridge to temporarily drop off the crest of the ridge but soon returns to it to continue south.

Take one last look because the trail soon heads downhill below the crest following along the western slope below Three Fools Peak, even though the trail is in and out just above the tree line. Follow PCT2000 south traversing now near the base of the steep Lakeview Ridge. In about 1.4 miles from the top of the Devils Staircase, the trail crosses over the western shoulder of the ridge. Fortunately, the trail holds fairly level for the next mile or so, hovering around the 6600' contour. Our next waypoint is Woody Pass, 1.7 miles down the trail past the shoulder of the ridge.

0695P 4.7mi 48° 53.111'N 120° 46.035'W 6660' PCT2000 @ Woody Pass

At Woody Pass we can see the ridge leading south up to Powder Mountain, which towers above the valley below us. We also see the trail along its ridge that we'll have to climb over in about 2.5 trail miles to the south. Since we can see that trail you might be tempted to bushwhack over the scree to Rock Pass and avoid the elevation gain and loss by following the main trail down into the valley. As one hiker noted, "Do not attempt … It has eroded to a dangerous slip-and-slide. I regretted taking it, and still have the scar to prove my folly."[GT] There is no reason to take the shortcut, which was barely visible in 2016.[CN] The main trail is open and simple.[48]

Some hikers have planned to camp at Woody Pass but the altitude and extremely high Pacific winds that funnel through the pass from the west make this a difficult camp spot. Hopefully you'll have good weather here.

Follow PCT2000 downhill south with switchbacks dropping almost 700' elevation to the base of the rocky cliffs. Keep working south on good tread another 0.6 miles to begin a series of major switchbacks to climb back up almost 500' to the crest of the ridge at Rock Pass. After climbing the eastern side of the ridge, follow the crest for a little over 0.1 miles to where the trail then drops along the western side toward our next waypoint, a camp spot with a spring.

0698P 2.9mi 48° 51.492'N 120° 44.628'W 6220' PCT2000 @ Camp With Spring

This waypoint is at a spring which offers a relatively good trail camp sitting in a high alpine meadow. There are some trees nearby and you are somewhat protected from the wind here with mountain ridges on three sides. There is also a way trail that starts us toward Goat Lakes, about 0.4 miles southeast. Goat Lakes are pristine, isolated, and it takes about half an hour to reach them. The way trail is pretty good up to the point where we can look down on lower Goat Lake. From there it's about a quarter mile up via a rock scramble beside the outlet stream to reach the scenic upper lake. This is a little less than a mile total to reach the upper lake, but worth the effort.[GT]

We continue on PCT2000 heading west downhill, dropping about another 500' elevation in just under 0.4 miles and into the trees. Don't try bushwhacking a shortcut downhill here because there is a large rock outcropping cliff that the trail works around before turning south again through the forest.

The trail stays level for 1.4 miles before going slightly downhill into our next waypoint at Holman Pass and the end of our journey on PCT2000.

0700P 2.2mi 48° 50.409'N 120° 44.228'W 5060' PCT2000 X Chancellor/ Canyon Creek Trail 754 @ Holman Pass

Holman Pass is a three-trail junction with the PCT2000 going due south, the Holman Pass Trail 472A coming from the east, and our PNT primary route, TR754 headed west. There is an old collapsed cabin about 100 yards down TR754 west of Holman Pass on the PNT.[49]

TR754 leads us west and slightly downhill as we enter the Mount Baker National Forest, but it is still designated the Pasayten Wilderness. In about 0.9 miles the trail reaches the valley floor and crosses Canyon Creek. Just prior to crossing the creek there is good spot for a trail camp and this junction might be a little confusing with side trails to other campsites.

After picking up the trail west we naturally climb again up on the ridge and onto the east shoulder of South Shull Peak. Hiking uphill about 500' elevation gain we break out of the trees onto a rocky slope. In this area we cross a small stream with another potential trail camp spot. Following the trail west for another 1.0 miles there is a saddle north of Shull Mountain, known as Sky Pilot Pass and our junction with the Devils Dome Trail 752.

0703P 3.2mi 48° 49.406'N 120° 46.296'W 6300' Trail 754 X Devils Dome Trail 752 @ Sky Pilot Pass

At the pass TR754 continues south to climb to the summit of Shull Mountain, but we stick to the primary PNT route and turn west on TR752. We drop down the ridge on TR752 for about 1.0 miles where we lose 750' elevation to a snow-melt stream crossing on a series of wood marsh bridges that are in disrepair—walk carefully. Blowdowns were reported near here in 2017.[ES] This takes us to a relatively undefined saddle shown on the map as Deception Pass.

Climbing west out of the pass we gain 200' elevation where the trail settles around the 5600' contour. In 1.8 miles from Deception Pass the trail crosses a stream fed by the melting snow above. It was dry in 2015.[50] There is a good trail camp spot near the stream. Continue southwest along the ridge to reach our next waypoint, the junction with the Jackita Ridge Trail 738.

0708P 4.8mi 48° 48.721'N 120° 51.214'W 6130' Trail 752 X Jackita Ridge Trail 738 @ Devils Pass

TR738 comes up the ridge from the south and is part of the popular Devils Dome Loop through the western Pasayten. Some hikers consider this a slightly shorter alternate route to Ruby Creek, but it is much steeper.

Look for the brand new sign right in the middle of the clearing at Devil's Pass—you can't miss it.[61] We'll stick to the primary PNT route hiking west on TR752, along the southern side of the ridge. Look for a campsite with logs forming a square around a fire pit just before this trail intersection. There is a new, very clear sign here. What is not so clear is where the tread is. Continue about 5 yards past the sign and then turn right, as if you are going uphill on a fainter trail. When you start to do this you'll see the real trail taking off to your left. This is a little confusing, but cast about with this clue and you'll find it.[66]

Next we climb again up the ridge on a couple of switchbacks to circle south of the 6262' knob shown on the map. Working west along about the 6000' contour the trail remains relatively level for about 0.6 miles before it climbs north a little higher on the ridge, never quite reaching the crest.

Next, TR752 breaks out of the trees to circle a bowl to the south for about 1.0 miles, at which point we cross over the south shoulder of Cinnamon Mountain. If the weather is bad, there may be a camp site in the trees where the trail turns northwest. Although without water, this maybe a better option than spending the night at Devils' Dome.[ES]

Crossing the shoulder, the trail turns northwest along the steep slope of the mountain to reach the spine of its western ridge in another 0.9 miles. Look to the west to see your first glimpse of Ross Lake. Hiking now on the sharp crest of the ridge, the trail climbs another 550' elevation in only 0.5 miles to reach the top of the Devils Dome, which offers a great campsite. *"This is arguably the most spectacular view on the entire PNT."[49]* Water is farther down the trail in small streams in late August 2017.[ES]

0712P 4.3mi 48° 49.470'N 120° 55.084'W 6950' Trail 752 @ Devils Dome

From Devils Dome the trail begins our massive 5200' descent down to Ross Lake. There is an adequate campsite in the first half mile on the descent from Devil's Dome where trail approaches a snowmelt stream.[GT] The trail begins by dropping quickly down about 1000' elevation north and then west onto a large, almost treeless rock bench on the south slope of Bear Skull Mountain.

This area is one of the PNT's most scenic segments. Look south to have a clear view of the Nohokomeen Glacier on the north face of Jack Mountain about 3.5 miles distant. Looking down the slope to the southwest we see the valley and Devils Creek, almost 2600' below the trail and just over a mile away. We hike across the rock bench to our next waypoint and the spur trail to the Bear Skull Cabin.

0713P 1.4mi 48° 49.731'N 120° 56.510'W 6090' Trail 752 @ Bear Skull Cabin

Note: This is the last campsite in the Pasayten Wilderness. After this waypoint we soon enter the Ross Lake National Recreation Area where camping permits are required. Bear Skull Cabin, or shelter, lies about 0.2 miles north on the spur Trail 752B. In 2012 the Bear Skull shelter was in fair condition, with built-in bunks, a small table and fire ring. There are some gaps in the roof but a large tarp behind the shelter can be used to cover it in the event of rain.[GT]

Our primary PNT route continues west on TR752 for about 0.3 miles over Dry Creek Pass where the trail begins a 4.6 miles descent down to Ross Lake. The trail circles west down the slope of Barnett Butte. There are no short cuts so keep going down on the trail as we leave the sparse forest and rock outcroppings and hike deeper into the Mount Baker National Forest.

About 3.0 miles after starting down from Dry Creek Pass, we have dropped almost 2700' in elevation and leave the Pasayten Wilderness to enter the Ross Lake National Recreation Area.

0716P 3.3mi 48° 49.713'N 120° 59.893'W 3470' Trail 752 @ Ross Lake Nation Rec Area Boundary

As mentioned above, when leaving Oroville call for your Ross Lake camping permits (360) 854-7245. Permits can be obtained via phone only; paper permits are not required. Your descent continues for another 1.3 miles, dropping another 1500' in elevation to reach our next waypoint, the Ross Lake East Bank Trail.

0718P 1.7mi 48° 50.222'N 121° 01.101'W 1820' Trail 752 X Ross Lake East Bank Trail 736 (signed)

Just as we come down here there are two sign posts. Take the one "Highway 20" pointing left. The other trail leads to Devils Creek Camp downhill near the lake.[66] All the camps on Ross Lake are small, with pit toilets and fire rings. Some camps allow stock.

Keeping to the primary PNT route, we turn south on TR736 along the shoreline of Ross Lake for the next 9.1 miles until the trail turns east along Ruby Creek. In 1.25 miles after the trail junction there is a suspension footbridge across Devils Creek as the trail progresses through the uncut forest. Still heading south we pass the "weeping" rock wall and in 1.8 miles past Devils Creek, where we reach the trail junction to Rainbow Camp.

Here the East Bank Trail 736 remains relatively level after leaving the trail junction but it turns inland away from the shore. In another 0.7 miles the trail crosses May Creek on a single log with a handrail. There are two May Creek Camps. The north one is a horse camp, while the second is a boat-in camp that can be reserved by hikers. It is reported to be the best camp along the East Bank Trail, with wide open views across lake from your tent pad, and a nice rock outcropping to take in the sun or to dive into the lake.[GT] The camp is west near the creek toward the shoreline.

In another 1.3 miles the trail crosses Roland Creek, with its camp, and begins to climb 800' elevation to cross over Hidden Hand Pass. After the pass the trail rounds to the southeast and to our next waypoint at the junction with the Jack Mountain Trail.

0728P 9.4mi 48° 43.622'N 121° 00.705'W 1930' Trail 736 X Jack Mountain Trail

Jack Mountain Trail cuts diagonally across our primary PNT route. If you want to climb Jack Mountain, take this trail northeast ascending about 7200' from the trail junction to reach the 9066' summit. Perhaps we should pass this one up and keep to the primary PNT route! If you need a place to camp, there is the Hidden Hand (rodent infested) and Ruby Pasture trail camps, about 0.5 miles to the southwest from our trail junction. Both camps are near the water along Ruby Arm.

Back on the TR736, the East Bank Trail, we head east away from Ross Lake staying on the north side of Ruby Creek. The trail crosses at least three streams flowing down from Jack Mountain as we head east to our next waypoint at the bridge over Ruby Creek. We hike east for the next 2.5 miles to the bridge and then backtrack west again on the other side.

0730P 2.4mi   48° 42.502'N 120° 58.542'W 1670'   Trail 736 @ Bridge Over Ruby Creek

At this 'T' junction turn south and cross the bridge, then climb 0.2 miles on the switchbacks up side of the ridge to the parking lot and our next trailhead. There is a vault toilet on the west side of the parking lot with the new Happy Panther Trail nearby.

We head northwest paralleling State Route 20, following the trail for just over 5.0 miles, through some erosion, but easily passable.[GT] Our next waypoint is at the base of the tourist trail down from the Ross Lake Resort parking areas. The observation parking area and viewpoint is 300' elevation above the trail. The trail ends at the Ross Lake Dam service road, which we follow to cross over the dam. Across the road is a picnic area and vault toilet.[50]

This waypoint ends our discussion of the primary PNT route for this section.

0735P 4.8mi   48° 44.059'N 121° 03.762'W 1690'   Happy Panther Trail X Ross Lake Dam Service Road

Alternate Route: Original PNT Route Harrison Camp on Trail 533

This alternate route takes us south on the original PNT route past Harrison Camp to the old Pasayten airfield, then west and up Soda Creek to rejoin the primary PNT route near the Chuchuwanteen Cabin.

Start: 0673P Trail 533 X Robinson Creek Trail.

Rejoin: 0681P Trail 533 X Trail 482 @ Chuchuwanteen Cabin.

Mileage: 8.1 miles; shorter than the primary route by 2.5 miles.

Highlights: Proven, passable route through some older burn area and avoids the unknown status of the Robinson Creek Trail and Trail 482.

Note: There has been confusion in the past about trail identification numbers from different resources. From this waypoint to TR533 at the old Chuchuwanteen Cabin, the trail numbers shown here are sourced from USFS published maps.

0673P 0.0mi 48° 58.168'N 120° 35.400'W 4000' Trail 533 X Robinson Creek Trail

Harrison Camp may be shown on the map in this area, but it has not been found in many years. There is, however, a good makeshift campsite 50' past Harrison Creek, marked with a cairn.[49]

Here we leave the primary PNT route and remain on TR533 to continue southwest paralleling the Pasayten River on the west bank, climbing on the ridge through thick forest for 1.0 miles past the trail junction. This area was burned in a fire in late 2006 that swept all the way into Canada. You will see evidence of the fire on the slopes to the west of the trail, with some better return growth closer to the river.

Here TR533 drops back down the ridge closer to the river. Keep working southwest passing the Holdover, Burn, Thompson and Honess creeks, one each about every half mile or so. After a total of 3.8 miles from our last waypoint you will come to a gate on the south side of Soda Creek.

Follow the cairns across the old airfield to find TR533 again. The airfield has not been used for many years as evidenced by the growth on the north end of the field that looks like a "Christmas tree lot."

PNT Factoid: The Pasayten Airstrip was built in 1931, with the first airplane to land on this remote sod strip in 1932. Horses were used to tow the aircraft after landing. The history of the airfield construction is lost and no one can figure how it was built with, or without, roads and bulldozers at this remote site.

0678A 4.6mi 48° 55.327'N 120° 37.804'W 4280' Trail 533 @ Pasayten Airfield

The airfield offers a good place to trail camp out of the burn area.[61] Follow TR533 out of the north end of the airfield to rejoin the primary PNT route in 3.5 miles. 2017 hikers report that TR533 was clear of blowdowns all the way to the junction with the PCT.[61] TR533 leaves the old airstrip from the northwest corner and follows along the south side of Soda Creek, thankfully out of the burn area. Hopefully you'll find ripe huckleberries along this trail!

Soon we are climbing again with a 340' gain over the next 0.9 miles to where the creek 'Y's into two branches. TR533 crosses Soda Creek to follow the northern branch and uphill. As the trail heads northwest into this steep ravine past the 'Y', we gain another 430' in 1.3 miles to reach the "shoreline" of Dead Lake (a dry swamp some seasons). Pass along the north side of the lake working downhill for the next 1.1 miles to reach our waypoint to rejoin the primary PNT route. As there is no bridge, we ford the creek just before our next waypoint.

0681P 3.5mi 48° 57.194'N   120° 40.620'W 4600'   Trail 533 X Trail 482 @ Chuchuwanteen Cabin - Trail Camp

RESUPPLY OPTIONS

None.

Trail Support

None.

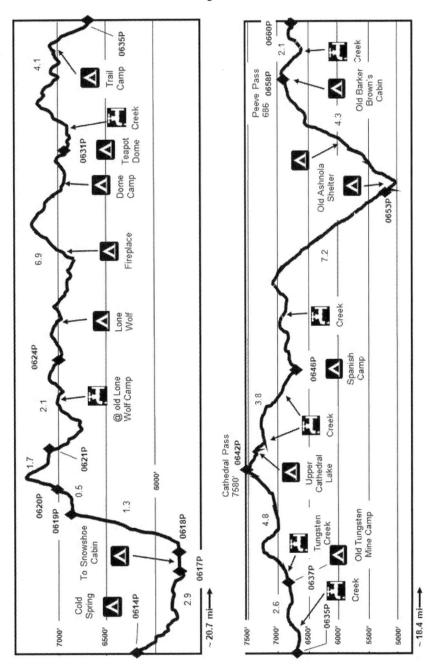

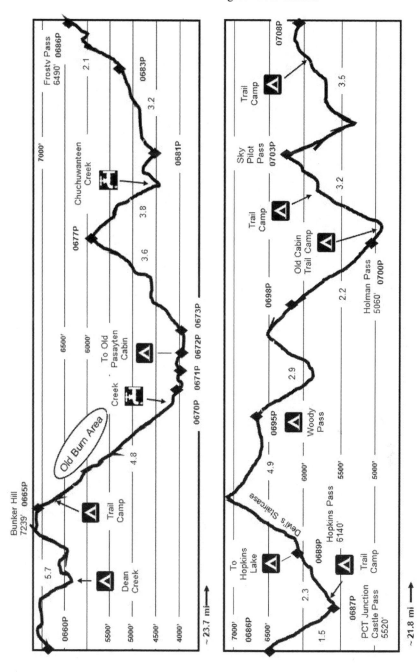

~ 23.7 mi →

~ 21.8 mi →

Tim Youngbluth

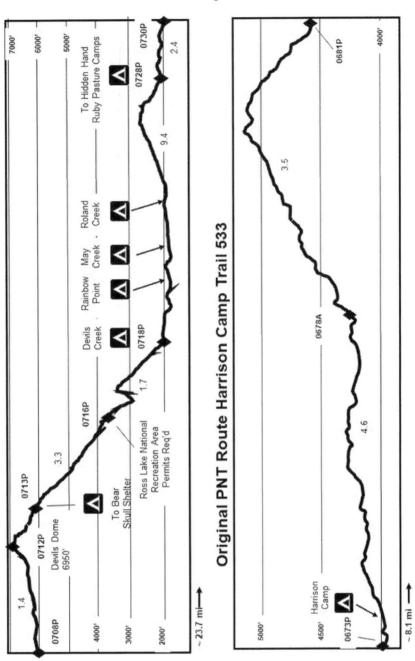

Original PNT Route Harrison Camp Trail 533

170

"So why not embrace the atmosphere of freedom taught to us by our time in the wild and really, truly, *hike your own hike.*

Hike because you love a range, because you've never heard an elk bugle, because you want to learn to be at ease with nothing between you and megafauna other than 50 denier ripstop. Do it for you, not the likes, and not a paper crown."

by Eric "Panorama" Wollborg

From "**Why I Gave Up My Triple Crown (to Hike the PNT)**" Blog Post, Jan 25, 2017, http://pnt.org/blog/why-i-gave-my-triple-crown/

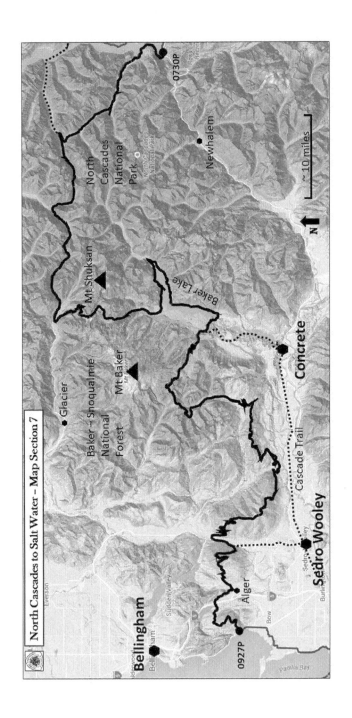

North Cascades to Salt Water – Map Section 7

~ 10 miles

N

0730P

Newhalem

North
Cascades
National
Park

Mt.Shuksan

Baker Lake

Glacier

Baker – Snoqualmie
National
Forest

Mt Baker

Concrete

Cascade Trail

Sedro Wooley

Alger

Bellingham

0927P

172

CHAPTER EIGHT
NORTH CASCADES TO SALT WATER– MAP SECTION 7
Ross Lake to Samish Bay

Ross Lake, Ross Lake National Recreation Area, Washington

Key Trail Notes

Highlights: All of North Cascades NP; Mount Baker; Chuckanut Trails – Oyster Dome

Primary Route Estimated Elevation Change: 25,757' climb / 27,337' descent

Route Alternates: Baker Lake - Mount Josephine, Cascade Trail

Possible Resupply: Ross Lake Resort; Newhalem; Glacier; Concrete; Sedro-Woolley

Parks/Forests: Ross Lake National Recreation Area; North Cascades NP; Baker NF; Mount Baker Wilderness; Timberland; Whatcom County Parks

Permits: North Cascades NP backcountry

Other Notes: Active logging operations may be in progress near Mount Josephine, Anderson Mountain and Blanchard Hill. Check with the PNTA at 877-854-9415.

The Washington Department of Natural Resources (DNR) manages state trust lands in Skagit County, which the PNT utilizes between Mount Baker-Snoqualmie National Forest and Interstate 5. These units are managed to

generate timber revenue to support important programs throughout the state, including public schools, state institutions, and county services. While the Forest Service, PNTA, and other partners work toward a permanently protected trail corridor with high scenic integrity in this region, the DNR has been a gracious and cooperative host on these lands, which are currently needed to maintain the continuity of the PNT.

While witnessing an active harvest may not fit within your expectations for a national scenic trail, it's important to recognize the critical need that these timber harvests serve for the communities of Washington state. It's also important to recognize that the DNR is under no obligation to manage for recreational use, but currently welcomes PNT hikers and equestrians to respectfully use these lands to "connect their steps" from Montana to the Pacific.

0735P 0.0mi 48° 44.059'N 121° 03.762'W 1690' Happy Panther Trail X Ross Lake Dam Service Road

From trail's end, the access road to the dam climbs up, winds around, and is easy to follow. We cross the top of the dam following the signs and turn north on the Big Beaver Trail in front of the sheer rock cliff. The trail starts near the shoreline but soon climbs to be 250' above the water. There is good water from a stream crossing the trail about 150 yards after crossing the dam. In 0.7 miles we come to the spur trail that will take us down about 200' to the shoreline and the Ross Lake Resort.

In 2018 the resort picked up and held hiker boxes for a $20 fee each. Since the staff only picks up mail about once a week and drives a nearly 100 mile round-trip to get it, it is best to plan ahead. There is a box size limit due to the limited storage space on this floating resort. Call ahead to let them know your plans. Their phone number is 206-386-4437 (May-November).

The resort is a series of 12 floating cabins, with no restaurant, store, nor laundry, but they now have Wi-Fi.[61] The cabins start at $150 per night with reservations needed well in advance. The resort also provides a water taxi that will take you for a fee north to the Little Beaver Trail. There is no cell service at the resort, but staff charges a $1 "hiker rate" to use their land line. Since they have a Seattle phone number, they do not charge if you want to call a number with area codes 206, 425 or 253. Only snacks and soda are available at the resort store.[48]

Back on the trail, we continue on the Big Beaver Trail for 1.3 miles where the trail turns inland away from the lake to skirt the hump west of Cougar Island. Soon thereafter we cross the Pierce Mountain Way (trail).

0739P 3.8mi 48° 45.387'N 121° 02.166'W 2080' Big Beaver Trail X Pierce Mountain Way (Trail)

Keep working northwest on a light downhill grade for another 1.4 miles to drop into a ravine as we follow the trail toward the lake. In another 0.6 miles there is a second ravine, and on the other side, we begin a series of switchbacks to take us down to Big Beaver Creek. Just prior to crossing the creek on a steel footbridge, there is a side trail that would take you east to the lake and Pumpkin Camp. This is a hiker-only camp with a small beach and the tent sites tucked back in the forest along the Big Beaver Creek inlet.[GT]

0742P 2.9mi 48° 46.497'N 121° 03.984'W 1610' Big Beaver Trail @ Big Beaver Creek

After crossing the creek on a footbridge, there is a trail junction. At the junction you can turn east toward the lake to reach Big Beaver Camp in 0.3 miles. This camp has 12 sites and a vault toilet. Our primary PNT route now turns west to follow the Big Beaver Trail up the creek. In about 3.0 miles after the bridge we enter one of finest stands of old growth red cedars in North America. Some of the cedars are 15 feet in diameter and well over 1,000 years old. The creek always flows and the mosquitoes always bite in this area.

In 4.9 miles from the bridge the trail comes to 39-Mile camp, which has 4 tent sites and a pit toilet. There is also a horse campsite nearby. We keep continuing west upstream on the Big Beaver Trail to come to the Ten Mile Camp in just about another 0.7 miles. Ten Mile Camp is also divided into two sections, one for hikers and one for stock. Our next waypoint is in 0.8 miles up the trail at the North Cascades National Park boundary.

0748P 6.4mi 48° 48.670'N 121° 10.254'W 1980' Big Beaver Trail @ North Cascades National Park Boundary

There is just a standard square post marking the park border.[50] As we hike in the North Cascades National Park be prepared to be a little disappointed by having only a few opportunities for a good view.

> *"You are almost always in a valley with very, very few views of the absolutely incredible mountains around. The old growth cedars and hemlocks are gorgeous but I wanted to be higher in the mountains. The two passes are short lived but amazing. ... I think the North Cascades is more of a climbing/mountaineering park than a hiking park, with most mountains above the tree line sheer rock and the glaciers coming down so low there aren't a lot of good places to build continuous trails."[BT]*

In another 0.75 miles we may get a view up McMillan Creek to the southwest and the McMillan spires, named after a mountain man who settled here in the 1880s.[16] The trail now turns northwest and climbs for 560' elevation gain over the next 1.9 miles to reach Luna Camp. Luna, like other trail camps has four sites and a pit toilet. Keep working uphill to the northwest for another 3.4 miles to reach the old, well-used Beaver Pass shelter, which is not an ideal camp. This three-sided shelter was constructed in 1938 and inherited by the NPS; it is for emergency use only.

0755P 6.6mi 48° 52.454'N 121° 14.920'W 3640' Big Beaver Trail @ Beaver Pass Shelter

The Beaver Pass Camp is just past the shelter with its four sites and a pit toilet. After the camp the trail is relatively level for the next 0.5 miles where it then begins to descend down into the Little Beaver Valley. At first the descent is easy but in another 0.5 miles there is a series of very tight, sharp switchbacks that drop you down over 800' elevation loss in 1.3 trail miles.

The entrance to the Stillwell Camp is found at the final switchback and is clearly signed with a post. Like the other North Cascade NP camps it has four sites, a pit toilet, and fire ring. Here we have a choice to take a shortcut north to the Little Beaver Trail by taking the trail towards the Stillwell Camp. East of the hiker camp is the horse camp. From here, make your way to the creek and cross it on a series of logs. Once on the opposite side we find the Little Beaver Trail, where head north to continue towards Whatcom Pass. (If heading eastbound, the routing across the creek into the Stillwell Camp is not at all obvious.)[CN]

Previously there has been discussion here and in trail blogs about the aforementioned shortcut down to Stillwell Camp and across the creeks to Little Beaver Trail. In 2017, any "shortcut" was essentially a bushwhack. The primary PNT is a lovely easy walk. All the PNT trails in North Cascades National Park were cleared and open.[CN]

0758P 3.2mi 48° 53.807'N 121° 15.149'W 2400' Big Beaver Trail X Little Beaver Trail

In 2017 the Little Beaver Trail was reported to be clear and in good shape.[49] Follow the Little Beaver Trail west and southwest for the next 6.1 miles to Whatcom Pass as it climbs up a rugged narrow valley made by a river etched into the heart of the North Cascades.[KC]

We keep to the north side of Little Beaver Creek and keep slowly climbing. The next camp is Twin Rocks, about 2.3 miles west of Stillwell. It has six sites, a pit toilet and fire ring, as well as a stock camp nearby.

In 2017 the trails through NCNP were reported to be in good shape.[ES] Be sure to fill up on water from Little Beaver Creek, about 1.5 miles past Twin Rocks Camp, as it may be our last chance for a while. The trail starts to climb the ridge away from the creek up into a very rugged valley. Just for a warm up the trail climbs 660' in the next 0.8 miles into our next waypoint.

0763P 5.6mi 48° 52.319'N 121° 21.173'W 3710' Little Beaver Trail @ Climb to Whatcom Pass

Our climb to Whatcom Pass is one of the toughest on the entire PNT with a 1700' elevation gain in about 1.0 trail miles to reach Whatcom Pass. The climb takes you to the headwaters of Little Beaver Creek on many tight switchbacks. While on the climb be sure to look west to the Whatcom Glacier and south to the massive Challenger Glacier. At the top enjoy some of the very best views of the PNT at Whatcom Pass.

0764P 1.0mi 48° 52.536'N 121° 21.816'W 5240' Little Beaver Trail X Brush Creek Trail @ Whatcom Pass

There is also an unofficial side trail at the pass that leads south to climb the Whatcom Glacier, but unless you're prepared with the proper equipment, this is probably not a good idea. Just 0.1 miles south on this trail takes you to a spectacular stealth campsite.[49]

Leaving the pass we head west downhill on the Brush Creek Trail, which will take us 5.4 miles to the northwest and to the Chilliwack River. The Whatcom Pass Camp is not right at the pass, but about 0.3 miles down the west slope after crossing a small creek where the spur trail to the camp is found. One site has a good view and all are on a first-come first-serve basis.[GT] Bears are seen frequently in this area and a good tree to hang your food is difficult to find, therefore, a bear canister is strongly recommended by the park service, but not required.

The Bush Creek Trail has been reported to be passable, with a new bridge and trail maintenance in 2014.[DV] In 1.5 miles we drop down about 1,000' as the trail descends on the south side of the ridge to cross Tapto Creek. We press on downhill along the ridge for another 1.4 mile to reach Graybeal Camp.

Graybeal is another camp with four sites, pit toilet, and fire ring. There is an associated stock camp nearby, with a good stream. In 2015, hikers reported blowdowns right in the camp.[48] We have descended almost 2,000' from the pass but still have a ways to go to get down to the river valley. From Graybeal the trail heads almost due north along the east side of Brush creek and fortunately begins to level nicely into our next waypoint.

0769P 5.9mi 48° 54.391'N 121° 25.298'W 2790' Brush Creek Trail X Chilliwack Trail

Note that some maps may indicate a trail junction with the Hannegan Trail, but that trail junction is further west on the PNT. Although not an official park trail camp, there is a pretty good place to spend the night near this trail junction.

The Chilliwack Trail takes us northwest and slightly downhill as it rounds back to the southwest and closer to the Chilliwack River. In about 0.75 miles, as you approach the river, the trail splits with the horse ford going west, while our trail keeps working south to the cable car crossing.

0770P 1.2mi 48° 54.254'N 121° 26.327'W 2540' Chilliwack Trail @ Cable Car Crossing

The cable car holds two people with a maximum weight of 500 pounds.[50] Use the cable to pull the basket over the Chilliwack River. After crossing the river, we keep hiking southwest, now on the west side of the river. In about 0.7 miles past the cable car, the trail takes us close to U.S. Cabin. This "cabin" is really a trail camp with the standard four sites, pit toilet, fire pit and stock camp nearby.

After U.S. Cabin the trail begins to climb toward Hannegan Pass, but first we get to the Copper Creek Camp in a little over 2.4 miles. Copper Creek Camp has sites on both sides of the creek and is a typical park trail camp with a pit toilet and fire ring. Right after the camp the trail turns northwest briefly and begins to climb to Hannegan Pass. Keep working up to the pass for another 2.3 miles and climbing about 1300' elevation gain to reach Boundary Camp and the junction with the Copper Ridge Trail.

0776P 5.6mi 48° 53.270'N 121° 31.438'W 4460' Chilliwack River Trail X Copper Ridge Trail @ Boundary Camp

The Copper Ridge Trail joins our trail coming down from the ridge to the northeast. The Boundary Camp has four sites, pit toilet, and bear box for food storage. No fires are permitted here. If you have time, and the inclination, a good side hike is to follow the Copper Ridge Trail east, climbing about 1000' in 1.5 miles. From here you can see south to the glacier on the north side of Ruth Mountain.

Just west of Boundary Camp we leave the North Cascades National Park and enter the Mount Baker Wilderness, also where no campfires are permitted.

Now pushing upward we go another 1.2 miles and keep climbing 630' elevation gain to reach the Hannegan Pass Trail and our next waypoint.

0777P 1.2mi 48° 52.974'N 121° 32.051'W 5080' Chilliwack River Trail X Hannegan Pass Trail 674 (aka Ruth Creek Trail)

At Hannegan Pass there is good trail campsite but not a lot of protection from the wind. There are also two short spur trails, one north Trail 674.1 which takes you up about 1000' vertical in 1.0 miles to the summit of Hannegan Peak 6197'. It is worth the climb for more incredible views—especially at sunrise![49] "Spectacular views. You'd be crazy to miss this side hike unless you were doing the Copper Butte route."[80]

From the pass, there is another mountaineering trail to the south leading to the top of the 5930' knob. Again, with better views than we might see from the pass. Either one is recommended and well worth the climb because they are "stupendous and highly recommended if the weather is clear."[GT]

From the pass follow the Hannegan Trail to the west as it zigzags down about 480' over the next 0.6 miles. Here it turns northwest along the ridge on the west side of Hannegan Peak, also staying north of Ruth Creek. This is one of the most enjoyable parts of the Baker Wilderness.[BT] The trail keeps descending along the ridge over the next 0.9 miles to settle around the 4000' contour. With luck the skies will be clear and you will see the glaciers to the southwest that come down from Nooksack Ridge and Mount Sefrit and the many waterfalls.

After a very brief respite on the level trail, we keep descending to reach our next waypoint at the trailhead on Ruth Creek Road and the Hannegan Campground, in a total of 4.0 miles from the pass.

0781P 4.0mi 48° 54.614'N 121° 35.498'W 3120' Trail 674 X Hannigan Pass Road (Road 32) - Hannegan Shelter Trail Camp

At the trailhead we exit the Mount Baker Wilderness and enter the Snoqualmie National Forest. The Hannegan Camp at the trailhead has four dispersed campsites with fire rings and picnic tables and a day-use shelter. Next we road walk west on the well-used FR32 through the steep valley, still staying on the north side of Ruth Creek. FR32 descends gently through thick forest for 4.0 miles to then cross Forest Road 34, which comes in from the southeast. We continue on FR32 for another 1.3 miles to our next waypoint at the junction with the Mount Baker Highway.

0787P 5.3mi 48° 54.387'N 121° 41.616'W 2030' Road 32 X Mount Baker Highway (State Route 542)

Resupply: About 13 miles west is the very small hamlet of Glacier, with several motels/chalets and Grahams Restaurant, with a somewhat expensive general store. There is also a post office for a mail drop. The best part of this little town is the "Chair 9" Restaurant. This pizza, steak, burger and beer place is that about a mile east, back towards the trail.[BT] The new Heather Meadows Café at mile marker 55 also gets good reviews for their fresh local food. Hitchhiking to town is an option.

But we're following the PNT, road walking along the SR542 to the south, and of course, uphill. The NFS Silver Fir Campground is off the access road about 0.2 miles after the bridge. It has 20 tent/trailer sites of which 13 can be reserved. The fee is $16 per night. Some hikers report, however, that there is a hollow giant red cedar to sleep in.

Be careful hiking the Mount Baker Highway. It is often busy with tourists looking at the scenery while driving and not looking around the curves. There is essentially little or no shoulder. Catch a ride if you can for safety.[ES] We climb 2.6 miles to reach Bagley Creek gaining 700' elevation. Over the next 5.3 miles the road twists every direction as it climbs up toward the Mount Baker ski area. Fun fact: this ski area received the world's greatest amount of seasonal snowfall in 1998-99 measured at 95 feet!

About 2.8 miles past Bagley Creek we come to the beginning of the ski lifts and a road to the east leading to the White Salmon Ski Lodge (closed in summer). Keep climbing southwest for another 2.1 miles on the highway to reach Picture Lake. Get your camera out. With an afternoon sun at your back and calm winds, you might capture a mirror image, "award winning" picture, of Mount Shuksan's reflection on the lake.

0794P 7.3mi 48° 51.976'N 121° 40.607'W 4140' Mount Baker Highway @ Picture Lake

It's time to get off the highway and away from the tourist traffic. After Picture Lake we have a short road walk to the Baker Ski Lodge, and to the south end of the parking lot.

0795P 0.7mi 48° 51.680'N 121° 40.955'W 4270' Wild Goose Trailhead

Here we find the Wild Goose Trail that takes us south, climbing for another 1.0 miles to our next waypoint and the junction with the Lake Ann Trail 600.

About a half mile along the trail we pass through a picnic area and a parking lot for the visitor's center. The visitor center near the top has no running water but gives out bottled water for a "donation".[GT] Find the Wild Goose Trail again on the south side of the visitor's center, and in another 0.5 miles we gain the final 320' of elevation to the trail junction.

0796P 1.1mi 48° 50.999'N 121° 41.160'W 4760' Wild Goose Trail X Lake Ann Trail 600

Most worthy side trip: stay on the Wild Goose Trail paved pathway for less than 15 minutes. About 1.0 miles beyond the Lake Ann trailhead is the final parking lot and view area. This spot is called "Artists Point" and a 2017 thru-hiker exclaimed, "This is not to be missed under any circumstances!" If you go directly down TR600 you'll miss these views.[ES]

Artist Point is the top competitor for best viewpoint in [Washington] state. The beautifully shaped Mount Shuksan is the star of the area, with a gorgeous summit pyramid and several impressive glaciers. Mount Baker dominates the skyline in the southwest. Artist Point also is a great viewpoint for the Cascades, with sweeping views of the valley of Baker Lake and in the far distance peaks like Whitehorse Mountain, Three Fingers, Sloan Peak and White Chuck Mountain. Immediately from the trailhead beautiful peaks in the north are visible, such as American Border Peak, Mount Larrabee, and Goat Mountain.[75]

Back to our PNT primary route. The trailhead for TR600 is at the second to last parking lot/view point on the Mount Baker Highway. The trail starts downhill to the east and circles around to the south on switchbacks dropping us down about 600' in the first 0.9 miles. The descent continues more slowly over the next 1.4 miles as we reach our waypoint at the junction with the Swift Creek Trail 607.

0798P 2.4mi 48° 50.022'N 121° 39.449'W 3930' Lake Ann Trail 600 X Swift Creek Trail 607

There is a good trail sign here with a PNT insignia[MS] but check carefully as the sign is reported to point 45° off in the wrong direction.[DV] Go about 10 yards downstream across a grassy area. Following TR607 southwest we begin climb along the ridge to rise above the south side of Swift Creek to reach a ravine in 0.3 miles. From here TR607 comes back downhill on a series of short switchbacks. The tread itself, though easy to follow, is at times narrow and has suffered some erosion.[GT]

About 2.0 miles past the trail junction TR607 turns south down the Swift Creek valley as the stream flows toward Baker Lake. We're hiking, however, well above Swift Creek at around the 3300' contour. This is a sharp 'V' valley with the trail tacked like a ribbon on the steep ridge.[KC] Our next waypoint is where the trail crosses a large crevice with glacier runoff creek from the snowfields above us to the east. In August 2013 the water was waist deep[KC] but in 2015 there was almost no water.[48]

0801P 3.0mi 48° 48.761'N 121° 41.166'W 3250' Swift Creek Trail 607 @ Large Crevice and Stream

After crossing the crevice TR607 turns west briefly downhill and into a turn to the south to parallel Swift Creek just above the 3000' contour, about 700' above the creek. Next we enter the steep ridge (almost canyon wall) following it downhill to our next waypoint where we ford the creek.

0804P 2.5mi 48° 47.144'N 121° 40.479'W 1620' Swift Creek Trail 607 @ Swift Creek Ford

At our waypoint TR607 transitions to the west side of the creek. Caution is advised because the creek holds to its namesake with a swift current in thigh-deep water.[GT] In 2015, a very dry year, the creek was only knee deep.[50] An inch of rain in the mountains can swell the creek very quickly.

There may have been a bridge at one time, but for now we must get wet. Some hikers have found spots to cross either up or downstream and then bushwhacked to the trail. Climb the west bank and pick up the trail south and downhill. In 1.6 miles TR607 crosses a creek again, this time on logs with a hand cable. The trail now levels for the next 0.7 miles to reach our next waypoint at the intersection with Forest Road 1144.

0806P 2.2mi 48° 45.739'N 121° 40.111'W 1360' Swift Creek Trail 607 X Forest Road 1144

The primary PNT route follows FR1144, a decommissioned road / trail, south to Baker Lake and then north around the lake, and back down the east side. Before we return to the PNT, note that the Baker Hot Spring is near this waypoint. Follow FR1144 north 0.3 miles to a parking area, and then follow the trail southwest another 0.3 miles. At one time this was a pristine spot but the NFS no longer maintains it. The water is a little less than 100°F and not much more than 2 feet deep.

Back to the PNT. FR1144 is pretty much an extension of the Swift Creek Trail 607 which keeps south downhill 1.6 miles to a short spur trail. The spur trail leads southeast to old unofficial camp area. We continue south for another 1.1 miles to reach our next waypoint at the intersection with Baker Lake Road - Forest Road 11. Just prior to Baker Lake Road you will find the NFS Park Creek Campground. This campground has 12 tent/trailer sites of which 6 can be reserved, and vault toilets. There is a $12 fee.

0809P 2.9mi 48° 43.985'N 121° 39.798'W 870' Forest Road 1144 X Baker Lake Road (Road 11)

Straight across the intersection, and 0.4 miles down toward the lake, you can find the newly reopened NFS Swift Creek Campground, formerly the Baker Lake Resort. There are 45 sites and beachside cold water outdoor showers. The fee is $18 per night, or $5 for day use only. In previous years there was a small store here, but it was not open in 2015.[49]

Back to the road, we turn east on the paved FR11, and along the way find a number of unofficial camps between the road and the shoreline, albeit very close to the road with dust and road noise.[ES] Hike 3.3 miles to cross Forest Road 1152. If we turned southeast on FR1152, it would take us in 0.3 miles to the lake and the Shannon Creek Campground. This camp has 17 sites, vault toilets and drinking water.

We keep hiking along FR11 to the east end of Baker Lake, in about another 2.6 miles. This takes us to trailhead for the Baker River Trail 606.

0815P 6.2mi 48° 45.029'N 121° 33.315'W 770' Forest Road 11 X Baker Lake Trail 606

The trailhead is in a large parking area with a vault toilet. TR606 and the East Bank Trail 610 share a common path for about 0.6 miles, going northeast along the bank of the Baker River. At this waypoint they split, with TR606 headed north while the primary PNT route takes TR610 east across the bridge.

0815.3P 0.5mi 48° 45.357'N 121° 32.895'W 830' Trail 606 X East Bank Trail 610 (Baker Lake Trail 610)

The trail for many years was known as the East Bank Trail, but it may have been confused with the trail of the same name on Ross Lake. You may see a trailhead sign that shows it as the "Baker Lake South Trail 610." Turn east where the trail forks from TR606 to cross the amazing 240+ foot long suspension bridge. Once over the bridge the trail turns south through a washout area, where hopefully the trail repairs are still in place. The old growth cedars in this area provide good cover on the relatively level trail.

In 3.7 miles pass the campground of the same name, then we cross the wood bridge over Noisy Creek. This is probably the best camp on the east side of Baker Lake.[51] While on the bridge you will get a great view of the backside of Mount Shuksan to the north. At this point TR610 is pointed almost due west and stays around 100' above the lake shoreline. Keeping west we next cross Silver Creek in 1.4 miles past Noisy Creek. Still west for another 1.5 miles the trail rounds the elbow of Baker Lake to turn due south.

In a little less than 2.5 miles after turning south we come to the spur trail that leads us to the Maple Grove primitive trail camp with six tent sites. But, we keep south on TR610, where in another 1.8 miles we find the spur trail to the Anderson Point campsites. This camp sits on the east bank of Baker Lake with exceptional views of Mount Baker. Next, we cross Anderson Creek on a single log and finish TR610, climbing slightly for the next 1.5 miles into our next waypoint, the south trailhead on Forest Road 1107.

0827P 12.1mi 48° 38.735'N 121° 40.479'W 970' Trail 610 X Forest Road 1107

We turn west and downhill from the trailhead on FR1107 to go 0.75 miles to the junction with the Baker River Road (Road 1106).

0828P 0.8mi 48° 38.607'N 121° 41.245'W 740' Forest Road 1107 X Baker River Road FR1106

Note: Baker River Road is an unofficial alternate route to the town of Concrete, which is 9.8 miles to the south. This road has less vehicle traffic than Baker Lake Road, which we meet at our next waypoint.

Back on the primary route we turn north to cross the Upper Baker Dam just under 0.4 miles on the single lane road, about 250' above the outlet to our west.

After the dam the road drops downhill passing the RV Kulshan Campground, and then slightly uphill to our next waypoint.

0829P 1.7mi 48° 39.632'N 121° 42.384'W 870' Forest Road 1106 X East Bank Road

Rather than staying straight ahead on the East Bank Road, the PNT turns left onto an abandoned forest road to get to Baker Lake Road quicker. We head west for only 0.3 miles, perhaps crossing the creek on a "bushwhack." If you're headed to the town of Concrete for resupply, you may want to take this shortcut.

0830P 0.3mi 48° 39.531'N 121° 42.783'W 860' Abandoned road X Baker Lake Road (Road 11)

Resupply: The town of Concrete is about 11 miles south; first going 7 miles on the Baker Lake Road, and then turning on Burpee Hill Road to State Route 20. The Big Apple food store and pizza place are about a mile west on SR20. This is not a pleasant road walk to say the least.

Decision Time. Some thru-hikers hike the "Cascade Trail Super Cutoff" route west from Concrete into Sedro-Woolley, but we'll stick to the primary PNT route for our discussion. This rail-trail alternate route is described at the end of this section.

Back to our primary PNT route which now takes us to the south side of Mount Baker. But before we begin, here is a comment about this route from a 2012 hiker:

> *"It was an 8 mile slog up gravel roads and around the other side had some rough and boring trail, but the few miles of alpine right in front of Baker were amazing. I had the best campsite of the PNT trip at the top of the switchbacks in the alpine (stealth site but hidden from view). I'd highly recommend timing it so you camp here; and then this 30 mile loop would be worth it. Otherwise, it was too forested for me."[BT]*

We begin by turning north and uphill on the paved Baker Lake Road – RD 11 for 0.6 miles to find the Forest Road 1114.

0831P 0.6mi 48° 40.008'N 121° 43.096'W 740' Baker Lake Road X Forest Road 1114

There is an unmarked gate at the entrance of this old forest road. Climb north then west on FR1114 gaining 800' elevation over the 1.5 miles to reach our next waypoint, the intersection with Forest Road 12, which is gated and signed.[MS]

0832P 1.3mi 48° 40.421'N 121° 44.130'W 1550' Forest Road 1114 X Forest Road 12

We turn right to hike west, climbing FR12 for 1.3 miles, gaining 360' elevation. Our next waypoint is at the intersection with Forest Road 13.

0833P 1.3mi 48° 40.918'N 121° 45.582'W 1910' Forest Road 12 X Forest Road 13

FR13 takes us up higher toward Mount Baker, climbing on major switchbacks for 2.1 miles, gaining another 710' in elevation. Our next waypoint is an unnamed forest road in the middle of another switchback 'U-turn'.

0835P 2.1mi 48° 41.293'N 121° 45.423'W 2620' Forest Road 13 X Old Forest Road

We keep hiking west on FR13 and uphill for another 3.1 miles to the end of the road and to the trailhead for the Park Butte Trail 603. Fortunately, this road walk has a lesser uphill grade, but we still gain another 750' in elevation. There are two campsites just before you reach the trailhead.[50]

0838P 3.1mi 48° 42.421'N 121° 48.765'W 3370' Forest Road 13 X Park Butte Trail 603 (best water at TH creek)

TR603 is a popular trail for hikers, backpackers and climbers in the summer months as it leads along the Easton Glacier to the climbing routes, and through Schreiber's Meadow. The NFS states that hikers must use the designated campsites, which are all north of the PNT. The meadow provides waist-high heather and huckleberries.[18]

TR603 enters the forest from the trailhead at the west side of the parking area. The best water for a while is at the creek under the bridge. If you plan to spend the night at Park Butte it is best to fill up here.[ES] The trail drops down to cross the creek and then begins its slow climb through the meadow. There are no official NFS campsites in the meadow.

Traversing the meadow area in 0.9 miles from the trailhead, TR603 comes to a rocky avalanche area. We cross the rocks and boulders on a northwest heading to begin a series of switchbacks in 0.6 miles. This "stairway" takes us up 600' elevation in 0.6 miles into the Upper Morowitz Meadow. Near the top of the switchbacks there is a distinctive "U-turn" in the trail at our next waypoint and the junction with the Scott Paul Trail 603.1.

0840P 2.1mi 48° 43.031'N 121° 50.385'W 4440' Trail 603 X Scott Paul Trail 603.1

One hiker reported that hidden "stealth" trail camps can be found up TR603.1 at the top of the switchbacks.[BT] TR603.1 leads north up a glacier carved valley to the Easton Glacier. Our primary PNT route TR603, however, turns briefly west and then northwest, climbing into the Morowitz Meadow. Here we should find some exceptional views of the Easton Glacier above us, and of the year-round snow on the summit of Mount Baker about 3.5 miles distant. Our next waypoint is a short 0.4 miles from the junction with TR603.1

0841P 0.4mi 48° 43.130'N 121° 50.385'W 4660' Trail 603 X Railroad Grade Trail 603.2

At this 'Y' trail junction TR603.2 also leads due north (right) about 0.4 miles and into the snowfield where climbers depart to climb up the Easton Glacier. This is considered a moderate climb, but you should have some glacier climbing experience and proper equipment to ascend Easton Glacier. The primary PNT route keeps us on TR603, the left portion of the 'Y,' which takes us in 0.35 miles to our next waypoint and trail junction.

0841.2P 0.4mi 48° 43.202'N 121° 50.839'W 4870' Trail 603 X Bell Pass Trail 603.3

TR603, which we have been following, turns southwest to terminate at the summit of Park Butte in 0.9 miles. Here's one hiker's description of the Park Butte Lookout:

> *"This is a 1 mile detour off route, but if camping in the area, the lookout tower is first come first serve. To spend the night there offers the most AMAZING views with the surrounding mountains,, glaciers, and valleys that seem close enough to touch. When the sun sets the clouds come up to the overlook so you feel like your cabin is floating in an orange cloud heaven. It was the most beautiful night and morning of my life that I experienced in that cabin. I exaggerate not. That would become a top highlight of anyone's trip. 100% highly recommended."*[31]

If you have your heart set on staying here overnight, plan on arriving early as there is stiff competition for it. If it is full, there are a few other campsites nearby.[51]

Back to the PNT primary route. At this trail junction we are staring into the rock face of Cathedral Crag with the choice of two routes around it. Here we have to differ from the maps that show a trail circling the north side of Cathedral Crag. The Bell Pass Trail to the south is the only option. You could bushwhack around the north side, but you are discouraged from doing so by the signs on the trail asking you to protect sensitive vegitations.[50]

The primary PNT route goes around to the south side of Cathedral Crag, on TR603.3, I presume, and climbs up through a treeless dry creek ravine for only about 0.3 miles. TR603.3 next turns west in a small saddle to drop us down over 400' in 0.4 miles. Here it turns back southwest and downhill for 0.25 miles. TR603.3 crosses the Ridley Creek Trail 696 at the NFS shelter.

0842P 0.8mi 48° 43.355'N 121° 51.241'W 4420' Trail 603.3 X Ridley Creek Trail 696 @ Mazama Park Shelter

Camping is permitted in the area of the shelter. We continue southwest descending on TR603.3 for 0.4 miles where the trail enters the Baker Wilderness on the west face of Park Butte. The trail was in good shape in 2015[51] and keeps to a slow descent for the next 2.0 miles and into our next waypoint at Bell Pass.

0845P 2.5mi 48° 42.475'N 121° 53.385'W 4000' Trail 603.3 @ Bell Pass

At the pass TR603.3 transitions from the western to the eastern slope, continuing to descend along the ridge above Forest Road 12 through fairly dense forest. In just over 1.4 miles the trail descends almost 850'. Here the road/trail heads west for 0.3 miles to parallel FR12. FR12 is officially closed to vehicle traffic here. Note: An alternative route would be to hike east, then south on

FR12, road walking for about 3.4 miles to rejoin the primary PNT route at the Pioneer Horse Camp described below.

0846P 1.9mi 48° 41.488'N 121° 54.671'W 3110' Bell Pass Trail 603.3 X Forest Road 12

The trail picks up again at the end of the road, where we follow the sign to Elbow Lake. Hike TR603.3 north along the slope of the ridge, climbing for an estimated 0.35 miles to then turn west to cross the dry creek. On the other side we intersect the Elbow Lake Trail 697, where there is a trail sign that points us toward Pioneer Camp.

0847P 0.5mi 48° 41.760'N 121° 54.820'W 3200' Trail 603.3 X Elbow Lake Trail 697

TR697 runs north-south. About 1.0 mile to the north are Lake Doreen and Elbow Lake. Our primary PNT route turns south, as we follow this horse trail, and in just under 0.5 miles we begin a steep descent on switchbacks down the ridge. This leads us to the beginnings of the South Fork Nooksack River, about 0.8 miles downhill. Next we follow TR697, not crossing the river, along the north bank. TR697 takes us southeast downhill along the east side of the river to the Pioneer Horse Camp in about 1.0 miles. There might be some trail number confusion here. The NFS describes the trail to Pioneer Horse Camp on the east side of the Nooksack River as TR697, whereas the maps show it as TR602.

0849P 2.0mi 48° 40.812'N 121° 53.843'W 2180' Trail 697 X South Fork Nooksack Trail 602 @ Pioneer Horse Camp (a parking lot)

Don't get excited over this camp; it is only a horse trailer parking lot with access to FR12. There is no toilet or campsite. In 2018 it was reported that there is a new, rebuilt trail to walk until Wanlick Creek in 2.9 miles.[80]
The NFS relocated TR602 higher on the slope away from the river.

0851P 2.6mi 48° 39.032'N 121° 52.439'W 2040' South Fork Nooksack Trail 602 X Forest Road 20

TR602 continues south on the east bank of the river to cross Wanlick Creek in 0.25 miles. From here things get tough. In 2018, the trail required some guesswork here.[80] Bushwhack, if required, south and downhill for about 0.4 miles to begin to pick up remnants of the old Mainline Road.[51] Keep following the road / trail south to our next waypoint in another 0.4 miles. Route finding is easy once on RD300 even though it is bushy at times.

0852P 1.0mi 48° 38.216'N 121° 52.412'W 1850' Trail 602 X Crown Pacific Mainline Road (Road 300)

To the west at this junction, the road crosses the South Fork Nooksack River, but sometime after 2009 the bridge washed out. We'll stick to the primary PNT route, continuing south on the unmaintained FR300, pushing through more bushes and alders until you reach a canyon with a possible stream 1.0 miles ahead.[51] Follow the road on a fairly level grade for 2.8 miles. There is evidence along the way of the old forested clear cut areas. As we approach our next waypoint, about 0.25 miles prior, look for the road to open into a massive new clear cut uphill on the eastern slope.

0855P 2.6mi 48° 36.540'N 121° 53.519'W 1870' Forest Road 300 X Forest Road 340

FR300 goes straight west, while our PNT route turns south and uphill on the signed FR340 through the clear cut. Climb for 0.75 miles to where the road turns back to the east for another 0.9 miles. We follow the road around to the south again to a road junction and the Huckleberry Trail. FR340 ends at an old road that veers and climbs southeast, while we embark on the new Huckleberry Trail.

Note: It appears that the Huckleberry Trail is now open and signed. If so, it begins 0.2 miles after FR301 turns east, negating the need for the longer 1.6 mile loop east.

0857P 0.8mi 48° 35.953'N 121° 53.831'W 2370' Forest Road 340 X Huckleberry Trail

Huckleberry Trail may have a new trailhead sign and/or be flagged. It is only about 0.5 miles long as it traverses along the north side of the ridge climbing through thick forest. The trail ends in a small clearing at the junction with Forest Road 317.

0858P 0.6mi 48° 35.662'N 121° 53.774'W 2820' Huckleberry Trail X Forest Road 317

The old forest road could in fact now continue the Huckleberry Trail. FR317 turns south and does not appear to be well used as it likely has some overgrowth on it. It looks more like a trail than a road. Follow it south climbing on a reasonable grade up the ridge for 0.2 miles where it turns east then rounds southeast. From here it is only 0.4 miles to our next waypoint at the intersection with Forest Road 310.

0859P 0.7mi 48° 35.245'N 121° 53.205'W 2980' Forest Road 317 X Forest Road 313

We turn west on FR313, a wide gravel road, on a slight downhill grade. In about 0.4 miles we break out into a clear cut area. We keep west on a slight downhill grade through the clear cut for the next 1.8 miles to our next waypoint at the junction with an old logging road

0861P 2.2mi 48° 35.299'N 121° 55.695'W 2630' Forest Road 313 X Logging Road

At this waypoint turn right for 30 yards to continue on FR313 to the west. This is the lesser used road. We follow this road/trail only a short distance into our next waypoint.

0861A 0.5mi 48° 35.167'N 121° 56.123'W 2870' Forest Road 313 X Spur Road to the Les Hilde Trail

Decision time. If we continue straight southwest in 0.15 miles we find the trailhead for the Les Hilde Trailhead at the end of the road. This trail is 5.4 miles long and shortcuts the primary PNT loop to the top of Mount Josephine. The alternate route is described at the end of this section.

Sticking to the primary PNT route we turn north staying with FR313 for 0.4 miles, following the edge of the clear cut to where the road turns west again. Here the road has forest on both sides as we progress west to the East Josephine Ridge Trail at our next waypoint. Just prior to the trailhead, to our south is the Upper Josephine Lake. There's a faint and steep but short trail down to upper Josephine Lake about 30 yards prior to our next waypoint. The lake sits about 70' below the road. There is no evidence of a camp near the lake.[GT]

0862P 0.9mi 48° 35.348'N 121° 56.732'W 3120' Forest Road 313 X East Josephine Ridge Trail

There is a sign where the trail starts, as we head west on the East Josephine Ridge Trail for just under 0.5 miles on the old road bed. The trail continues for another 0.5 miles up the ridge toward Mount Josephine. We follow the trail along the crest of the ridge to reach the summit in another 0.2 miles and our next waypoint.

0863P 1.0mi 48° 35.297'N 121° 57.709'W 3957' East Josephine Ridge Trail X Mount Josephine Truck Trail (MJTT)

From the Mount Josephine summit we look to the north to see Mount Baker dominating the skyline, but unfortunately there are some trees that have grown up blocking some of the view.[GT] To our south is the sheer cliff of the south wall of the mountain, and the Skagit River valley below.

We descend on the MJTT as it winds down the north side of Mount Josephine for 1.3 miles before turning to the southwest. The "trail" on this old road is easy to follow as it continues to descend 1000' into our next waypoint. About 1.6 miles into our descent the road opens into the clear cut area on the west side of the road. Shortly thereafter the MJTT turns west and into three road crossings, all within 0.1 miles of each other. The primary PNT route bypasses these to keep straight west, but the second road crossing is our next waypoint. If we had gone north on the bad-weather alternate FR310 mentioned above, we would return to the primary PNT route here.

0865P 2.0mi 48° 35.239'N 121° 58.790'W 2740' Mount Josephine Truck Trail X Forest Road 310

In another 0.6 miles the trail turns south then west in a zigzag through a clear cut, continuing to descend through more patches of clear cut on both the north and south side. After about 1.5 miles west, on a relatively straight stretch, there will be three major switchbacks before the road turns southeast as it leads into our next waypoint at a triangle road intersection.

0869P 4.1mi 48° 34.075'N 122° 00.711'W 1500' Mount Josephine Truck Trail X Unnamed Forest Road

The primary PNT route keeps to the road southeast to pick up a new trail. The new route is in the Washington State Harry Osborne Forest, and most of the trails are maintained by the Skagit Country Backcountry Horseman. In 2015 the PNT Association with the DNR installed "confidence" signage along the PNT route with PNT stickers. This should make the navigation easier and the hiking here more enjoyable.

At this triangle road junction, bear left (east) for 150 yards to find another road junction, where you bear right (southeast). Follow the road for 0.5 miles east downhill to cross a DNR forest road (truck tracks) coming in from the north. This is our waypoint. If you find yourself hiking around a turn directly east, you've missed the waypoint.

0870.5P 0.5mi 48° 34.004'N 122° 00.051'W 1350' Mount Josephine Truck Trail X New – PNT

This new PNT trail descends southwest over the first 0.5 miles through thick forest. Here the trail turns more to the south to parallel a creek basin about 100' below us to the west. There are no reports of good access or water.

The trail follows the creek basin for another 1.0 miles into our next waypoint where we meet an old forest road.

0870.8P 1.5mi 48° 33.234'N 122° 00.930'W 610' PNT-New Trail X Old Forest Road

We turn southwest at the road, which is not much more than a pair of truck tracks. In only 0.15 miles the tracks turn directly south. About 100 yards after that we come to the trailhead for the Lost Creek Trail. As shown on the PNTA map, this trail is an alternate route northwest.

We, however, stick to the primary PNT route by keeping south on the truck tracks for another 160 yards to find the trailhead at our next waypoint for Mary's Trail. If you miss the trailhead you will find yourself at a 'T' road junction with the Crown Pacific Mainline Road.

0871P 0.3mi 48° 33.054'N 122° 01.057'W 510' Old Forest Road X Mary's Trail

Decision Time. If at this point you have had enough of trudging through timber company property, you can bail out of the trail and follow the road southeast for about 2.0 miles to find State Route 20 near the town of Hamilton to pick up the Cascade Trail alternate route, then to Sedro-Woolley for resupply.

Nevertheless, we'll describe that primary PNT trail route. Head west on the trail, which initially parallels the Mainline Road to our south, and then after about 0.3 miles, the trail turns northwest to climb about 100' elevation gain. After the short climb the trail wanders back down the hill south, finally returning back northwest. After a total of about 1.2 miles the trail crosses the Mainline Road at an intersection.

0872P 1.5mi 48° 33.343'N 122° 02.141'W 580' Mary's Trail X Crown Pacific Mainline Road X Forest Road

At this point the PNTA map shows a "shortcut" by sticking to the timber roads. Hike northwest on the Crown Pacific Mainline Road northwest for 0.5 miles and then west on Forest Road 110 for 0.4 miles to rejoin the primary route. FR110 is reported to be in good shape except for several washed out areas, which are easily crossed. FR110 has little traffic with places to camp on the many turnouts. Water was plentiful along the many small creeks on FR110. You can find a PNT sign and decal at the junction of FR110 and the Crown Pacific Mainline Road.[DV]

Back to our PNT primary route using road and trails. We cross the intersection and keep following the trail to the southwest on the old forest road. The road stays level and southwest for about 0.7 miles. We count the road crossings. At the third road intersection we turn due we on the more established road. Look for the 'Y' in 0.3 miles where we turn north until the end of the road. The trailhead for the Jones Creek Trail is our next waypoint.

0873P 1.3mi 48° 32.898'N 122° 03.063'W 490' Forest Road End X Jones Creek Trail

Look for the trail on the west side of the dead-end turnaround. The trail takes us southwest and immediately descend down toward Jones Creek. There are no reports of water. After crossing the creek, we are at our next waypoint.

0873.5P 0.3mi 48° 32.820'N 122° 03.309'W 360' Jones Creek Trail X Pipeline Trail

Pick up the trail north. In all likelihood this is the same trail we are hiking. The Pipeline Trail climbs slightly to turn back northeast after 0.2 miles, after to slightly climb north through a clearcut on a forest road until we reach 'Y' road junction.

0874P 0.5mi 48° 32.805'N 122° 03.483'W 480' Pipeline Trail X Unnamed Forest Road

Turning right (northeast) we keep on our gentle climb up to our next waypoint at the junction with CP Road 110.

0875P 1.1mi 48° 33.378'N 122° 02.914'W 570' Pipeline Trail X CP Road 110 - Trail Camp

Before we turn west on CP Road 110, note that hikers report a location for an unofficial trail camp down in the trees on the side of the creek, about 0.15 miles east of this waypoint.

We begin with a forest road that soon turns into two truck tracks. Washouts and slides have been reported on this section of the road in the past. Hiking west for 0.9 miles we can enjoy thick forest. After crossing the creek, with no reports of water, we enter a massive clearcut to the north side of the road. In another 0.4 miles the next waypoint is at a road junction still in the clearcut.

0876P 1.2mi 48° 33.000'N 122° 04.268'W 1140' CP Road X Scott Paper Road FR110

Continuing due west on FR110, in 1.8 miles there is a major creek crossing. Sorry, but there are no reports of water in the creek here either, but it is very possible. Keep west for another 0.8 miles where the road winds north and back east into our next waypoint.

0880P 3.2mi 48° 33.433'N 122° 06.939'W 2210' Scott Paper Road 110 X Forest Road 130

Next, we follow FR130 north for 0.8 miles, climbing to where it turns west to cross two creeks. There may be a small flow of water here in the summer. In 0.6 miles after the creeks, FR130 crosses signed Forest Road 138 coming from the north, followed shortly thereafter by the 'Y' intersection with an unnamed forest road. Bear right (northwest) at the slim 'Y' junction. Then 1.0 miles past FR134 we come to our next waypoint, crossing Forest Road 150.

0882P 2.5mi 48° 34.515'N 122° 08.695'W 3510' Forest Road 130 X Forest Road 170

FR150 runs north, but the PNT stays generally west on FR130 into a tricky intersection. A 2012 hike report states that, "Trail signage improves on latter part of Lyman Hill with PNT stickers and blazes."[GT] In 0.35 miles past FR150 there is a 'Y' with Forest Road 170, where we take the right fork northwest. In another 0.1 miles there is a second 'Y' at our next waypoint.

0883P 0.5mi 48° 34.398'N 122° 09.185'W 3590' Forest Road 170 X Forest Road 171

PNT Factoid: At this waypoint you are at the closest point on the PNT to the Pacific Northwest Trail Association headquarters. The PNTA is 4.0 miles southwest of this waypoint on the north side of Sedro-Woolley, but there is no direct or easy way to get there to visit.

At this second 'Y' intersection Forest Road 172 joins us from the north, but we bear left (northwest) on FR171. Follow this road, which is reportedly in need of trail maintenance, for 0.8 miles to find the intersection with an unnamed forest road that comes downhill from the west. Keep following the old road tracks of FR171 northwest on a relatively level grade about another mile on a newly built logging road to our next waypoint.

0884P 1.2mi 48° 35.191'N 122° 09.897'W 3650' Forest Road 171 X Old Forest Road

At this 'Y' road junction bear right (straight north) and uphill on the main road. The road straight ahead descends, which we do not want to take. In only 0.15 miles the road enters a very ugly clearcut area, but fortunately we exit it in quickly at another 'Y' junction. Keep straight this time following the main road due north. We enter the thick forest growth with a gentle climb into our next waypoint and a trail.

0885P 0.7mi 48° 35.879'N 122° 09.975'W 3970' Forest Road 171 X Gurdgieff Connector Trail (GCT)

The new logging road turns into the GCT; the trail is well marked as a future surveyed logging road and then with white blazes. The road gradually turns back into an old forest road. The GCT goes due north climbing to the top of the ridge. Hikers report that after about 0.8 miles or so the trail fades periodically, but if we keep following the top of the ridge, we will pick up the trail. The next waypoint is not far away but it will help us stay on track. This waypoint is where the trail ends at a 'U' turn in the gravel forest road.

0886P 1.0mi 48° 36.685'N 122° 09.801'W 4160' Gurdgieff Connector Trail (GCT) X Gravel Forest Road

At this junction the trail splits and you enter a heavily rocked road.[50] The left side, the primary PNT route, bears northwest and slightly downhill. Follow the maintained road downhill for 0.9 miles, losing 560' elevation to the point where the trail does a sharp 'U-turn" back to the southwest. Keep working downhill for another 0.7 miles, losing another 300' elevation, to where the road returns back to the north, then traverses a clearcut. In another 1.9 miles, after working generally north along the twisting downhill road, we will come to a quarry to the north side of the road.

0890P 3.5mi 48° 38.004'N 122° 10.948'W 2470' Gravel Forest Road X Road W1000

Keep to the road past the quarry, now designated W1000, for about 5.0 miles through five major switchbacks, dropping almost 2,000' elevation. Navigation here is easy but the road walk is tedious through old and new logging operations. Look for another quarry on the west side of the road about 1.1 miles past the last switchback. This will be 0.6 miles before the next waypoint.

0894P 4.9mi 48° 39.168'N 122° 12.278'W 280' Old Forest Road X Innis Creek Road X Wickersham Road

We face more roads ahead. On Wickersham Road turn west to reach Valley Highway – State Route 9. Wickersham is a small hamlet with only a small church and no stores for resupply. Note: SR9 is a dangerous road walk with a narrow shoulder.[48]

Turning south on the paved SR9 in 1.15 miles we look for a gravel turnoff with a pull through drive with an old section of split rail fencing on the west side of the road. This is our next waypoint.

0897P 3.2mi 48° 36.841'N 122° 13.618'W 260' State Route 9 X Old Forest Road/Trail entrance to Anderson Mountain

You will find an open forest road to the west with switchbacks.[31] There is a white gate, known as the Bloedel gate, with a clear cut on the north side of the road. (This is not the same Bloedel gate discussed below). Just past the white gate there is a white blaze on the left marking the PNT route.

We'll continue with the description of the new trail (albeit perhaps through private land). Follow the forest road south and uphill past a couple of homesteads on the left, and then again, farther down, two homesteads on the right in 0.8 miles. Here the road enters the forest as you begin to climb Anderson Mountain. In 1.3 miles from SR9, Road A-1900 intersects another unnamed forest road. We keep hiking uphill southwest for another 0.9 miles. At this point FR A-1900 begins a series of ten major switchbacks to climb the eastern slope of the mountain. Our next waypoint is about half-way up at the point on the sixth switchback, about 2.2 miles after the switchbacks begin.

0902P 4.1mi 48° 37.849'N 122° 14.912'W 2600' Forest Road A-1900 X Anderson Mountain Shortcut

There are now two PNT signs at this junction. An alternate shortcut route is to stay on the road for another 0.8 miles. The primary PNT route to get to the same point is 3.5 miles, but provides you with the Anderson Mountain overlook.

For about the next 20 miles, the primary route is marked with white blazes to help your navigation.[51] For now we'll stick to hiking the longer route on FR A-1900. This section of the "road" has been closed for years and the trail is not maintained. It will be more like a bushwhack at some points. Follow the trail north for another 1.2 miles, on a relatively level grade, before beginning more switchbacks. As the trail turns back south for about 0.3 miles it intersects with Forest Road FR A-1000K at our next waypoint.

0903P 1.5mi 48° 38.516'N 122° 14.869'W 2690' Forest Road A-1900 X Forest Road A-1000K

There are reports of a PNT sign here, but this has not been confirmed. We turn north at this road junction, climbing for 0.4 miles to connect to the Anderson Mountain Trail.

0904P 0.4mi 48° 38.813'N 122° 15.027'W 2820' Forest Road A-1000K X Forest Road A-1810

The trail starts at the end of the road parking area. Hikers report that there is a "Wickersham/ Alger sign" at this junction. The trail starts north, perhaps for only a short distance, before rounding back to the south to climb near the crest of the ridge toward the summit. We climb south for 0.4 miles to the Anderson Mountain "overlook," with nothing to look at because the trees have grown too tall.[50] Looking north through the trees you should see Lake Whatcom and to its west the PNT across the west side of I-5. Continue west then south uphill for another 0.5 miles to reach the junction with Forest Road A-1810.

0905P 1.1mi 48° 38.331'N 122° 15.466'W 3210' Anderson Mountain Trail X Forest Road A-1810

This old road branches back up to the northeast and uphill to climb to the east side of Anderson Mountain. But, we keep heading due south, although the road/trail may very well look much like trail that we have been hiking. The road keeps a level grade for about 0.3 miles where it then descends into a clearcut with possible tank traps the last 100 yards.

0906P 1.9mi 48° 37.710'N 122° 15.383'W 2990' Forest Road A-1810 X Anderson Mountain Shortcut

This is a four-way road junction. At this waypoint the shortcut described above rejoins our route coming up from the east. The primary PNT route now turns north hiking along the maintained road on a fairly level grade hovering around the 3000' contour for about 0.7 miles. In 2012 a hiker reports that the PNT trails on Anderson are OK, although better on west-side descent, and well-signed.[GT]

From here the road starts its descent north for another 0.7 miles to a "U-turn" in the road. There is a car "parking" area on a short rock bench north of the turn. In the 'U' you can see a spur trail that cuts north through trees about a quarter-mile to a flat gravel patch. That spot boasts one of the best views in the county outside of the North Cascades - you can see the San Juan Islands, Bellingham, Canada, and even the tip of Mount Baker. There is no water, but it would make for an excellent trail camp and a rare spot with built-in fireproofing.[81]

After the 'U' south we continue downhill for about 0.25 miles looking for a trail to the west, which is well marked with a post and a PNT decal.[DV]

0907P 1.5mi 48° 38.529'N 122° 16.054'W 2570' Forest Road A-1810 X Unnamed Trail

As we turn west off the road, look for the white painted blazes marking the trail through this sction.[49] The trail drops down into the thick forest for just less than 0.2 miles to break out into a clear cut area. In 2015, after a major wind storm, hikers reported blowdowns for about 0.2 miles after the clear cut area.[48] The trail meanders through the clear cut as we cross the many skid tracks, reentering the forest in about 0.9 miles. Keep working downhill and southwest for another 0.15 miles to cross Forest Road A-1600 at our next waypoint. Thanks go to those who maintain this trail as it is in great shape all the way down to Alger Creek Road.[DV]

0908P 1.2mi 48° 38.299'N 122° 16.794'W 1920' Ken Rosencrantz Trail X Jim Futrelle Trail

We keep to the trail in heavy forest downhill for the next 0.4 miles, dropping almost 360' elevation. You can expect areas of deep, eroding ruts in the tread due to motorcycle use on this trail.[DV] We exit on a southwest direction onto a forest road at a bend in the road and follow the road southwest as it comes to a 'T' road junction. We turn north for only 60 yards to another 'T' junction, where we turn west.

We follow this road as it bends south for 0.2 miles, on a relatively level grade, to pick up the trail where the road ends.[50] This short trail takes us down the slope, first to the north and then back to the south. In 0.4 miles it breaks into a clear cut, and then down to a forest road, where we turn left, having lost about 300' elevation into our next waypoint.

0910P 1.7mi 48° 38.236'N 122° 17.864'W 1050' Jim Futrelle Trail X Art Reinhardt Trail

Next we hike north on the road for 0.3 miles, losing 200' to a 'Y' road junction, where we turn southwest and keep going downhill. This road takes us southwest for 0.5 miles, losing another 300', to turn sharply back to the north. In another 0.3 miles the road comes upon a quarry (an informal shooting range), which hikers offer as a trail camp. Next we turn west for 0.2 miles to get us to our next waypoint.

0911P 1.0mi 48° 38.191'N 122° 18.560'W 470' Unnamed Forest Road X Alger Creek CCC Road

Turn southwest on Alger CCC Road for 0.25 miles to intersect the signed Alger-Cain Lake Road, which we follow for 1.5 miles to our next waypoint at the Trillium Gate. Trillium Gate sits just east of the first house that you come to after a break in the forest. The road with the gate is about 0.1 miles west after crossing the highway bridge over Silver Creek. If you need water, you can get to the creek with some meandering down the rocks, perhaps making you feel like a hobo under a bridge, but will likely be the last water source for the next 3 miles.[31]

0912P 1.7mi 48° 37.207'N 122° 20.092'W 300' Cain Lake Road @ Trillium Gate

Trail Angel (Alger): See details at the end of this chapter.

Hungry? The Alger Bar & Grille is a quarter mile west on Cain Lake Road. It serves breakfast, lunch, and dinner. This is not a recommendation, just letting you know it's there. There is also a motel in Alger. The nearest convenience store is 0.5 miles south of Alger on Old Highway 99, or another one 0.7 miles west of Alger where Lake Samish Road crosses under I-5.[49] Here you can also find the Skagit Park and Ride to catch the bus to Bellingham.[50]

Back to the PNT. At our waypoint, we turn north and climb to bypass the yellow gate. In another 40 yards there is a trail sign that points the way to Little Mount Baldy. We climb this gently rising road due north for 0.5 miles where the road works west and continues to then climb at a steeper rate. In 0.3 miles the road returns to the northwest along the western slope. Keep climbing into our next waypoint at a 'Y' road junction.

0914P 1.5mi 48° 38.082'N 122° 20.567'W 910' Forest Road 1100 X Forest Road 1300

At the 'Y' junction one branch turns northeast and uphill to climb to the summit. We, however, bear left (southwest) on Road 1300 to descend as the road turns back quickly to the northwest. In a short 0.1 miles we come a 'Y' junction. Turn west so that we can hike the west side of the ridge. Soon the trail (road) turns back north to hike along the ridge to our next waypoint.

0914.5P 0.8mi 48° 38.411'N 122° 21.092'W 730' Forest Road 1300 X South Ridge Trail

Looking to the west we can see Old Highway 99 and the trailhead, but it is more than 300' below us on this steep slope. Keep hiking on the South Ridge trail until we reach the northwest corner of the lake. Unfortunately, the water in Squires Lake looks a little "scummy."[GT]   Just before the trail to the west to descend to the trailhead parking lot, there is a water fountain/spigot about 20 yards beyond the trail junction.

Descend the ridge on the trail as it heads south and then north again for 0.2 miles to get safely down the ridge on the Squires Lake Trail to the trailhead. There is a toilet at the trailhead.

0915P   0.8mi 48° 38.633'N   122° 21.345'W   270'   Squires Lake Trail X Old Highway 99

Trail Angel (Lake Samish): See details at the end of this chapter.

We hike north 0.35 miles on this paved road where it rounds west and is now named Nulle Road.   There is forest on both sides and traffic is moderate, depending on the time of day. In less than a quarter mile Nulle Road passes under I-5 at Exit 242. This is a residential-farm area and there are no service stations or mini-marts at this exit.

Keep west on Nulle Road for 0.7 miles past I-5 to merge with Summerland Road. This road transition is at the junction with Appaloosa Lane. Climb along Summerland Road northwest for 0.6 miles to the next waypoint at the Bloedel Gate.

0917P   2.1mi 48° 39.037'N 122° 23.257'W   510'   Summerland Road @ Bloedel Gate-Private Logging Road

There is a white gate across the logging road to prevent vehicle traffic and an official PNT emblem and white blaze. The white gate is across the street from a small driveway to a homestead back in the trees.

In 0.1 miles there is 'Y' in the road. The PNT bears left (west) as shown on the PNTA map as a "private logging road." Follow this road generally west through thick timber land, passing by all side roads.

0918P   0.9mi 48° 38.964'N 122° 24.203'W   630'   Bloedel Forest Road X Unnamed Forest Road

Here it gets a little tricky. This waypoint appears to be at the end of the logging road at a turnaround point. Keep hiking on the same road southwest, then following it as it curves back to the northwest. The last part of this "trail" is straight south on what appears to be a section line cut. This straight section south is about 0.3 miles into our next waypoint.

0918.5P 1.1mi 48° 38.678'N 122° 24.876'W 1100'   Unnamed Forest Road X Spur Trail

This is a four-way trail junction. The short segment we want is the trail turning sharply northwest for only about 0.1 miles. Next, we turn southwest for 100 yards into the next waypoint.

0919P 0.2mi 48° 38.730'N 122° 25.019'W 1030' Spur Trail X DNR Road BL48

At this 'T' junction onto Road BL48, we turn left (south). In 0.3 miles there is forest road at a 'T' road junction coming in from the east. We stay straight south on the road we were hiking for another 0.2 miles to find the British Army Trail. A local hiker says that this section is well marked and "no map should be needed."[31]

0920P 0.5mi 48° 38.321'N 122° 24.964'W 1310' DNR Road BL48 X British Army Trail (BAT)

Depart the road and follow the BAT uphill southeast for 0.8 miles to come to the west side of Lizard Lake. The lake sits down in a shallow boggy bowl and you will likely find it a little unattractive. The trail passes along the south side of the lake and in less than 0.1 miles past the lake we should cross the Incline Trail, coming in from the east. The Washington DNR operates the Lizard Lake Backcountry Campground near this trail junction. An annual ($30) or Day-Use ($5) Discover Pass is required for both Lizard and Lily Lake Camps.

0921P 0.9mi 48° 37.845'N 122° 24.248'W 1870' British Army Trail X Lizard Lake Trail (DNR - Lizard Lake)

There are reports of a new connector trail between Lizard and Lily Lakes, with a good spring at the start of the trail above Lizard Lake.[49] But for now, we'll stick with the primary PNT route as we circle around to the east and south side of Chuckanut Mountain on the DNR's well-maintained trail. In about 0.5 miles we should come to the junction with the Lily Lake Trail, which joins coming uphill from the southeast. We keep west, on the Lily Lake Trail for about 0.3 mile. We find two close trail junctions in quick succession. The first is the junction with Max's Shortcut. The second is at our next waypoint with the Oyster Dome Trail and the spur trail to the DNR Lily Lake Backcountry Campground. The campground is on the northside of the lake on the Connector Trail. This lake is a little more pristine than Lizard Lake, but still relatively dark and unattractive.[GT]

0922P 2.1mi 48° 37.381'N 122° 24.401'W 1990' Lily Lake Trail X Oyster Dome Trail X Connector Trail

We continue west for only 0.4 miles to the junction with the Oyster Dome Trail. There are reports of all new trail signs in this area, including those for the PNT.[49]

0924P 0.4mi 48° 37.453'N 122° 24.849'W 1890' Oyster Lily Trail X Samish Bay Trail X Oyster Dome Trail

If we turn north the trail climbs about 150' elevation to the top of Oyster Dome. Sometimes water can be found in the creek about 0.25 miles from the top, but it is not guaranteed. From the top of Oyster Dome we have one of the best views of Puget Sound and the San Juan Islands. There is an unofficial place to camp on top with magnificent views of Puget Sound at sunset.[49]

To keep on the PNT route, follow the now Samish Bay Trail west and then south downhill for 1.1 miles to intersect with the Larry Reed Trail from Max's Shortcut.

0926P 0.35mi 48° 36.901'N 122° 25.658'W 1070' Samish Bay Trail X Larry Reed Trail

Continuing directly south, and downhill, we're now on the Pacific Northwest Trail (perhaps the one and only place the PNT is the actual trail name). We drop 200' elevation, along the west side of the mountain for 0.5 miles, to the first major switchback to the north. Follow this well-maintained trail back north for 0.4 miles descending another 310' elevation. Here, the trail turns south again for another 0.4 miles, losing another 360' elevation.

There is one final major switchback to the north, and then we complete the trail in about 0.1 miles at our waypoint with the intersection with State Route 11. As you exit the trail, look back and find the rock with the Pacific Northwest Trail inscription carved into it.

0927P 1.5mi 48° 36.468'N 122° 25.979'W 110' PNT X State Route 11

This completes the primary route for this section; now on to the alternate routes.

Alternate Route: Mount Josephine – Les Hilde Trail

This alternate route uses the original stock route to hike south of Mount Josephine, using the developed horse trails in the Washington's Harry Orborne State Forest. This is a horse trail / hiker only system maintained by the Back Country Horsemen of Skagit and Whatcom counties.

Start: 0861P Forest Road 310 X Forest Road 313

Rejoin: 0870.5P Heritage Hill Trail X rejoin PNT

Mileage: 4.5 miles; shorter than the primary route by 4.5 miles

Highlights: A useable bad-weather alternate but the many trails may be a little confusing

0859P 0.0mi 48° 35.299'N 121° 55.695'W 2630' Forest Road 310 X Forest Road 313

We follow the FR313 southwest uphill for 0.5 miles to a corner where the road turns north. This is the northern trailhead for the Les Hilde Trail.

0861A 0.5mi 48° 35.167'N 121° 56.123'W 2870' Forest Road 313 X Forest Road

We follow the horse trail, an old forest road, southwest downhill for only 0.2 miles to reach the trailhead at the end of the road.

0861.5A 0.5mi 48° 35.123'N 121° 56.309'W 2920' Forest Road X Les Hilde Trail
The trail drops sharply downhill for the next 0.2 miles on a series of switchbacks. First, the trail traverses a clearcut, and then halfway, it enters the forest. The trail exits into an end-of-road turnaround area.

0862A 0.2mi 48° 34.926'N 121° 56.438'W 2520' Les Hilde Trail X Forest Road 2000

We follow the relatively straight forest road southwest to continue our steep downhill quest. The next waypoint is at a junction with a more established forest road.

0862.5A 0.4mi 48° 34.503'N 121° 56.960'W 1950' Forest Road 2000 X Forest Road

The PNT continues straight west on the more established road, but is still designated FR2000. Our descent continues, too. There is thick forest to the north of the road with patches of clearcut to the south.

0863A 0.6mi 48° 34.478'N 121° 57.817'W 1790' Forest Road 2000 X Les Hilde Trail

At this way point there is a junction with an abandoned old forest road coming in from the south. The trail should be found about 20 yards past the road junction.
We turn south on a steep downhill run for the first 0.7 miles, but then, the descent levels off significantly. We hike through a mixture of both new and old growth forest.
We follow the trail as it alternates from west to south for another 0.5 miles to intersect with Forest Road 2000, again.

0864A 1.5mi 48° 33.850'N 121° 58.843'W 1050' Les Hilde Trail X Forest Road 2000

We turn west on the road for just under 0.4 miles to a 'T' road intersection at our next waypoint.

0865A 0.4mi 48° 33.760'N 121° 59.260'W 990' Forest Road 2000 X Heritage Hill Trail

Decision Time. There is an option at this waypoint to turn south to join the Cascade Trail Super Cutoff route at the town of Hamilton. The routing is described at the end of this chapter.

We turn north on the Heritage Hill Trail, climbing again for 0.2 miles, gaining 100' elevation, and looking for the Heritage Hill Trail that breaks into the trees to the west. The trail should be just after the bend in the road. We follow this horse trail initially west and then north for about 0.3 miles, climbing another 100' elevation, to where we intersect a forest road.

We turn west on the road for only about 120 yards, looking for the continuation of the trail to the north. Back on the trail we climb for about 0.2 miles to where the horse trail rounds back to the south. This northern point on the trail is known as "Picnic View.' There is a picnic table there with a fine view of the clearcut below.[50] Now working south, the trail crosses the forest road—yes, the one we just walked about 120 yards a ways back to round to the west. We hike on the horse trail west for 0.4 miles to our next waypoint and to rejoin the primary PNT route.

0870P 0.7mi 48° 33.997'N 121° 59.802'W 1160' Heritage Hill Trail X Forest Road

Hike west a short 0.2 miles looking for the primary PNT route off the road to the south. The PNT trail should be about 50 yard west of a horse trail/road junction that heads north from the road and uphill. We want to find the trail just beyond that takes our south and downhill.

0870.5P 0.2mi 48° 33.850'N 121° 58.843'W 1050' Heritage Hill Trail X rejoin PNT

Alternate Route: Cascade Trail Super Cutoff - Concrete to Sedro-Woolley Rail Trail

As noted in our description above, that if you make it into the town of Concrete, Washington, there is the alternate rail-trail route used by several PNT thru-hikers. The rail-trail extends 22.8 miles to Sedro-Woolley. It by-passes the majority of the Mount Josephine routing. The trail somewhat follows the winding, scenic Skagit River.

Established under the Rails-to-Trails Conservancy, it is described as:

"The Cascade Trail follows the Skagit River along an old rail bed of the Burlington Northern line, between Sedro-Woolley and Concrete. The trail parallels State Route 20 through cultivated fields, open space, scattered woodlands and river bottoms."[19]

Start: 0830P Abandoned Road X Baker Lake Road (Road 11)

Rejoin: 0870.5P Heritage Hill Trail X rejoin PNT

Mileage: 41.1 miles; shorter than the primary route by 25.4 miles

Highlights: Seems like all road walking and little camping opportunity. Offers multiple opportunities for resupply, restaurants, and motels.

From Baker Lake Road to Concrete:

0830P 1.8mi 48° 39.531'N 121° 42.783'W 860' Abandoned road X Baker Lake Road (Road 11)

Continue south on Baker Lake Road for another 0.6 miles to cross Forest Road 1106. Keep road walking south, then west, to cross Rocky Creek. From the bridge over the creek you get one of the most iconic views of Mount Baker to the west. Access to Rocky Creek is difficult. Keep road walking south on the Baker Lake Road to our next waypoint.

0834D 4.3mi 48° 37.215'N 121° 44.892'W 940' Baker Lake Road (Road 11) @ Bear Creek

There are few landmarks to identify this waypoint except that it is the only bridge on the highway after Rocky Creek. Access to Bear Creek is best from the forest road on the north side of the bridge.
From here it is another 3.1 miles southwest to find Burpee Hill Road, by Lake Tyee, and the most direct route into the town of Concrete.

0837D 3.1mi 48° 34.821'N 121° 46.555'W 940' Baker Lake Road (Road 11) X Burpee Hill Road

We turn south on Burpee Hill Road through a small "residential" area. There is not much on the road between here and Concrete. The road goes uphill for most of the way, but then drops sharply downhill on a curvy road into our next waypoint. At the first 'T' road intersection, turn south again on North Superior Avenue to reach the Cascade Trail in four blocks.

0841D 4.1mi 48° 32.183'N 121° 45.543'W 220' North Superior Ave. X Cascade Rail-Trail @ Concrete

The Cascade Trail parallels the north side of State Route 20 and is straight and flat. In 6.7 miles west of Concrete there is a Skagit County trailhead at the intersection of Baker Lake Road and SR20. The trailhead has information and a toilet. Tip: In another 1.2 miles, look for the Birdview Brewing Company. It is on the south side of SR20 at the intersection with Wyatt Lane.

The trail then crosses to the south side of SR20 about 1.1 miles east of Hamilton.

From Forest Road 2000 to Hamilton

0865A   0.0mi   48° 33.760'N   121° 59.260'W   990'   Forest Road 2000 X Heritage Hill Trail

Instead of turning north on the Heritage Hill Trail, we turn south at this junction to follow the forest road downhill.   In 1.4 miles there is a 'T' intersection where we turn left (east) for only 0.1miles to cross Muddy Creek. There are no reports of water here.   Follow the road south for another 0.1 miles to join the paved Medford Road.

Medford Road heads southwest until it leaves the forest and enters into a residential area in 1.2 miles.   At a 'T' junction with Hamilton Cemetery Road, turn east.   In short order we turn south again, this time on Petit Street.   We follow Petit Street south to cross SR20.   Note that there is a bike path on the north side of SR20, but this is not what we are looking for.   The Cascade Trail is 0.3 miles south after crossing SR20.

R852   3.6mi   48° 31.522'N   121° 59.412'W   100'   Petit Street X Cascade Trail

From Cascade Trail to Rejoin PNT at Anderson Mountain

R864   11.8mi   48° 30.387'N   122° 14.315'W   60'   Cascade Trail X Metcalf Street @ Sedro-Woolley

The western trailhead is on Metcalf Street in Sedro-Woolley. We, however, are looking to return to rejoin the PNT.   The primary PNT is north on SR9, about 8.2 miles, at the waypoint to Anderson Mountain. The most direct route is to hike directly north on SR9.   In Sedro-Woolley SR9 begins on the Cascade Trail at Township Street, about 0.6 miles east of the Cascade Trail western terminus.

The best landmark to recognize Township Street is when hiking west on the trail, there are pine or fir trees planted on each side of the trail for about 150 yards. After exiting the trees, on the south side, across from the trail and the parallel Polte Road, there is a large Methodist Church.   The next street crossing to the west is Township Street.

It is straight forward to hike directly north on SR9 to the rejoin waypoint.

0897P   8.2mi   48° 36.841'N   122° 13.618'W   260'   State Route 9 X Old Forest Road/Trail entrance to Anderson Mountain

RESUPPLY OPTIONS

0735P 48° 44.059'N 121° 03.762'W 1690' Happy Panther Trail X Ross Lake Dam Service Road **Ross Lake Resort:** In previous years the resort offered to accept hiker packages for a mail drop. But, in 2015 they stopped this service because of limited staff. In 2018 hikers could send resupply boxes with permission in advance for size limits and for a $20 fee. The mail for the resort is picked up only periodically in the town of Rockport. Their resort's phone number is 206.386.4437 (May-November). There is no store for resupply at the resort. The closest town for very limited resupply is in Newhalem, about 13.5 miles west on SR20. There is no post office there.

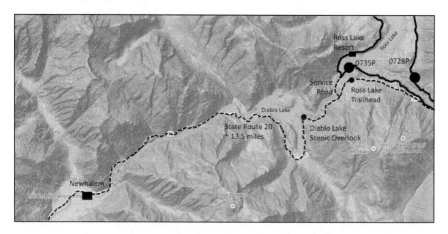

0787P 48° 54.387'N 121° 41.616'W 2030' Road 32 X Mount Baker Highway (State Route 542) **Glacier:** About 13 miles west on the Mount Baker Highway lies this very small hamlet, several motels/chalets and the Grahams Restaurant, with a somewhat expensive general store. There is also a post office for a mail drop. The best part of this little town is the "Chair 9" Restaurant. This pizza, steak, burger and beer place is about a mile east, back towards the trail. Hitchhiking to town is an option.

0830P 48° 39.809'N 121° 43.034'W 900' Forest Road 1106 X Baker Lake Road (Road 11) **Concrete:** The town is about 11 miles south; first going 7 miles on the Baker Lake Road, and then turning on Burpee Hill Road to State Route 20. The Big Apple food store and pizza place are about a mile west on SR20. This is not a pleasant road walk, to say the least. The grocery store can be found about 1 mile west of town. Here you can also find great pizza and a motel nearby.

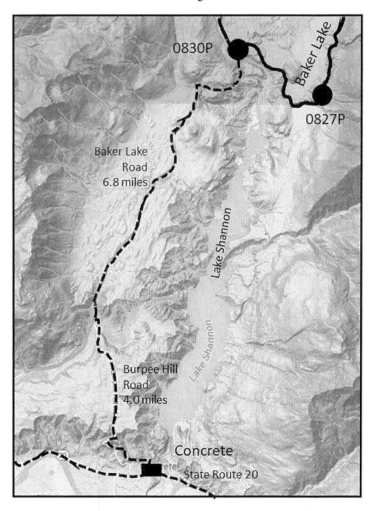

0912P 1.7mi 48° 37.207'N 122° 20.092'W 300' Cain Lake Rd @ Trillium Gate **Alger:** Restaurant and convenience store .02 miles west, then 0.5 miles south on Old Highway 99N

Trail Support

0912P Alger: Hunter Dunn, (360) 389-0296, hunterjdunn@gmail.com. Can provide a ride, food, or local suggestions about the PNT.

0915P Lake Samish (Bellingham): Mary Walker, mkwalker@live.com, (360) 393-9971. Located just west of I-5 off Nulle Road. (House under renovation for 2019, but can provide welcome packages.)

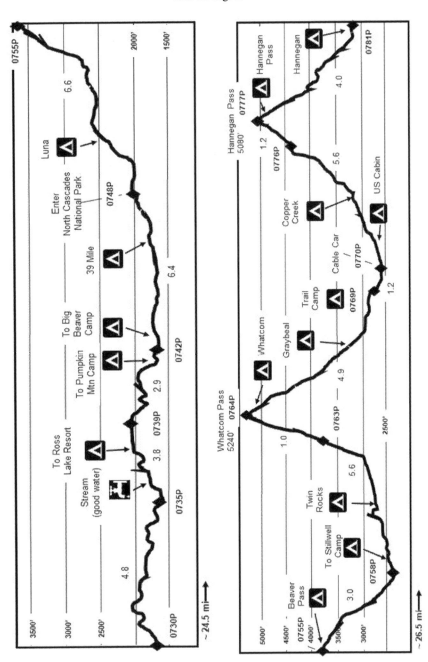

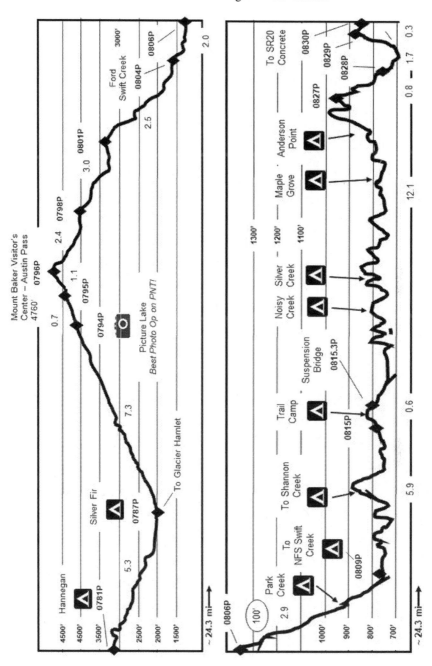

Tim Youngbluth

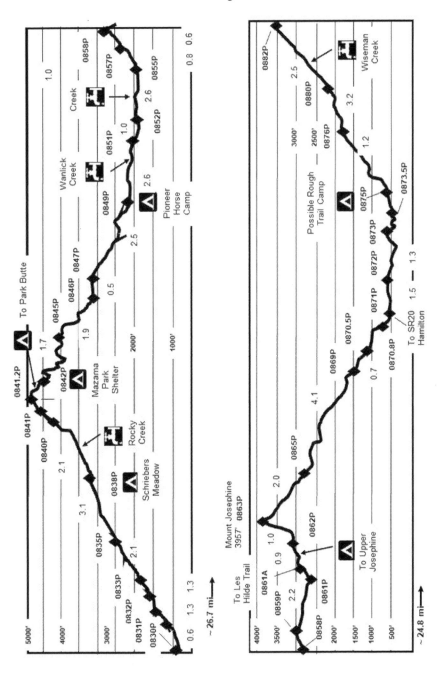

210

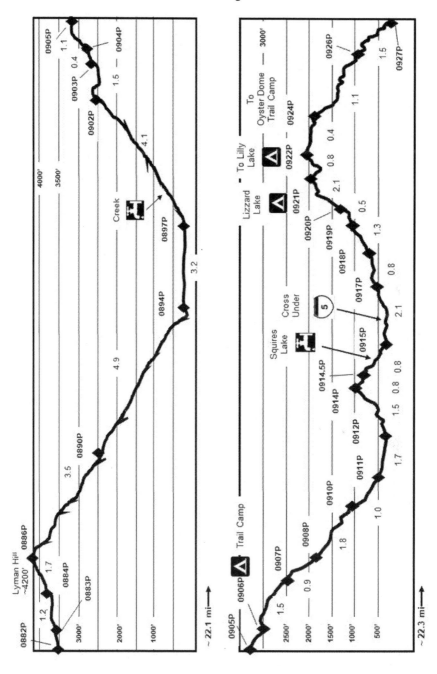

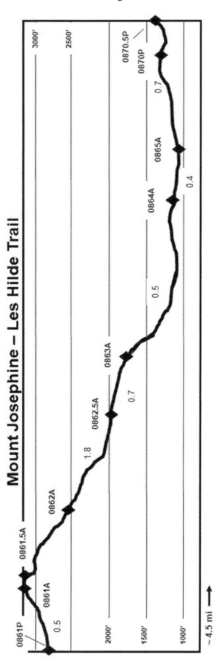

Mount Josephine – Les Hilde Trail

****

On July 8, 2017, a Pacific Northwest Trail hiker named "Sockeye" wrote the following verse in a Forest Service journal located high on a pass in the Yaak:

"Through biting bugs and searing heat,

we've traveled far on weary feet,

wandered through the Yaak,

with good friends and a pack.

Forward now to Bonners for a treat."

****

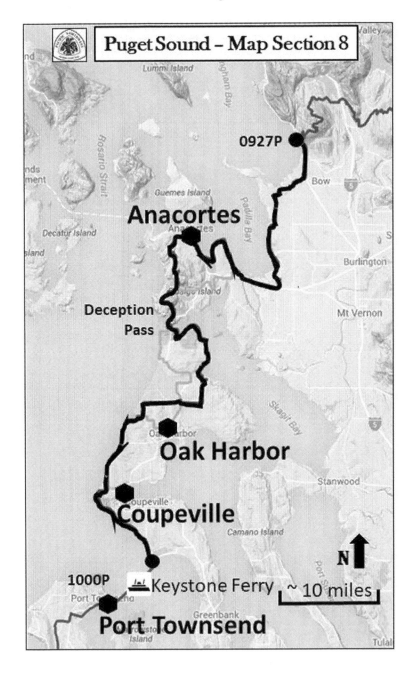

CHAPTER NINE
PUGET SOUND – MAP SECTION 8
Samish Bay to Admiralty Inlet

Goose Rock Perimeter Trail near Deception Pass, Whidbey Island, Washington

Key Trail Notes

Highlights: Tommy Thompson Trail; Deception Pass; Keystone Ferry

Primary Route Estimated Elevation Change: 925' climb / 1,025' descent

Route Alternates: Oak Harbor

Possible Resupply: Anacortes; Oak Harbor; Coupeville; and many stores along State Route 20 in this section.

Parks/Forests: Anacortes Community Forest Land; Washington State Parks,

Permits: Overnight state park fees

Other Notes: Trail Angels in Coupeville and Oak Harbor. In Anacortes call ahead for Olympic National Park reservations (360) 565-3100

0927P 0.0mi 48° 36.468'N 122° 25.979'W 110' PNT X State Route 11, Chuckanut Drive

A word of caution to begin: SR11 has a narrow shoulder so be careful as you hike south and downhill into the flat lands of Samish Bay, but it does improve to the south. In 0.5 miles after leaving the trail you come to the Chuckanut Manor Restaurant, which may be a little upscale for "hiker trash," but it is an option for a good sit-down meal.

Once on the flat section of SR11, heading due south, be sure to look up. At Murrow Drive the field to the east is a designated landing zone for paragliders launching from the Blanchard Hill parking area, off Max's Shortcut. We keep south on SR11 for another 1.8 miles to our next waypoint.

0930P 2.8mi 48° 33.927'N 122° 25.331'W 10' State Route 11 X Bow Hill Road / East Edison Road

There may be a small store for resupply at this road intersection. Here we turn west for 0.9 miles to follow the road into the town of Edison looking for McTaggart Avenue and the 'T' intersection in town.

0931P 1.1mi 48° 33.740'N 122° 26.619'W 10' McTaggart Ave X Farm to Market Road [Note: The PNTA map shows a second 0931P in the description below.]

A PNT hiker encourages us to visit Tweets Café at the corner of McTaggert and Gilkey Avenues. "The staff is extremely kind and stopped me on my way by to give me a free coffee and free cookies, which can't be expected for all, but they deserve your business if anyone does."[31] Tweets menu offers sandwiches for around $12-$18. Next door, however, is the Longhorn Saloon which serves fabulous meals, with large portions, around $7-14. The Longhorn is claimed by a PNT trail angel to have the best the fish and chips within 70 miles.[37]

From the center of "town" head south on Cains Court for three blocks and then as it rounds west into Farm-to-Market Road. This begins our flat country road walk, looking for the Bayview Edison Road in 0.25 miles. Follow this west to a jog south and west. We come to a 'T' road junction where the road continues straight as Samish Island Road. Turn south keeping to the Bayview Edison Road. Keep road walking for another 2.2 miles through farm country to our next waypoint.

0933P 2.2mi 48° 31.018'N 122° 28.350'W 10' Bayview Edison Road @ Joe Leary Slough

After this final jog the road is very near the bay. Follow the Bayview Edison Road south for another 2.3 miles to find the Bayview State Park.

0937P 2.3mi 48° 29.253'N 122° 28.809'W 40' Bay View-Edison Road @ Bay View State Park

Bayview State Park has 46 tent spaces and four cabins with $12 hiker/biker sites.[49] Showers are available for $.50. Next, we follow this paved road for only 0.6 miles to the trailhead for the Padilla Bay Shore Trail.

0938P 0.6mi 48° 28.815'N 122° 28.378'W 20' Bay View-Edison Road X Padilla Bay Shore Trail

Finally, we're off the road for a while. From the state park we keep south for 0.6 miles to pick up the Padilla Bay Shore Trail. This paved hard-packed gravel bicycle trail has a signed trailhead; it is hard to miss. The trail follows along the top of the dikes for just under 2.3 miles through the mud flats and ends at the La Conner and Samish Road. This is just an extension of the Bay View-Edison Road we were walking before. There is a privy here at the south end trailhead.

0941P 3.2mi 48° 26.877'N 48° 26.877'N 10' Whitney-Bay View Road X State Route 20

Caution: SR20 is a very busy divided highway. We head west on SR20 for 1.0 miles looking for an obvious bike path that parallels the main highway. Take the bike path 2.0 miles to reach the elevated highway bridge over the Swinomish Channel with the pedestrian walkway/bike path. After the bridge, in 0.5 miles we exit onto South March Point Road. Follow this road northwest for 0.8 miles and into our next waypoint at the junction with East March Point Road.

0944P 3.4mi 48° 27.939'N 122° 32.207'W 10' State Route 20 X East March Point Road

The primary PNT route hikes around the March Point oil storage area, across the Tommy Thomson Trail bridge into Anacortes. Another option is to bypass the oil tanks on March Point by staying west on East March Point Road for 1.6 miles to reach March Point Road. Along the way you will pass an old, closed drive-in theater, then a coffee shop called Moca Joe's with WiFi, on the south side of the road. At March Point Road we would turn north for 1.0 miles to pick up the Tommy Thompson Trail.

Let's get back to our primary PNT route and turn north on March's Point Drive. Although this route requires more road walking, it does offer some of the best views of Padilla Bay and the mountains to the northeast, which we hiked a few days ago.[80] In 2.6 miles we reach the north tip of the point which offers a great view of Mount Baker almost 40 miles to the northeast. Rounding the point we turn south, now named March Point Road, following it past the oil tanks for 2.1 miles to our next waypoint and the east end of the Tommy Thompson Trail.

0949P 4.8mi 48° 28.614'N 122° 34.352'W 20' March Point Road X Tommy Thompson Trail

The trail begins on a 0.9 mile long converted rail trestle bridge across Fidalgo Bay. Immediately after leaving the bridge, the trail cuts through an RV park. There are no tent sites, but there is free Cable TV (oh sure ... just thought I'd throw that in!) Press past the RV park following the trail for another 1.7 miles into Anacortes and to our next waypoint at 22nd Street. Note that the parking area for the trailhead is one block south, opposite 23rd Street.

There is a nice public restroom on the NE corner of 22nd & R Street. There is also a fabulous supermarket called The Market on 17th, between Q and Commercial Streets. Lots of natural and organic food, as well as a large bin (pay by the pound) area that has 8 different types of trail mix, among other things. The Market also has a coffee shop with free WiFi and outlets.[37]

0952P 2.7mi 48° 30.270'N 122° 36.547'W 30' Tommy Thompson Trail X 22nd Street @ Anacortes

Planning Note: From Anacortes (or around this point) it is a good idea to call the Olympic Wilderness Center to get the required permits. Call the WIC at (360) 565-3100 to check on station hours and seasons, or for more information about getting your permit. The PNT trek through Olympic National Park is a long stretch. For 2019 the permit fee is expected to be $8 per person per night. An annual pass, which covers all permit fees for a year, is $45. Reservations are required for some backcountry campsites. Also, bear canisters are required at some camps and along the coast beach walk in Olympic National Park due to racoons.

Back to Anacortes. Most of the stores and restaurants can be found on the north-south Commercial Avenue/SR20. At the Cap Sante Marina (1019 Q Ave.), about 0.6 miles north, with $10 pay showers and $3 laundry.

To get to our next waypoint and the trailhead for Trail 100 on the west side of Anacortes, the map portrays the route directly through on 23rd Street, which unfortunately stops and starts in a maze through a residential area of the town.

My recommendation is that once you have finished your rest and resupply we hike west uphill on 22nd Street for 0.75 miles to G Avenue. Go one block south on G Avenue to reach 23rd Street, which we take 0.4 miles west. The trailhead is on the south side of the street just prior to entering Forest Ridge condominiums.

0953P 1.2mi 48° 30.231'N 122° 38.077'W 260' 23rd Street X Trail 100 @ Anacortes Community Forest

Hiking the PNT through the community forest can feel much like a bit of a corn maze. Detailed maps of the next few waypoints can be found at the Pacific Northwest Trail Association website under maps for Cranberry and Heart Lakes at **https://www.anacorteswa.gov/588/Biking-Trail-Maps.** The trails have been developed and maintained by the community in this park, and are generally for horses, bicyclists, and hikers.

We start hiking south on TR100 for just under 0.5 miles to join Trail 104 very close to the 29th Street access. Follow TR104 southwest past the water tank to the bridge between Little Cranberry Lake and Big Beaver Pond. After you cross the bridge follow Trail 106 southwest for 0.1 miles to the junction with Trail 11 and Trail 10.

0955P 1.1mi 48° 29.757'N 122° 38.648'W 320' Trail 106 X Trail 10

Turn south on TR10 as we hike along the west side of Big Beaver Pond. Keep working south on TR10 for about 1.1 miles as it circles south of Mitten Pond and intersects Trail 126.

0955.5P 1.0mi 48° 29.144'N 122° 38.517'W 320' Trail 10 X Trail 126

We take TR126 east for just over 0.5 miles to come to our next waypoint at the trailhead on Havekost Road and Trail 241. As we come to the end of TR126, it skirts just south of a housing area.

0956P 0.4mi 48° 28.999'N 122° 38.221'W 340' Trail 126 X Havekost Road X Trail 241

Next, we cross the road and pick up TR241 as it angles south on a very thin stretch of public land between residential areas and then turns east into the junction with Trail 224 in 0.5 miles.

0956.5P 0. 48° 28.805'N 122° 37.895'W 350' Trail 241 X Trail 224

Turn south on TR224 for only 0.2 miles to join Trail 210. Eventually we pass through the two posts that designated TR210 for hikers only, and keep south into the heavy forest along the west side of Heart Lake.

TR210 takes us south 0.6 miles to the junction with Trail 243. The PNT route turns back northeast continuing with TR210 around the south shore of Heart Lake. After about 0.3 miles TR210 turn due south and climbs through the woods to a signed junction with Trail 212.

There are two posts for TR210 at this junction. We stay keep south on TR212 for just another 0.2 miles to the end on an unsigned old forest road designated Trail 25. Although it seems we could bushwhack down the ridge to our next trail, we follow TR25 southwest for just under a 100 yards to the junction with Trail 220 and our next waypoint.

0958P 1.8mi 48° 28.054'N 122° 37.849'W 420' Trail 212 (Trail 25) X Trail 220

We follow TR220 south for 0.8 miles, crossing two foot bridges as we progress slightly downhill. TR220 then intersects Trail 249.

0958.2P 0.8mi 48° 27.572'N 122° 378.164'W 340' Trail 220 X Trail 249

We follow TR249 east to immediately cross Heart Lake Road. After crossing the road, the trail is now Trail 247 and climbs slightly. It then turns south again to parallel Heart Lake Road on the east side of the road. Climb about 200' on TR247B south for a total 0.8 miles from the road to the junction with Trail 248. Time to drop back west to Heart Lake Road on TR248 for about 0.2 miles. Now we must road walk south for just under 0.2 miles to our next waypoint at the junction with Campbell Lake Road.

Note that just prior to the next waypoint we pass the Lake Erie grocery store for resupply. They are open until 8 pm in the summer. Some hikers report that it is a little expensive and advise not to drink the water from the outside tap![80] From the Mt Erie Store, go slightly left onto the Campbell Lake Road for only 0.1 mile to Donnell Road.[62]

0959P 1.8mi 48° 26.841'N 122° 37.955'W 110' Heart Lake Road X Campbell Lake Road X Donnell Road

In 2016 trail crew volunteers from SWITMO (Skagit-Whatcom-Island Trail Maintaining Organization) continued their long legacy of trail service to the PNT by completing the John Tursi Trail in Deception Pass State Park. This new trail connects with the Pass Lake Trail to eliminate 2.8 miles of PNT road walking.

Go right on the Donnell Road and walk south 0.45 mile to a private property gate which has a property number of 13998 on a sign to the right of the gate to the trailhead.

0960P 0.5mi 48° 26.457'N 122° 38.063'W 90' Donnell Rd X John Tursi Trail

We head into the woods climbing the ridge on the Tursi Trail. Along the way you might find the remnants of a 100 year-old miner's cabin just inside the state park boundary.[63] Follow the Tursi Trail for south for 0.9 miles, exiting onto a driveway.

0961P 0.9mi 48° 25.844'N 122° 38.391'W .340' John Tursi Trail X Ginnet Trail

Next we go left, south again, to the site of an old homestead. Find the Ginnett Trail, which is mostly downhill for 0.9 miles to a four-way trail intersection.

Go straight ahead on the Pass Lake Trail for another 0.67 miles to the trailhead parking lot. There is a privy at the fisherman's parking lot before crossing Rosario Road. Our next waypoint crossing is about 35 yards west of the intersection with SR20.[62]

0963P 1.4mi 48° 25.017'N 122° 38.680'W Pass Lake Trail X Bowman Hill Trail X Rosario Road

Cross the parking lot and the street. The trail starts behind the big Deception Pass State Park sign right about where Rosario Road and Hwy 20 intersection. We follow the trail southwest as it parallels, but drops down below the elevation of SR20. The trail turns back to the east and uphill to meet SR20 after 0.6 miles. We hike on the pedestrian walk across the Deception Pass Bridge. Make sure that any loose items are strapped down on your pack—including your hat—as strong winds funnel through the pass! The bridge is about 180' above the water. The flow of the water under the bridge depends on whether the tide is coming in or going out. Our next waypoint is at the south end of the bridge.

0964P 0.9mi 48° 24.296'N 122° 38.680'W 170' State Route 20 X Goose Rock Perimeter Trail @ Deception Pass Bridge

After crossing the bridge, go down the steps under the super structure to find the Perimeter Trail, complete with its small PNT insignia. We head east as the trail starts downhill on an excellent tread to take us around the peninsula, and then south to Cornet Bay. There is a signed shortcut route near the start that offers better views from the top on the Goose Rock Summit Trail, then we descend to rejoin the PNT at Cornet Bay.[49] The Summit trail has PNT markers and has views on top of the Strait of Juan de Fuca, the Olympic Mountains and the San Juan Islands are the best on the island. If you take this route you round the trail on the east side there is an unmarked intersection. Take the steep trail to the right because the trail that stays low peters out and you meet a dead end.[68]

Back to the primary route on the Perimeter Trail. The Goose Rock Perimeter Trail is an enjoyable easy hike that is fairly level. You'll find good views of Cornet Bay and even Mount Baker peeking above the eastern horizon. The trail ends at an old picnic area near the bay and the Lower Forest Trail.

0965P 1.2mi 48° 23.837'N 122° 38.321'W Goose Rock Perimeter Trail X Lower Forest Trail

Continuing south for only about 150 yards, the primary PNT route turns west on a new trail. If you miss this trail junction you'd soon come to a wooden gate that leads to the Cornet Bay Retreat Center. Do not hike through the Center. Rather, find the new trail west for about 0.2 miles to find another trail junction, which has not been reported as signed. We turn south crossing seasonal wetlands on puncheon-style platforms, ending the trail at Cornet Bay Road.

0965.5P 0.5mi 48° 23.530'N 122° 38.418'W 80' Lower Forest Trail X Cornet Bay Road

Although the PNT primary route turns east here, there is a State campground 0.2 miles west off Cornet Bay Road with a hiker/biker site for $12 a night. Look for Quarry Pond Loop Road and turn north into the campground, a satellite of Deception Pass State Park. The hiker site is one site away from the bathroom/showers.

Back to the PNT, turn northeast on the paved Cornet Bay Road as it takes you past a tiny fishing community. There is a small general store on the bay side of the road. After 1.0 miles on the road, we reenter Deception Pass State Park. Heated toilets are available by the boat ramp, and pay showers for 50 cents![37] Our next waypoint is at the east end of the public boat launch at the closed gate.

0967P 1.1mi 48° 24.080'N 122° 37.318'W 10' Cornet Bay Road X West Hoypus Point Trail @ Deception Pass State Park

The Hoypus Point Trail begins at a blocked road just past the boat launch ramp and goes northeast for about 0.7 miles. Look for the trail as it bears to the right off the road, just past the old maintenance area. The trail turns due east for about 0.4 miles and climbs higher along the peninsula before descending back down toward the shoreline.

0967.5P 0.8mi 48° 24.561'N 122° 36.682'W 60' Hoypus Point Trail X East Hoypus Point Trail

We find the East Hoypus Point Trail at the end of the maintenance road. The trail takes us to the Point where it soon turns south for about 0.6 miles and stay about 100' higher than the bay to the east. The trail stays on a finger of Deception Pass State Park until the end where it turns east and drops down 100' toward Angler's Haven Drive, and our next waypoint.

0968P 1.0mi 48° 24.056'N 122° 35.935'W 230' East Hoypus Point Trail X Spur Trail to Alngler's Haven Drive

There is a short spur trail at this junction that cuts downhill between houses for access to Angler's Haven Drive. We'll keep south on the trail above the housing area for another 0.6 miles. On this section there are two trail junctions. The first in 0.2 miles is the Fireside Trail heading west. The second, in another 0.2 miles, is unnamed and heads east. We turn east and downhill to the "trailhead" on Angler's Haven Drive.

0969P 0.6mi 48° 23.707'N 122° 35.770'W 110' East Hoypus Point Trail X Angler's Haven Drive

Time for road walking, again. Follow Angler's Haven Drive south for just 0.1 miles to reach Troxel Road, where we turn east for another 0.4 miles.

0970P 0.7mi 48° 23.648'N 122° 35.332'W 50' Troxell Road X Jones Road

Here we pick up Jones Road, which takes us south along Puget Sound, with some pretty good views of the Cascades far to the east. This is a long but pleasant road walk for 3.1 miles into our next waypoint at Dike Road.

0972P 2.7mi 48° 21.541'N 122° 36.027'W 60' Jones Road X Dike Road

We turn south and downhill as Dike Road takes us to the shoreline of Dugualla Bay and into East Frostad Road in 0.7 miles. The primary PNT route turns east, but one option, with much higher traffic, is to road walk west 0.9 miles to SR20 and then south for 1.7 miles to Ault Field Road.

But for now, we'll follow the primary PNT route by turning east on Frostad Road for 0.3 miles to find Taylor Road. Turn to the southwest and follow Taylor Road 0.5 miles to where it turns due south and we go another 1.3 miles as Taylor Road rounds the bend into Fakkema Road. Take Fakkema road due west for 1.6 miles to intersect State Route 20. Here we turn north for 0.2 miles to Ault Field Road and our next waypoint. Look for the two Navy jet fighters on pedestals on the corner.

0976P 4.7mi 48° 19.731'N 122° 37.772'W 120' State Route 20 X Ault Field Road

Trail Angel (Oak Harbor): See details at the end of this chapter.

Before we discuss the route west on Ault Field Road, you might want to note that the town of Oak Harbor is less than 2 miles south on SR20. Since you're going to be road walking for the next ten miles anyway, you may consider following SR20 south into Oak Harbor with the shopping areas and multiple fast food places right on the highway.

Back to the PNT. We turn west on Ault Field Road, again road walking on the road shoulder and sidewalk. In about 1.7 miles there is a pizza place and a gas station mini-mart. Go west another 1.2 miles to the end of the road as it rounds south into Golf Course Road, which we follow for 1.0 miles. Next, we turn west on Crosby road for a little over 0.5 miles as it then rounds south. As the road rounds south there is a dirt parking area on the northwest side of the road. At the south end of the parking lot we take the Moyer's Loop Trail into Joseph Whidbey State Park and to our next waypoint.

0981P 4.3mi 48° 18.659'N 122° 42.118'W 60' W. Crosby Road @ Whidbey State Park

There are several dirt paths in this area and you just need to pick the one that takes you southwest into the trees and to the beach. This is only about 0.6 miles where we find the beach trail to the south for 0.1 miles into a small parking lot and West Beach Road with a pit toilet and water spigot.

0983P 1.6mi 48° 17.898'N 122° 43.491'W 10' West Beach Road X West Beach (Beachwalk)

From the parking lot the primary PNT route is a beach walk south. As an alternative entrance to the beach, we can hike south on West Beach Road for 0.7 miles to find private homes between us and the ocean. Once we are clear of the homes we can walk on the beach for the next 5.6 miles down to Ebey State Park. The beach is very rocky slowing your pace and maybe impassable if the tide is up.[DV]

If the weather or tides aren't right, then we have the option of staying south on West Beach Road for 4.9 miles to Libbey Road.** Turn west for 0.6 miles into a picnic area to rejoin the beach walk. Or, go west only 0.3 miles on Libbey Road to Hill Valley Drive and follow it south to Ebey State Park.

**Trail Angel (Coupeville): See details at the end of this chapter. The "Happy House" is a quarter mile east of the intersection of West Beach Road and Libbey Road.

0987P 4.6mi 48° 13.634'N 122° 46.152'W 5' Beach Trail @ Fort Ebey State Park

The primary PNT route has us continuing the beach walk south for the next 2.3 miles. This waypoint offers the opportunity to climb the bluff into Fort Ebey State Park, as described here. But, be advised, you will need to scamper down the steep bluff to the beach in about 1.7 miles to avoid trespassing on private property prior to our next waypoint.

Here is the description if you chose to climb the bluff here. We're at the north end of the park near the picnic area. Fort Ebey has campsites for hikers, about 0.9 miles south and a little inland from the Bluff Trail, just past the old gun battery. The state camping fee is about $12 per night. If you keep to the trail we will come to another picnic area with water and vault toilets, just north of the old gun battery. Keep south past the gun battery to the signed Bluff Trail with a small PNT insignia on it. Within another 0.5 miles there are group camping sites right near the trail on the bluff.

There is a picnic area on the PNT in Ebey State Park, where you can divert inland (east) to head into Coupeville, as described below. Follow the Kettle Trail through the State Park to SR 20, then south on the paved, non-motorized bike path into town.[DV and 46]

Hiking above the beach, we keep south on the Bluff Trail for another 0.1 miles just past the group camping site where the Bluff Trail ends and the PNT continues on the Cedar Hollow Trail. Continue down Cedar Hollow Trail past the old DNR campsites and outhouses until you get to the bottom of the saddle. A wooden fence bars your way if you want to slide down the hill to the beach below. If you look over the edge you can see two pink flags where some intrepid PNT hiker flagged the trail previously. The fence is easy to crawl through or go around if you want to go that way. Be sure NOT to go through any of the earlier fences with the warning signs. Those trails were washed out several years ago and are seriously undercut. They are dangerous![37] A 2015 hiker reported that, *"Personally I think getting down to the beach here, even on the safer route, is too dangerous. I walked the Kettle Trail back to the bike path along SR20 and then road walked to Ebey's Landing."*[50]

While on the beach at this short section there is private property above you. Do not try to bushwhack along the top of the bluff here.[49]

0989P 2.3mi 48° 12.240'N 22° 44.311'W 0' Beachwalk X Bluff Trail

The primary PNT route now climbs the bluff with three short switchbacks climbing the bluff, or you can stay on the beach. I recommend the Bluff Trail as it is a little easier and faster, and with a better view, rather than continuing the beach walk. Either way we keep working south for 1.6 miles to the end of the Bluff Trail and to our next waypoint. There is a small parking lot at the trailhead.

0991P 4.0mi 48° 11.550'N 122° 42.518'W 20' Beach Walk @ Ebey's Landing

Resupply: Off the PNT route you can hike about 2.4 miles north on Ebey's Landing Road to reach the small town of Coupeville, a quiet farming, waterfront community. There are no chain restaurants in town. They do have good food and B&Bs, but they might be a little upscale for most "hiker trash." There is also, however, the very mediocre Tyee Motel, at 405 South Main Street, with room rates around $75. The attached restaurant serves all three meals and the town grocery store is right across the street.[GT]

Trail Angel (Coupeville): See details at the end of this chapter.

Back to the primary PNT route as we beach walk south from Ebey's Landing, but we can also walk down Hill Road paralleling the beach. If you take the road, to get back to the beach you'll have to scramble down the 150' bluff to the beach when the road turns east. Beach walk south for a total of 2.5 miles from Ebey's Landing, looking for the point where the bluff rises significantly higher. There is an old concrete gun battery at this point if you can see it from the beach. Note that along the way there is a "Private Beach Next ½ Mile" sign, so presumably you may be trespassing.[50]

You can continue to beach walk around Admiralty Head, but I recommend you climb the bluff into Fort Casey State Park and follow the well-defined trails. If you leave the beach walk early, you will pass through part of old Fort Casey that is now owned and operated by Seattle Pacific University. Once you start to climb the bluff you should see the Lighthouse and the PNT marked trail. Water and vault toilets are available in the picnic area. Once past the lighthouse follow the roads east to the RV campground and step over the cable to the Port Townsend-Keystone ferry parking lot and our next waypoint.

0995P   3.6mi   48° 09.544'N   122° 40.354'W   10'   State Route 20 @ Port Townsend-Keystone Ferry

The Port Townsend – Keystone Ferry operates from 6:30 am to 9:15 pm seven days a week making ten round trips per day, once about every 90 minutes. The passenger-only fee in early 2019 is expected to be $3.45 one-way for a walk-on passenger. There is galley food service on the ferry during the summer.

RESUPPLY OPTIONS

0952P   48° 30.270'N   122° 36.547'W   30'   Tommy Thompson Trail X 22nd Street @ Anacortes   **Anacortes:** Directly on the PNT primary route, most of the stores and restaurants can be found on the north-south Commercial Avenue/SR20.

0976P   4.0mi   48° 19.731'N   122° 37.772'W   120'   State Route 20 X Ault Field Road   **Oak Harbor:** This town provides multiple opportunities for resupply and lodging along the two mile stretch of SR20, south of the waypoint.

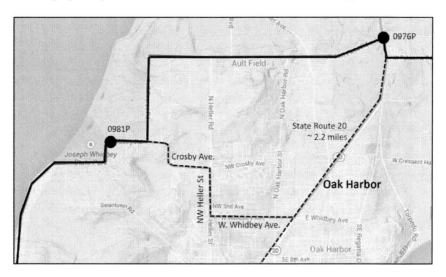

0991P   48° 11.550'N   122° 42.518'W   20'   Beach Walk @ Ebey's Landing **Coupeville:** Hike about 2.4 miles north on Ebey's Landing Road to reach this small, quiet, farming and waterfront community. Look for the Tyee Motel, at 405 South Main Street, with an attached restaurant that serves all three meals and the town grocery store is right across the street.

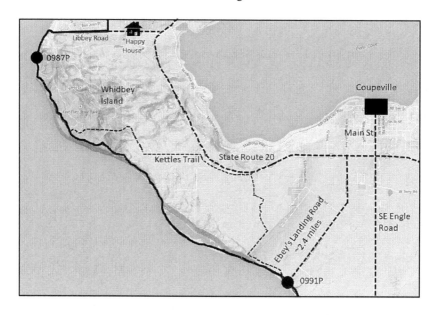

Trail Support

0976P Oak Harbor: Skip LeMay, skiplemay@hotmail.com, (360) 632-0629. Contact by phone or email. Located 1.7 miles south of where the beach walk and West Beach Road separate at mile 0982. Two guest bedrooms and lots of room in the yard to camp if the guest rooms are full, wifi, laundry, showers, and rides to Oak Harbor for resupply. Pet friendly. Feel free to contact for local area information. Will accept and hold hiker packages - contact via email for mailing address. Would appreciate an estimated ETA/updates. Note: Access only from West Beach Road; do not attempt to scale the cliff from the beach walk at this point.

0987P Whidbey Island, Coupeville: "The Happy House" lernr730@aol.com, Rebecca cell (360) 632-1701; John cell (360) 632-3169. Hiker box, loaner clothes, loaner swim suits for the hot tub, showers, laundry, wifi, maps of Olympic Park for permit planning, two guest bedrooms and lots of room in the yard to camp if the guest rooms are full. Send hiker packages to: (your name), c/o The Happy House, 2396 Libbey Rd, Coupeville, WA 98239. An estimated ETA would be helpful.

If you are traveling westward, our home is 3 miles **BEFORE** Coupeville. We are a quarter mile east of the intersection of West Beach and Libbey Road.

Tim Youngbluth

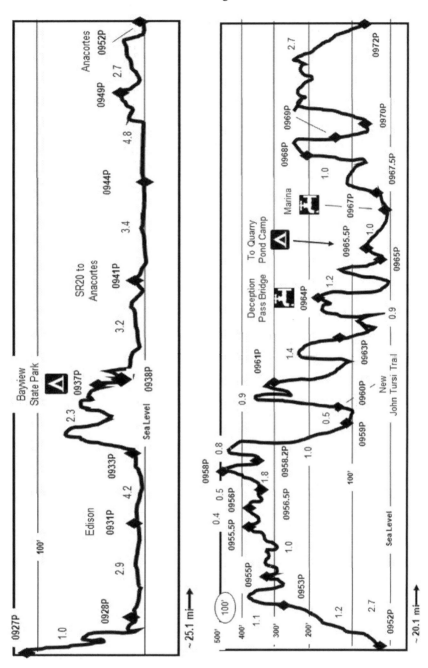

228

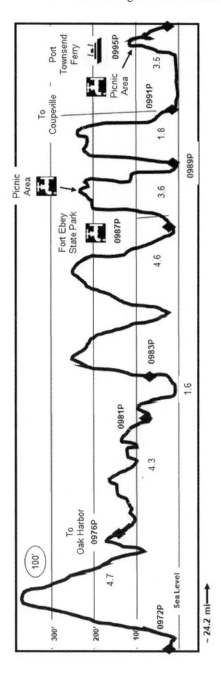

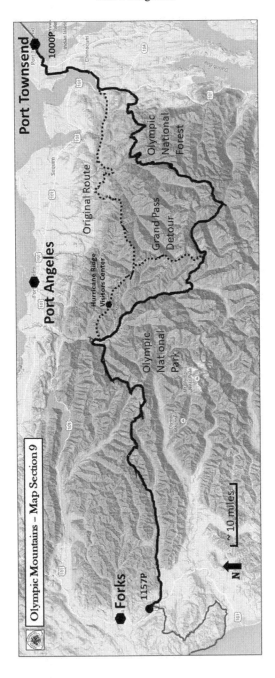

CHAPTER TEN
OLYMPIC MOUNTAINS – MAP SECTION 9
Admiralty Inlet to Bogachiel River

PNT at Grand Pass, Olympic National Park

Key Trail Notes

Highlights: All of Olympic National Park

Primary Route Estimated Elevation Change: 20,100' climb / 19,870' descent

Route Alternates: Olympic National Park Hurricane Ridge; Grand Pass detour

Possible Resupply: Port Townsend; Hurricane Ridge Visitors Center (minimal); Forks

Parks/Forests: Olympic NF; Olympic NP

Permits: Olympic NP Backcountry camping and reservations by submitting the form: http://www.nps.gov/olym/planyourvisit/upload/Wilderness-Reservation-Form.pdf

Other Notes: Bear canisters recommended.

"DO NOT under any circumstances shortcut the Olympics. The park is simply amazing and was my favorite part of the entire PNT."[BT]

1000P 0.0 mi 48° 06.745'N 122° 45.672'W 10' Port Townsend Ferry Dock X Water Street

Trail Angels (Port Townsend): See details at the end of this chapter.

Let's assume that we have just disembarked from the ferry and want to go straight to the trail. You'll, however, likely want to spend some time in Port Townsend and afterward, we turn south on Water Street–State Route 20. In about 0.5 miles SR20 bears to the right (toward the Safeway grocery store), while we bear left onto Washington Street. Follow Washington Street, which is now one block east of SR 20, for 0.3 miles to cross into the public parking and then past the marina. In 0.2 miles after entering the public parking you come to the Larry Scott Trail and our next waypoint.

If perhaps you decide to continue on SR20 to get to Safeway, then from the grocery store cross the street at the traffic light onto Haines Place. Walk through the boat yard to find the trailhead parking area and a public toilet. This entry is about 0.15 miles southwest of the waypoint described below.

1002P 1.0mi 48° 06.357'N 122° 46.737'W 10' Larry Scott Trail @ Port Townsend

The Larry Scott Memorial Trail (LST) is an extension of the Olympic Peninsula Trail, as well as the primary PNT route. It is a relatively smooth multi-purpose non-motorized trail. It is under long term development and you'll have to see how far it goes.

Follow the LST southwest along the bay for 1.0 miles on a slow uphill grade to where it turns inland, just before the paper mill. Continue west and uphill along this old railroad bed for another 0.8 miles, past Thomas Street, to where it rounds to the southwest again and crosses Mill Road.

1003P 1.0mi 48° 05.931'N 122° 48.677'W 120' Larry Scott Trail X Mill Road

Just after Mill Road the LST jogs northwest, paralleling the road up towards SR20 for 0.1 miles, then turns south, just east of SR20. Follow the LST south for 0.6 miles to where it crosses under SR20 and soon turns west. Keep west on the LST as it passes under Discovery Road and then another 0.5 miles to our next waypoint, at the Cape George Road Trailhead.

1005P 1.7mi 48° 05.503'N 122° 50.132'W 220' Larry Scott Trail X Cape George Road

This is a three-way intersection with Cape George Road to the north and Nelson's Landing Road to our south, with Woodduck Way crossing both. Follow the trail west for a little more than 0.1 miles as it parallels Cape George Road. We want to be on the south side of the fence.

The Larry Scott Trail is part of the longer Olympic Discovery Trail, a designated non-motorized, multi-use trail spanning the north end of the Olympic Peninsula. The route spans around 140 miles between Port Townsend,

Washington and La Push, Washington. As of 2017, 80 miles of this trail are complete and additional miles under construction.

The trail winds south and west, past a parking area, for about 0.5 miles where it turns due south to hike next to South Edwards Road. This well-established trail keeps south but then turns east to hike next to Douglas Way with another trailhead. We keep east on the trail to cross South Discovery Road, where the trail turns south again for 0.2 miles.

Here, the LST turn east for only 0.1 miles to turn south away from streets and through a greenbelt. The trail ends in a parking area trailhead on South Discovery Road. Turn east on Discovery Road for 0.3 miles to State Route 20 and our next waypoint.

1009P 4.2mi 48° 02.958'N 122° 49.178'W 130' State Route 20 X Four Corners Road

There is a gas station and mini-mart on the southeast corner as we turn south on SR20. Caution: this section of SR20 has heavy traffic with narrow shoulders. An alternate route is being explored, but it is not official and not drawn on the map. There is a bus stop at Four Corners which will take hikers south to US Highway 101. This is highly recommended--SR20 is too dangerous to road walk.

Nevertheless, sticking to the primary PNT route from Four Corners, we hike south for 2.5 miles to cross Anderson Lake Road, which comes in downhill from the east.

1012P 2.6mi 48° 00.822'N 122° 49.818'W 100' State Route 20 X Anderson Lake Road

Keep hiking along SR20 through a heavily wooded screen on both sides of the road for another 1.9 miles to reach Eaglemount Road.

1013P 1.9mi 47° 59.550'N 122° 51.106'W 420' State Route 20 X Eaglemount Road

From here SR20 continues to the west slightly downhill for another 1.8 miles to reach our next waypoint at the junction with US Highway 101.

About 100 yards before the junction with US101, SR20 spits at a 'Y' to facilitate traffic entering US101. In between the 'Y' on US101 there is a small local food joint with a giant 4' hamburger out front – it must be good!

1015P 1.8mi 47° 59.263'N 122° 53.207'W 10' State Route 20 X US Highway 101

Decision Time. The original PNT route at this waypoint takes on a west route into the Olympic National Forest and Olympic National Park. This alternate route is described at the end of this section. For now, we'll follow the primary PNT route which turns us south on US101. FYI: 0.2 miles northwest at the junction of US101 and Uncass Road there is the Village Store. It is not large but it is there just in case you need to top off with resupply, or fresh coffee, etc.

Back to the primary PNT route and US101. We turn east and follow it as it rounds to the south, through the valley with Snow Creek. To our west is private farm land. In about 2.2 miles US101 comes to an overpass with State Route 104. Keep to US101 south under the over pass for another 0.9 miles to West Snow Creek Way, and our next waypoint.

1019P 3.5mi 47° 56.414'N 122° 53.079'W 210' US 101 X West Snow Creek Way @ US101 Mile Marker 286

Turn west on the unsigned W. Snow Creek Way for only about 130 yards to the junction with Skidder Hill Road. Turn southwest on the unsigned Skidder Hill Road for only 15 yards or so, to find the junction with Camp Talbot Road (just a dual track driveway), which we follow southwest for 0.2 miles to pick up the unsigned Little Skidder Trail. [47° 56.239'N 122° 53.187'W] Keep straight; do not turn up hill on the dual tracks to the trailer.

The LSHT is a 2.9 mile trail along the east side, then south side, of Skidder Hill which traverses through old logging areas. The trail climbs consistently on a reasonable grade into a confusing area. Look carefully to cross several old skid tracks and logging roads.

1022P 3.1mi 47° 54.926'N 122° 55.277'W Little Skidder Trail X Snow Creek Road FR2850

The primary PNT route turns north on FR2850, which crosses Anderson Creek in about 110 yards, which may have water. Keep north on FR2850 for 1.3 miles where it rounds to the west for another 1.1 miles and into our next waypoint at the junction with Forest Road 2889. Just before our waypoint you will enter the Olympic National Forest.

1024P 2.3mi 47° 56.073'N 122° 56.736'W 1070' Forest Road 2850 X Forest Road 2889

We turn south on FR2889 as it climbs through heavy forest about 150' elevation above Rixon Creek to the southeast. After 1.2 miles FR2889 technically ends, but we continue to follow the tracks southwest for another 0.6 miles gaining 340' elevation.

Here the trail jogs briefly to the north on Forest Road 2847 in a small saddle. Given the thick forest surrounding us at this point, we may not even recognize the rising terrain on either side. Follow FR2889 around the "hump" and to the southwest on a slight uphill grade for another 0.8 miles to where it turns north and into our next waypoint.

1026P 2.8mi 47° 55.107'N 122° 58.623'W 2210' Forest Road 2889 X Bushwhack Point

Just after the old forest road FR2847 turns north, look for the small creek that flows from the west to the east. Bushwhack along the creek, following it upstream and steeply uphill as it rounds to the southwest. Your bushwhack route through the thick forest and along the creek is about 0.3 miles, partly through new growth of a 2006 clear cut. Follow the edge of the new growth, hopefully by the creek, to the junction with Forest Road 2814 and our next waypoint.

1027P 0.3mi 47° 54.952'N 122° 58.776'W 2380' Bushwhack X Forest Road 2814

Hike north only about 0.5 miles looking for the trailhead for the Snow Creek Trail 890 on the west side of the road.

1028P 0.5mi 47° 55.323'N 122° 58.974'W 2340' Forest Road 2814 X Snow Creek Trail 890

There are no reports of signage at the trailhead, nor of the trail conditions. TR890 immediately climbs to the south through thick forest.

1029P 0.9mi 47° 54.764'N 122° 59.128'W 2840' Snow Creek Trail 890 X Deadfall Trail 849

At this trail junction we turn directly west, continuing on TR890 for about 0.8 miles. The trail climbs to the 4000' contour where we then follow the trail north to the summit of Mount Zion in another 1.1 miles.

1030P 1.8mi 47° 55.403'N 123° 00.636'W 4270' Snow Creek Trail 890 X Mount Zion Trail 836 @Mount Zion

There once was a fire tower on the summit, but it is long gone and the forest is reclaiming the views. Through the trees though, you might see the San Juan Islands to the north. TR836 is reported to be one of the best trails for wild flowers in the Pacific Northwest in the early summer and "rhodies" later in the summer.

At the trail junction we follow TR836 northwest along the western slope of Mount Zion on a reportedly good tread and well-maintained trail. It follows the ridge below the crest for about 0.6 miles to where it turns back to the south and begins to drop us downhill before quickly returning back to the northwest. In another 0.4 miles the trail decidedly turns back south and down the ridge, where we lose 700' elevation over the next 0.7 miles. This brings us to the trailhead at Forest Road 28.

1032P 1.7mi 47° 55.374'N 123° 01.558'W 2960' Trail 836 X Sleepy Hollow Trail 852 (signed) @ Gold Creek Road - Road 28

The Olympic NF shows this waypoint to be a trailhead for Trail 836 and Trail 852.[29] There is a parking area with a toilet and picnic table[ES] on the west side of the road. Note that some maps show this as Forest Road 2849. It is not.

We cross the parking area to find TR852 as the old forest road – jeep trail leads us south, winding downhill for 0.7 miles and losing about 400' elevation. Here the road/trail turns to the northwest, hovering around the 2500' contour. The last 0.1 miles of the road turns back to the southeast to intersect old Forest Road 2830.

1034P 2.1mi 47° 55.341'N 123° 02.880'W 2230' Trail 852 X Old Forest Road 2830.

This old forest road has not been used by vehicles for 10-15 years, although on some maps it is shown as Gold Creek Road – Road 28. Clearly there are no dual vehicle tracks visible on this road, now Trail 852.

We turn back northwest on TR852, going slightly downhill, for only 0.6 miles. Here we meet the end of Forest Road 2830 and a parking area. While FR2830 continues north, we turn west following TR852 as it winds back to the south temporarily to cross a creek in 0.15 miles.

After the creek, TR852 climbs west for 1.3 miles where it crosses an old forest road and then circles to the south. In another 0.4 miles, after turning back south and dropping downhill, TR852 intersects with old Forest Road 030. At this point neither road has shown much vehicle traffic in a few years.

1037P 2.5mi 47° 55.693'N 123° 04.569'W 2680' Trail 852 X Old Forest Road 030

FR030 heads east uphill while the primary PNT route on TR852 keeps working south on a level grade for 1.2 miles. Near a bend in the trail we cross an unnamed forest road that runs east and uphill. Within about 70 yards after the bend there may be a small creek with water. Keep south on TR852 on a slight downhill grade for another 0.5 miles to where the trail turns back to the north as it crosses a creek.

TR852 now climbs north along the eastern ridge with several PUDs for about 1.4 miles, gaining a total of 200' elevation, putting us near the crest of the ridge. Here the remnants of the old forest road, now TR852, turn southwest downhill for 0.2 miles to intersect with the Gold Creek Trail 830 at our next waypoint.

1040P 3.3mi 47° 55.118'N 123° 05.294'W 2620' Trail 852 X Gold Creek Trail 830 (Note: Trail may be signed as Tubal Cain Trail 840)

Turn south on TR830, following it for 3.6 miles along the western slope of the ridge above the Dungeness River, which lies about a quarter mile to our west and about 900' below. There are large old-growth Douglas fir trees in this part of Olympic NF. The trail climbs on a relatively good grade for the first 2.0 miles, gaining about 800' in elevation to where it then descends to level around the 3200' contour. TR830 heads southeast to finish by crossing Forest Road 2870 at the trailhead for the Tubal Cain Trail 840.

1043P 3.2mi 47° 53.172'N 123° 05.494'W 3260' Forest Road 2870 X Tubal Cain Trail 840

The trailhead is a small parking area with no toilets. TR840 is 8.6 miles of leg burning climbs, tracing the route miners took to get to their camps in the early 1900s. At first it is about 8% grade but then turns to a 10-15% grade up toward Buckhorn Pass. So, let's press on. The trail departs the parking area on a short leg south and downhill to cross the creek on a log bridge. You may see indications of the old Silver Creek Shelter in this area.

Soon the trail turns back to the northwest on a long switchback and into the Buckhorn Wilderness. In 0.7 miles from the trailhead, after gaining about 200' elevation, the trail turns south following Copper Creek up into Marmot Pass. As you climb along the ridge up the valley, you should have great views of Buckhorn and Iron Mountains towering in front of you.

About 3.0 miles from the trailhead TR840 crosses an unnamed trail that heads east straight uphill. This spur trail is 0.7 miles long and heads into Tull Canyon with a 480' elevation gain. If you're up for a side trip, there is an old mine shaft just up the spur trail but deemed to be extremely dangerous to enter. Further along the spur trail you can discover the ruins of an old mining town and the wreckage of a WWII B-17 bomber.[20] Past the crash site there is beautiful lupine filled alpine meadow which makes a great backcountry campsite.

Back on TR840, we keep south past the spur trail and we keep climbing into our next waypoint in 0.4 miles. Here TR840 crosses Copper Creek to transition and climb along the far ridge.

1047P 3.5mi 47° 50.938'N 123° 06.124'W 4320' Tubal Cain Trail 840 @ Copper Creek

At the crossing there is a popular trail campsite near the old mine. The trails in this area may be a little confusing due to previous hikers camping in this area. The Washington Trail Association reports that, "…the Tubal Cain Mine is a private inholding within the wilderness and is still active (somewhat); respect all postings and leave any equipment alone."[20]

After crossing Copper Creek the trail does a short zigzag north-south up about 100' to settle on a north track climbing for 0.5 miles. You'll gain 400' elevation above the creek going north to the point where the trail does a sharp switchback to the south. This southbound leg is through a relatively treeless meadow along the side of the slope for 1.3 miles, gaining only another 500' elevation. This takes us into our next waypoint where there is a spur trail to Buckhorn Lake.

1049P 2.0mi 47° 50.477'N   123° 06.940'W 5200' Trail 840 X Spur Trail to Buckhorn Lake

Look for the "Buckhorn Lake" sign and arrow tacked to a cedar tree. The spur trail heads southeast and east downhill, dropping 150' elevation to the lake, which is tucked into thick timber[20]. The lake does provide a good trail camp under cover.

Next, TR840 does a series of switchbacks in and out of the trees over the next 0.7 miles, moving west away from Copper Creek. TR840 then settles back to the southwest, continuing its climb up to Marmot Pass as it comes near the crest of the ridge. The views are exceptional along this treeless portion of the trail. Even in August you may find lingering portions of snowfields on this ridge. Keep south into our next waypoint at the junction with the Upper Big Quilcene Trail 833.1 at Marmot Pass.

1052P 3.0mi 47° 49.084'N   123° 08.003'W 5980' Trail 840 X Upper Dungeness Trail 833.2 X Upper Big Quilcene Trail 833.1 @ Marmot Pass

As TR840 ends and TR833.2 begins at Marmot Pass, we descend south on TR833.2. About 0.9 miles from the pass we enter a series of four switchbacks, dropping 400' elevation over 0.6 miles. Here the trail resumes its course south for 0.3 miles to come into our next waypoint at the Boulder Shelter and the Home Lake Trail 893.

1053P 1.7mi 47° 48.351'N   123° 08.601'W 4920' Trail 833.2 X Home Lake Trail 893 @ Boulder Shelter

The Shelter is about 100 yards down TR893, then off another 70 yards or so on another spur trail.[GT] The shelter is old but substantial with a table and bench, and wires in the rafters. It is located on an open knoll and there are grass tent sites nearby in the cedars. There is a small stream flowing west nearby.

We pick up TR893 as it rounds south on a relatively level grade to enter Olympic National Park in 0.9 miles.

1054P 1.0mi 47° 47.735'N   123° 08.993'W 4830' ONP Boundary Constance Pass Trail

From here, backcountry camping permits are required in the park, but reservations are not required in this area. Bear canisters are recommended in this subalpine area because the surrounding trees are not tall enough to hang food the recommended 12' high. Open fires are prohibited—stoves only.

After entering the park the trail begins a gradual descent along the western slope of the Cloudy and Warrior Peaks far above you to the east. Follow the trail downhill for another 1.4 miles to cross Home Creek, but along the way you should find many small streams and waterfalls above you. The trail in this portion is very rocky and may cross some lingering snowfields.

After crossing the creek, the trail climbs along the spine of a minor ridge for another 0.7 miles to reach Home Lake. Home Lake is a very nice small lake— good for a quick dip—and a good trail camp but you can expect bugs even at this altitude. After the lake TR893 climbs on switchbacks 500' in a little over 0.3 miles to crest at Constance Pass and our next waypoint.

1057P 3.7mi 47° 46.030'N 123° 09.988'W 5840' Constance Pass Trail @ Contance Pass

We head due west on the CPT, following the trail along the open ridge, climbing another 600'. The views to the south offer one of the best along the entire PNT, but there will be more to come. Note that we're not done climbing once we reach Constance Pass as we proceed up the ridge.[GT] About 0.7 miles after the pass there is reportedly a rock shelter built by hikers that may give us some temporary relief from the winds along the ridge. The views here are reported to be amazing, too.

Soon after the shelter the trail turns southwest and begins a series of twists, turns and switchbacks to take us down the steep ridge. In about 1.0 miles the trail drops us over 900' elevation into Sunnybrook Meadows.

There is an Olympic NP trail camp in the meadows area with a good creek. From here the CPT drops like "crazy" over the next 3.2 miles with too many switchbacks to count, losing a total of about 4,300' elevation from the top of the ridge. This takes us into our next waypoint at the junction with the Dosewallips River Trail.

1062P 4.8mi 47° 44.875'N 123° 12.399'W 2190' Constance Pass Trail X Main Fork Dosewallips River Trail

The DRT runs northwest and southeast paralleling high above the steep bank of the Dosewallips River below. About 1.1 trail miles east is the Olympic NP Dose Forks trail camp. The primary PNT route, however, takes us the other direction, to the northwest and upstream. The trail has ups and downs along the ridge but overall gains elevation for the next 3.4 miles as we hike through very thick forest. Along the trail we will cross four creeks, flowing west into the river below, providing good opportunity for water. Our next waypoint is crossing Burdick Creek on the DRT.

1065P 3.1mi 47° 46.476'N 123° 15.403'W 2640' Dosewallips River Trail @ Burdick Creek

Here the DRT turns north, still following the river upstream and climbing. Over the next 1.8 miles the trail gains about 520' elevation as it takes us into the Olympic NP Deception Creek Camp. No reservations are required for this camp. In 2017 there was a pit toilet and the bear wire is a little further up the trail on the way to the toilet.[ES]

We follow the trail as it rounds to the west still on the steep slope of the high ridge to our north. In an estimated 0.7 miles past Deception Creek there is Camp Marion, which also offers a trail camp and shelter. Then in another 0.7 miles past Camp Marion, the trail crosses the Gray Wolf Trail, which heads up the canyon wall to the east. We, however, keep to the primary PNT route following the river upstream. At this point the river is now more a creek, but we follow it on the trail west for another 1.7 miles and into our next waypoint at the Olympic NP Bear Camp. Streams on the map in this portion of the trail are not reliable enough for water.

1070P 4.8mi 47° 48.557'N 123° 18.877'W 3870' Dosewallips River Trail @ Bear Camp

Bear Camp offers a toilet and bear wire, and like other camps along the DRT, no fires are permitted. We keep hiking west on the DRT, still following along the north side of the river, as the canyon seems to narrow and we continue to climb. As the trail breaks through the thick forest we should be able to see Mount Fromme straight ahead. In 1.7 miles past Bear Camp there is the Dose Meadows camp, with the customary trail toilet and bear wire.

"Dose Meadows is the best camp on the Dosewallips River Trail."[ES] There is also a nice little stealth camp up towards the pass, right before the trail leaves the more brushy-forested area and crosses the large open meadow for the final climb.[ES]

1071P 1.7mi 47° 47.864'N 123° 20.650'W 4470' Dosewallips River Trail X Lost Pass Trail @ Dose Meadows Camp

Decision Time: The popular and highly recommended Grand Pass Detour is described in the alternate section at the end of this chapter.

Sticking to the primary PNT route, we continue climbing toward Hayden Pass on the DRT. This trail was reported to be "beautiful" after extensive restoration by the ONP trail crews.[80] After Dose Meadows the trail gains 320' elevation in the first 0.5 miles. Here the trail turns southwest to climb to the top of the ridge and into Hayden Pass. We head south, winding our way up to the crest of ridge for about 1.8 miles, gaining another 1050' in elevation. This is our next waypoint at the junction with the Hayden Pass Trail.

1074P 2.1mi 47° 46.954'N 123° 21.025'W 5850' Dosewallips River Trail X Hayden Pass Trail (HPT) @ Hayden Pass

Follow the sign arrow "Whiskey Bend 25.0." The primary PNT route turns northwest as it transitions onto the HPT and we cross into the meadow, now along the south slope of Mount Fromme. Unfortunately, we're going to be hiking in and out of the burnt area from the 2017 wildfire for the next four miles. The trail hovers around the 5600'-5700' contour for the first 1.0 miles until crossing over the southern shoulder of the mountain. After that it drops down 300' in 0.4 miles, but then our descent steadies as the trails straightens, too. We keep hiking down along this massive ridge for the next 4.1 miles, losing 1,900' elevation.

Look for the trail to cross a creek and turn west for 0.6 miles, losing another 300' elevation, and then turn on switchbacks to the south. We continue downhill for the rest of the trail. The only feasible campsite on the Hayden Pass Trail is near the creek crossing, about 1.0 miles from the lower end of the trail.[GT] As we come into our next waypoint, we have hiked 8.3 miles from Hayden Pass and lost 4,050' elevation to our junction with the Elwha River Trail.

1081P 8.3mi 47° 48.639'N 123° 27.172'W 1800' Hayden Pass Trail X Elwha River Trail (ERT)

There are numerous Olympic NP camps along the Elwha River Trail (ERT). All require permits, but none require reservations, and fires are permitted. The first camp is about 170 yards south of the trail junction at the Hayes River Guard Station. This camp has a pit toilet and bear wire. The ranger and his/her horse may be there when you arrive.

The ERT provides a dramatic change from hiking along the high rocky ridgelines into the lush bottom, wet lowlands of Olympic NP. The ERT, of course, follows the east bank of the Elwha River as we head downstream. This was the first white settler's trail to be blazed across the Olympic Mountains. It was first marked by explorers of the Seattle Press Expedition, in April 1890, and some of their distinctive three-slash blazes can still be found on trees along the route.[21]

Turn north on the ERT, following the marked trail with its well-maintained tread. Spring floods have been known to wash out parts of the trail, but Olympic NP works hard to keep the ERT passable as it is one of the more popular trails in the park. In short order we will pass the Chateau and Tipperary trail camps within the first mile.

We continue hiking north along the river and downstream for 4.9 miles from the trail junction to our next waypoint at the Elkhorn Ranger Station and camp. Just south of the junction is the Olympic NP Stony Point Camp.

1087P 4.9mi 47° 52.369'N 123° 28.172'W 1420' Elwha River Trail @ Elkhorn Camp

Elkhorn Camp has a pit toilet and bear wire, and is found just south of the ranger cabin. But on we go, hiking north downstream along the river for another 1.1 miles to reach Canyon Camp, again with a pit toilet and bear wire.

Continue north still for about 1.5 miles to reach Mary's Falls trail camp, with a pit toilet and bear wire. There is a falls view point off the trail closer to the river where you can find Mary's Falls far up on the ridge to the west. This waterfall has both great height and volume.

We continue our PNT trek northbound on the ERT, where in 0.3 miles north of Mary's Falls Camp the trail turns uphill away from the river, and we climb almost 500' over the next 1.1 miles. The trail grade moderates over the next mile, and then begins to descend slightly, then sharply, into Lillian Camp. Note that trail crosses a footbridge about 0.1 miles east of the map position.

1093P 6.2mi 47° 56.313'N 123° 31.889'W 1370' Elwha River Trail @ Lillian Camp

This camp, like the others, has a pit toilet and bear wire. There is a bridge over the Lillian River with access to water. We keep hiking north on the ERT and cross the Lillian River Trail in 0.3 miles. In another 0.7 miles we cross a footbridge over a creek, as the trail turns west, but still following high above the Elwha River below. We progress down the trail another 1.3 miles into our next waypoint at Michael's Ranch and spur trail to the Hume Ranch Camp.

1095P 2.0mi 47° 57.204'N 123° 33.240'W 1120' Elwha River Trail @ Michael's Ranch

The spur trail to Humes Ranch Camp backtracks southeast down toward the river for about 0.6 miles. This camp has a bear wire but no toilets. Here's a little Olympic trivia for you. The old cabin at Hume Ranch was first built in the early 1900s and was used in the early 1940s by a filmmaker who shot wildlife footage, which became Walt Disney's "Olympic Elk" movie. The park has since restored the cabin, but the wet environment is tough on wood structures. Elk and bear still inhabit this area of the small meadow with good water.

Back to the ERT and Michael's Ranch (old cabin site). Michael's Cabin was occupied by 'Cougar Mike', a local sharpshooter who made a living hunting mountain lion and maintaining trails and phone lines for the Geyser Valley community.[13] I know--enough trivia--time to move on down the trail.

The ERT continues west on a fairly level tread where we cross the Kraus Bottom Trail that would take us back down to the river. We keep hiking for another 0.3 miles looking to cross the Krause Bottom Trail again that heads south to Goblins Gate. Goblins Gate is a rocky outcrop that stands over a tumultuous point where the river is forced through the high, narrow walls of Rica Canyon.

The ERT at this point remains relatively level, but the Elwha River drops well below us, through the sheer canyon walls. In another 1.0 miles we come to the end of the ERT and the trailhead at our next waypoint and Whiskey Bend Road.

1097P 1.9mi 47° 58.069'N 123° 34.945'W 1160' Elwha River Trail X Whiskey Bend Road

The Whiskey Bend Horse Camp has two sites and a small corral for use by backcountry horsemen. We hike along the road following the primary PNT route north and downhill along the side of the ridge. On the map it looks like we are about 500' above Lake Mills to our west and the road generally follows the shoreline.

Lake Mills, however, is gone. In 2011-2012 Olympic NP removed the 100 year-old dam, as well as the Lake Aldwell Dam down river to the north, to restore the natural salmon run from Puget Sound up the Elwha River. All that is left is the gravel sediments of the former lake bottom. Eventually nature, with the help of Olympic NP, will reclaim the vegetation along the banks of the river.

About 2.0 miles north of the Whiskey Bend trailhead you may find on your map the Windy Arm Camp, but Olympic NP does not recognize any official campsites in this area. Another mile past Windy Arm you will pass the site of the old dam. The primary PNT route is just on the other side of the old dam, but we can't cross the Elwha River here, so we keep hiking north to for another 1.2 miles to Olympic Hot Springs Road.

1101P 4.0mi 48° 00.882'N 123° 35.398'W 370' Whiskey Bend Road X Olympic Hot Springs Road

This waypoint is also where the alternate route discussed at the end of this section rejoins the primary PNT route. Just north of the road intersection is the Elwha Ranger station which is manned all summer. In early 2016 the NPS shows both the Altair and the Elwha car campgrounds "destroyed" by flooding from the Elwha River. Removing the dam in 2014 has unleashed the river to find its own course. The Olympic Hot Springs Road was washed out about 1.4 miles north of this waypoint. There is an interim trail east of the road to get you to a new trailhead and past the washout if you are headed north.

Resupply: The closest store for provisions is a small mini-mart 7 miles northeast: 4 miles north on Olympic Hot Springs Road, and then 3 miles east on US101. The nearest grocery store is Safeway in Port Angeles, about 9 miles east on US101.

Back to the PNT. Turn south on the paved Olympic Hot Springs Road to cross the bridge in 0.3 miles and past the previous Olympic NP Altair car campground on the other side. After crossing the bridge, the road begins an uphill grade as it winds higher along the ridge following now the north side of the Elwha River. In 1.1 miles past the bridge the road takes us to the site of the old dam.

Follow the paved road north as it keeps us climbing up the ridge to gain 220' elevation over 0.5 miles. Here, the road turns back south for another 2.0 miles as it climbs another 700' into our next waypoint at the overlook.

1105P 4.0mi 47° 58.984'N 123° 36.808'W 1520' Olympic Hot Springs Road @ Overlook

From this high vantage point we can look to the southeast and see the Elwha River valley and the trail we've just come from. Above the valley to the east is Hurricane Ridge and the alternate PNT route. Leaving the overlook we turn west and uphill, and still on the paved road. In about 0.6 miles past the overlook the road is no longer paved, right about where we find the trailhead for the Happy Lake Ridge Trail.

Although not part of the PNT, the Happy Lake Ridge Trail offers a circular diversion from the PNT, taking you over 3000' higher in elevation and into a more remote section of Olympic NP. The trail circles back and rejoins the primary PNT route by Boulder Creek camp.

We continue to hike west on Olympic Hot Springs Road for another 0.9 miles on a relatively level grade and to our next waypoint.

1107P 2.0mi 47° 59.178'N 123° 38.676'W 1730' Olympic Hot Springs Road X Boulder Creek Trail

The PNTA maps show this as the trailhead, however, it is another 0.4 miles west on the road. Nevertheless, we hike west on the Boulder Creek Trail. Follow this well-marked trail for about 2.4 miles, still on a slight uphill grade into the Boulder Creek Camp and to our next waypoint. About 0.1 miles before the camp there is a spur trail that takes us downhill to the hot springs.

1109P 2.4mi 47° 58.662'N 123° 41.285'W 2150' Olympic Hot Springs Trail @ Boulder Creek Camp, Olympic Hot Springs

First the camp, and then the hot springs. Boulder Creek Camp has a pit toilet, bear wire, and fires are permitted. Reservations are not required. If there is a road closure the Olympic hot springs are hard for everyone else to get to, so you'll likely have them all to yourself. One hiker described them as, "Awesome hot sulfur pools, but lots of 'muck' on the bottom kind of ruins them a bit."[BT] The hot springs are 21 pools, or seeps, several of which have been trapped by rock-lined depressions. The depth of these pools is about one foot and water temperatures vary from lukewarm to 138 degrees F (54 degrees C).[22] Olympic NP advises hikers to bathe at their own risk due to concentration of bacteria that can build up in the summer.

Back to the PNT and the Appleton Pass Trail. As we leave Boulder Creek Camp, bear right through the tent sites continuing west for about 0.8 miles to cross the Boulder Lake Trail, which comes down the ridge from the northwest.

1110P 0.8mi 47° 58.470'N 123° 42.159'W 2420' Boulder Lake Trail X Appleton Pass Trail

We bear left (southwest) at this trail junction on what is now called the Appleton Pass Trail. The trail remains on a relatively level grade around the 2500' contour, still on the north side of Boulder Creek. In 0.8 miles past the trail junction, the Appleton Pass Trail turns south and we must ford North Fork Boulder Creek. In another 0.5 miles we find a short spur trail, and if you choose, follow it to the Little Boulder Falls and a series of cold water swimming holes.[23]

About a mile past the spur trail we re-enter the no fire, stove-only zone of Olympic NP. For a the next 3.6 miles the trail consistently climbs through huckleberry country, gaining almost 2500' elevation, as we enter Appleton Pass and our next waypoint. The last half mile is a tough climb.

1114P 4.4mi 47° 56.322'N 123° 43.396'W 5050' Appleton Pass Trail @ Appleton Pass

At the pass we can see most of central Olympic NP. Look to the southwest and find the High Divide that we'll be hiking soon. At the pass there is a spur trail that leads east to Appleton Pass Camp toward Oyster Lake. There are several sites, a bear wire, but no toilets.

After we cross over the pass the trail turns west and southwest, descending gradually and then far more rapidly. We are now in the Olympic NP Sol Duc area where all food, garbage and scented items must be stored in park approved bear canisters, and reservations for backcountry camping are required. The trail descends almost 2000' over the next 2.2 miles into our next waypoint at the trail junction with the Sol Duc River Trail.

1116P 2.3mi 47° 55.942'N 123° 45.031'W 3090' Appleton Pass Trail X Sol Duc River Trail

Be bear aware! The PNT at this waypoint begins to circle the Seven Lakes Basin. In 2017, bears were sighted daily in this area, even double digit counts in a single day.[ES]

As we turn east and begin uphill again you'll have the Sol Duc River to the south and many Olympic NP camps along the trail. In order of appearance they are Appleton Junction, Rocky Creek, Seven Mile Group Camp, Upper Sol Duc Bridge, Lower Bridge Creek, and Sol Duc Park. All require reservations and bear canisters. Only Sol Duc Park has a toilet and a ranger station.

We hike east for about 0.8 miles to where the trail turns south past the water falls gaining only about 350' elevation. From here the trail climbs another 780' for 2.1 miles into our next waypoint at Sol Duc Park Camp.

1119P 2.1mi 47° 55.170'N 123° 43.724'W 4200' Sol Duc River Trail @ Sol Duc Park Camp

More climbing ahead as we keep south on the Sol Duc River Trail past the Heart Lake Camp through an open meadow. This camp has seven sites, some on both sides of the trail. There is a pit toilet in the southeast side. Bear canisters are required, and of course, reservations. Our next waypoint is only 0.2 miles past Heart Lake Camp, and only 1.0 miles from our last waypoint, but 600' elevation gain.

1120P 1.0mi 47° 54.513'N 123° 44.090'W 4830' Sol Duc River Trail X High Divide Trail (HDT)

At this 'Y' intersection we bear right (west) onto the HDT. Note that ONP advises that there is little opportunity for water on the HDT over the next 8 miles while hiking on the ridge. Keep climbing through the subalpine meadows for 0.6 miles to the crest of the ridge, gaining 430' elevation.

Here we can look north into the amazing Seven Lakes Basin below us, and to the south, Mount Olympus. From here the views get even better as the HDT follows west along the crest of the ridge. Many thru-hikers have proclaimed this to be the best part of the PNT. May the "trail gods" give you fair weather and a clear sky.

On the crest it is a relatively level grade. Down the trail we crest the south shoulder of Bogachiel Peak. The best view of the Seven Lakes region is from the summit of Bogachiel Peak. Look for a spur trail heading northwest to climb the peak. The trail takes us to the summit and is at most a 5 minute hike.[GT]

Back on the HDT we keep southwest briefly, where on the south side of Bogachiel Peak we cross the Hoh Lake Trail.

1121P 1.3mi 47° 54.260'N 123° 46.701'W 5260' High Divide Trail X Hoh Lake Trail

The Hoh Lake Trail would take us south about 1.2 miles to the Hoh Lake Camp. This camp has a pit toilet, bear wire; and reservations are required.

PNT Factoid: To reach the quietest place in the Continental United States (47° 51.959N, 123° 52.221W) follow the Hoh Lake Trail south for a total of 6.0 miles to reach the Upper Hoh River Trail. Turn west, past the Olympus Ranger Station, for 5.6 miles. This proclamation was made by acoustic ecologist Gordon Hempton after a 30 plus year study.[45]

We, however, stay high and keep working west on the HDT along the southern slope of Bogachiel Peak. Our next way point is the spur trail to camps in the Seven Lakes Basin.

1122P 0.8mi 47° 54.715'N 123° 47.383'W 4910' High Divide Trail @ Seven Lakes Spur Trail

There are three trail camps down in the basin: Round Lake, Lunch Lake, and Clear Lake. Lunch Lake is the most popular with a pit toilet and ranger tent. All three require bear canisters and reservations. Again, no fires are permitted in this section of the park. Clear Lake is the furthest from the HDT, a little over 1.2 miles north and down 650' elevation. If you have the supplies, one of these camps is a great place to rest for a day.

On with our PNT trek as we hike west still on the HDT, which keeps us on the southern slope of the ridge, and then around a shallow bowl, always below the crest. In about 1.5 miles the HDT turns north and begins to descend. Go another 0.9 miles downhill, losing 560' elevation to reach a small "unpublished" Olympic NP camp called the Potholes. Here there is a group of tarns among pink and white heather and beargrass, and a wonderful place to soak for a spell.

From the Potholes the HDT keeps north and downhill for another 1.0 miles, losing another 550' elevation to take us into our next waypoint, crossing the Deer Lake Trail, the Deer Lake camp and the Little Divide Trail.

1125P 3.2mi 47° 55.547'N 123° 49.355'W 3550' High Divide Trail X Little Divide/Deer Lake Cutoff Trail

Let's start with the camps around Deer Lake. There are Deer Lake and Canyon Creek 1, 2, and 3 Camps, although the Canyon Creek Camps are north along the Deer Lake Trail and not on the primary PNT route. All camps require reservations, bear cannisters, and no fires are permitted. Only Deer Lake has a pit toilet and a ranger tent.

The trail junction is by the southeast corner of the lake, where we turn left (west) taking a boardwalk across a marshy area to soon find the trail sign for the Mink Lake Trail; the Little Divide/Deer Creek Cutoff Trail has no sign.[DV]

We follow the primary PNT route as it transitions west along the Little Divide Trail for 3.6 miles to reach the Bogachiel River Trail. Note that your map may indicate the Little Divide Trail instead of the Deer Lake Cutoff Trail. The trail turns south temporarily and climbs away from the lake up the ridge before switching back to the west and crossing over the ridge. We'll be hiking about 0.8 miles from the camp and gaining 600' in elevation crossing the crest of the ridge.

The PNT does not go all the way to Bogachiel Lake, but instead the trail stays high on the hillside above that lake. Due to the thick forest we really can't see the lake.[GT] We keep working west climbing again along a ridge up to a high bowl, where we can see the Bogachiel River at least 2,000' below us. About 2.4 miles from Deer Lake, the trail sits on the top of the Low Divide ridge and keeps west for another 0.7 miles, Here, we cross the Mink Lake Trail coming uphill from the north at our next waypoint.

1129P 3.6mi 47° 55.917'N 123° 52.466'W 4080' Little Divide Trail X Bogachiel River Trail (BRT)

About 0.3 miles past the Mink Lake Trail junction, we exit the Olympic NP Sol Duc area, and where camp reservations are no longer required. The BRT follows near the crest of the ridgeline west on a relatively level grade for another 1.3 miles past the trail junction, to a point where it descends on some switchbacks, but keeps west for 0.8 miles. Here we follow it north for 1.9 miles as it descends down to the Bogachiel River and into our next waypoint at the Twenty-one Mile Camp.

1132P 3.9mi 47° 55.923'N 123° 55.393'W 2210' Bogachiel River Trail @ Twenty-one Mile Camp

The camp is located near the old forest service shelter erected in 1930. The 21-mile Shelter is now just a pile of logs, lumber and nails. There is room for two or three tents here.[DV] Fires and camping are permitted along the North Fork Bogachiel River in designated sites and along the various gravel bars. Permits are still required and bear canisters are recommended.

Follow the BRT northwest and then southwest as it parallels the rivers along the southern bank. From this point west we'll be close to the river, but high water should not be a problem from mid to late summer and fall.

The forest changes with the elevation, finally becoming a temperate rainforest of moss-cloaked maples, giant spruces and cedars. Likely if you are hiking in September, the maples will have already been losing leaves as you walk through a papery fall orange on a crunchy trail.[KC]

In 2.9 miles the BRT takes us to the Hyak Shelter Camp. There is no toilet at this camp. There has been work done on the shelter and it is in good shape with some limited camping around, but most of the area is overgrown.[CN] The Hyak Shelter is a better option than the Fifteen Mile Shelter down the trail[49] and looks to be the best along the trail in this area.[GT]

The trail here is overgrown, not well maintained, and has landslide damage. Expect slow going here on the Bogachiel River Trail—it will take much longer than you expect.[ES] Be prepared to get soaked from the brush.[51] This was actually one of the roughest parts of the PNT, but it eventually does smooth out.[80] Hiking west, we're still on the river's southern bank, following it downstream. Although there are some small creeks to ford or rock-hop along here, the only time we need to cross the river is on a bridge before the Fifteen Mile Shelter.[GT] We come to the Fifteen Mile Shelter, just after the bridge to the north side of the river.

1138P 6.0mi 47° 54.128'N 124° 01.354'W 1040' Bogachiel River Trail @ Fifteen Mile Shelter

This is another of the usable shelters along the BRT, with holes in the roof and a slanted dirt floor. There is room for one or two tents in front[CN] but with no toilet or other amenities. This shelter works fine even in the pouring rain, with room to hang clothes to dry.[48] The BRT continues southwest, climbing slightly higher along the north bank and in 0.7 miles, we pass the confluence of the North Fork into the Bogachiel River, below us to the south.

Keep working downhill following the river for another 3.1 miles as the gravel bars grow and the river seems to widen near the Flapjack Shelter, which like the other camps, has no toilet. Be cautious of planning to camp at the Flapjack Shelter as one hiker reports that despite hiking the spur trail to it, there is no "shelter," but there is good camping on land and gravel bars.[CN] To get to the camp turn left (south) toward the river for 0.15 miles to find a fire ring in a huge grassy area plus the sand bar down near the river.[DV] Fires are permitted and bear canisters are recommended.

We continue hiking west, as the BRT drops us now closer to the river bottom, for another 3.7 miles to reach our next waypoint at the Bogachiel Camp and cross the Indian Lakes Trail. Stay straight west to continue on the PNT.[DV]

Good news: in 2017 trail crews have clear the BRT of all blowdowns from about two miles west of Flapjack all the way to the trailhead.[CN]

1146P 7.5mi 47° 53.008'N 124° 10.060'W 450' Bogachiel River Trail X Indian Pass Trail

The junction with Indian Pass Trail, which comes downhill from the north, is about 100 yards west of the camp. We stick to the primary PNT route, following the BRT and the river downstream, still along the northern bank. In 2017, the trail was reported to be in pretty good condition, especially the last 3 miles to the trailhead.[ES]

As we hike west, the gravel bar continues to widen on a slight downhill grade. In 4.0 miles past Bogachiel Camp we exit the Olympic National Park at our next waypoint.

1150P 4.0mi 47° 52.935'N 124° 14.821'W 360' Bogachiel River Trail @ Exit Olympic National Park

Our next waypoint is not very far away at the trailhead for the BRT on North Bogachiel Road. Over time the river has changed its flow and perhaps washed out part of the trail as shown on the map. Keep following the trail west through the lush river bottomland for about 1.2 miles. Here the trail turns north near Morganroth Creek. Follow the muddy tracks uphill for 0.3 miles to North Bogachiel Road and the trailhead, which sits about 140' elevation higher than the river at our next waypoint.

1151P 1.5mi 47° 52.925'N 124° 16.534'W 490' Bogachiel River Trail X North Bogachiel Road - FR 2932

The parking area for the trailhead is about 70 yards east of where the trail exits to the road. We, however, turn west to follow the road downhill through second generation timber and private property on either side of the road. Keep west on FR2932 for 1.9 miles to exit the Olympic National Forest.

The road is renamed Undi Road for the Undi family that homesteaded in this area. There is now private property on both sides of the road and in another 0.3 miles we pass a homestead on the south side. Recent flooding has disintegrated Undi Road from this point west for about 2.5 miles. Look for the Undi Road bypass to the north. There should be stop sign at a 'T' road junction. Taking the bypass we turn north until the next road junction. This should be a DNR road that takes us west back to Undi Road.[ES] This may add a mile or so to your hike but it will save you time. Once back on Undi Road hike northwest for another 2.1 miles as it exits into US Highway 101 at our next waypoint.

1157P 5.2mi 47° 53.695'N 124° 21.859'W 240' North Bogachiel Road X US Highway 101 @ Bogachiel State Park

The nearest grocery store, motel, and restaurants are about 6 miles west/north on US101 in Forks, Washington. The primary PNT route turns east and south on US101, which will be described in the next section. For now, this waypoint concludes our discussion of the primary PNT route for this section.

Alternate Route: Original PNT Route Uncas Road - Hurricane Hill Trail

This alternate route, based on the original PNT, takes us on a northern route through the Olympic National Forest and Olympic National Park and to the waypoints of Dungeness Forks, Deer Park, Hurricane Ridge, and then the Hurricane Hill Trail into the Elwha River to rejoin the primary PNT route. In 2013 a thru-hiker wrote that this route was "amazing, view-saturated, eye-ball-strain-from-staring beautiful."[KC] This route is recommended.

Start: 1015P State Route 20 X US Highway 101

Rejoin: 1101P Hurricane Hill Trail X Olympic Hot Springs Road

Mileage: 51.3 miles; shorter than the primary route by 34.4 miles

Highlights: Most direct route into Olympic National Park, Hurricane Ridge and visitors center

1015P 0.0mi 47° 59.263'N 122° 53.207'W 10' State Route 20 X US Highway 101

At our junction of State Route 20 and US Highway 101, turn northwest for only 0.2 miles to find West Uncas Road. Don't forget the burger stand at this intersection, and there is also a mini-mart, on the northwest corner of West Uncas Road. Follow the paved West Uncas Road as it turns south for 0.9 miles. We first pass Casselary Road on your right and several farms. As the road opens to a field on the east side of the road near our waypoint, look to the west for Salmon Creek Road – Road 2986. You'll see a row of trees and what appears to be a driveway just after.

1016A 1.1mi 47° 58.718'N 122° 53.789'W 70' West Uncas Road X Salmon Creek Road – Road 2986

Trail Angel (Discovery Bay): See details at the end of this chapter.
Hikers report that the road looks like a driveway that goes between the house and the barn on the south side. Look for the PNT sign on the mailbox at 922 West Uncas Road! The owner, Greg, is a nice, friendly guy. If he is out in the yard, he will point you in the right direction. Use the maps he provides that can be found in the covered shed above the metal gate for the route to stay off the property of unfriendly neighbors. In 2019 he is fixing up the shed for a trail cabin to be used over night if you desire. Greg has placed tags along the route to follow to get you successfully through onto the logging road at our next waypoint.

There are some new cattle gates in this field as you hike uphill. You're looking for the second gate and the marshy area, while avoiding the bright shiny gates which are tempting to cross. Follow the tracks as we go under the double power lines for about 70 yards, and reach the edge of the southern power line. Here the predominant tracks turn west, but we should see an obscure road almost hidden in the trees. Do not follow the power line.

After entering the tree line we can then follow the old forest road for 0.7 miles to break out into an open field at the intersection of an unnamed forest road and our next way point. Note that this route crosses private property for about 50 yards, so please be respectful.

1017A 1.2mi 47° 58.380'N 122° 55.133'W 470' Forest Road 2986 X Unnamed Forest Road

The unnamed forest road comes in from the southeast. It actually looks like this is the "new" FR2986, but nevertheless, we turn west. There are a lot of confusing side roads in this area so we just keep hiking west on the best road. In 0.8 miles there is a 'Y' junction with our road to the right (west) and double tracks going left (southwest). We bear right for another 0.15 miles, looking for an old obscure forest road on the left, just past the wooden bridge and creek. We continue west hiking through thick forest for 0.2 miles where the trail opens into an older clearcut area. At the clearcut, we enter the Olympic National Forest. Soon the trail ends on an old spur forest road. We turn northwest and soon find our next waypoint at a 'T' road junction.

1019A 1.6mi 47° 58.572'N 122° 57.435'W 860' Forest Road 2986 X Forest Road 2905

Despite the numerous spur roads navigation is relatively easy as we hike west on the main forest road FR2905. Our next waypoint is with Snow Creek Road – Forest Road 2850, which runs north-south.

1020A 1.3mi 47° 58.451'N 122° 58.229'W 980' Forest Road 2986 X Snow Creek Road – Forest Road 2850

A little more road walking ahead as we turn north on FR2850 and downhill for about 0.8 miles as it rounds to the west. Snow Creek will be on the south side of the road. We hike the road west for another 1.3 miles, still downhill, and into our next waypoint at the junction with Jimmycomelately Road. As we approach this junction, FR2850 turns north and our new road turns sharply back to the south in a tight "U-turn."

1022A 2.1mi 47° 59.142'N 123° 00.328'W 620' Forest Road 2850 X Jimmycomelately Road – Forest Road 2855

FR2855 drops us downhill and south for only about 100 yards before turning back to the west. As we hike on the road we'll pass several other old forest roads, but the one we're on is the best and on a very slight uphill grade. In about 1.8 miles FR2855 turns due west and begins a little steeper grade. Here it comes parallel to Jimmycomelately Creek on the south side of the road. Keep hiking west for another 2.2 miles past some ranches and to our next waypoint at the junction with Palo Alto Road – Road 39. As we approach the junction we enter a large triangle intersection with houses on the south side. Keep west past the houses and onto our next road.

1027A 4.1mi 47° 59.581'N 123° 04.674'W 1400' Forest Road 2855 X Palo Alto Road (paved) FR2909

We now hike due west on the paved Palo Alto Road past ranches in this remote farming area. In 0.6 miles the road turns 90° due south to follow the section line for 0.5 miles, and then southwest and into the trees. In 0.15 miles after entering the trees there is 'Y' intersection, where we bear right (more southwest than south). In another 0.25 miles we find a second 'Y' intersection at the junction with Forest Road 310 and our next waypoint.

1028A 1.6mi 47° 58.916'N 123° 05.970'W Palo Alto Road X Junction Forest Road 2880

Continue southwest on FR2880 on a downhill grade for 1.1 miles to past the NFS Dungeness Forks Campground. This campground has 10 tent sites and a vault toilet. The Fee is $14 per night. Water must be drawn from the Gray Wolf River that flows nearby.

Continue south on FR2880 for another 0.6 miles uphill past the campground to Forest Road 2927, where we turn west and downhill to the Gray Wolf River in another 0.6 miles. Cross the road bridge over the river and climb up the road. We keep north on FR2880 hiking uphill for about 0.3 miles to where the road turns back south. We follow it for another 0.3 miles as it winds west. Here FR2880 turns again north and into our next waypoint at Forest Road 2870, having gained almost 500' elevation.

1031A 1.9mi 47° 58.029'N 123° 07.643'W 1430' Dungeness Road FR2870 X Gray Wolf Trail 34 (Buckhorn National Wilderness)

The original route would have us follow TR834 crossing the Gray Wolf River, as shown on the PNTA maps. The bridge is washed out over the river on this trail and it has been declared impassable by the Forest Service. The trail extends 4.2 miles and then you will have to turn back. There have been no reports of any hikers successfully scaling down to the river and then back up the steep canyon wall in the last six years. This route is not recommended, and therefore, will not be described.

We are now in the Buckhorn National Wilderness until we reach Olympic National Park. Turn north and follow FR2870, still climbing for 1.2 miles, where the road turns west. We climb for another 1.2 miles to where the road turns to the northwest and starts back downhill. This takes us on the final leg for 1.6 miles to cross Forest Road 2878. Keep working west and north, passing Pats Creek. In 0.6 miles past FR2878, on a relatively level grade, we come to the junction with Forest Road 2875 at our next way point.

1036A 4.5mi 47° 59.933'N 123° 10.533'W 1390' Old Forest Road 2880 X Forest Road 2875

We turn left (west), following R2875 for 0.3 miles, passing Pats Creek along the way. Here we start to turn back to the south, and in another 1.3 miles we cross Forest Road 2877, joining FR2875 from the west. We keep hiking due south, now uphill, for another 2.0 miles to the trailhead parking area for the Deer Ridge Trail 846.

1039A 3.5mi 47° 57.888'N 123° 11.642'W 2550' Forest Road 2875 X Camp Trail 838 X Deer Ridge Trail 846

Dispersed camping is allowed near the trailhead in this three unit rustic camp with no toilet or water. We'll hike TR836 for about 3.6 miles to enter Olympic National Park beginning in a forest and ending in an alpine meadow at Deer Park Camp. As we leave the trailhead TR846 climbs south higher on the ridge as it enters a forest of rare yew trees. In about 1.4 miles the trail turns west with good views of the Gray Wolf River canyon.

In another 1.1 miles the trail crests on the top of Deer Ridge and enters the Buckhorn Wilderness, having gained over 1700' elevation in the first 2.5 trail miles. The trail takes us near the crest of the ridge for 0.6 miles before descending along the southern slope for about 0.8 miles. About half way along this slope we enter Olympic National Park.

1042A 2.8mi 47° 56.798'N 123° 13.634'W 4640' Trail 846 @ Olympic National Park Boundary

As a reminder, permits are required, and fires are prohibited in this section of the ONP.

TR846 continues west, near the crest of the ridge, but only for a short while as it drops down along the southern slope below the crest. But then, back up we go as the trail reaches its highest elevation around the 5400' contour, or about 2,850' above the trailhead. From here TR846 descends slightly over the next 0.6 miles to enter a small overview parking area at Deer Park. Follow the lower road downhill west past the campground and past the ranger station to our next waypoint.

1044A 2.2mi 47° 56.984'N 123° 15.890'W 5230' Trail 846 @ Deer Park Camp, Olympic National Park

The Deer Park Campground has 16 tent sites and pit toilets, and two hiker's shelters. Water is available at the trailhead for the Obstruction Point Trail, just past the Ranger Station. There is a spring in the campground, in the drainage west of the hiker/biker sites. The water is cold and clear, but you may have to travel downstream a bit to find a good place from which to draw.[CN] While in this area of Olympic NP, reservations, bear canisters, and permits are required. The camp fee at Deer Park is $15. Remember that we're in a no-fire zone here above 3500' elevation.

Obstruction Point/Deer Park Trail is the one we're looking for. I highly recommend that you carry water, sun block and bug repellant on this high ridge hike. There are few trees, and if the winds are strong, bugs will be the least of your concerns. The trail begins by descending 0.5 miles, then climbs to the crest of the ridge in 0.3 miles, and follows near the top for 3.0 miles, as we gain only about 600' elevation.

Here the trail turns south, as we climb another 320' elevation over the next 0.4 miles to where the trail then turns west, and skirts around the summit of Maiden Peak. Still climbing, we hike along the treeless slope west and south around the bowl. About 0.7 miles after the trail turns south we come to the Roaring Winds Camp.

This very appropriately named Roaring Winds Camp is the only campsite permitted along this trail. As per other Olympic NP camps, it requires reservations and bear canisters. Keep following the trail west, after climbing higher on the ridge, for about another 0.9 miles to come to our next waypoint crossing the Badger Valley Trail.

1050A 5.4mi 47° 55.405'N 123° 20.857'W 6620' Trail 836 X Badger Valley Trail

At the 'Y' junction the Badger Valley Trail would drop us down 1,300' elevation into the valley to then climb back up 700' to join our route in 2.0 miles, very near Obstruction Peak. Olympic NP recommends ice axes along this route if you see any snow down in the valley. There is a very difficult climb at the end of the trail.

For now, we choose to stay on the higher route along the treeless Hurricane Ridge, hiking west and downhill very slightly. In 1.5 miles the trail turns south to round the giant bowl formed on the eastern slope of Obstruction Peak. As we hike south along the ridge, and go slightly downhill, we cross the Badger Valley Trail coming up from the east. From here it is another 0.3 miles uphill into the Obstruction Point observation parking lot and trailhead at our next waypoint. There is a vault toilet at the trailhead.

1052A 2.1mi 47° 55.107'N 123° 22.928'W 6130' Trail 836 X Obstruction Point, Olympic National Park

If you have the energy and want to "bag" another peak along the PNT, Obstruction Peak is a relatively easy one to climb. Find the trail behind the toilet. It is about 0.9 trail miles and 350' elevation gain to up to the summit, but expect your route to be slowed by the tourists in plaid shorts and flip flops. Awesome views![49]

Back to our original PNT route, we head west out of the parking lot for some road walking along the Obstruction Peak Road. Soon this popular gravel road turns northwest downhill along Hurricane Ridge, and then north. There is no water readily available on this road march. Grind it out downhill enjoying the views of the valley and the mountains to the west.

1056A 2.1mi 47° 55.907'N 123° 24.676'W 5990' Obstruction Point Road X Eagle Point Trail

The Eagle Point Trail, at 0.7 miles to the summit, is a popular side trip to the second highest point on the Obstruction Ridge. I bet you want to get to the Hurricane Ridge Visitors Center, so let's continue on our way.

On our way downhill, there is one last side trip to consider in about 1.6 miles. There is a trailhead to take you east to PJ Lake. The trailhead is near mile post 3.8. This is the site of the old Waterhole Picnic area. Sorry, but heading to the lake may not a good option for water in my opinion. The trail would take you about 0.6 miles to the lake, but downhill to the "lake" with about 600' elevation loss.

Keep road walking another 4.0 miles to the end of the road into the massive parking lot of the Hurricane Ridge Visitors Center and our next waypoint.

1059A 5.6mi 47° 58.149'N 123° 29.908'W 5250' Obstruction Point Road @ Hurricane Ridge Visitors Center

We made it! The visitor's center has water, flush toilets and a snack bar. Rangers and phones are also available. Hurricane Ridge Visitor Center has a decent but expensive grill (free soda refills!), and a small selection of chips, bars, candy, muffins, etc. You could resupply snacks here (expensive) but there are no real dinner options.[BT] This is the most popular attraction in the park, being an easy drive from Port Angeles to view Mount Olympus and the surrounding mountains. Note: If you want to go to Port Angeles, this is the best point to hitch a ride.[49]

Hiking out of the visitor's center to the west we follow the road for 0.6 miles to cross the Wolf Creek Trail to the south. This trail is a steep 8.1 miles trail that would take you downhill to end at the Whisky Bend trailhead and rejoin the primary PNT route. We, however, hike west and slightly downhill on the road for another 0.7 miles past the observation parking lot on the south side and into the trailhead parking for the Hurricane Hill Trail and our next waypoint.

1059A 1.4mi 47° 58.595'N 123° 31.057'W 5090' Heart of the Hills Road X Hurricane Hill Trail (HHT)

Just follow the tourists, past the toilet, as they slowly climb along the paved trail, admiring the views and the subalpine terrain. In 1.5 miles you reach the end of the "trail" gaining almost 700' elevation. Leave the tourists behind as we hike west on the far less traveled trail. We remain high on the ridge for about 1.9 miles where we make the most dramatic descent of any parts of the PNT.

Follow the trail as it switchbacks down the ridge, dropping almost 1,500' elevation over the next mile. Here the trail rounds to the northwest and continues downhill for another 1.6 miles to intersect Whiskey Bend Road, losing another 2,500' elevation. The total drop is a mile of elevation from leaving the paved trail above! Once on Whiskey Bend Road we follow the road northwest another 0.15 miles to come to our waypoint and rejoin the primary PNT route.

1101P 5.7mi 48° 00.882'N 123° 35.398'W 370' Hurricane Hill Trail X Olympic Hot Springs Road

Alternate Route: Olympic National Park Grand Pass Detour

This alternate route takes us north to join the original PNT route to Hurricane Hill. This detour was originally recommended because the Hayden Pass Trail was closed due to a wildfire in 2016. It is now recommended because it is one of the most remote, rugged, and scenic routes in Olympic National Park. This alternate route will then also bypass the Elwha River Trail.

Note: Due to the lack of trees along this route, bear canisters should be used for food storage.

Start: 1071P Dosewallips River Trail X Cameron-Lost Pass Trail @ ONP - Dose Meadows Camp.

Rejoin: 1052A Grand Valley Trail @ Obstruction Point

Mileage: 13.2 miles.

Highlights: This popular route may be one of the most remote, rugged and difficult in the park, but it offers absolutely superb views seen by few visitors to Olympic National Park.

1071P 1.7mi 47° 47.864'N 123° 20.650'W 4470' Dosewallips River Trail X Cameron-Lost Pass Trail @ ONP - Dose Meadows Camp.

There is the customary trail toilet and bear wire at Dose Meadows.

Taking the detour to avoid the closed Hayden Pass Trail, we turn northeast on the Lost Pass Trail. This trail may be one of the most rugged and difficult in the park, but it offers absolutely superb views as we climb up it almost 1100' in just 0.8 miles where we reach Lost Pass.

You can enjoy an easy hike for the next 1.0 miles as the trail traverses the treeless western slope of Lost Peak. This section on a clear day offers exceptional views down the steep valley of the Lost River. Soon, however, the trail begins a 1,000' ascent up the left shoulder of Lost Peak to reach the crest in 0.7 miles.

Once on top we are well above the tree line. The trail descends to cross the barren landscape of Cameron Pass. Here, the trail name changes to the Cameron Pass Trail. You can expect spots of snow and ice fields for the next 0.7 miles. In the summer, the trail should easily be visible on the other side of these short patches. Snow could cover this short section of the trail here in mid-September and later.

Past the snow field we keep heading north on a slow descent for about 1.3 miles into our next waypoint.

1075A 4.8mi 47° 50.548'N 123° 21.953'W 4940' Cameron Pass Trail @ Upper Cameron Basin Camp

The campsites are in the basin below the trail. There are no toilets and ONP requires that you bury waste 6-8" deep and 200 feet from water sources and campsites.

The Upper Cameron Basin with the camp is perhaps the most scenic, if not remote, places in Olympic National Park. There are not toilets. Water is available from Cameron Creek.

Back to the detour route, we turn northeast on the trail and descend into the valley and lose our views.

1077A 1.5mi 47° 51.429'N 123° 20.692'W 4180' Lost Pass Trail X Grand Pass Trail X Cameron Creek Trail

Lost Pass Trail ends here at a 'Y' junction. There are no reports of signage. Our detour routes heads north (left) uphill. If you find yourself continuing east sharply downhill into a clearing, then you have missed the junction.

The Grand Pass Trail climbs steeply and turns northwest for the next 1.2 miles on multiple switchbacks to reach the crest at Grand Pass. The last 0.5 miles is through anther treeless expanse. As we reach the top, be sure to stop and look to the south for amazing views of valley below where we just hiked and the Cameron Glaciers beyond.

On top there is an unnamed spur trail that runs southwest for better views of the valley and the glaciers. We keep north through this treeless section on the Grand Pass Trail through more small snow and ice patches for the next 0.7 miles. Again, after the snow field, the trail works downhill turning northeast into our next waypoint.

1080A 3.1mi 47° 52.703'N 123° 21.093'W 5060' Grand Pass Trail X Spur Trail to Gladys Lake Camp

Gladys Lake Camp is another primitive backcountry camp with no privy. It is about 0.1 miles south on the east side of the small lake.

Continuing on the Grand Pass Trail, we keep descending heading northeast. Shortly we come to Moose Lake Camp. This is a nicer lake and the camp is near the water. It has bear wires and a privy.

1081A 0.6mi 47° 53.005'N 123° 21.093'W 5060' Grand Pass Trail @ Moose Lake Camp

Leaving the camp the trail keeps north and is relatively level for the next 0.5 miles into our next way point.

1082A 0.5mi 47° 53.416'N 123° 20.988'W 4940' Grand Pass Trail X Grand Valley Trail X Badger Valley Trail

The Grand Pass Trail ends at this junction. Grand Lake and its camp are 0.3 miles east. To get to the camp keep right on the Badger Valley Trail for 75 yards looking for a spur trail downhill to the lake and the camp. This is a popular camp and reservations are required in the summer.

Note: Grand Lake Camp is the last official ONP campground near the trail that is open for the next 23 miles. Camps along the Elwha River are closed indefinitely due to the changing Elwha River after the dam was removed several years ago. The next available camp is Boulder Creek.

Back to the final leg of our detour route. Keep northeast (bear left) on the Grand Valley Trail, which is just an extension of the Grand Pass Trail. There are no reports of signs at this junction. The trail climbs relatively easily for 0.3 miles before reaching a plateau. Across the short plateau we climb through more remote ONP, gaining about 1100' elevation over the next 3.2 miles.

The trail turns west briefly before turning north to tackle a very steep grade on multiple switchbacks. At the top of the switchbacks the trail turns west on the south side of a barren ridge. At the point where the trail crosses over the shoulder, there is a knife-edge spur trail to the southwest. This spur trail of 0.2 miles takes you out to overlook the valley and mountains to the south and west.

On the detour route we follow the trail northwest across another barren ridge, on good tread, for another 1.3 miles into Obstruction Point.

1052A 3.6mi 47° 55.107'N 123° 22.928'W 6130' Grand Valley Trail @ Obstruction Point

RESUPPLY OPTIONS

1000P 48° 06.745'N 122° 45.672'W 10' Port Townsend Ferry Dock X Water Street **Port Townsend:** Immediately after exiting the ferry you will find that this eclectic small seaport offers the last best accommodations and resupply directly on the PNT. The grocery store is one mile south of the ferry dock on SR20, one block west of the trail. Try a movie in the Starlight Room in the Rose Theater, four blocks north of the ferry terminal. They have loveseats, cocktails and hor d'oeuvres.[51]

1101P 48° 00.882'N 123° 35.398'W 370' Whiskey Bend Road X Olympic Hot Springs Road **Port Angeles**: Follow Olympic Hot Springs Road 4 miles north to US101, then 3 miles east to find a small mini mart. The nearest grocery store is Albertsons, about 8 miles east on US101.

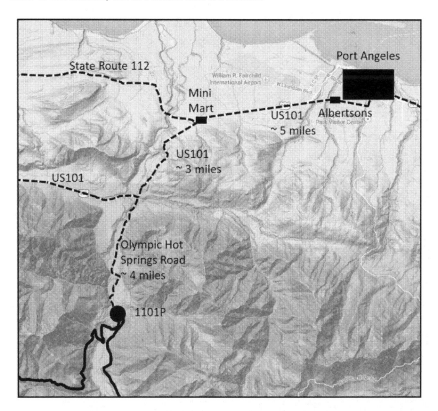

1157P   47° 53.695'N   124° 21.859'W   240'   North Bogachiel Road X US Highway 101 @ Bogachiel State Park   **Forks:** The town is about 6 miles west and north on U.S. Highway 101. At the south end of town is a small shopping center with the Forks Outfitters, Thriftway Supermarket, Ace Hardware, and a bakery with espresso.

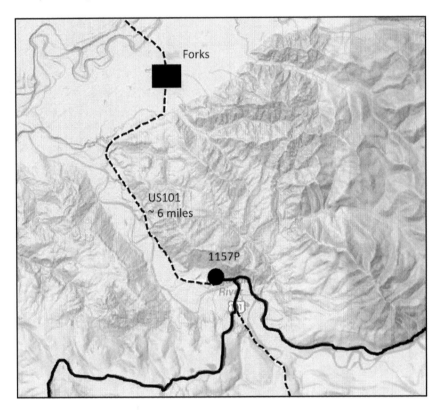

Trail Support

1000P Port Townsend: Dan & Lys Burden, wpburden@aol.com, (360) 301-0982, 310 Willow Street. Can provide transportation, lodging, laundry, showers, food, resupply drop, and meals. [Note: Dan and Lys are also members of Warm Showers, a free worldwide hospitality exchange for touring cyclists.]

1000P Port Townsend: Anne and Dave Krabill, annekrabill@gmail.com, cell (360) 821-1227. We can offer a shower, a drive to a grocery store, or other help as needed.

1016A Discovery Bay: Greg Reseck, 922 W. Uncas Road, Port Townsend, WA 98368. greseck56@gmail.com, (360-385-0150). Look for the PNT sign on the mailbox. Will receive and hold packages. Please contact in advance. Possible rides to Port Townsend, trailheads, and camping in the yard or in a small trail cabin. Look for maps in the covered shed above the metal gate to stay off the property of unfriendly neighbors.

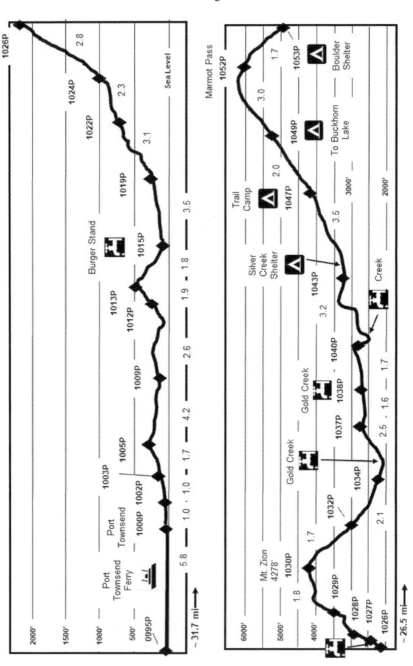

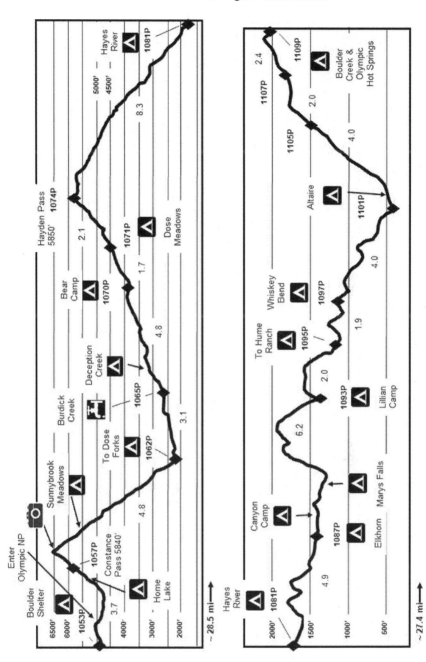

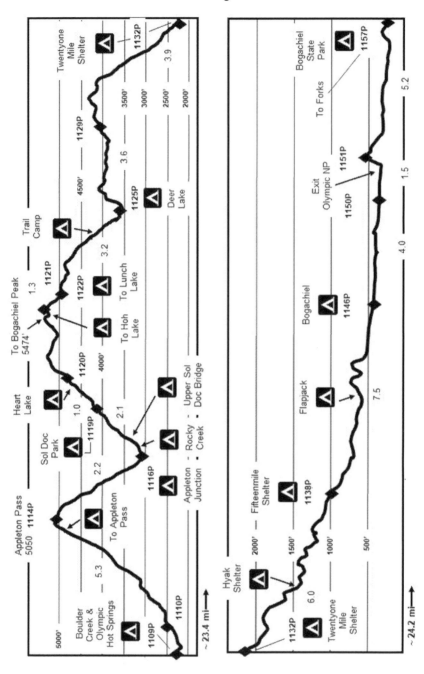

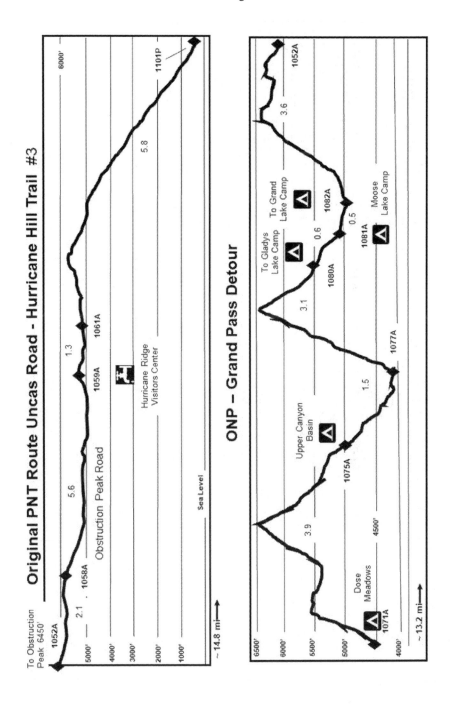

Original PNT Route Uncas Road - Hurricane Hill Trail #3

To Obstruction
Peak 6450'

1052A

2.1 . 1058A

5.6

Obstruction Peak Road

1.3

1059A

1061A

Hurricane Ridge
Visitors Center

5.8

1101P

6000'
5000'
4000'
3000'
2000'
1000'
Sea Level

~ 14.8 mi

ONP – Grand Pass Detour

1052A

3.6

To Grand
Lake Camp

1082A

To Gladys
Lake Camp

0.6

0.5

1081A

Moose
Lake Camp

1080A

3.1

Upper Canyon
Basin

1077A

1.5

1075A

3.9

Dose
Meadows

1071A

6500'
6000'
5500'
5000'
4500'
4000'

~ 13.2 mi

265

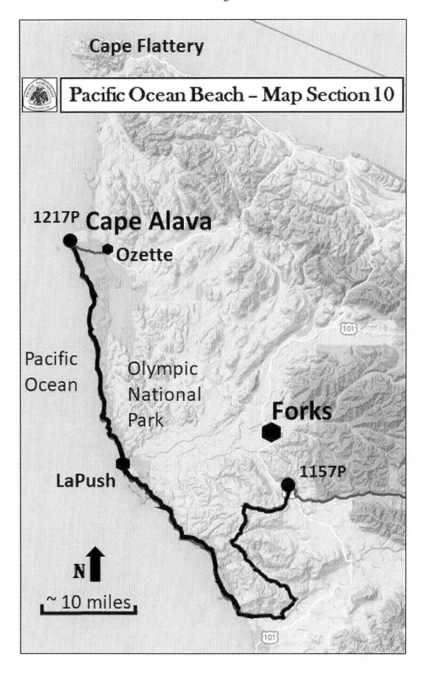

CHAPTER ELEVEN

PACIFIC OCEAN WILDERNESS BEACH – MAP SECTION 10

Bogachiel River to Cape Alava

Low Tide Near Cape Alava, Olympic National Park, Pacific Ocean

Key Trail Notes

<u>Highlights</u>: Beach walk, PNT western terminus

<u>Primary Route Estimated Elevation Change</u>: 1,350' climb / 940' descent

<u>Route Alternate</u>: None

<u>Possible Resupply</u>: Forks, La Push

<u>Parks/Forests</u>: Olympic NP, timberland

<u>Permits</u>: Olympic NP Backcountry permit; Reservations for north coast Olympic NP campsites. Advance reservations are accepted beginning April 1 for camping between May 1 and September 30. The form must be submitted: http://www.nps.gov/olym/planyourvisit/upload/Wilderness-Reservation-Form.pdf

<u>Other Notes</u>:   Bear canister required (protection from beach raccoons); tide charts required (see the tide chart graph example in Chapter 1.)

1157P 0.0mi 47° 53.695'N 124° 21.859'W 240' North Bogachiel Road X US Highway 101 @ Bogachiel State Park

This waypoint is on U.S. Highway 101 six miles south of the town of Forks, Washington. Before we return to the trail, let's discuss the town of Forks, and then Bogachiel State Park.

Resupply: Forks is about 6 miles west and north on U.S. Highway 101. At the south end of town is a small shopping center with the Forks Outfitters, Thriftway Supermarket, Ace Hardware, and a bakery with espresso. One block up is Pacific Pizza. There are nine motels and B&Bs in the small town of Forks, as it was depicted as the home for Vampires and Werewolves in the Twilight series books and movies.

Bogachiel State Park sits on the edge of the Hoh rainforest with up to 160 inches of rain each year, but fortunately most of that is in the spring and fall. The campground has 36 sites, a community kitchen shelter without electricity, as well as picnic tables for day use. Sites 3 and 4 are for hikers/bikers for $12 in 2015. Pay showers are available using quarters (like a carwash!).[DV]

Now back to the primary PNT route and a little more road walking. Turn east and follow US101 as it rounds to the south on the bridge over the Bogachiel River. Fortunately, we only stay on US101 for about 0.9 miles as we come to Anderson Ridge Road – G2000. Look for the street sign across from it showing "Kalman Road." We turn west on the paved Anderson Ridge Road, hiking alternately south and west, uphill for about 1.5 miles.

Here we hike predominantly west on Road G2000, on a slight uphill grade, passing seven side roads over the next 2.3 miles. At the junction with Road G2400, which branches to the south about 0.75 miles east of our next waypoint, there is a white gate. This is not the white gate we're looking for; keep hiking west.[51] Next, look for a 'Y' junction with Forest Road G2500, and another white gate, at our next waypoint. There is no road sign at this junction.[DV]

1161P 4.5mi 47° 52.164'N 124° 24.558'W 800' Road G2000 X Forest Road G2500

We pass through the white gate and turn left (southwest) on G2500 on a relatively level grade as it soon turns west and then back northwest. On G2500 we pass the first road junction in 1.2 miles, at Forest Road G2530. Next, turn south on G2530, following it through second generation growth timberland. Hike downhill for 3.0 miles to cross Forest Road G3200, which intersects from the north. Keep west for only another 0.15 miles into a 'Y' junction, where we bear left (southwest) for 1.0 miles into our next waypoint. Here we approach the 'T' intersection with Forest Road G3000.

1165P 4.1mi 47° 49.930'N 124° 27.499'W 120' Road G2500 Forest Road G3000

Turn south for a short distance, crossing Goldman Creek, and to the junction with Forest Road RY3300. This sets us up for two alternative choices.

1166P 0.1mi 47° 49.802'N 124° 27.417'W 540' Road G3000 X Forest Road RY3300 and Goodman Creek

The is an alternative where we follow RY3300 south around the bend to a 'Y' junction in 150 yards and then bear left (south) for 1.4 miles to rejoin the primary PNT route and G3000 again at 1164P. I'm not sure why the primary PNT route takes the direction it does, unless it is a more defined road.

Back to the primary PNT route, we bear left (southeast) into a clear cut area on the more traveled road. The road begins an uphill grade after crossing the creek. G3000 follows the northern edge of the clear cut of 0.8 miles where it enters the trees as it turns south. Navigation is fairly easy as we road walk another 0.75 miles. Next, G3000 winds around from east to south and into our next waypoint crossing Forest Road RY3300.

1167P 1.6mi 47° 49.174'N 124° 26.209'W 540' Road G3000 X Forest Road RY3300

There has been a lot of logging in this area with many roads crossing this harvested timberland. This road intersection can be described as an extended 'X', with RY3300 coming in from the northwest. At this junction bear left (due east) on G3000 but only for 0.2 mile along the "crest" of the ridge to where there is another intersection. Bear right (south) and downhill as the road winds through open clear cut for 0.8 miles. Here G3000 rounds to the east and we go another 0.5 miles to cross Forest Road RY3400.

1168P 1.4mi 47° 48.554'N 124° 25.438'W 290' Road G3000 X Forest Road RY3400

Keep hiking directly south across the road intersection and then southeast on G3000 as it enters the trees. In 0.6 miles we come close to the creek on the southwest side of the road, which may offer water. In a little over 1.1 miles from our last waypoint we cross Forest Road G3600, which 'Ts' from the southwest. We keep to G3000, road walking southeast through secondary growth forest on both sides of the road. We're on a long, level, dry stretch of road for 4.2 more miles to finally come to our next waypoint, a triangle junction with the Oil City Road.

1174P 5.3mi 47° 46.039'N 124° 20.524'W 400' Road G3000 X Oil City Road

Just a little more road walking on the Oil City Road south and west for the next 5 miles to enter Olympic National Park. Note that there is no "city" in Oil

City and no stores to resupply. This is a very sparsely populated area of the Olympic peninsula.

We turn southwest on the Oil City Road and follow it for 1.4 miles to where it turns due south toward the Hoh River. Hike south downhill for another 0.75 miles where the road makes a hard turn to the west. In 0.5 miles after turning west, you'll pass a homestead and 0.2 miles thereafter the road comes near the river bank. This may be our first opportunity for water.

For the next 2.0 miles the road stays close to the Hoh River as we pass one last homestead and come to the end of the road and our next waypoint, where we enter Olympic NP. There is a parking lot and a pit toilet at the end of the road. There is also good stealth camping on the gravel bars on the Hoh, reachable via a social trail across the parking lot from the privy.[CN]

1179P 5.2mi 47° 44.968'N 124° 25.221'W 40' Oil City Road X Olympic National Park - Oil City Trail

As we enter Olympic National Park remember that permits and bear canisters are required for camping on the coast. No reservations are required along the coast. The park service also warns that the light tan color of the creek water originates from tannin leached from leaves. Cryptosporidium and giardia exist in coastal streams and rivers; therefore, always filter or boil water. Iodine is ineffective against cryptosporidium.

Another caution is worth repeating. Always carry a tide table and know how to use it; plan your hike around the tide schedule, which may mean some night hiking. The shoreline can be rocky and wet, so go slow and concentrate on your footing. A twisted ankle here could mean serious trouble in this very remote area. There are numerous authorized camp spots along the beach, as well as established trail camps, but there won't likely be many other hikers here.

Here's a handy tip for those who have not camped on a beach in the Northwest: Don't pitch your tent with the door toward the ocean. The damp ocean air will fill your tent and sleeping bag, leaving you wet in the morning.[KC]

As we enter the park on the Oil City Trail there is no ranger station or facilities. We hike west 0.7 miles to the trail end. Congratulations! We made it to the Pacific Ocean and our westward hiking. Now, to finish the PNT we'll hike north for a few days.

Once again, high tides are common at the mouth of the Hoh River. Turn north to hike the shore of the Pacific Ocean, checking the tide on the beach past Diamond Rock and around Jefferson Cove. One 2012 hiker reported, "The Diamond Rock area can be tricky at high tide. Although the ranger will tell you a 2 foot or lower tide is needed, I found it passable on the water side at between a 5 and 6 foot tide by scrambling and jumping from rock to rock, timing it in between the waves - and stayed dry."[GT] This brings us to our next waypoint.

1181P 1.9mi 47° 46.009'N 124° 27.427'W 30' Beach Walk @ Hoh Head Trail @ Ladders

We must leave the beach and climb the three sections of sand ladders at the north end of Jefferson Cove. This takes us to a 3.5 mile long trail through the rain forest on the bluff and slightly inland. The trail is usually muddy and parts have been washed out. Olympic NP has provided a rope assist in some areas. There are hiker reports of a trail camp on the bluff above Jefferson Cove, but Olympic NP does not recognize it as such.

About 1.1 miles on the trail we come to a small creek that may offer water. Look for a spur trail west to the beach about 0.1 miles past the creek. This will take us down to an Olympic NP beach camp spot, but we will stick to the higher trail.

Keep hiking north on the trail where it ends in another 1.7 miles to reach the first Olympic NP established camp at our next waypoint.

1184P 3.2mi 47° 47.908'N 124° 28.833'W 70' Hoh Head Trail @ Mosquito Creek Camp

Fortunately there are few mosquitoes here. The camp can be very busy in the summer and has a pit toilet. Beach fires are allowed. Walk over the boardwalk through the marshy area. Mosquito Creek can be difficult or impossible to ford in deep water, especially after a heavy rains. Crossing the mouth of the creek in low tide is advised, when the water is usually knee to waist deep at that time.

1185P 1.5mi 47° 49.126'N 124° 29.424'W 20' Beach Walk @ Alternate Goodman Creek Bypass [Private Property Easement Revoked in 2018].

We continue hiking north on the beach for another 0.5 miles to where it turns due west toward Goodman Point. *Caution*: Six foot tides are possible in this area. Consult your tide table to schedule your hike through here. Next, we climb the bluff as this is a very rocky point. Even at low tide, crossing the mouth of Goodman Creek is nearly impassable. At high tide it is dangerous. To be safe we clamber over the driftwood and turn inland at bull's eye marker, to head up a hillside.[24]

After our climb to the bluff on the trail, it drops back down, requiring us to ford Goodman Creek. In late 2015 there were a number of blowdowns on the trail due to a recent storm.[51] Apply caution in fording Goodman Creek because it can get deep and fast after a heavy rain and at high tide. Even though we are inland from the beach, the creek at the trail crossing is only a few feet above sea level. Also, hikers have reported using a camp spot near Goodman Creek.

The trail climbs about 170' elevation gain in the first 0.2 miles into the thick protected forest. Here the trail goes north, away from the coast, another 0.2 miles inland and downhill to ford Goodman Creek.

Next, we hike west along the trail, crossing the minor Falls Creek in about 0.2 miles, and then climbing to gain 210' elevation over the next 0.4 miles. Finally the trail turns southwest and downhill toward the ocean, but returns to the north along the bluff for about 0.2 miles to the end of the trail as it slides back down to the beach.

We beach walk west about 0.8 miles to reach Jackson Creek and the Toleak Point Camp at our next waypoint.

1188P 2.9mi 47° 50.079'N 124° 32.246'W 15' Beach Walk @ Toleak Point Camp

Sorry, the shelter is long gone but Toleak Point is the nicest beach camping on this stretch. It can be crowded on weekends.[GT] There are tent sites on both sides of the point. There is a pit toilet and beach fires are allowed. Like all the camps along the Olympic NP coast, bear canisters are required. The north toilet at Toleak Point is located around midway behind the string of wooded campsites; the south toilet is located up the access trail behind the logs on the north side of Jackson Creek, just below and to the left of the deteriorating A-frame shelter.

Leaving Toleak Point Camp, cross over the low bluff to the beach and beach walk north for 1.2 miles to Strawberry Point through a rocky stretch. There is an ONP camp at Strawberry Point, which straddles two coves frequented by seals and otters. Hike past the sea stacks and past Giants Graveyard for another 1.2 miles past Strawberry Point into Scotts Creek Camp at our next waypoint.

1191P 2.4mi 47° 51.614'N 124° 33.469'W 10' Beach Walk @ Scotts Creek Camp

This Olympic NP camp, like the others, has a pit toilet and beach fires are allowed. The path to the toilet at Scott Creek is about 30' south of the last campsite before we climb Scotts Bluff, using the ropes if needed. The beach near Taylor Point is a high-tide area. Walk on the beach about 0.5 miles north, to once again climb the bluff because Taylor Point is impassable.

1192P 0.9mi 47° 52.053'N 124° 34.074'W 10' Beach Walk X Taylor Point Trail

The Taylor Point Trail is marked with the round orange and black marker. The trail gains 240' in elevation over the first 0.3 miles. Follow the trail north and downhill for another 0.9 miles to descend on stairs and ladders to Third Beach. Hikers have reported making camp before starting back down to the beach. _Caution_: Five foot tides are possible in this area. Consult your tide table to schedule your hike through here.

Hike the beach, known as Third Beach, north another 0.5 miles into our next waypoint looking for the Third Beach Trail. Short of our next waypoint there was a landslide creating a pinch point. At high tide you'll have to scramble up and over the slide.[49] Just prior to finding the trail off the beach we come to the Third Beach Camp. This camp has a toilet and fires are allowed on the beach.

1193P 1.6mi 47° 52.724'N 124° 35.319'W 10' Beach Walk X Third Beach Trail

The ONP Third Beach Camp is tucked into the bluff with a pit toilet. Reservations are not required, but keep using your bear canister.

The trail should be located just past the small creek or in that area. Climb the bluff, gaining 260' elevation in the first 0.2 miles. Follow the trail north through the forest on a level grade for the next 1.2 miles to exit at the trailhead and our next waypoint on La Push Road.

1194P 1.4mi 47° 53.428'N 124° 35.941'W 270' Third Beach Trail X La Push Road -WA110

We exit the trail at the trailhead parking and hike west on the paved La Push Road. After 0.6 miles we enter the Quileute Indian Reservation. In about 1.2 miles from our last waypoint, there is a bike path protected from the road by a guard rail that lets us safely walk west and north on the paved La Push Road. It is about another 1.3 miles downhill to reach the center of La Push via the road. The primary PNT route, however, takes us off the road before reaching La Push.

In 1.6 miles the road turns north and changes its name to Ocean Front Drive. While on the bike path, just after the turn north, there is a trial leading west to the beach. The trail is about 15 yards prior to the fenced overlook point on the bike path.

This unnamed trail takes us to the Second Beach Camp, which also has a pit toilet. Enjoy the hike on the beach north toward La Push.

Resupply: Although short of the center of La Push, we come to the Lonesome Creek general store and post office. From the beach you'll see the RV parking and the rental cottages. Follow the road between the two to find the store. This is our best opportunity to resupply for the remainder of the PNT. Hike along the road, or the beach, another 0.5 miles to reach the center of town.

Another option is to take a 30-minute bus ride from the Third Beach Trailhead to Forks, provided by both the Clallam Transit (Route 15) and the Quileute Reservation bus systems. It may be necessary to flag down the bus. The Quileute shuttle is free.

1197P 2.0mi 47° 54.559'N 124° 38.231'W 20' Center of La Push @ Quillayute River

The town of La Push is on the Quilleute Indian Reservation and is small. However, it is the largest town that the PNT traverses on the coast.

PNT Factoid: The Indians have inhabited this part of the Olympic peninsula for an untold number of centuries. The Quileute were once one of the great whaling tribes in the Pacific Northwest, using only cedar canoes. Being isolated along the coast, the Quileute were not introduced to the white man until 1855.

The primary PNT route crosses the river, but there is no bridge. The best option is to find the Harbor Master to arrange a ride across the river. His office is at 71 Main Street, (360) 374-5392, cell (360) 640-8621.[71] Be sure to offer gas money in return.[49]

Another option, far from ideal, is to backtrack to the Third Beach trailhead and road walk east on La Push Road to Mora Road and then west for a 9 mile circuit to come to the other side of the Quillayute River.

Once on the north side, we beach walk to reenter Olympic National Park on Rialto Beach, where the first mile of the beach is a no camping zone until you pass Ellen Creek. Reminder: check the tide table. Past the creek we may camp along the beach for the next 0.75 miles as we hike north to Hole-in-the-Wall, which is an Olympic NP camp with a pit toilet. Fires are allowed on the beach and bear canisters are required to keep out those pesky raccoons.

Caution: From here to the end of the PNT at Cape Alava, four to six foot tides are possible. Consult your tide table to schedule your hike through this portion of the PNT.

Hole-in-the-wall is a natural carved arch right near the shore—at low tide you will walk through![GT] There is a short trail over the bluff if the tide is too high to beach walk around the arch. We beach walk on the rocky shore over and around the large driftwood logs for another 2.2 miles. Here we come to the Chilean Memorial and our next waypoint. Beach camping is allowed about half way along this leg.

1201P 3.8mi 47° 57.887'N 124° 39.929'W 20'   Beach Walk @ Chilean Memorial Camp

The Chilean Memorial Camp is the same as the other Olympic NP beach camps with a pit toilet and beach fires are permitted. The memorial commemorates the *W.J. Pirrie*, a Chilean ship that wrecked in 1920 with no survivors, and is marked by a simple plaque that's quite easy to miss.

Continuing our beach walk, note that the black or brown rocks are especially slippery, so beware.[GT] Follow the beach west temporarily as it rounds Cape Johnson and then turns north. Hiking through here is likely to be slower than you might estimate. Head north 2.0 miles from Cape Johnson to an unnamed point where we have to climb a short bluff trail to cross over to the beach. Camping is permitted in the trees inland from this short trail.

After the trail we keep hiking the beach for another 2.3 miles to come to our next waypoint at the Cedar Creek Camp.

1206P 4.8mi 48° 01.114'N 124° 40.771'W 20' Beach Walk @ Cedar Creek Camp

Bet you figured it out—this camp has a pit toilet and fires are allowed on the beach. Let's keep hiking north on the beach for another 1.2 miles to come to the Allens Bay Trail and the Norwegian Memorial and camp. The Allens Bay Trail goes northeast inland to Allens Bay on Ozette Lake, but that's it. There are no stores or facilities on the lake.

The Norwegian Memorial Camp has a pit toilet with fires allowed on the beach. A bear canister is still required. The memorial is in honor of the Norwegian Bark *Prince Arthur* which struck the reef and broke apart in 1903. A granite obelisk, designated the Norwegian Monument, is set to honor the dead sailors. It is one of the many tragic events along the Washington coast in this area known to mariners as the Graveyard of the Pacific.[25]

We keep hiking north, again probably a lot slower than you might expect for a beach walk. Double check the tide tables, as the bluff (i.e., cliff) along the shore becomes higher and steeper. We beach walk for the next 3.9 miles north on the rocky shore to where the shore rounds into the Yellow Banks, so named for the color of the dirt bluff. About half way around the cove look for a small stream and our next waypoint at Yellow Banks Camp.

1211P 5.5mi 48° 05.653'N 124° 41.203'W 20' Beach Walk @ Yellow Banks Camp

This Olympic NP camp requires reservations since it is close to Ozette and is a popular beach camp. There is no toilet, and <u>no</u> beach fires are allowed. Follow the beach north about 0.5 miles to cross around Point 5, a particularly rocky and slow area of the beach. After the beach improves we hike northwest another 0.9 miles to the South Sand Point Camp.

The South Sand Point Camp requires reservations and <u>no</u> fires are allowed in this area, but it does have a pit toilet. Soon after the camp, as we hike north along the shore, we find the Sand Point Trail, which heads east to Ericson Bay on Ozette Lake, but that's it.

Continuing to hike the shoreline in about 0.6 miles past the Sand Point Trail, we come to the Sand Point camp, which also requires reservations, with no fires and a pit toilet. If you have the energy, you can scramble to the top of Sand Point to find some great, and perhaps final overall views of the Pacific Ocean coastline. There are a few stellar campsites just after the first low tide area just north of Sand Point.[CN] Next we cross the North Sand Point Trail, which would take us directly to the Ozette Ranger Station in 3.1 miles. We, however, want to finish the PNT up to Cape Alava, so we continue north along the beach for 2.2 rocky miles to come to the Wedding Rocks Camp and our next waypoint.

1216P 4.6mi 48° 08.932'N 124° 43.177'W 20' Beach Walk @ Wedding Rock Camp

There are actually two campsites here, neither with a toilet, nor are fires allowed. You must have reservations. At the wedding rocks you can find dozens of Native American petroglyphs on the southwest side near the ocean at the high tide line. As an example, one depicted a marriage scene with a man and a woman and some fertility symbols, and another with whales and orcas.

Let's press north on the shoreline to the final waypoint on the primary PNT route. We hike north for 1.2 miles to the Cape Alava Trail. As we hike north you can see Ozette Island to our west about a mile away, and as we pass it, the shores turns north. Straight ahead we see the large sea stack of Tsakawahyah

Island ahead in front at the official point of Cape Alava. The trail, however, should come in on our right from the southeast.

Note: If you venture north along the beach, you can find outstanding views from Tsakawahyah Island all the way up to Vancouver Island, Canada.[49]

1217P 1.2mi 48° 09.645'N 124° 43.902'W 20' Beach Walk @ Cape Alava Trail

Open the Champagne and celebrate—you've earned it, big time! This is the official end of the primary PNT route, but we need to return to civilization. Some hikers want to venture north along the shore to Cape Flattery, which is possible. But this puts you into an even more remote section on the Makah Indian Reservation. Transportation from Cape Flattery is difficult.

If you are in need of an overnight camp, the Olympic NP Cape Alava Camp is about 140 yards north on the shoreline. It has a pit toilet and beach fires are allowed. Reservations are required.

To finish our trail description, we turn southeast on the trail, climbing slightly. The trail is almost continuous cedar boardwalk for the 3.3 miles east to Ozette. Here you will find an Olympic NP ranger station and a car campground. The Olympic NP Ozette Campground has 15 sites.

Just outside the park is The Lost Resort, which claims to be the most western outpost in the lower 48! They have 36 tent sites for $15 a night, cabins, and showers. But more importantly they have a restaurant, espresso and beer.

This concludes the description of the primary PNT route into Ozette, Washington.

Special Note: In 2015 Backpacker Magazine proclaimed the 15 miles of beach walking, from Cape Alava north to Shi Shi Beach, as some of the best 100 miles in Olympic National Park. Your Olympic National Park Wilderness Pass is required. To park at the trailhead, vehicles will need a Makah Recreation Pass which may be purchased for $10 at businesses or the museum in Neah Bay.

"Although not part of the PNT, you might consider extending your hike. Green Trails Map #89S 'Cape Flattery' can be purchased at the La Push Resort Office. This route is highly recommended at least as far as going up to Shi Shi Beach. The terrain is fairly easy with 75/25 percent beach walk/trails. Take the knife edge side trail that leads to the huge sea arch at The Point of Arches, just south of Shi Shi Beach. Follow the two-mile access trail at the north end of the beach through the Makah Indian Reservation to Hatchery Road parking lot."[49]

From the parking lot you can road walk to Neah Bay, about 6.5 miles, for resupply and public transportation.[ES]

RESUPPLY OPTIONS

1194P 47° 53.428'N 124° 35.941'W 270' Third Beach Trail X La Push Road **La Push:** Although south of the center of La Push, by about 0.5 miles on Ocean Front Drive, there is the Lonesome Creek general store and post office. This is our best opportunity to resupply for the remainder of the PNT.

1217P 1.2mi 48° 09.645'N 124° 43.902'W 20' Beach Walk @ Cape Alava Trail **Ozette:** Sorry, the Lost Resort on the east side of this village has a restaurant but no general store. The nearest resupply point is back in Forks, about 53 miles via Ozette Lake Road to State Route 113, and then south on US101. Port Angeles is 78 miles from Ozette, using the same route but turning east on US101.

Trail Support

None.

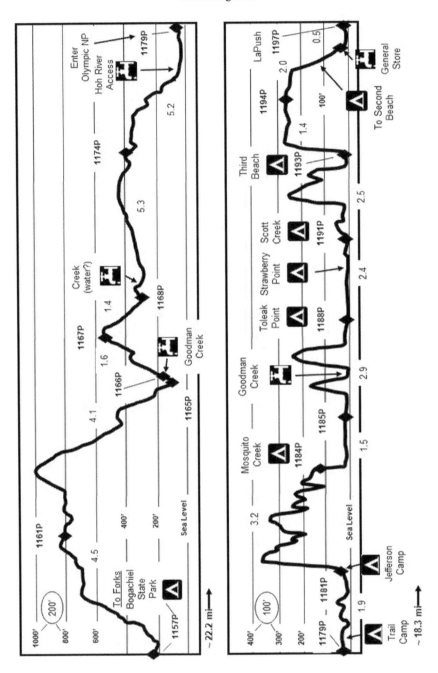

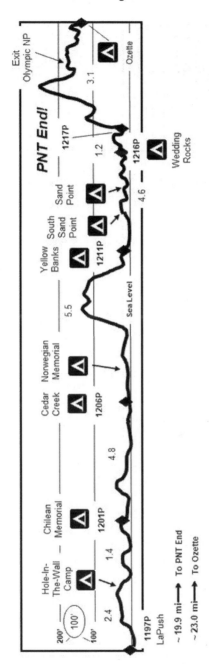

Tim Youngbluth

****

Dear Lord, if you pick 'em up, I'll put 'em down.

Hiker's Prayer

****

CHAPTER TWELVE

PLANNING RESOURCES and REFERENCES

Trail sign, Bluff Trail, Fort Ebey State Park, Whidbey Island, Washington

Books about the Pacific Northwest Trail

The Pacific Northwest Trail Guide: The Official Guidebook for Long Distance and Day Hikers by Ron Strickland (maps by Ted Hitzroth); ©2001 by Ronald Gibson Strickland; out of print; ISBN 1-57061-177-7; Sasquatch Books, 615 Second Avenue, Seattle, WA 98104; www.sasquatchbooks.com.

Pacific Northwest Trail Town Guide by Melanie Simmerman © 2015 by Melanie Simmerman; $11; The Town Guide includes detailed information of re-supply towns and is illustrated with maps and photos of places such as Eureka, MT and Port Townsend, WA. ISBN 10: 1507838263; ISBN 13: 978-1507838266; www.amazon.com.

Grizzly Bears and Razor Clams: Walking America's Pacific Northwest Trail by Chris Townsend [Paperback] © 2012 Chris Townsend; ~$20; The story of Chris Townsend's walk along the 1200 mile Pacific Northwest Trail with the author's photographs; ISBN: 978-190-8737-04-5; Sandstone Press Ltd, P.O.

Box 5725 One High Street, Dingwall IV15 9WJ, Scotland; www.sandstonepress.com.

Summit to Sea: *From the Continental Divide to the Pacific Ocean on the Pacific Northwest Trail* by Harly Drum [Paperback and ebook] © November 2013. The trail journal of Harly and Dan Drum's thru hike in 2004. ISBN-10: 1493717936; ISBN-13: 978-1493717934 from Amazon.com.

Recent Videos

THRU It's Not Just Hiking (Trailer), by Andy Laub and Peter Hochhauser. Posted 11/5/18, 2:31. Feature film to be released in 2019. Experience every step as four strangers embark on a 1,200-mile journey THRU | The Pacific Northwest. **https://www.hiking-thru.com/**

PNT 2017 Thru Hike, by David Zermeno, 2/20/18. A well-documented journey of my Pacific Northwest Trail thru-hike in 2017 (1,217 miles), 12:00. https://www.youtube.com/watch?v=dXRDRGYmI6Q&feature=youtu.be

Pacific Northwest Trail Montana, by Iceberg The Yak, posted 1/22/18, 14:26, https://www.youtube.com/watch?v=oVShKhfovuQ

The Pacific Northwest Trail: Crest to Coast, by Dylan Ivens, [Publish ate to be determined.] Teaser, 1:26, can be found at: **https://www.youtube.com/watch?v=5i0-rvWqB0s&app=desktop**

"Beautiful Washington" Scenic Nature Documentary Film about Washington State, by Pro Art, Inc. on the 4K Relaxation Channel, youtube.com

Episode 2: @ 28:06 Olympic Peninsula; @ 32:20 Hoh Rain Forest;

Episode 3: North Cascades, first 14 minutes;

Episode 4: @ 33:34 Olympic National Park Hurricane Ridge Visitors Center; @ 34:24 Hurricane Hill Trail; @39:20 Olympic Peninsula Coast, Ruby Beach and Hole-in-the-Wall; @ 47:32 Ozette Triangle Trail.

[Authors Note: These 4K HD documentaries show the spectacular scenery of parts of the PNT in Washington. Not every trail on the video is on PNT but much of it is. If this doesn't make you want to saddle your pack and head out and trek the PNT, nothing will!]

What It's Like to Hike the Pacific Northwest Trail, by Julie Holtz, posted on 6/8/16, 3:18, https://www.outsideonline.com/2089651/what-its-hike-pacific-northwest-trail

Parker Ridge USFS Camp, by Scott Rulander, USDA/USFS, posted on 7/9/16, 3:20, https://www.youtube.com
Author's comment: Every step a hiker enjoys on the trail was proceeded by someone—usually a volunteer—who prepared the way for them, foot-by-foot.

Wandering Thru – The Pacific Northwest Trail, by Terasu and Julie Hotz, posted on 2/18/16, 3:18, https://vimeo.com/155931598

Barely Hiking on the PNT, by Kurt Bramel (Fitty Shrimp), posted on 12/16/15, 4:57, https://www.youtube.com/watch?v=p25nnLmF1lU

The Pacific Northwest Trail, Oroville, Washington to Glacier National Park, Montana, by Zed Nek, posted 12/21/14, 13:06; http://vimeo.com/115093202

Legend's Pacific Northwest Trail (PNT) thru hike 2014, by Jeff Garmire (aka 'Legend') Eastbound, posted 10/1/14, 11:19; http://youtu.be/u05l_DILIl8

Pacific Northwest Trail (PNT), by Seattle SirHikesALot, posted 9/22/14, 13:13; http://www.youtube.com/watch?v=wdZPXy1mBzc

PNT 2014, by Stephan Berens (Section hiker from Germany), three videos, http://vimeo.com/user31481372

Pacific Northwest Trail 2013, by Dbirdyurtdog, posted 1/10/14, 10:59; http://www.youtube.com/watch?v=k3GtOPl33K4

Pacific Northwest Trail, by Glaucoma Patient, posted 8/18/13, 2:25; http://www.youtube.com/watch?v=kC8p7KPbdGA

Creating the 1,200 Mile Pacific Northwest Trail – Ron Strickland – Pathfinder, by Better World Films, posted 5/29/12, 9:57 ; http://www.youtube.com/watch?v=bpuIIRjAKvU

Pacific Northwest Trail (PNT) 2012 – August – September, by backpacker1964, posted 10/12/2012, 50:22; http://www.youtube.com/watch?v=NUr8tstmq0M

Nimblewill Nomad - Odyssey 2010 - PNT - Part 1, by Nimblewill Nomad, 8/8/10, 9:33; http://www.youtube.com/watch?v=SbVnv94jglo

Pacific Northwest Trail, by Sam Haraldson, posted multiple videos for 2007 thru hike; www.youtube.com

Useful Websites and Trail Journals

Pacific Northwest Trail Association: www.pnt.org

Pacific Northwest Trail Association: https://www.facebook.com/pacificnorthwesttrail

Pacific Northwest Trail:
https://www.facebook.com/groups/PNTHikers/#!/pacificnorthwestnationalsceni
ctrail

PNT Hikers: https://www.facebook.com/groups/PNTHikers

Ron Strickland Website: http://www.ronstrickland.com/rs/Home.html PNT.
Check both his section on the PNT and his Blog for tips and resources.

PNT History and Planning Overview by the U.S. Forest Service:
http://www.fs.usda.gov/Internet/FSE_DOCUMENTS/stelprdb5425480.pdf

Interagency Grizzly Bear Committee: igbconline.org. The IGBC was formed in
1983 to help ensure recovery of viable grizzly bear populations and their habitat
in the lower 48 states through interagency coordination of policy, planning,
management, and research. The PNT crosses through three of their recovery
areas.

Snow Levels:

   http://www.wcc.nrcs.usda.gov/cgibin/westsnow.pl

   http://nrmsc.usgs.gov/files/norock/research/FlattopSWE2013_2014.pdf

   http://postholer.com/gmap/gmap.php?trail_id=27&lat=47.412987&lon=-
   118.428496&zoom=7&dist=0&vw=0.

2018

Blog: The Pacific Northwest Trail by Einav Bloom:
   https://milky10.wixsite.com/einavbloom/blog

Blog: Hike-Minded by Jared Stewart: https://hike-minded.com/ and Instagram
@jaredhikes

Instagram: griggsdomler on the Pacific Northwest Trail:
   https://www.instagram.com/griggsdomler/

Instagram: #crowntocoast, group posts & photos of the PNT
   https://www.instagram.com/explore/tags/crowntocoast/

2017

Blog: Zucchini Walking by Zucchini:
https://zucchiniwalking.wordpress.com/pnt-2017/

Blog: Charlie and Niv's Big Wander: https://cpntadventures.wordpress.com/ [A
Scottish pair that just married before their PNT trek.]

Blog: In Jungle Heat by Austin: https://injungleheat.wordpress.com/trail-
journal/

Blog: Tinker Run by Madeleine Weatherhead: tinkerrun17.wordpress.com

Blog: Sterling R. Deck (Vagabond Veteran), 2017 PNT thru-hike narrative and pictures, http://www.riderunroam.com/2017/09/23/pacific-northwest-trail-final-thoughts/

Facebook: Jordan Newton (Samaritan), Album – Thruhike Pacific Northwest Trail, pictures and narrative, 6/29/17 thru 8/22/17 (posted 8/22/17)

Blog: Hiking Dude by Paul Kautz (My Pacific Northwest Trail Hike: http://hikingdude.com/pacific-northwest-trail.php

Picture Journal: PNT 2017 by Tyler M. Yates (thru-hiker): https://www.flickr.com/photos/tmyprod/sets/72157687358058684/

Blog: Pacific Northwest Trail: North Cascades National Park and Three Weeks on the Pacific Northwest Trail: Traversing Olympic National Park, by **Cathe Neuberger: http://www.pounceonlife.com/2017/09/21/pacific-northwest-trail-north-cascades-national-park/**

Blog Post: Thru-Hike The Pacific Northwest Trail; Interview with Jeff Kish, Executive Director of the Pacific Northwest Trail Association: by Columbia Sportswear. http://blog.columbia.com/thru-hike-pacific-northwest-trail/

2016

Blog: Thru-Hiking the PNT: The Last Hike on the Pacific Northwest Trail by MSR Team, 3/7/17. This is an amazing accomplishment of Triple Crowner Quoc Nguyen, who undertook the PNT in the fall. This is a feat for expert thru-hikers and those with extensive avalanche education and winter backcountry experience. https://thesummitregister.com/thru-hiking-pnt/

Magazine Article: The Pacific Northwest Trail – The Last Wild National Trail by Seattle Backpackers Magazine, 6/23/16: http://seattlebackpackersmagazine.com/the-pacific-northwest-trail-the-last-wild-national-trail/

Blog: Northwest of Here by Trent Banks and Jenna Walenga (PNT thru-hike): http://www.northwestofhere.com/blog/

PNT Photos and Notes: David Parks, https://www.facebook.com/david.parks.5473

Blog: Crown to Coast by Jeremy and Sarah Lange: https://crowntocoast.wordpress.com/

Blog: Northwest of Here by Strauss Matchen: http://www.northwestofhere.com/blog/

Blog: Crosby on the Trail – Pacific Northwest Trail by Andrew Frei: https://andrewfrei.wordpress.com/

PNT Photos, Short Videos and Notes: Matt Sweeney, facebook.com/Matt Sweeney

Blog: "Epic" and "Fancy Pants" PNT Adventure by Doug Carducci: https://epicpantz.wordpress.com/

Trail Journal: Brianle - Pacific Northwest Trail Journal – 2016, by Brian "Gadget" Lewis: **http://www.postholer.com/user/brianle/2808**

Blog: "Jess Hikes the PNT," by Jess, a section hiker in 2015 and 2016: https://jesshikesthepnt.wordpress.com/

2015

Crown To Coast 2015: Hiking the Pacific Northwest Trail by Ashley 'Bluebird' Davis and Eric 'Spice Rack' Oliver: https://crowntocoast2015.wordpress.com/

Take a hike with Mike, Pacific Northwest Trail by Michael, et.al.: http://takeahikewithmike.blogspot.com/

Trail Journal: Mark on the PNT by Mark Davis: http://postholer.com/markdavis

Blog: SOBO-HOBO, How Many Miles to the Next Bloody Mary? By Ashley Hill: http://www.sobohobo.com/

Blog: Bike from LA to Glacier National Park then Hike the PNT by Julie Hotlz: http://www.juliehotz.com/about-bike-hike/

Blog: Team Astro – 2015: http://www.pnt2015.blogspot.com/

Blog: Free on the PNT by Matt Hopkins: https://www.facebook.com/freeonthepnt

Blog: Jess Hikes the PNT by Jess : https://jesshikesthepnt.wordpress.com/

Trail Journal: Alistair and Gail: http://www.postholer.com/journal/Pacific-Northwest-Trail/2015/aandg/2589

Trail Journal: Melanie Simmerman (Lemstar): www.trailjournals.com/entry.cfm?trailname=19213

Trail Journal and Photo Journal: 2015 PNT by Len Glassner (Al H.): www.trailjournals.com/entry.cfm?trailname=19013
https://len5742.smugmug.com/Len/2015-PNT/i-qXkzhsG

Trail Journal: Jeremy Delong (Brown Bag): www.trailjournals.com/entry.cfm?id=503236

Blog: Abby Otherworld: trekkinlady.wordpress.com/

Blog: takeahikewithmike.blogspot.com

Article: Pacific Northwest Trail Challenges: Mosquitos, Staying Dry, Navigation & More by Ashley Hill: http://blog.hyperlitemountaingear.com/pacific-northwest-trail/

2014

Blog: Hiking the Pacific Northwest Trail 2014 by Ignacio Mendez Nunez: http://pntbound.wordpress.com/

Blog: PNT 2014 by Cedar: pacificnorthwesttrail2014.wordpress.com/

Blog: Hiking the Pacific Northwest Trail and Great Divide Trail by Zed Sychrava: http://fordingriver.wordpress.com/

Blog: The Long Trails by Jeff Garmire (start Jul 2, 2014 West to East): jgar15.blogspot.com

Trail Journal: The PNT by Brian "Gadget" Lewis (West to East): http://postholer.com/journal/viewJournal.php?sid=d41c15799b0e1fc1f454f7b51 b004723&entry_id=46461

Text References:

BT Brian Tanzman	GT Greg Thompson
MS Melanie Simmerman	KC Katherine Cook
DV Dick Vogel	CN Cathe Neuberger
ES Ellie Stevenson	

Note: Reference number 1 – 9 not used. References are not necessarily in numerical sequence in the chapter text.

10. Washington Trails Association, Slow Loris and Walks Ahead, 7/10/2010 http://www.wta.org/go-hiking/trip-reports/trip_report.2010-07-11.7934584666

11. The Priest Lake Ranger District Trails: http://www.geocities.ws/ralph_schooley/priest_lake_trail_index.html

12. Summit Post.org, Thoma Lookout and Abercrombie Mountain: http://www.summitpost.org/thoma-lookout-point-7104/749253 http://www.summitpost.org/abercrombie-mountain/152166

13. Out There Monthly: Callie Fraser and Dale Tessin http://www.outtheremonthly.com/?p=2032

14. The Trailhead News, Vol. 33 Issue 1, Jan/Feb 2009, page 5, Trygve Culp http://www.bchw.org/Trailhead%20News/bchw_janfeb_09_web.pdf,

15. Trimble Outdoors, Pacific Northwest Trail, Cold Springs Campgroundhttp://www.trimbleoutdoors.com/ViewTrip/1447976

16. National Park Service, North Cascades National Park, Big Beaver Trailhttp://www.nps.gov/noca/planyourvisit/big-beaver-trail.htm

17. Oh Ranger, North Cascades National Park, Little Beaver Trailhttp://www.ohranger.com/north-cascades/poi/little-beaver-trail

18. USDA, National Forest Service, Easton Glacier Climbing Route http://www.fs.usda.gov/recarea/mbs/recreation/recarea/?recid=30322&actid=38

19. Trail Link, Cascade Trail, http://www.traillink.com/trail/cascade-trail.aspx

20. Washington Trails Association, Tubal Canyon Mine and Buckhorn Lakehttp://www.wta.org/go-hiking/seasonal-hikes/hikes/buckhorn-lake

21. Elwha Destinations - Elwha River Trail, http://www.windsox.us/ELWHA/elriver.html

22. GORP, Olympic National Park http://www.gorp.com/parks-guide/travel-ta-olympic-national-parksidwcmdev_067767.html

23. Washington Trails Association, Appleton Passhttp://www.wta.org/go-hiking/hikes/appleton-pass

24. Trimble Outdoors, Olympic National Park, Hoh River to Third Beachhttp://www.trimbleoutdoors.com/ViewTrip/55411

25. History Link, http://www.historylink.org/index.cfm?DisplayPage=output.cfm&file_id=8998

26. Idaho Panhandle National Forests, Ball and Pyramid Lakes Trail (43) http://www.fs.fed.us/ipnf/rec/activities/trails/d7ballpymd43.html

27. Trail Journals, Apple Pie's 2012 Pacific Northwest Trail Journalhttp://www.trailjournals.com/entry.cfm?id=389042

28. Matt McGrath Photography, Pacific Northwest Trail 2012; http://www.flickr.com/photos/mattmcgrath/collections/72157627626008616/

29. USDA, Olympic National Forest, Sleepy Hollow Trail http://www.fs.usda.gov/recarea/olympic/recreation/hiking/recarea/?recid=47933&actid=50

30. Ted Murray, Okanogan County Outdoor Recreation Coordinator, via email.

31. Brigham Lazalde, local hiker, via email

32. Glacier Park, Inc. http://www.glacierparkinc.com/howtogethere.php

33. All Trips Glacier National Park, http://www.allglacier.com/transportation/public_transportation.php

34. A slow hiker's guide™ to Glacier National Park's free shuttle
http://www.glacierhikers.com/shuttle.html

35. Clallam Transit http://www.clallamtransit.com/route-maps.html

36. Olympic Bus Lines http://www.olympicbuslines.com/

37. Rebecca Roberts, "Whidbey Duo" via email.

38. Jefferson Transit, "Taking the Bus from Port Angeles to Seattle,"
http://jeffersontransit.com/files/PA-to-Seattle-Brochure-1-13-2013.pdf

39. Eden Valley Guest Ranch,
http://www.edenvalleyranch.net/accommodations/cottages.html

40. Dianne Roth, http://democratherald.com/lifestyles/columnists/the-rules-of-
hiking/article_78b3aabc-030c-11e3-867b-001a4bcf887a.html

41. Ten Lakes Scenic Area,
http://www.libbymt.com/areaattractions/tenlakes.htm

42. Stahl Peak: http://www.summitpost.org/stahl-peak-mt/646809

43. Wilson, Trail notes from 2013 thru-hike, Feb 7, 2014:
http://pnta.proboards.com/thread/315/2014

44. USDA, Colville National Forest North Fork Trail 507:
http://www.fs.usda.gov/recarea/colville/recarea/?recid=67950

45. The Huffington Post, Suzy Strutner1/24/15: http://www.msn.com/en-
us/travel/news/this-is-the-quietest-place-in-america/ar-AA8z53p

46. Kettle Trails PDF 2015:
www.islandcounty.net/publicworks/Documents/Kettles%20trails%202015.pdf

47. Len Glassner, PNT Hiker 2015, from posts on Facebook PNT Hikers and
emails.

48. Bev Britt, 2015 Thru-Hiker, edits to manuscript.

49. Dave Osborn ("Freebird") from email notes on 2015 PNT thru-hike.

50. Mark Davis, 2015 thru-hiker, email notes on 2015 PNT Digest.

51. Ashley Davis, 2015 thru-hiker, email notes on 2015 PNT Digest.

52. Kristin Ackerman, via email 3-1-2016; and PNTA-Okanogan
https://www.facebook.com/pnta.okanogan.trailcrew/

53. Matt McGrath, USFS PNNST Program Manager via email

54. Lynda V. Mapes, Seattle Times, 3-11-2016, "Elwha Valley access limited after
undammed river wrecks campgrounds, road"

55. *Out There Monthly,* article by Callae Frazier and Dale Tessin, 5/1/10, http://www.outtheremonthly.com/hiking-and-camping-on-the-pacific-northwest-trail-three-great-routes-for-crossing-the-inland-northwest-on-foot/

56. http://www.idahoconservation.org/events/explore-idaho/north-idaho/long-canyon-parker-ridge

57. USFS Idaho Panhandle National Forest, http://www.fs.usda.gov/recarea/ipnf/recreation/hiking/recarea/?recid=6832&actid=51

58. Steve Petesch, Trails and Recreation, Forest Service, Idaho Panhandle National Forests, Bonners Ferry RD, via email.

59. Strauss Manchen, PNT thru-hiker on facebook.com/PNT Hikers, 2016

60. Cathe "Pounce" Neuberger, PNT thru-hiker on facebook.com/PNT Hikers, and via email 2016

61. Mike Unger, PNT thru-hiker via email, 2016

62. Joan Melcher, PNTA volunteer via email, 2016

63. Skagit County Land Trust Brochure: John Tursi Trail

64. Diane Broackway, PNT section hiker, 2016 via email

65. Vince Devlin, Pacific Northwest National Scenic Trail: From Glacier to the Pacific, PNT is one rugged hike, albeit with amenities, Missoulian, 10/29/16.

66. Brian Lewis, PNT thru-hiker via email, 2016

67. Jeremy and Sarah Lange Blog: Crown to Coast 2016: https://crowntocoast.wordpress.com/

68. Rebecca Roberts "Scout," local hiker, via email 2017.

69. Jeff Kish, Executive Director, Pacific Northwest Trail Association, via email 2017.

70. Terry R. Borden, Senior Operations Manager, Boundary/Lucky Peak Dams, via email 2017.

71. Email from Eric Wollborg, 7/20/2017.

72. Email from Jeff Kish, 7/21/2017.

73. Email from Ken White, 8/25/2017.

74. Email notes from 2017 thru-hiker, Ellie Stevenson.

75. Washington Trails Association, https://www.wta.org/go-hiking/hikes/artist-point-snowshoe.

76. Betty Holder, Facebook, PNT Hikers, 2/25/18.

77. Email from Chris Metcalf, 7/26/18.

78. Message from Matt Hodson, PNT hiker, 11/26/18.

79. Email from Eric Wollberg and Tom Harris, 12/10/18.

80. Robert Paul Kendall, PNT thru-hiker 2018, via email 1/8/19

81. Hunter Dunn, PNT Hiker 2019, via email 1/24/19

Cover Design

Gail C. Youngbluth, Colville, Washington

Photo Credits

Front Cover: Photo courtesy Jeff Kish, Director Pacific Northwest Trail Association, PNT thru-hiker, 2014. View of Mount Olympus, from the Pacific Northwest Trail, on the High Divide Trail, Olympic National Park. Approximately mile 1121P, near the trail junction with the Hoh Lake Trail, below the summit of Bogachiel Peak.

Chapter 1: Jordan Newton, 2017 PNT thru-hiker, *Double PNT trail sign near Deception Pass, Washington.*

Chapter 2: Tyler M. Yates, 2017 PNT thru-hiker, *Pacific Northwest Trail, Glacier National Park*

Chapter 3: Greg Thompson, *Bushwhack on ridge, Tuchuck Mountain in background, Flathead National Forest*

Chapter 4: Greg Thompson, *Ascending Abercrombie Mountain, Colville National Forest*

Chapter 5: Tim Youngbluth, *Kettle Crest National Recreation Trail 13, from Sherman Peak, Colville National Forest, Washington*

Chapter 6: Greg. Thompson, *Trailhead sign for Trail 10, Okanogan County*

Chapter 7: Greg. Thompson, *Amphitheater Mountain from Cathedral Pass, Pasayten Wilderness*

Chapter 8: A. Porter, *Ross Lake from Lightning Creek Trail, Ross Lake National Recreation Area, Washington*

Chapter 9: Tim Youngbluth, *Goose Rock Perimeter Trail near Deception Pass, Whidbey Island, Washington*

Chapter 10: Jordan Newton, 2017 PNT thru-hiker, *Grand Pass, Olympic National Park (approx. waypoint 1078A)*

Chapter 11: Corky Robinson, 2017 PNT thru-hiker, *Low Tide near Cape Alava, Olympic National Park, Pacific Ocean*

Chapter 12: Tim Youngbluth, *Trail sign, Bluff Trail, Fort Ebey State Park, Whidbey Island, Washington*

Last Page: Stirling R. Deck, 2017 *Thru-Hiker, photo on the Pacific Ocean Beach in Olympic National Park, Washington*

****

When thinking back on the whole planning and execution experience, I can say with certainty that without the updated books and maps, I would not have attempted this trail last year. Some of the most memorable and rewarding times were when I was solo hiking and relying only on your Digest. Using no electronics, I would just peek at the paper map/compass for reassurance occasionally. The amount of detail [in the Digest] is incredible. As a beginner from Chicago with fewer than 10 days backpacking experience in my life, I made it through the PNT in 65 days (including just 2 zero days). I had a lot of luck and plenty of great help from hiking buddies and others along the way, but it started with knowing that trustworthy resources were available as a guide. So, thank you. *John Flowers, 2017*

The Digest has been invaluable, I can't imagine the fun people must have had in years prior to publication. The elevation profiles are key in setting realistic expectations for forward progress. I keep the current Digest page visible on one side of my gallon ziploc, and the current map visible on the other side. Works great. *Len Glassner, 2015*

My hiking partner and I really appreciate your PNT Digest. Without it we would still be wondering around in Montana like Lewis and Clark, trying to find a route west, to the Pacific Ocean. *Dick Vogel, 2015*

■■

May the "trail gods" be with you.

SUPPORT THE
PACIFIC NORTHWEST NATIONAL SCENIC TRAIL

If you would like to support the trail, or need more information, please contact the Pacific Northwest Trail Association at:

https://www.pnt.org

info@pnt.org

1851 Charles Jones Memorial
Circle #4
Sedro-Woolley, WA 98285
Phone: (360) 854-9415

Made in the USA
Lexington, KY
16 March 2019